The Shakespearean Archive

Why is Shakespeare so often associated with information technologies and with the idea of archiving itself? Alan Galey explores this question through the entwined histories of Shakespearean texts and archival technologies over the past four centuries. In chapters dealing with the archive, the book, photography, sound, information, and data, Galey analyzes how Shakespeare became prototypical material for publishing experiments and new media projects, as well as for theories of archiving and computing. Analyzing examples of the Shakespearean archive from the seventeenth century to today, he takes an original approach to Shakespeare and new media that will be of interest to scholars of the digital humanities, Shakespeare studies, archives, and media history. Rejecting the idea that current forms of computing are the result of technical forces beyond the scope of humanist inquiry, this book instead offers a critical prehistory of digitization read through the afterlives of Shakespeare's texts.

ALAN GALEY is Associate Professor in the Faculty of Information at the University of Toronto. His research focuses on intersections between textual scholarship and digital technologies. He has published in journals such as *Shakespeare Quarterly* and *Archival Science*, and his article "The Enkindling Reciter: E-Books in the Bibliographical Imagination," in *Book History* (2012), was awarded the Fredson Bowers Prize by the Society for Textual Scholarship. He is also the co-editor of *Shakespeare, the Bible, and the Form of the Book: Contested Scriptures* (2011).

The Shakespearean Archive

Experiments in New Media from the Renaissance to Postmodernity

ALAN GALEY

CAMBRIDGE
UNIVERSITY PRESS

CAMBRIDGE
UNIVERSITY PRESS

University Printing House, Cambridge CB2 8BS, United Kingdom

Cambridge University Press is part of the University of Cambridge.

It furthers the University's mission by disseminating knowledge in the pursuit of education, learning and research at the highest international levels of excellence.

www.cambridge.org
Information on this title: www.cambridge.org/9781107040649

© Alan Galey 2014

First published 2014

Printed in the United Kingdom by TJ International Ltd, Padstow, Cornwall

A catalogue record for this publication is available from the British Library

Library of Congress Cataloguing in Publication data
Galey, Alan, 1975–
The Shakespearean archive : experiments in new media from the
Renaissance to postmodernity / Alan Galey.
  pages cm
ISBN 978-1-107-04064-9 (hardback)
1. Shakespeare, William, 1564–1616 – Criticism and
interpretation – History. 2. Shakespeare, William,
1564–1616 – Criticism,Textual. 3. Shakespeare,
William, 1564–1616 – Bibliography. 4. Shakespeare, William,
1564–1616 – study and teaching – Technological innovations.
5. Shakespeare, William, 1564–1616 – In mass media.
6. Archives – Technological innovations.
7. Archival materials – Digitization. 8. Literature and technology. I. Title.
PR2965.G35 2014
822.3′3–dc23   2014019406

ISBN 978-1-107-04064-9 (hardback)

For Gerry and Joan Galey
and in memory of Evelyn Galey, 1919–2006

Contents

Figures

Preface

The inspiration for this book came from a rare opportunity I was given a few years ago to create a digital interface for the Electronic New Variorum Shakespeare (ENVS), the Modern Language Association's continuation of Horace Howard Furness's series of variorum editions begun in 1870, itself a descendant of the work of Malone, Boswell, Capell, Johnson, and other eighteenth-century editors. As I worked with the meticulously crafted XML code of the ENVS editions created by Julia Flanders and Kitto Weikert, I became distracted (productively, one hopes) by the rich cultural history of the project in which I found myself working, whose edges kept receding into the shadowy space of what I came to think of as the Shakespearean archive. That curiosity took shape in 2009 as a project funded by the Social Sciences and Humanities Research Council of Canada (SSHRC) titled *Archive and Interface in Digital Textual Studies*. That project had a twofold rationale: first, that we cannot build and study digital archives without giving serious thought to interfaces as cultural artifacts; and second, that such inquiry might profitably be carried out by a multi-modal project that combines hands-on digital experimentation with a reconsideration of the cultural history of archival interfaces. The digital experimentation has taken the form of my online project www.VisualizingVariation.ca, and the cultural history has primarily taken the form of this book. A shorter version of Chapter 6 and a few passages in Chapter 7 were published as "Networks of Deep Impression: Shakespeare and the History of Information," in *Shakespeare Quarterly*, 61.3 (2010), 289–312, and two paragraphs in Chapter 1 are taken from "The Human Presence in Digital Artifacts," in Willard McCarty (ed.), *Text and Genre in Reconstruction: Effects of Digitalization on Ideas, Behaviours, Products, and Institutions* (Cambridge: Open Book, 2010), pp. 93–117.

I wish first to express thanks to SSHRC, the University of Toronto's Faculty of Information, and the University's Connaught Fund for financial and other forms of support. I am also grateful to Julia and Kitto for the opportunity to learn from them, and to Kathleen Fitzpatrick, David Nichols, Judith Altreuter, and the members of the MLA's Committee on the New Variorum Shakespeare (past and present) for their encouragement. My chief scholarly debt is to Paul Werstine, whose intellectual generosity, time, enthusiasm, and wisdom made this project possible, and who contributed more to this book than I can record.

At Cambridge University Press I am especially grateful to Sarah Stanton for her encouragement, patience, and guidance, and to Rosemary Crawley, Caroline Drake, Fleur Jones, Anna Lowe, and Tom O'Reilly for their attention to detail at every stage in the process. To Noeline Bridge I am grateful for her careful work on the index. I also wish to thank the anonymous readers for the Press, who in many ways understood the book better than I did, and whose insights and detailed advice saved me from many mistakes. Any remaining errors are my own.

Over the past several years I have accumulated an archive of debts to others. For their help in the form of information, conversation, critique, and encouragement I am grateful to Jon Bath, Michael Best, Peter Blayney, Christie Carson, Anne Coldiron, Terry Cook, Travis DeCook, Peter Donaldson, Gabriel Egan, Julia Flanders, Suzanne Gossett, Jonathan Hope, Paul Israel, Christopher Keep, Kathryn Kerby-Fulton, Eric Ketelaar, M. J. Kidnie, Matthew Kirschenbaum, Ian Lancashire, Chaya Litvack, Kathleen Lynch, Bonnie Mak, Daniel Martin, Sonia Massai, Jeff Masten, Scott McLaren, Randy McLeod, Barbara Mowat, Martin Mueller, Andrew Murphy, Scott Schofield, Sydney Shep, Bill Sherman, Peter Stallybrass, Carlene Stephens, Sarah Werner, and Michael Whitmore. I am deeply grateful to those who took time to read chapter drafts, especially Fiona Coll, Jennifer Esmail, Jenny Kerber, Zachary Lesser, Randy McLeod, Heather MacNeil, Katherine Rowe, and, again, Paul Werstine and the anonymous readers for the Press.

I also wish to thank the many overlapping scholarly communities that encouraged this project in various ways: my co-editors on the Architectures of the Book project; the other members of the Floating Academy blog; the Folger Institute, especially the members of the 2013 Early Modern Digital Agendas seminar, led by Jonathan Hope and supported by the National Endowment for the Humanities; and audiences and seminar groups at the conferences of the Canadian Association for the Study of Book Culture, the Modern Language

Association, the Renaissance Society of America, the Society for the History of Authorship, Reading, and Publishing, the Society for Textual Scholarship, and especially the Shakespeare Association of America. I am also grateful to the organizers and audiences of the many invited talks that helped me develop the ideas in this book over the past several years.

I am fortunate to be part of so many stimulating intellectual communities at my home institution, such that they require their own paragraph. At the University of Toronto I am especially grateful to the students, faculty, and other members of the Book History and Print Culture collaborative graduate program, the Jackman Humanities Institute, the Centre for Reformation and Renaissance Studies, and the McLuhan Coach House Institute. I owe a special debt to the University of Toronto's Faculty of Information (iSchool), not only for its institutional support but also for the adventurous, interdisciplinary, and intellectually hospitable community created by its students, faculty, staff, and alumni. I hope that a great many of my colleagues will see their influence reflected in this book, and I particularly wish to thank Joan Cherry, Wendy Duff, Patricia Fleming, Steve Hockema, Lynne Howarth, Heather MacNeil, Matt Ratto, Seamus Ross, Brian Cantwell Smith, and my students over the past several years. I was also privileged to work with outstanding research assistants on this project, namely Peter Gorman, Sarah Lubelski, Emily Monks-Leeson, Rebecca Niles, and Matthew Wells.

The staff of several libraries and archives made all the difference in this research, and I am grateful to those at the Bodleian Library, the Horace Howard Furness Memorial Library at the University of Pennsylvania, the Library of Congress Manuscript Division, Massey College Library at the University of Toronto, the National Library of Scotland, the New York Public Library, the Smithsonian National American History Museum, the State Library of New South Wales, George Eastman House at the International Museum of Photography and Film, and the Thomas A. Edison Papers Project at Rutgers University. Special thanks go to Nancy Shawcross of the University of Pennsylvania Library for granting permission to use the image of H. H. Furness's annotated copy of the Cambridge *Romeo and Juliet* for the cover. My warmest gratitude goes to the Thomas Fisher Rare Book Library at the University of Toronto and the Folger Shakespeare Library, the two quiet yet sociable havens where much of this book was written, whose staff have been unstintingly generous with their knowledge and energy.

On a personal note, I wish to thank the many friends and family who supported me in this project through good times and bad. My parents, Gerry and Joan Galey, to whom this book is dedicated, provided moral and material support beyond reckoning and without reservation. This book is also dedicated to my grandmother, Evelyn Galey, whose struggle with Alzheimer's disease taught me new respect for memory's fragility and durability alike. Most of all, I would not have finished this project were it not for Jenny Kerber's wisdom, enthusiasm, advice, patience, impatience, and humour. I cannot repay the debt I owe her, but look forward to trying anyway.

Abbreviations

All parenthetically cited Shakespeare quotations are from Jowett, *et al.* (eds.), *The Oxford Shakespeare.*

F1	*Mr. William Shakespeares Comedies, Histories, & Tragedies* (London, 1623)
F2	*Mr. William Shakespeares Comedies, Histories, & Tragedies* (London, 1632)
Bell Family Papers	Alexander Graham Bell Family Papers, 1834–1974, Library of Congress, Manuscript Division, www.loc.gov/collection/alexander-graham-bell-papers/
Furness Family Papers	Furness Family Papers (Ms. Col. 481), University of Pennsylvania, Rare Book and Manuscript Library
NVS	*New Variorum Shakespeare*
OED	*Oxford English Dictionary Online*, www.oed.com

1 Introduction: scenes from the prehistory of digitization

When our poet's entire library shall have been discovered, and the fables of all his plays traced to their original source, when every temporary allusion shall have been pointed out, and every obscurity elucidated, then, and not till then, let the accumulation of notes be complained of.

Edmund Malone, preface to the 1790 Variorum[1]

Had the Shakespeare editor Edmund Malone written these words in the early twenty-first century instead of the late eighteenth, he might well have used the word *archive* instead of *library*. Malone was certainly interested in Shakespeare's actual library of source material, but his ambition to recover all possible traces of Shakespeare's originary acts of authorship can best be described as archival. Between Malone's time and ours, the archive has replaced the library as the dominant metaphor for cultural memory, extending to specific institutions and technologies, and to memory as a personal and social phenomenon. While libraries tend to order their materials according to abstract systems premised upon Enlightenment models of an ideal world of knowledge, modern archives instead take a forensic approach, ordering their materials according to a reconstructed model of the typically unideal conditions in which an author's unpublished records lived and had their being. In other words, libraries usually order the world of knowledge as it should be; archives order the many little worlds of documentary traces as they actually were (as far as we can determine). The figure of the archive provides a useful set of metaphors for thinking about the transmission and preservation of literary texts like Shakespeare's, given that an archive is at once a physical thing – that is, a material gathering-together of documents, artifacts, and data – and an imaginary thing, a symbol for cultural investments in memory, preservation, and an available past. Malone may have envisioned Shakespeare's library as a real

---

[1] Malone (ed.), *Plays and Poems*, vol. I, part I, p. lvi.

space, but the object of Malone's own recovery project was an imagined Shakespearean archive – the sum of all the recoverable traces of the author's literary life.[2] This book explores the convergence of texts, technologies, documents, data sets, and new media experiments that have come to constitute the Shakespearean archive in the digital age.

Archives also embody our preoccupation with human presences in the documents that outlive us. With the possible exception of the Bible, that preoccupation is nowhere more intense than in the study of Shakespeare's textual remains. Jacques Derrida famously called this tendency *mal d'archive*, the archive fever or disorder which means "to have a compulsive, repetitive, and nostalgic desire for the archive, an irrepressible desire to return to the origin, a homesickness, a nostalgia for the return to the most archaic place of absolute commencement."[3] Derrida's characterization captures the nature of Malone's preoccupation with Shakespeare, as does Pierre Nora's description of memory's social and institutional dimensions:

Modern memory is first of all archival. It relies entirely on the specificity of the trace, the materiality of the vestige, the concreteness of the recording, the visibility of the image … [S]ociety as a whole has acquired the religion of preservation and archivalization. What we call memory is in fact a gigantic and breathtaking effort to store the material vestiges of what we cannot possibly remember, thereby amassing an unfathomable collection of things that we might someday need to recall.[4]

The road by which we arrived at this condition has been a long one, and amounts to more than just a chronicle of media and technologies. As Thomas Richards notes, for those living at the height of the British Empire, "The archive was not a building, nor even a collection of texts, but the collectively imagined junction of all that was known or knowable, a fantastic representation of an epistemological master pattern."[5] The inaccessibility of the ideal archive, in the sense Richards describes, makes it both an object of desire and the principle by which that desire is frustrated.

What role does Shakespeare play in this archival picture of cultural memory, in the Victorian period but also within the more general scope of modernity that Nora considers? How does the preoccupation with archiving, as described by Derrida and Nora and embodied by Malone,

---

[2] On Malone's encyclopedic project, see de Grazia, *Shakespeare Verbatim.*
[3] Derrida, *Archive Fever*, p. 91.   [4] Nora, *Realms of Memory*, vol. I, p. 8.
[5] Richards, *Imperial Archive*, p. 11.

shape the ways we understand and represent Shakespeare's texts? This book explores these questions in ways that shed light not only on historical instances of Shakespearean archive fever, like Malone's variorum edition, but also on their connections with digital tendencies in the present. Shakespeare's texts give a habitation and a name to the spectres of forgetting and loss that haunt any archival enterprise.

What I call the Shakespearean archive can be defined as the imagined totality of playbooks, documents, versions, individual variants, commentaries, sources, adaptations, and other preservable records that underwrite the transmission of Shakespeare's texts. The Shakespearean archive serves as an answer – or at least a response – to the bibliographic koan attributed to F.W. Bateson, "If the *Mona Lisa* is in the Louvre, where [is] *Hamlet* ... ?"[6] The essential characteristic is the persistent sense, evident in Malone's words above, of the Shakespearean archive as an *imagined totality*, and specifically as what Nora calls an "an unfathomable collection" of information that cannot be remembered in its totality, but may be grasped in fragments with the help of memory technologies – including the format of the variorum edition, in Malone's case. In this sense, one could just as easily speak of the James Joyce archive, or the archive of English common law, but Shakespeare stands as an exceptional case given the degree to which his unstable textual archive is made to bear the weight of cultural heritage in the Western tradition. This form of Shakespearean exceptionality has received less attention than the more traditional kind, which takes Shakespeare to be the apex of English literary achievement and insight into human nature. Whatever else Shakespeare may be, his works stand as an exceptional problem for the idea of the straightforward transmitting and archiving

---

[6] Quoted in Greetham, *Textual Scholarship*, p. 342, and in slightly different forms in Bornstein, "How to Read," p. 29, Robinson, "Is There a Text," p. 99, and probably many more publications. However, it is unclear what they are quoting; as Sukanta Chaudhuri points out, it appears that F. W. Bateson never formulated this idea as the question so often attributed to him, and that the closest he came in any printed source was a statement (accompanied by a decided answer), not an open question, in "The New Bibliography and the 'New Criticism,'" pp. 9–10 (but see also Bateson's exploration of the *Hamlet-Lycidas*-Louvre thought experiment from ten years prior, in "Modern Bibliography and the Literary Artifact," p. 74, and Joseph Grigely's discussion in *Textualterity*, pp. 84–5); Chaudhuri, *Metaphysics of Text*, p. 53. However, literary critics and textual scholars such as Chaudhuri, Greetham, Bornstein, and Robinson have also demonstrated the value of considering the received question as such, regardless of attribution.

of cultural texts, and the various responses to this problem reveal human insights of a different kind.

The absence of the most archival of authors' records – Shakespeare's dramatic manuscripts – often prompts a necessary over-compensation in other areas of archival management. A specifically Shakespearean form of archive fever manifests in the interplay of time, desire, and data that runs through Malone's language in the epigraph above: "entire library"; "all his plays traced"; "every . . . allusion"; "every obscurity" – this is the language of philological encyclopedism, inflected through the context of variorum editing as the building of a new kind of Shakespearean editorial interface. Though Malone makes an appeal to the spatial metaphor of Shakespeare's own library, his emphasis here is on temporality, on the archive as both an experiential state (responding to the "accumulation of notes" on the page) and an unfolding process (the sum of the verbs "discover," "trace," "point out," "elucidate," and "accumulate" as archival energies behind the notes). The tone of apocalypticism in Malone's words bears out Derrida's point that archives exist not for the past but for the future.[7] Malone looks ahead to a moment of final revelation and escape from the squabbles of Shakespearean editorial history ("then, and not till then"), to be reached only through the medium of time with all its repetitions and accumulations.

Yet Malone apparently cannot account for a phenomenon that now seems commonplace, that the passing of time and accumulation of data generate more questions than answers. That accumulation defines the conditions of digital textual scholarship today. Over fifteen years ago, as digital editing and archiving were becoming the viable pursuits that humanists now accept them to be, Julia Flanders posed a question that textual scholars are still working to answer: "what pressure does the term 'archive' . . . put on the conceptualization of the 'edition'?"[8] Archives seem to offer unconstrained access to vast stores of primary materials, but at the expense of the scholarly selectivity and synthesis that readers value in editions. As the twenty-first century brings more digital Shakespeare projects, Flanders's question remains with us. It is clear that all digital textual scholarship takes place within the long

---

[7] Derrida, *Archive Fever*, pp. 33–4. Peter Shillingsburg makes the similar point that "The purpose of editing is not to replicate the past" in his defense of authorially focused editorial theory, "The Semiotics of Bibliography," p. 21.

[8] Flanders, "Body Encoded," p. 136.

shadow of the archive, but that does not mean that we understand the shape of the figure casting that shadow.

The Shakespearean Archive explores the entwined histories of Shakespearean texts and archival technologies over the past four centuries, and asks why one finds Shakespeare so often associated with new information technologies and with the idea of archiving itself. In a sequence of chapters dealing with the archive, the book, photography, sound, information, and data, this book explores how the inherited texts of Shakespeare's plays (and to a lesser extent his poems) became prototypical material for publishing experiments, new media projects, and tech demos, as well as for theories of information and computing from the seventeenth century to the present. The chapters delve into specific examples of what could be called Shakespearean sites of memory, in reference to Nora's concept of *lieux de mémoire*: the various sites, whether documents, places, or ritual practices, "in which memory is crystallized."[9] As Nora describes, "An archive is a purely material site that becomes a *lieu de mémoire* only if imagination invests it with a symbolic aura."[10] Shakespeare's texts bring with them a symbolic aura like no other, and yet also function as sites of forgetting and loss, even in the context of digitization projects that appeal to the modern archive fever that Nora and Derrida describe.[11]

This book offers a critical prehistory of digitization read through the technological afterlives of Shakespeare's complex and imperfect textual archive. In taking modern digitization as a point of departure for historical inquiry, I regard the present state of computing not as a given, but as the result of cultural investments that bestow value in some ways and withhold it in others. The most consequential of those investments – in ideas such as the transmissability of culture through new media, and the translatability of cultural texts into data – were made earlier than one might expect, and many preceded and set the stage for modern Shakespeareans' narratives about the transmission of the texts.

Attempts to manage the Shakespearean archive inevitably take technological form. The book itself is the most obvious technology to consider in this regard, and there has been a resurgence of scholarly energy

---

[9] Nora, *Realms of Memory*, vol. I, p. 1.
[10] Nora, *Realms of Memory*, vol. I, p. 14.
[11] For a general discussion of the role of loss in the history of books and libraries, see the chapters in Raven (ed.), *Lost Libraries*, and especially Raven's introduction, "The Resonances of Loss," pp. 1–40.

in this area in recent years.[12] However, there has been less attention given to Shakespeare's strange ubiquity in the history of information and media, especially from the nineteenth century onward.[13] He shows up in the strangest places. When an 1856 advertisement pitches the stereoscope as a new invention for domestic entertainment, it quotes *Hamlet* ("Seems Madam! Nay, it IS!"). When the editor and librarian (and forger) John Payne Collier undertook the first photographic reproduction of a complete book, the book he chose was the rare *Hamlet* first quarto. When the Royal Ordnance Survey published a pamphlet detailing their own newly discovered methods of photozincographic reproduction, a page from the 1623 First Folio led the triumphal procession of sample images (followed by reproductions of *Domesday Book*, an indenture document, topographic maps, and photographs of Egypt). When Alexander Graham Bell demonstrated early versions of the telephone on the stages of public theatres and music halls, audiences heard *Hamlet* recited over the line, along with newspaper reports and live music. Later, when Bell and his collaborators went to the Smithsonian to deposit a prototype of what would become the dictaphone, they returned to *Hamlet*, recording lines of the play on the wax cylinder that went into storage with the prototype. When Thomas Edison demonstrated an early prototype of a device much like a fax machine, he chose the opening line from *Richard III*, underscoring the temporal efficacy of the machine with Shakespeare's powerful opening word, "Now."[14] It is as though Shakespeare wrote the script for new media's introduction into the cultural imagination.

Shakespeare has been recruited to legitimate not only new technologies but also new ideas about the nature of information and data. When Alan Turing first published his groundbreaking ideas about artificial intelligence in 1950, he imagined the composition of a Shakespearean sonnet to represent the boundary between human and machine

---

[12] Examples include Kastan, *Shakespeare and the Book*; Scott, *Idea of the Book*; Chartier, *Inscription and Erasure*; and Stallybrass, Chartier, Mowrey, and Wolfe, "Hamlet's Tables." See also the works cited in note 24 below.

[13] Exceptions include the work of Katherine Rowe and Peter Donaldson. Rowe cites Donaldson's survey of Shakespeare as "launch content" for new media from the nineteenth century to the present; Rowe, "Media History," p. 306.

[14] These examples are cited and discussed in greater detail elsewhere in this book. On the stereoscope advertisement, Collier *Hamlet* facsimile, and Royal Ordnance Survey experiments, see Chapter 4. On Bell and Edison, see Chapter 5; on Edison's use of *Richard III* specifically, see also Gitelman, *Scripts, Grooves*, pp. 161–2.

intelligence.[15] When other postwar theorists of information and cyber-netics explained their ideas to each other and to the public, Shakespeare regularly furnished examples. When Jeff Rothenberg published one of the foundational articles on digital data preservation in *Scientific American* in 1995, Shakespeare's Sonnet 18 ("So long lives this, and this gives life to thee") served to exemplify preservable data, illustrated by a page from the 1609 quarto.[16] A recent pamphlet by Franco Moretti for the Stanford Literary Lab uses *Hamlet* to illustrate the application of network theory to literary studies, though it does so by detaching *Hamlet* from its history of textual transmission.[17] The most well-known example of all comes from decades earlier: when physicist Arthur Eddington first conjured up the image of innumerable monkeys at typewriters generating literary works by accident, the works were *not* Shakespeare's – Eddington's original example was the contents of the British Museum Library – but somehow Shakespeare colonized the metaphor as it propagated through the twentieth century.[18] That is what Shakespeare does.

Reciprocally, our understanding of the transmission of Shakespeare's texts underwent radical changes immediately after the nineteenth century, in what were also formative decades for modern information culture. Twentieth-century Shakespearean textual studies and its disciplinary progeny, the New Bibliography, have shaped scholarly and popular ideas about the transmission of literary texts under the generally unacknowledged influence of information culture and technology. It was under these conditions that the leading figures of the New Bibliography, W. W. Greg, A. W. Pollard, and John Dover Wilson, inherited the nineteenth century's preoccupation with Shakespeare's quartos and folios as an encyclopedic mass of documents. They inherited an empty archive, given the absence of surviving Shakespeare manu-scripts, but filled it with inferentially reconstructed documents, whose precise details they deduced from patterns of information left by machines

---

[15] Turing, "Computing Machinery and Intelligence," p. 446. Turing and information theory are among the subjects of Chapter 6.

[16] Rothenberg, "Ensuring the Longevity of Digital Documents"; a revised version is posted in the Council on Library and Information Resources online archive: www.clir.org/pubs/archives/ensuring.pdf. I am grateful to Yuri Takhteyev for bringing Rothenberg's article to my attention.

[17] Moretti, "Network Theory, Plot Analysis." This example, along with the Rothenberg article on digital preservation cited above, is discussed in greater detail in Chapter 7.

[18] On Eddington, see Butler, "Monkeying Around with Text," p. 113–14.

and humans working together in the early modern printing house. Following Greg's first major work on memory as an agent of textual transmission in 1910, bibliographers increasingly viewed Shakespeare's textual problems in terms of information technology.[19] Joseph Loewenstein characterizes the New Bibliography not simply as an editorial and bibliographical movement, but as a "research program in industrial history," and argues that "new information technology and a legal crisis [over copyright] which that technology exacerbated were somehow determining for a twentieth-century bibliographical scholarship [with the result that] problems in modern intellectual property somehow motivate research into *early* modern information technologies and *early* modern intellectual property."[20] With these changes, as well as the rapid extension and consequent breakdown of the British Empire's networks of information gathering and dissemination, the technologizing of human memory in Freudian psychoanalysis, and the apocalyptic vision that spawned a knowledge preservation industry following the First World War, Shakespeare's material texts acquired unprecedented importance for all Shakespeareans, not just bibliophiles. Memory, textual transmission, and the preservation of knowledge became subjects of a Shakespearean bibliographic narrative, just as the practice of editing became a vital epistemological activity. It prompted the formation of an imagined archive: a fantasy of recoverable histories of textual transmission to buttress cultural monuments under threat from error, loss, and overload.

Digital humanists of the present stand to learn from how Shakespeareans have confronted those spectres, and how they negotiated their own imaginative engagements at the threshold between human and machine. The digital humanities now occupy much the same position in which the New Bibliography found itself in the mid-twentieth century. Then as now, the cultural pressures that went with social and technological change required the assimilation of vast amounts of knowledge about the transmission of texts – and by extension, the seemingly transmissible parts of culture itself – into a coherent narrative. This narrative had to account not only for the literary documents that survive, and for the positive explanatory power they bring to the idea of a transhistorical humanities archive, but also for the practical means by which culture

---

[19] Greg (ed.), *Merry Wives of Windsor*.
[20] Loewenstein, *Author's Due*, pp. 251–2, emphasis in original.

could be preserved and disseminated into the future through editing and related activities. Like digital humanists today, the New Bibliographers lived in a time of new media; they had to articulate their work to a changing academy that often did not understand it; they were obliged by their material to command a detailed knowledge of how text interacts with machines; and they had to respond to the often contradictory imperatives of explaining and making.

Shakespeareans have a unique perspective on the complex relationships between technology and textuality, given that, as Barbara Mowat has pointed out, all of the Shakespeare texts we have inherited from the past (with the possible exception of part of the manuscript for *Sir Thomas More*) are print artifacts.[21] All of the New Bibliographers' hypothesizing about Shakespeare's authorial manuscripts cannot change a basic fact: the Shakespeare we have inherited is the product of a mechanical process – or, to be more exact, the system of linked mechanical processes that constituted early modern printing. There is a large body of scholarly literature on Shakespeare and publishing, building upon the research of eighteenth-century editors such as Edward Capell and Edmund Malone. In recent decades, Shakespeareans have made a concerted effort to see the supposedly stable and familiar form of the book with new eyes, linking the material forms of the text to interpretive questions. In particular, Peter Stallybrass and Margreta de Grazia's provocative 1993 article "The Materiality of the Shakespearean Text" challenged critics to read the plays and poems in the light of knowledge about printing and scribal practices being uncovered by bibliographers and book historians. The materialist turn in Shakespeare studies – exemplified most controversially, perhaps, in Stallybrass and de Grazia's article – coincided with two other key developments: the widespread challenges to the orthodoxy of the New Bibliography's ideas about scholarly editing; and rapid changes in computing technology through the 1990s, which promised new frontiers for the transmission, representation, and analysis of Shakespeare's texts.[22] The link between Shakespeare and the book has become a central topic, exemplified

---

[21] Mowat, "The Problem of Shakespeare's Text(s)."

[22] See De Grazia and Stallybrass, "The Materiality of the Shakespearean Text," and Marcus, *Unediting the Renaissance*. Gabriel Egan provides a skeptical overview of what he calls the New Textualism in his chapter "Materialism, Unediting, and Version-Editing, 1990–1999," in *The Struggle for Shakespeare's Text*, pp. 190–206.

in recent studies by David Scott Kastan and Charlotte Scott.[23] In retrospect, all of this scholarship served to establish the history of the book as no longer merely background or context for Shakespeare's work, but as essential knowledge for understanding the very nature of the texts as cultural artifacts.

What has not yet been attempted on a broad historical scale is an examination of Shakespeare's entanglement with information technologies and structures generally, including books but also encompassing archives, libraries, databases, and other knowledge infrastructures that underpin modernity. With that difference as a point of departure, the present book builds upon studies of the editorial and bibliographical dimensions of Shakespeare by de Grazia, Kastan, Laurie Maguire, Andrew Murphy, Sonia Massai, Lukas Erne, Gabriel Egan, Paul Werstine, and most recently Zachary Lesser.[24] All of these authors concern themselves in different ways with the roles of scribes, players, printers, and publishers in transmitting Shakespeare's texts, and with editors in reshaping those texts for readers. The story of Shakespeare editing and publishing has been told thoroughly and well in these volumes, but *The Shakespearean Archive* seeks to tell a different story, one that focuses instead on textual agents who are not quite editors: the technologists, experimenters, inventors, and other information workers who were the first witnesses of Shakespeare's complex afterlife through information technology. Their stories inform present-day digital projects from the margins of Shakespearean history, and these technologists of the past have their counterparts in the information workers of the present: the encoders, programmers, project managers, database specialists, interface designers, archivists, and librarians who increasingly populate the ranks of the digital humanities. What they teach us is that the range of textual mediations commonly grouped under the word *editing* can take many forms, and can happen in places one might not think to look.

---

[23] Kastan, *Shakespeare and the Book*; Scott, *Idea of the Book*. On the related theme of reading and writing in Shakespeare's works, and in their transmission, see Goldberg, *Writing Matter*, and the essays in Bergeron (ed.), *Reading and Writing*.

[24] De Grazia, *Shakespeare Verbatim*; Maguire, *Shakespearean Suspect Texts*; Murphy, *Shakespeare in Print*; Erne, *Shakespeare as Literary Dramatist*; Massai, *Shakespeare and the Rise of the Editor*; Egan, *The Struggle for Shakespeare's Text*; Werstine, *Early Modern Playhouse Manuscripts and the Editing of Shakespeare*; Lesser, *Hamlet After Q1*.

However, this book is not just a history of how publishers, scholars, maverick inventors, and proto-digital Shakespeareans have applied new technologies to the transmission and study of Shakespeare. My approach is similar to Massai's exploration of the quasi-editorial influence of annotating readers of early modern playbooks, and I share her sense of the larger goal being not simply "to tease these elusive textual agents out of anonymity, but to reflect on the principles which informed the annotation of dramatic copy as a practice and the implications of such practice for contemporary editors."[25] Although I look for different kinds of textual agents and in largely different periods, my goal is also to recover their histories as lessons for the present. Chief among those lessons is that digital Shakespeare in the present is not only a matter of using new tools to read Shakespeare differently, but also of using Shakespeare to see those tools and their underlying epistemologies with different eyes: as new media assimilate Shakespeare, so does Shakespeare assimilate new media.

That reciprocality is central to my argument in this book, and specifically to my critique of instrumentalist definitions of the digital humanities, which often characterize the field as the one-way application *of* digital tools *to* humanities materials – an active-passive binary that encourages the reduction of all humanities texts to the condition of data.[26] The strong current of historical exceptionalism running through the digital humanities makes it difficult to realize that we are not the first to work through questions of Shakespeare's transmission through new media. Although this is not a book about the digital humanities, in the usual sense of contemporary projects and methods, I hope it nonetheless serves as a constructive critique of a rapidly changing field which sometimes overlooks the instructive potential of materials that resist straightforward digitization. In many of the scenes from the prehistory of digitization that I shall examine, Shakespeare's texts are not merely passive content for new information technologies to prove themselves upon. In those meetings of technologies and materials, the imaginative power of Shakespeare's texts also shapes our understanding of information itself. That is what literature does.

---

[25] Massai, *Rise of the Editor*, p. 201.
[26] See Johanna Drucker's critique of misuses of the concept of data in "Humanities Approaches to Graphical Display."

Much of the rationale for calling this book a critical prehistory comes from an argument put forward by Ronald Day in *The Modern Invention of Information*, which holds that information culture systematically forgets its own history. The reason, according to Day, is that "information in modernity connotes a factuality and pragmatic presence ... that erases or radically reduces ambiguity and the problems of reading, interpreting, and constructing history."[27] I call this book a prehistory of digitization not to hint at any supposedly natural or inevitable progression from past to present, but rather, in the spirit of media archaeologists like Wolfgang Ernst and early modernists like Terence Cave, to highlight the difficulty of approaching the digital era as continuous with the past. As Ernst argues, "when media archaeology deals with prehistories of mass media, this 'pre-' is less about temporal antecedence than about the technoepistemological configurations underlying the discursive surface ... of mass media."[28] Narrative is a tool by which humans order their understanding of phenomena, but prehistory, as a critical approach, makes a virtue of the fragmentary – sometimes intractable – aspects of the past that resist easy aggregation into historical narratives. In a similar vein, Anna Holland and Richard Scholar point out that Terence Cave's notion of "afterlives" shares with prehistories "the capacity to probe the (often seductive) myths of origin attached to a particular cultural object."[29] A corollary of these arguments that we might draw from media archaeology is that the stronger the origin myths in question, the greater the need for critical prehistories to tunnel beneath their foundations.

The rest of this introduction lays out some of the foundational concepts that are developed in the rest of the chapters, beginning with *the archive* as a critical term that brings its own challenges. The discussion then turns to a detailed reading of a specific late Victorian

---

[27] Day, *Invention of Information*, p. 3.

[28] Ernst, *Digital Memory*, p. 55. For this reason, although my approach shares obvious affinities with Jay David Bolter and Richard Grusin's *Remediation*, I depart from them in at least two ways. For one, as a textual scholar I try to read the characteristics of media at a level of granularity appropriate to material artifacts; for another, as a Shakespearean I tend to accord more importance than Bolter and Grusin to remediated materials – or content, though I dislike the term – as agents in the making of meaning.

[29] Holland and Scholar, *Prehistories and Afterlives*, p. 5. See also Max Horkheimer and Theodor W. Adorno's use of the term in relation to their own project on modernity and anti-Semitism in *Dialectic of Enlightenment*, p. xvii, and Gerhard Schweppenhäuser's gloss of their use of the term in *Theodor W. Adorno*, pp. 32–3.

edition of *Hamlet* that exemplifies this book's approach to sites of Shakespearean memory. The final section outlines the way those examples are structured in the rest of the book's chapters.

The archive as a critical term

It has become a critical commonplace to speak of *the archive*, using the definite article, as though the term names an ideal epistemological form that stands behind the diversity of memory technologies and institutions. However, after decades of invocations of the archive by critical theorists, historians, and literary scholars – largely in response to Foucault's *Archaeology of Knowledge* and Derrida's *Archive Fever* – the term needs some justification as a central concept in this book. The problem, according to Paul Eggert, is that

> the term *archive* has been generalized, abstracted, extruded into filaments so fine that, like a perfect spider's web, it draws itself into nearly everything that wafts by ... If we are to regard the archive as nearly everything ever remembered, or repressed, or written, or turned into narrative, if it is drawn this wide, pulled this thin, then in a particularlized form that can be dealt with empirically it is almost nothing at all.[30]

In his frustration with *the archive*'s gradual slide into indistinction, Eggert expresses a traditional textual scholar's impatience with inexact terms, a sentiment that runs through the many pointed critiques of Derrida's *Archive Fever* in particular.[31] Although some of that criticism can be dismissed as territoriality on the part of some historians, archivists, and others who feel a disciplinary prior claim to the idea of the archive, one can see Eggert's point, especially given the critical tendency to describe any collection of vaguely interesting objects as an archive.[32]

The crux of the vocabulary problem is the duality of the archive, in that it functions simultaneously as a technical term and as a resonant symbol. Paul Voss and Marta Werner note this duality when introducing their special issue on the archive for the journal *Studies in the Literary*

---

[30] Eggert, "Brought to Book," p. 13.   [31] See Steedman, *Dust*, 1–12, 67–8.

[32] Geoffrey Yeo offers a helpful discussion of the archival concept of the *collection* in "Conceptual Fonds." As Chapter 2 will consider in more detail, the scholarly literature of archivists such as Yeo can ameliorate the vagueness of which Eggert complains, yet that literature also does not shy away from the poststructuralist understanding of archives as political, discursive, and symbolic constructions. For many archivists, these are not contradictory perspectives.

Imagination: "The archive is both a physical site – an institutional space enclosed by protective walls – and an imaginative site – a conceptual space whose boundaries are forever changing."[33] It is exactly this duality that makes the archive a useful concept for analyzing technologies of memory, despite its inherent risk of spinning off into sublime metaphor. The answerability of a "physical site," such as a Shakespeare quarto, to a "conceptual space," such as any of the scenarios of memorial reproduction imagined by Alfred Pollard and the New Bibliographers, reminds us that textual scholarship deals with verifiable facts and indeterminate concepts alike.[34] My use of the term *archive* throughout this book proceeds from this understanding of the word's irreducible duality.

Sorting things out and pinning them down is not always the best use of the humanistic imagination, but there is nonetheless a valid case against loose uses of the term *archive* by those who ignore the experiential aspects of archiving and archival research, as well as those who neglect the differences among archives, libraries, and museums as distinct kinds of institutions, each with their own histories, scholarly literatures, and communities of practice. Although this book was inspired by my early encounter with Derrida's *Archive Fever* and other theoretical explorations of archives, I have become wary of invoking *the archive* as metaphor while ignoring *archiving* as practice, not to mention ignoring archivists as theorists of their own practices. For example, soon after Rebecca Comay's landmark collection *Lost in the Archives* appeared in 2002, the volume's reviewer in *American Archivist* found occasion to lament the "all-too-common habit of invoking archives without listening for the voice of any archivist."[35] Even a full decade later, a similar collection such as Gunhild Borggreen and Rune Gade's *Performing Archives/Archives of Performance* manages to cite only two archivists, and Richard Burt and Julian Yates's *What's the Worst Thing You Can Do with Shakespeare?* cites none at all, despite invoking the archive at several points.[36] As an

---

[33] Voss and Werner, "Poetics of the Archive," p. i.

[34] For similar discussions of the archive with regard to textual studies, see Greetham, "Who's In, Who's Out: The Cultural Poetics of Archival Exclusion," in *Pleasures of Contamination*, pp. 117–51; Bjelland, "Editor as Theologian"; and Assmann, "Texts, Traces, Trash."

[35] Horton, review of *Lost in the Archives*, p. 296.

[36] In the *Performing Archives/Archives of Performance* collection, edited by Gunhild Borggreen and Rune Gade, Heike Roms cites Terry Cook in her chapter, "Archiving Legacies: Who Cares for Performance Remains," pp. 35–49, and

analogy, imagine trying to do research in the field of science and technology studies (STS) without referencing any writing by scientists – it would be just as misleading as accepting *only* the accounts of scientists themselves as evidence of their practice. Responsible STS scholarship steers between these extremes. Likewise, this book is intended not as a riposte against theory on behalf of practicing archivists, but rather seeks a middle ground where ideas such as Derrida's archival "Freudian Impression" can remain provocative without becoming the limit of one's thinking about archives.

To put Eggert's reservations in context, it may be helpful briefly to consider the archive as what Mieke Bal calls a "travelling concept" by examining three different uses of the term *archive* from separate fields that share similar investments in the term.[37] The figure of the archivist is most readily identifiable with the disciplines of library and information science, and museum studies (though archives constitute a distinct field and scholarly discourse of their own, as I shall discuss in more detail in Chapter 2). Here is a tripartite definition of *archives* as it appears in *A Basic Glossary for Archivists, Manuscript Curators, and Records Managers*:

(1) The noncurrent records of an organization or institution preserved because of their continuing value . . . (2) The agency responsible for selecting, preserving, and making available archival materials . . . (3) The building or part of a building where such materials are located.[38]

The glossary offers synonyms for each of these three senses of *archive*, but the metonymic elasticity of *archive*, which folds "records," "agency," and "building" into the same word, remains unavoidable even here, in a standard professional glossary where one might expect only no-nonsense positivism.

Another permutation of the term *archive* came with the rise of digital humanities projects such as *The Rossetti Archive* and the *William Blake Archive*.[39] One might question the appropriateness of the term in these cases, given that these projects include published texts, whereas archives traditionally limit themselves to unpublished, noncirculating records. However, one of the clearest rationales for the concept of digital

---

Rachel Fensham cites Francesca Marini in her chapter, "Choreographic Archives: Towards an Ontology of Movement Images," pp. 146–61.

[37] Bal, *Travelling Concepts*.

[38] Evans, Harrison, Thompson, and Roffes, *Glossary for Archivists*, p. 417.

[39] In addition to the sources referenced below, see McCarty, "Humanities Computing," p. 14.

archives comes from Sonia Massai, herself a digital Shakespeare editor, who notes that "a change brought about by the electronic medium is that the end result of an editor's labours is not a critical *edition* but a critical *archive*":

A critical edition is structured hierarchically and privileges the modern text over other textual alternatives, which are cryptically and partially summarized in the textual apparatus. The critical archive provides accurate and searchable digital versions of the editions from which those textual alternatives derive ... A printed critical edition helps the reader approach the text by establishing a clear hierarchy of meanings and interpretations ... [but] [t]he structure of the archive is open-ended and the virtually endless combinations of pathways ... utterly arbitrary.[40]

Massai's use of the term *archive* marks an especially important distinction in Shakespeare studies, where the editorial and critical traditions have periodically drawn new energy from an influx of archival materials (Malone's 1790 variorum and Sam Schoenbaum's *Shakespeare: A Documentary Life* are but two examples).[41] Peter Donaldson, in his discussion of the terms *expanded text* and *electronic archive*, makes the related point that "the term 'archive' ... is one that evokes distinctions that belong to the familiar world of printed text, bound books, and physical artefacts, distinctions that do not apply exactly in the domain of electronic texts and digital documents."[42] This may be true, but Massai's use of the term puts the right name to the desire to provide (or acquire) unrestricted access to the mass of pre-editorial materials from which Shakespeare editions emerge.[43] Whether the archive is digital or paper, the scholarly desire for unconstrained access remains the same, despite the constraints inherent to all archives.

That brings us to a third permutation of the term *archive*, which is just as important as the others, even if less clearly defined. Speaking of the tasks of digital humanists in the coming years, Jerome McGann offered a prophecy in his 2002 acceptance speech for one of humanities computing's top honours, the Lyman Award: "There's a slow train

---

[40] Massai, "Scholarly Editing," p. 103.   [41] Schoenbaum, *Documentary Life*.
[42] Donaldson, "Digital Archive," p. 177.
[43] The *HamletWorks* project, for example, seeks to put online the materials assembled by the editors of the New Variorum Shakespeare *Hamlet*, including those that could not fit into the NVS's already compendious format: www.hamletworks.org.

coming and its song goes something like this: *In the next 50 years the entirety of our inherited archive of cultural works will have to be re-edited within a network of digital storage, access, and dissemination.*"[44] McGann apparently uses the term in the same sense as Grant Williams and Christopher Ivic, who, in the introduction to their collection *Forgetting in Early Modern English Literature and Culture*, echo many literary and cultural critics by treating the archive broadly as "the space of documents with which scholarship is preoccupied."[45] In McGann's example, the specific meaning of "our inherited archive" matters less than the phase's rhetorical context and even the cultural work it performs. McGann deliberately uses *archive* as a word whose power derives not from critical currency or theoretical sophistication so much as from the place the archive holds in the cultural imagination. This sense of the word *archive* most strongly embodies the archive fever of which Derrida speaks, and its manifestation in the increasingly large-scale projects of the digital humanities lends urgency to McGann's use of the term. Yet the confidence with which McGann and other digital humanists invoke the figure of the archive – as though archives are not also symbols for the loss, partiality, and unmanageable overload of knowledge – should prompt us to interrogate not only the technological keywords in McGann's statement, like "network, "digital," and "dissemination," but also the words that quietly deploy imaginative power, including "archive" but also "inherited," and most of all, the pronoun "our."

Each of these three examples pushes the term *archive* in different directions – indeed, the archivists' glossary pushes it in three directions at once. What unites them is the symbolism attached to the idea of the archive. Even if textual scholars were to retreat toward a purely empirical conception of archives, as Eggert seems to advise, they would find their path blocked by the intellectual advances of archivists themselves, whose own critical literature in journals like *Archivaria* and *Archival Science* has embraced the theoretical, cultural, and social dimensions of their subject. Likewise, G. Thomas Tanselle, who represents what could be

---

[44] McGann, "Textonics: Literary and Cultural Studies in a Quantum World," www.nhc.rtp.nc.us/newsrel2002/mcgannwebcast.htm, emphasis in the original; published in Nash (ed.), *The Culture of Edited Collections*. Variations on this theme appear throughout McGann's recent work; see *Radiant Textuality*, pp. 2, 18, and 184; "Note on the Current State of Humanities Scholarship," p. 410; and "Information Technology," p. 114.

[45] Williams and Ivic, "Sites of Forgetting," p. 10.

called a conservative tradition within textual scholarship, nonetheless praises an expansive use of the term *archive* – though with a sense of precision and a critical attitude toward the trustworthiness of archives as sources of evidence.[46] Tracing the material interconnectedness of publishing history, using methods such as the analysis of paper stocks and the public and private records of publishers, leads, in Tanselle's words, to "the understanding that all artifacts form one vast archive, the tangible residue of the activities of humanity"; "as one thinks about these connections, the idea of 'archive' inexorably expands."[47] It is essential to understand the technical aspects of archives, but as archivists and textual scholars alike maintain, that understanding cannot be isolated from the narratives that invest archives with encyclopedic capacity and imaginative force.[48]

That connection and its Shakespearean inflections will be the particular focus of Chapter 2, but this book as a whole deals with the power of the archive in the cultural imagination. Michael O'Driscoll points to the position of mastery that Enlightenment encyclopedists sought to attain by trading the tree of knowledge for the map, and quotes Jean Le Rond d'Alembert's version of the metaphor: encyclopedic arrangement "consists of collecting knowledge into the smallest area possible and of placing the philosopher at a vantage point, so to speak, high above this vast labyrinth, whence he can perceive the principal sciences and the arts simultaneously."[49] The encyclopedic ideal thus lends itself to spectacle, though the actual conditions of archives are harder to visualize. When scholars like McGann self-consciously use *archive* as a term on the edge of metaphor, they draw upon iconic representations of cultural memory that visualize what Tanselle calls the "one vast archive" of artifacts, and Nora calls "an unfathomable collection of things."[50]

An iconic representation of one such vast archive appears in a shot near the end of Orson Welles's film *Citizen Kane* (1941) in which the camera floats above a huge collection of artifacts in the deceased Charles Foster Kane's mansion, inventorying the material accumulations of the publishing magnate's misspent life, and finally picking out Kane's long-lost childhood sleigh "Rosebud" just before the beloved object is thrown in the incinerator. D. F. McKenzie takes this shot as a lesson for textual scholars,

---

[46] Tanselle, "World as Archive."   [47] Tanselle, "World as Archive," p. 405.
[48] See Manoff, "Theories of the Archive."
[49] D'Alembert, *Preliminary Discourse*, p. 47. See also O'Driscoll, "Derrida, Foucault," pp. 289–90.
[50] Nora, *Realms of Memory*, p. 8.

and emphasizes Jorge Luis Borges's insight that Kane's accumulated hoard of art objects is analogous to the archive as "a world of fragments without unity," challenging order and provoking fears of the failure of the editorial and archival enterprise.[51] Similar fears and desires underpin the final moments of the 1981 film *Raiders of the Lost Ark*, in which the Ark of the Covenant, recovered by Indiana Jones from the Nazis, is crated up and numbered by an anonymous workman, and wheeled down the aisle of a vast US government warehouse into a shadowy expanse of identical crates that mirrors the Egyptian temple where Jones found the Ark. Like many of the nineteenth-century anxieties about the failure of archives to preserve the past, this figure of the archive represents a failure of centralized authority to organize its information and to bequeath it securely to the future. "They don't know what they've got there," says Jones in his final line (later confirmed in the franchise's fourth film by the Ark's fleeting cameo during the warehouse chase sequence, in which the crate goes unnoticed by all but the camera).

The idealization of the archive thus remains incomplete without its attendant anxiety that once something important gets lost in a mass of information, it stays lost, and error creeps into its place. For Thomas Richards, writing of the late Victorian era, this archive anxiety crystallizes in the image of the British Museum's basement, where steadily incoming data and artifacts accumulated in a heap – the conditions where the informatic death-drive can do its work, as Derrida describes in *Archive Fever*.[52] To recall Voss and Werner's description of the archive's duality, mentioned above, the British Museum basement was important as both an actual place and a conceptual space, especially after what Richards calls the "information explosion" of the late nineteenth century.[53] According to Richards, "By 1900 not even the librarians at the British Museum seriously believed they would be able to chip away at this backlog of knowledge."[54] This backlog took literal and figural form in the British Museum's basement, the material substrate for the overworked knowledge-processing institutional mechanism above it, and became "a peripheral zone of lost or forgotten knowledge buried deep within the catacombs of the London archive."[55] The situation Richards describes

---

[51] McKenzie, *Bibliography*, p. 64.
[52] Richards, *Imperial Archive*, p. 16; Derrida, *Archive Fever*, pp. 11–12.
[53] Richards, *Imperial Archive*, p. 5.   [54] Richards, *Imperial Archive*, p. 4.
[55] Richards, *Imperial Archive*, p. 16.

could be considered part of what Richard Terdiman calls a broader crisis of memory in the nineteenth century, one whose various factors, technological and social, amounted to "the realization that *nothing* is natural about our memories, that the past – the practices, the habits, the dates and facts and places, the very furniture of our existences – is an artifice, and one susceptible to the most varied and sometimes the most culpable manipulations."[56] That crisis of memory affected nineteenth-century Shakespeare editing, as I shall discuss in subsequent chapters on the memory manipulations of new media in that period, but the sense of crisis also persists today, giving modern representations of archives their resonance.

Representations of the archive implicate us as viewers, too, and configure our relationships to technologies of memory. The *Citizen Kane* shot mentioned above is very much about the power of the mobile camera, and specifically its ability to locate and reveal the object named "Rosebud" that has eluded researchers throughout the film. Even though Rosebud is cast into the fire, the camera itself preserves the knowledge of the object from destruction, and the power of technically enhanced human vision triumphs in the end. *Raiders of the Lost Ark*, however, places the viewer in a different position altogether, as the camera remains stationary and the warehouse custodian wheels the Ark of the Covenant away from us, finally turning left into the stacks of identical crates and disappearing. The tablets of Moses contained in the Ark become lost objects of desire all over again, like Shakespeare's manuscripts.

Both examples are about the effect that lostness has on us as viewers of these scenes. Most Shakespeare editors and digital textual scholars would like to think their digital tools are like Welles's camera, always finding meaningful patterns against a chaotic background of noise, but digital tools may have as much in common with Steven Spielberg's camera in the *Raiders* shot, registering only the horizon of our knowledge and the ghostly traces of what has been lost.

Questioning computing essentialism: the case of Teena Rochfort Smith's *Four-Text Hamlet* (1883)

The tension between surfaces and depths is a theme that connects many of the examples above, from the *Kane* and *Raiders* shots to Richards's account of the British Museum basement, and even to Ernst's characterization of

---

[56] Terdiman, *Present Past*, p. 31, emphasis in original.

media archaeology as a recovery project that unearths "technoepistemological considerations underlying the discursive surface ... of mass media."[57] In all these examples, the archive represents a semi-structured but overwhelming mass of materials that requires an interface: some form of technology that mediates between the human and the masses of information that exceed human capacities.[58] In my cinematic analogies, the camera itself provides this technological mediation, creating what Margaret Hedstrom calls "interfaces with the past," where "power is negotiated and exercised ... consciously and unconsciously, over documents and their representations, over access to them, over actual and potential uses of archives, and over memory."[59] Interfaces with the past take many forms, and the surface–depth metaphor also describes the ways that disciplines interface with their own pasts – including the tendency in some quarters to present the digital humanities as a pristine, shining city on the hill that appeared on the landscape only recently.[60] This book, as a prehistory of digitization, explores the digital humanities' shadowy basement, as it were: the forgotten layers of technical and imaginative infrastructure beneath the surface of modern digital technologies, built by information cultures that predate the Internet by decades and even centuries.

Even the word *computer* has a forgotten basement of its own. Beneath the immediate, surface definition that is likely to come to mind – a digital device with a screen, memory, and processing power (which even within this definition may take multiple forms) – there lie nearly four centuries of accumulated meanings deriving from the word's original referent, according to the *OED*: "A person who makes calculations or computations ... *spec.* a person employed to make calculations in an observatory, in surveying, etc." (*computer* n.1). Only with the second *OED* definition does one arrive at "A device or machine for performing or facilitating calculation" (first attested in 1869); and only with the third

---

[57] Ernst, *Digital Memory*, p. 55. See also Peter Shillingsburg's chapter "The Dank Cellar of Electronic Texts," in his *Gutenberg to Google*, pp. 138–50.

[58] See Hedstrom, "Archives, Memory, and Interfaces."

[59] Hedstrom, "Archives, Memory, and Interfaces," p. 22.

[60] For example, a 2010 newspaper article on the digital humanities boils down to the following question and answer: "The next big idea in language, history and the arts? Data"; Patricia Cohen, "Digital Keys for Unlocking the Humanities' Riches," *New York Times* (16 November 2010). This article is discussed in more detail in Chapter 7.

definition does one arrive at "An *electronic* device" (first attested in 1945; emphasis added).[61] This successive overwriting of the meanings of *computer* exemplifies what Lauren Rabinovitz and Abraham Geil call information culture's "rhetoric of newness" and "rhetoric of amnesia," which shadows all discourse about new media and information technology.[62] Accordingly, most discussions of digital humanities projects naturally focus on the present, sometimes taking current forms of computing to be the result of technical forces beyond the scope of humanist inquiry, thereby forgetting the history of the word *computing* itself.

For that reason, the ongoing history of digital Shakespeare research stands somewhat at the edges of my focus on lesser-known examples of proto-digital innovation, even though new digital Shakespeare projects provide the impetus for this discussion.[63] Instead of privileging recent digital work, I aim to show that Shakespearean textual studies builds on a long history of technological experimentation in response to the perceived complexity of the Shakespearean archive. New dimensions of technology, past and present, open up when one takes computing as a practice that transcends any particular device. How might Shakespeare's past and future look different if we placed less emphasis on the recent distinction between digital and print editions, and instead took words like *computing* and *interface* to describe historical practices with long-term continuities? Let us consider an example that demonstrates the value of understanding the history of Shakespearean editorial interfaces in broad terms, without limiting ourselves to digital tools.

Few digital Shakespeareans are likely aware that the most visually complex edition of Shakespeare ever attempted – to this day – precedes the rise of the personal computer by nearly a century. In 1883 a young woman named Teena Rochfort Smith created a prototype of a four-text edition of *Hamlet*.[64] She pursued this project under the auspices of

---

[61] The *OED*'s record of attestations should never be taken as the last (or first) word on the matter, but its general progression of the meanings of *computer* holds true. On the dual human/mechanical meanings of *computer*, see Hayles, *My Mother*, p. 1, and Balsamo, *Technologies*, p. 133.

[62] Rabinovitz and Geil (eds.), *Memory Bytes*, p. 2.

[63] Overviews of recent and older digital Shakespeare projects can be found in Murphy, "Shakespeare Goes Digital"; Best and Rasmussen (eds.), *Monitoring Electronic Shakespeares*; Galey and Siemens (eds.), *Reinventing Digital Shakespeare*; and Carson, "The Evolution of Online Editing."

[64] Rochfort Smith, *A Four-Text Edition of Shakespeare's Hamlet*. Throughout, I follow Ann Thompson in using the shortened title *Four-Text Hamlet*. The Folger

Frederick Furnivall and the New Shakespeare Society, having presented a paper on "The Relation of the First Quarto of *Hamlet* to the Second, and on Some of the Textual Difficulties of the Play" to the Society the year before.[65] Her goal, evidently, was not to establish a best text of *Hamlet* but to visualize the differences between the texts of the first quarto (Q1, 1603), second quarto (Q2, 1604/5),and First Folio (F1, 1623). She did this using a four-column parallel-text layout extending across the opening of an oblong book, with the fourth column given to a "Revised Text" in the form of her own editorial conflation (Figure 1.1).

Parallel-text layouts had been attempted before 1883, and later became an interface strategy for multiple-text digital editions, but what sets Rochfort Smith's work apart is the elaborate typography by which she visually encodes *Hamlet*'s textual relationships within the play's own lines. She accomplishes this typographic encoding with a mix of Roman, italic, Clarendon, sans-serif, gothic, bold, and small-capital type, sometimes merging different types in the same word, and sometimes in combination with various diacritical marks. These pages from 1883 look like a postmodern typographical riot. Yet there is method in it, with each kind of visual flag signalling not only each text's variations from the modern "Revised" text in the fourth column, but also variations between the other source texts. In other words, Rochfort Smith undertook a complete collation including orthographical variants, unlike modern critical editions, which rarely collate widely variant sources against each other. Astonishingly, she represents all this intellectual labour without recourse to conventional textual notes.[66]

History has treated Rochfort Smith primarily as a footnote in Furnivall's biography because of her evident role as his mistress during this period,

Shakespeare Library holds what may be the only surviving copy (call no. PR2807 1883b Sh.Col.). A digitized version of the full document can be found at luna.folger. edu (search "teena"). I am grateful to the Folger's Curator of Rare Books, Goran Proot, and the Folger staff for expediting its digitization in late 2012.

[65] Rochfort Smith's tragic story is told by Ann Thompson in a 1998 *Shakespeare Quarterly* article titled "Teena Rochfort Smith, Frederick Furnivall, and the New Shakespeare Society's Four-Text Volume of *Hamlet*." Thompson's is the only other original scholarly work on Rochfort Smith's *Four-Text Hamlet* of which I am aware, and I am much indebted to her research.

[66] To be precise, although Rochfort Smith evidently collated every text against every other one, her representation of variants is not absolutely complete. For example, her prefatory guide to the typographical codes indicates that Q1 variants are flagged only when Q2 or F disagree with each other and agree with Q1 instead. Even so, her work is still remarkably thorough.

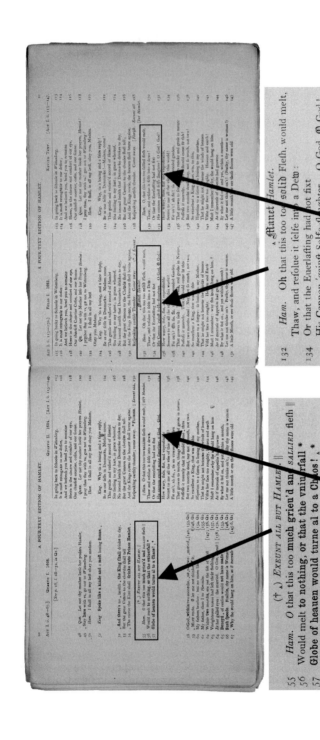

Figure 1.1 Teena Rochfort Smith's *Four-Text Hamlet* (1883).

which has distracted historians from the value of her editorial work as an experiment in Shakespearean interface design. Rochfort Smith's edition may be an obscure one in the annals of editorial history, but it anticipates and even outdoes the complex editorial layouts of the latter twentieth century, both print and digital, and in the *Four-Text Hamlet* one finds a long-lost ancestor of digital projects like *Juxta* and the *Versioning Machine*, and especially Bernice Kliman's *Enfolded Hamlet*.[67] Even by the standards of today's digital projects, Rochfort Smith's typographic interface was an exceptionally ambitious one. Had she completed her edition, it would have been, in Ann Thompson's words, "the most complex presentation of the texts of *Hamlet* ever attempted."[68] Although Thompson makes this claim in an article published in 1998, it still stands even after many years of digital editing. Given *Hamlet*'s unique complexity in the Shakespeare canon as the only play with three authoritative variant texts, one might extend Rochfort Smith's accomplishment beyond *Hamlet* to call it the most visually complex presentation of Shakespeare texts ever attempted. That she achieved that distinction at the age of twenty-one, and as a woman in the predominantly male world of Victorian textual scholarship, makes her accomplishment all the more remarkable.

Sadly, Rochfort Smith did not complete her edition, which proved too elaborate for the New Shakespeare Society's regular printer and publisher, N. Trübner & Company of London, and she died tragically soon after.[69] All that survives of her work on the *Four-Text Hamlet* is a thirty-six-page paper-bound prototype, showing only the play's first three scenes (up to "Be something scanter of your maiden presence"), probably prepared so that Furnivall and other Shakespeare Society members could comment on the project. That prototype survives in only one known copy, held by the Folger Shakespeare Library. Had that copy not survived, digital humanists

---

[67] Juxta is open-source collation software published by the *Nineteenth-Century Scholarship Online* (NINES) project: www.juxtasoftware.org. The *Versioning Machine* is a Web-based interface, designed by teams led by Susan Schreibman, for displaying the kind of variation of interest especially to genetic critics: v-machine.org. The Enfolded Hamlet is a Web-based synoptic reading interface, designed by Bernice Kliman, that combines colour-coded variants from the *Hamlet* texts within the same lines: www.hamletworks.org.

[68] Thompson, "Teena Rochfort Smith," p. 131.

[69] Her story is told in Furnivall's 1883 biography, *Teena Rochfort-Smith*. This pamphlet does not give Furnivall as an author; the attribution is by Thompson, who also notes some inaccuracies in Furnivall's account of the circumstances of her life and death.

would have lost an important if unknown part of their history.[70] What remains can be described as a prototype in the strict sense: an incomplete, small-scale experiment that demonstrated an innovative technology or method using a recognizable example. As a bibliographic artifact without accompanying documentation, the booklet that survives in the Folger Library raises the kinds of interpretive challenges that we will encounter throughout this book as we examine similar examples. In this case, the challenge takes the form of potentially unanswerable questions about how Rochfort Smith imagined her edition might be used. Did she conceive of it as an interface for continuous reading primarily in one column, perhaps with occasional glances left or right to the others, as one reads textual notes in a critical edition? Did she think of it as a reference interface for consultative or discontinuous reading, similar to the Shakespeare Variorums that Furness was editing during the same years in America? Could she even have imagined reading for patterns rather than details? (Given Rochfort Smith's collation of substantive and orthographical variants alike, her prototype could support linguistic and bibliographic patterned readings alike.[71]) Was the *Four-Text Hamlet* a kind of late Victorian paper computer – a "paper machine," in Derrida's phrase?[72]

Answers to these questions can only be inferred from the primary evidence of the surviving prototype itself at the Folger Library (at least in the absence of archival materials such as Rochfort Smith's correspondence

---

[70] An announcement in the periodical *Science: A Weekly Newspaper of All the Arts and Sciences* (17.417; 30 January 1891) mentions that the Shakespeare Society of New York was aware of the *Four-Text Hamlet* project of their London counterparts, "which succumbed to the typographical difficulties of the work." The announcement goes on to claim that "The New York Shakespeare Society believes it has surmounted those difficulties, and undertakes to furnish its subscribers, in or about the fall of 1891, with the four texts – a volume in folio, about 16 x 10, printed on laid paper, de luxe, in the best style of The Riverside Press, about 200 pages, and bound in boards, parchment back, Bankside or Roxburge style. One hundred and fifty copies only are to be printed from the types, and hand-numbered under the society's direction" (p. 69). If the New York Shakespeare Society succeeded in their plan to complete Rochfort Smith's project, they left no record that I have found.

[71] On patterned reading and algorithmic criticism, see Ramsay, *Reading Machines*. An example of reading for patterns in a bibliographic context would be Charlton Hinman's analysis of press variants using his optical collation device (described in more detail in Chapter 6). An example of patterned reading for linguistic patterns may be found in Hope and Witmore, "Hundredth Psalm."

[72] See Derrida, *Paper Machine*, especially the chapters "Machines and the 'Undocumented Person'" and "Paper or Me, You Know … (New Speculations on the Luxury of the Poor)" pp. 1–3, 41–65.

with Furnivall and Trübner). This so often becomes the predicament of prehistory, whether one is a media archaeologist uncovering lost contexts of strange new (old) media or a New Bibliographer reconstructing lost authorial and publishing processes behind a print artifact. There may be archival records that would shed light on Rochfort Smith's project, but my larger point here and throughout this book is that the prehistory of digitization requires interpretive work; it cannot be reduced to any simple progressivist chronology of digital projects leading up to the present. The prehistory of digitization is as elusive as Rochfort Smith's intentions, and emerges largely in the encounter between the cultural historian's gaze and the present artifact.

The textual artifact, in this case, suggests how Rochfort Smith mixed textual scholarship and editing with experimentation using the technology of her day. Regarded in this manner, her pushing of Victorian typography to its limits could be considered a kind of visual markup, like the tags that text encoders use to embed structural and descriptive information in digital texts.[73] She may have used typography instead of XML (eXtensible Markup Language), but her edition nonetheless encodes information about textual relationships at the most granular level, interpenetrating the words of the play. The similarity to digital markup becomes even clearer in Furnivall's description (from his posthumous memoir for Rochfort Smith) of the manuscripts that Rochfort Smith prepared for the press. As Furnivall relates, she took "infinite care" to prepare the manuscript version of her edition "with four different kinds of ink, and with three different forms of underline" to indicate variance among the four texts, as well as various other marks to indicate

---

[73] For example, a very simple XML encoding of a textual variant might look like the following:

Oh that this too too
<app>
        <lem wit="F1">solid</lem>
        <rdg wit="Q2">sallied</rdg>
        <rdg type="emendation">sullied</rdg>
</app>
flesh would melt,

This example combines variants from different sources in a single transcription, following the guidelines of the Text Encoding Initiative, but one could also use XML to link variants spread across different transcriptions of sources, as Rochfort Smith does with typographic markup.

omission, transposition, and other particulars.[74] If one could look at those manuscripts, one would probably see something akin to the XML tagging applied to digital texts of *Hamlet*. To be specific, I suspect Rochfort Smith's manuscripts would look remarkably like the so-called paper prototyping stage of markup that my students and I undertake when tackling a particularly challenging textual artifact to represent using XML, and would reflect a similar wrestling with both the materials and the constraints of the representational system. Rochfort Smith was thinking like an encoder and information designer, even if she would not have recognized the names we now assign to those roles.

The relationship of Rochfort Smith's hypothetical manuscripts to print is also proto-digital, in that Trübner's printing house functions much like the digital interfaces that translate marked-up texts for the screen (not always perfectly). Trübner had some prior experience with layouts for multiple-text Shakespeare editions, including parallel-text editions of *Romeo and Juliet* and *Henry V*, but as Furnivall notes, "The plan [of the *Four-Text Hamlet*] proved too elaborate for the printer, who, though he used six varieties of type, could not show in the same word perhaps three differences the Editress wisht him to; and the preparation of more simplified 'copy' became necessary. This, Miss Rochfort Smith undertook without a murmur."[75] As she prepared her manuscripts, Rochfort Smith must have found herself in a situation faced by nearly all encoders of digital editions, trying to balance an accurate, if ambitious, model of textual relationships, on the one hand, with the limited capabilities of technical infrastructure, on the other – all the while imagining an ideal interface between the reader and the archive of *Hamlet* variants. In this sense, the remarkable thing about the *Four-Text Hamlet* is not primarily the surviving prototype itself, but the intellectual capacity it reveals on Rochfort Smith's part. Furnivall's memoir praises her philological acumen, but also describes her ability to look beyond the page and model performance texts in her mind: "Her power of translating the printed words into action on the stage, was extraordinary, specially [*sic*] in the case of one who, like herself, had hardly ever seen a play on the boards."[76] As remarkable an interface as

---

[74] Furnivall, *Teena Rochfort-Smith*, p. 5.
[75] *Ibid*. For examples of Trübner's prior work on parallel-text facsimiles, see Daniel, (ed.), *Romeo and Juliet* and *King Henry V*.
[76] Furnivall, *Teena Rochfort-Smith*, p. 7.

the *Four-Text Hamlet* prototype may be, it is the human aspect of the work that forms the strongest continuities with the present.

The example also reveals that previously marginal parts of the Shakespearean tradition take on new importance when considered as part of digitization's prehistory. Andrew Murphy compares Rochfort Smith's technological vision to that of Vannevar Bush, popularizer of the proto-hypertext Memex machine, and calls them "kindred spirits" who "both sought a way of organizing and coherently presenting large bodies of information" – and who both failed, to a degree, but in productive ways.[77] Murphy's point is apt, but there are other comparisons to make, too. While computer scientists recognize another nineteenth-century woman, Ada Lovelace, as the first programmer for her work with Charles Babbage, Rochfort Smith might well stand as the Ada Lovelace of the digital humanities, and an alternative to the established male technologist-scholars, such as Vannevar Bush and Roberto Busa, who usually serve as the *fons et origo* of the digital humanities' origin myths.[78] By the time Bush published his proposal for the Memex in 1945 – an uncredited adaptation of the work of earlier thinkers – he had been head of the United States's Office of Scientific Research and Development, had contributed to key phases of the Manhattan Project, and would eventually stand beside Robert Oppenheimer during the first test of an atomic bomb.[79] When Rochfort Smith made her primary contribution to what we would call interface design, she was a twenty-one-year-old woman who had nonetheless won respect in a highly patriarchal field, and whose insights into the nature of information, visualization, and textuality, were, as far as we know, all her own.

In the same spirit, there are some digital humanists who find themselves drawn to the past not just in search of materials to subject to computational analysis but also with a sense of continuity with the challenges and questions faced by earlier technologists, such as Rochfort Smith.[80] That

---

[77] Murphy, "Electric Shakespeares," p. 411.

[78] See the website for Ada Lovelace Day, celebrated annually by advocates for women in computing: www.findingada.com.

[79] Bush, "As We May Think"; first published in different versions in *Life* and *Atlantic Monthly* in 1945. For critical readings of Bush and the Memex, see Buckland, "Emanuel Goldberg," and Harpold, *Ex-foliations.*

[80] For example, Melissa Terras begins her book *Digital Images for the Information Professional* with a historical chapter that starts not with personal computing in the eighties or computer typesetting in the seventies, but with optical telegraphy in the late eighteenth century and other precursors; pp. 15–17.

productive search for continuities has been stronger, however, among early modernists such as Peter Stallybrass, William Sherman, Ann Coldiron, Ann Blair, and others who detect echoes of the future in the past, and perform the historical and bibliographical work necessary to understand those echoes properly.[81] Their more recent work builds upon the collection *The Renaissance Computer*, published in 2000, whose essays by various early modern literary scholars explored what the book's subtitle called "knowledge technologies" in the sixteenth and seventeenth centuries, as the effects of print worked their way through early modern culture.[82] The book's deliberate embrace of anachronism productively shifted the millennial discussion away from grand claims about *the* computer, as a single essentialized device, and toward computing as a historically embedded range of practices. Such a conception of paper-based computing would presumably include projects like the *Four-Text Hamlet*. However, *The Renaissance Computer* also reflects some of the pitfalls of looking for the future in the past. Despite the credentials of its contributors in Renaissance studies, the volume's approach to computing is largely observational and, for the most part, confined to the non-specialist's experience of personal computing tasks such as email, word processing, multimedia consumption, information seeking, and what we now call social networking. Computing, as an activity not limited to any specific device like a desktop PC, calls for a broad sense of the topic's diversity. My account seeks to provide more balance in that regard, as well as more emphasis on the historical layers of computing practice and new media that stand between postmodernity and early modernity, like Rochfort Smith's late Victorian experiment.

Late nineteenth- and twentieth-century technologies, in particular, sit just on the edge of direct continuity with the present, both in terms of actual technological development and in the cultural imagination. As Lisa Gitelman points out, "looking into the novelty years, transitional states, and identity crises of different media stands to tell us much, both about the course of media history and about the broad conditions by which media and communication are and have been shaped."[83] To

---

[81] See Stallybrass, "Books and Scrolls," p. 42; Sherman, *Used Books*, p. 40, and his afterword, "The Future of Past Readers," pp. 179–82; Coldiron, *Printers Without Borders* (forthcoming); Blair, *Too Much to Know*, pp. 2–3, 229, and 265–8.

[82] Rhodes and Sawday (eds.), *Renaissance Computer*.

[83] Gitelman, *Always Already New*, p. 1.

Gitelman's premise I would add that studying media in these crucial historical moments, when their meaning was still contestable, and their future still unwritten, is best pursued in close proximity to hands-on experimentation and design.[84] Early non-electronic computers serve as helpful provocations to modern design thinking by still remaining visible as machines. In their awkward materiality and lack of familiar interfaces (such as screens, keyboards, and mice), early computers confront the assumptions about computing that have become naturalized through consumer culture. Although I use the phrase *new media* throughout this book, it is worth always keeping in mind how the word *machine* resonates differently from the word *medium*. Media, especially new ones, conjure up images of transmission, communication, and connectivity – the smoothly functioning world of technology marketing – while machines connote an intractability and even resistance to the purposes of their makers.[85] In computing, the word *machine* also suggests a certain pastness, as in the name of computer science's most venerable society, the Association for Computing Machinery (founded in 1947). Supposedly, machines are what computers used to be.

The example of Rochfort Smith's wrestling with the affordances and constraints of Victorian typography illustrates an encounter not just between Shakespeare and computational thinking, but also between Shakespearean textuality and the material forms that computing inevitably take. As a representative example of *The Shakespearean Archive*'s subject as a whole, the *Four-Text Hamlet* serves to remind digital humanists generally that the history of their field is measured not in years or funding cycles, but in centuries. Historicizing information technology in this manner can be a healthy antidote to a problem that Shakespeareans face as they reckon with new media, which Willard McCarty describes as "the common notion that *the* computer has a single nature we should regard as its essence and emergent evolutionary form, whether this be modeling machine, interactive environment, appliance or

---

[84] This book received financial support from the Social Sciences and Humanities Research Council of Canada as part of a multimodal project titled *Archive and Interface in Digital Textual Studies*, whose premise was that historical approaches to new media should go hand in hand with experiments in digital interface design. My online project *Visualizing Variation* serves as the experimental counterpart to this book: www.visualizingvariation.ca.

[85] On the cultural role of the machine in the early modern period, see Sawday, *Engines of the Imagination*.

whatever."[86] As with the phrase *the archive*, the definite article when placed before *computer* creates a term that is all too easy to use, leading to an intellectual tendency I call *computing essentialism* – another of this book's major themes, and its principal object of critique in the light of the specific challenges posed by Shakespeare's texts as prototypical material.

The crux of the problem of computing essentialism, as McCarty describes it, is how we respond to "the implication, that having discovered what the single nature of computing is, we must either take it or leave it." On this point McCarty draws upon Michael Mahoney's argument that (as McCarty puts it) "there is not one but many computings," and "that the computer, unlike other machines we have known, does not have [an essential] nature."[87] One of the consequences of Mahoney's argument about critical discussions of computing is that digital humanists should be wary of accounts of computing in the form of what McCarty calls "device-histories in which whatever is thought to be the prevailing form of computing is traced back to a particular evolutionary origin," such as Charles Babbage's Analytical Engine or other machines devoted to the processing of regularized data.[88] McCarty and Mahoney's approach resonates with the thinking of media archaeologists such as Ernst and Parikka, and historical examples like Rochfort Smith remind us that computing has histories yet to be explored.

Plan and scope of this book

The digitization of Shakespeare's texts represents the meeting of two culturally constructed essentialisms: Shakespeare idealized as transmissible code and translated into digital networks which are, themselves, idealized communications channels. It is the premise of this book that we are now after computing essentialism in the same sense that some have argued we are after theory: both chronologically subsequent to it and therefore inheriting its influence, but also, at the same time, positioned to reevaluate computing essentialism critically and move beyond it.[89]

[86] McCarty, *Humanities Computing*, p. 10, emphasis in original.
[87] McCarty, *Humanities Computing*, pp. 10, 14; see also Mahoney, "Histories of Computing(s)."
[88] McCarty, *Humanities Computing*, pp. 14–15.
[89] The phrase "after theory" is probably most recognizable as the title of Terry Eagleton's 2003 book *After Theory*; Evelyn Cobley points out some of the difficulties of his position in "Hard Going After Theory."

Exploring digital Shakespeare's historical and imaginative foundations – its shadowy basement – provides one of the best means of resisting computing essentialism, and thus of awakening the humanistic imagination to the possibilities of computing. I have attempted to counter the historical exceptionalism and narrowness with which I see ideas about computing, information, and data being deployed in the digital humanities by considering their historical antecedents from a range of perspectives. Although this is at heart a work of Shakespearean textual studies, it also reflects lessons I have learned from archival theory, book history, Victorian studies, media archaeology, science and technology studies, critical information studies, and historical epistemology.[90] More often than not, I write as a visitor to these fields, not an expert.

This may also be a digital humanities book, though I have reservations about the liberatory claims attached to the term, and especially the way it has been wielded as a category after its sudden rise in popularity following the 2008 economic crash.[91] As a practitioner of humanities computing, I see in recent forms of digital humanities the return of the repressed, despite their advocates' emphasis on their own newness and futurity. Specifically, in the recent emphasis on large, data-driven projects based on supposedly scientific models of collaboration, many digital humanists are simply aping the militarized big science of the Cold War – often doing it in ways unrecognizable to present-day scientists. As Steve Joshua Heims's history of cybernetics describes, the period immediately following the Second World War "was a time when human sciences rather than humanistic studies were in the ascendancy, solving problems rather than reflecting on meanings. Normally the humanistic and scientific modes of understanding coexist, overlap, and are seen by the generalist as complementing each other. Yet the two modes also compete . . ."[92] It is fair to say that the scientific side of what C. P. Snow

---

[90] Historical epistemology is a term associated primarily with Lorraine Daston; see the references collected in Poovey, *Modern Fact*, p. 332, n. 11.

[91] To let a few influential examples stand for many, see N. Katherine Hayles's sorting of humanistic work into the capitalized categories "Traditional Humanities" and "Digital Humanities" in her chapter "The Digital Humanities: Engaging the Issues," in *As We Think*, pp. 23–54, as well as the divisive tone and overwhelmingly postwar sense of history of Burdick, Drucker, Lunenfeld, Presner, and Schnapp in *Digital_Humanities*, esp. pp. 122–3, and the various digital humanities manifestos that have emerged since the field's sudden takeup by mainstream humanists after late 2008.

[92] Heims, *Cybernetic Group*, p. 4.

called "the two cultures" won that competition, with the result that one sees its power at work, as Ronald Day puts it, "in the privilege that a certain 'factual' and 'clear' information is given in communication (in writing in general, in the media, in organizations, in education, and in politics), in the demand that the arts represent reality rather than 'distort' it (realism), and even in the claim that history is the transmission of the past to receivers in subsequent generations (cultural heritage)."[93] Whenever a digital humanist premises her or his approach on a generalization along the lines of "that's just how computers work" – i.e. computers exist to analyze data; they require data to be normalized; they tolerate no ambiguity; they matter only when networked within big data environments; they demand division of labour into teams of specialists – the appeal to technological determinism usually hides either an ignorance of, or a contentment with, the human choices that have shaped computing as a form of labour.

Many digital humanists, computer scientists, and other uncategorizable scholars resist easy generalizations about computing, and *The Shakespearean Archive* shares with other recent interdisciplinary work a desire to discover alternatives to the hardening orthodoxies of digital humanities as a field – especially the notion that computers are inherently scientific instruments, whose successful importation into the humanities requires scientific forms of project design and management.[94] Very often these arguments appeal to a form of pseudo-scientism, such as the scientific management ideas of the early twentieth century, rather than the actual practices of scientists. My target, then, is not science, technology, or empiricism – all of which are longstanding core elements in textual studies, along with humanistic interpretation – but rather the mix of positivism, instrumental rationalism, and historical exceptionalism that

---

[93] Day, "Conduit Metaphor," p. 810. See also C. P. Snow's 1959 Rede Lecture, *The Two Cultures.*

[94] Recent major works that critique aspects of the digital humanities, while sometimes also building on their foundations, include Drucker, *SpecLab* (2009), esp. chapters 1.1 and 1.2; Golumbia, *Cultural Logic of Computation* (2009); Liu, *Laws of Cool* (2004); Ramsay, *Reading Machines* (2011); Earhart, *Traces of the Old* (2014 forthcoming); and Svensson's series of articles in *Digital Humanities Quarterly*: "The Landscape of Digital Humanities" (2010); "From Optical Fiber to Conceptual Cyberinfrastructure" (2011); and "Envisioning the Digital Humanities" (2012). Even McCarty's *Humanities Computing*, a foundational book for digital humanities from its first appearance in 2005, advances arguments that challenge what have now become truisms in the field.

has given digital humanities its dark side.[95] In that sense, this book is similar in spirit to the preceding generation of Shakespearean textual scholarship, which was motivated by similar frustrations with (and debts to) the New Bibliography.

In seeking out the exceptions to computing essentialism, I have followed Mahoney's advice that "the past can be a good place to look for the future," but depart from mainstream digital humanities by not simply accepting Roberto Busa's work with IBM in 1949 as the single origin of a single field.[96] The scenes from the prehistory of digitization that structure this book take the form of various information experiments and technological prototypes involving Shakespeare, like Rochfort Smith's paper computer. Some experiments were specifically technological, embodied in artifacts such as the *Four-Text Hamlet*; others were thought experiments and conceptual forays, such as the pattern of Shakespearean references made by cyberneticists and information theorists. All of the Shakespearean information experiments described in this book share one trait: each represents a foray into the stacks of the Shakespearean archive, often in an attempt to bring it under control by managing the perceived problem of information's susceptibility to loss, noise, overload, and entropy. Evaluating their successes is beside the point, and their failures can be far more instructive, especially in the light of Ernst's point that media archaeology deliberately resists an uncritically celebratory approach to technological narratives, just as it resists the curiosity-cabinet approach to treating the past as a collection of strange nostalgia objects.[97] Archives represent the traces of the past that cannot easily be reduced to the condition of data, which means that digitization forces Shakespeareans to confront that which has been lost, or remains untranslatable, in the Shakespearean archive as much as confronting new opportunities.

The following chapters will explore the Shakespearean archive as it casts its shadow over a range of sites in Shakespeare studies, from

---

[95] The dark side metaphor became popularized by a panel at the 2013 MLA conference in Boston titled "The Dark Side of Digital Humanities." A summary of the panel, along with links to the participants' papers and spirited debate in the readers' comments, may be found in William Pannapaker's blog post for the *Chronicle of Higher Education* (5 January 2013), chronicle.com/blogs/conversation/2013/01/05/on-the-dark-side-of-the-digital-humanities.

[96] Mahoney, "Histories of Computing(s)," p. 119.

[97] Ernst, *Digital Memory*, pp. 55–6.

eighteenth-century uses of Shakespeare editions as proto-databases, to the late Victorian culture of preservation, through the New Bibliographic mobilization of textual studies, to the present challenges of digitization and electronic editing. The selection of sites of inquiry in the following chapters by no means exhausts the topic, but rather provides a strategic analysis of areas of Shakespeare studies where preservation, transmission, and error have special bearing on the reception of Shakespeare's texts. After Chapter 2, which lays out a theoretical framework, the order of chapters is roughly chronological, though the book does not lay out a comprehensive history like Murphy's *Shakespeare in Print*. Instead, the chapters are strategically chronological, selecting examples that instantiate the Shakespearean archive within specific historical contexts, but which also use categories of media (such as sound and image) to link to digital practices of the present.

Chapter 2 maps the complex middle ground between textual theory, editing, and archiving. Specifically, the chapter uses Shakespeare to work through the implications of the under-recognized fact that archivists and editors share fundamental questions about the authenticity of texts and records, the stakes of representation, and the connections between cultural heritage and new technology. The chapter begins with an analysis of poststructuralist conceptions of the archive as they pertain to Shakespeare, and then moves to reconcile the professional practices and vocabulary of archivists, on the one hand, with the poststructuralist theorizing of archives. Given Shakespeare's unique importance in the history of scholarly editing, this chapter locates that uniqueness within larger contexts for cultural memory, and connects the form of the edition to the institutional structures of archives and libraries, as well as to the poststructural understanding of archives that has developed in response to Derrida's *Archive Fever*. This chapter introduces terms that will prove essential throughout the rest of the book, including *encyclopedism*, *substrate*, *archiviolithism*, and the distinction between *textual management* and *epistemic management*.[98]

Chapter 3 discusses Shakespeare's connection to the most ubiquitous of information technologies, the codex book. Differing in approach from other accounts of Shakespeare and the book, this chapter applies the perspective of information architecture to Shakespeare's most consequential bibliographic transformation: the shift from the supposed

---

[98] The latter distinction is O'Driscoll's, detailed in "Derrida, Foucault," pp. 288–93.

textual and codicological unity of the seventeenth-century folios to the dispersed fragments of information that made up the eighteenth-century variorums. The variorum format, pioneered for vernacular literature in the eighteenth century and further developed in the nineteenth, represents an attempt to reckon with a perceived excess of information about Shakespeare. This chapter builds on Margreta de Grazia's foundational work on Edmund Malone's 1790 variorum, and explores new territory by reading these instantiations of Shakespeare in book form as proto-digital experiments in the management and visualization of an archive. Horace Howard Furness's New Variorum Shakespeare editions of the late nineteenth century (which continued into the twentieth and twenty-first) have received less attention than Malone and his immediate predecessors, and this chapter will also explore their proto-digital aspects within the relatively neglected context of late nineteenth-century Shakespeare editing.

The next two chapters are paired, each dealing with Shakespeare's connection to different forms of new media that emerged in the nineteenth century. Chapter 4 explores how Shakespeare quartos and folios were among the first books to be reproduced through photographic means, beginning with John Payne Collier's project to reproduce the Devonshire copy of Q1 *Hamlet* in 1858. This work was followed by the Royal Ordnance Survey's photographic experiments on rare books and manuscripts (including *Domesday Book* and the Shakespeare First Folio) in the 1860s. Early responses to these facsimiles bear out Allan Sekula's characterization of photography as a technology of "instrumental realism."[99] As one commentator in *The Athenaeum* puts it (speaking of Collier's 1858 Q1 *Hamlet* facsimile), "the book now about to be distributed is complete in every respect and gives a perfect representation of the original, even to the minutest point, line, or speck impressed by the antiquated types."[100] By the end of the century, this fantasy of perfect mediation would extend to interpretation and criticism as well, with photographic facsimiles offering supposedly direct access to the Shakespearean archive in ways that editions could not. However, a closer analysis of the Collier and Ordnance Survey facsimiles reveals a capacity and willingness to manipulate the photographic representations of

[99] Sekula, "The Body and the Archive," p. 7.
[100] Article signed "C.", "Our weekly gossip," *The Athenaeum* (4 September 1858), p. 300.

Shakespeare books, in which the camera is used partly to construct the objects it represents. In other words, these early experimenters were using the camera not just to represent but to edit.

Chapter 5 introduces the theme of the Shakespearean tech demo in relation to new technologies for sound transmission and recording, taking the work of Alexander Graham Bell and Thomas Edison as its examples. Both inventors understood new technology as a performance, and both exploited Shakespeare's popular appeal and theatricality when staging their own inventions for the public. Bell, for one, repeatedly used *Hamlet* when demonstrating prototypes of the telephone in theatres and music halls, where audiences thrilled at hearing Shakespeare and other familiar sounds transmitted to them live from distant locations. This chapter also describes Edison's use of Shakespeare in tech demos, with particular focus on a first-hand account of a scene from *Julius Caesar* in a 1913 kinetophone demo, in which audiences experienced some of film's earliest syncronizations of moving images with sound.

Chapter 6 takes us fully into the twentieth century, by which time Shakespeare's texts had come to stand as both an ideal and a limit-case for the concept of information. Whereas the previous chapters explore the cultural and interpretive repercussions of Shakespeare's mechanical *reproduction* in print, this chapter examines what happens when the texts become machine-*readable* structures of information in the middle of the twentieth century with the rise of electronic computing. Specifically, this chapter explores how Shakespeare's texts became *code*, readable by machines and algorithms, even while bearing traces of the human. Mid-century bibliographers and information scientists alike were pursuing remarkably similar lines of thought in the years leading up to and immediately following the Second World War, with both fields deeply invested in the durability and mobility of texts. These currents converged in cryptographic approaches to Shakespeare's texts and their debunking by US Army cryptographers William and Mary Friedman, whose wartime activities mirrored those of Shakespearean bibliographers Fredson Bowers and Charlton Hinman. This chapter accounts for relatively unexplored aspects of the New Bibliography's technological and epistemological underpinnings, and also sets up the next chapter, which deals with the consequences of these events for digital Shakespeare today.

Chapter 7 considers the transformation of Shakespeare's texts into data, in an epistemological trade-off that often sacrifices historical and material specificity for the sake of computational tractability. Many digital Shakespeareans make that trade with full knowledge of the stakes, yet still face the contradiction that the texts resist digitization even as they embody a history of ideal transmissibility. Beginning with *Henry V*'s depiction of information overload in the opening Salic Law scene, the chapter considers the Shakespearean dimensions of recent debates over the term *data* in the digital humanities. The second half of the chapter takes a media-archaeological approach to the Globe Shakespeare of the 1860s and its transformation into the Moby Shakespeare, the ubiquitous public-domain Shakespeare text used by many digital projects, scholarly and otherwise. When Shakespeareans casually reach for digitized Shakespeare texts to use as data in digital humanities projects, they usually find some version of the Moby Shakespeare ready to hand. How did a Victorian Shakespeare text, designed to serve the specific needs of empire in the middle of the nineteenth century, become central research infrastructure in twenty-first-century digital humanities? More to the point, how has the misapplied concept of data obscured the historicity of digital Shakespeare texts like the Moby as artifacts themselves? These questions lead back to the concept of computing essentialism, and also set up the themes of the book's conclusion.

A different book might deal with figures of the archive or archival technologies as depicted in Shakespeare's works, and the field would benefit from more work along those lines.[101] In this book I am concerned less with the technologies in our Shakespeare than with the Shakespeare in our technologies: my object is Shakespeare's afterlives within information culture, and the productive vexations that Shakespeare brings to comfortably progressive narratives of transmission and computation. However, even though this is not a book that sets out to reinterpret the works of Shakespeare directly, it nonetheless emphasizes the imaginative potency of Shakespeare's works in their encounters with new media. Literature may be construed as content or data, but something important in the texts always resists, and Shakespeare in particular challenges the very conceptual frameworks by which we assign meaning to the words *content* and *data*. When one studies the use of *Hamlet* as prototypical content for an information experiment, one must acknowledge the power not only of the technology to grant new affordances, but also the power

---

[101] See Scott, *Idea of the Book*; Cohen, *Shakespeare and Technology*; and Kinney, *Shakespeare's Webs*.

of a work like *Hamlet* to shape ideas about memory, technology, and subjectivity. As one of the Association for Computing in the Humanities's most unlikely keynote speakers, Northrop Frye, argues in *The Educated Imagination*, "literature belongs to the world man constructs, not to the world he sees; to his home, not his environment."[102] This is why we can never merely apply computing to the study of humanities materials unidirectionally: our materials *are* our tools. If that realization slows down a digitization project, and prompts researchers to reconsider their materials and tools alike with new eyes, there is hope that the conventional wisdom of twentieth-century managerialism may give way to the deeper wisdom that leads us to seek meaning in literature in the first place.

The transmission of Shakespeare's texts persists at the centre of our imaginative engagement with memory and forgetting, preservation and loss. For that reason, there is a certain unpredictability in taking Shakespeare as the object of information experiments and technology prototypes, given the myth of inexhaustibility that has attached itself to Shakespeare since the Romantic period. That quality of Shakespeare's works is usually described in interpretive terms, in the sense that the works' capacity to generate new meanings will (happily) always exceed their critics' interpretive capacities. Yet there is a textual myth of inexhaustibility, too. Plays like *King Lear, Othello, Sir Thomas More, Romeo and Juliet,* and especially *Hamlet* present textual mysteries that seem almost insurmountable, yet not so much that textual scholars despair of solving them. Those two forms of inexhaustibility – textual and interpretive – inevitably mingle, as in Paul Werstine's comparison of play title and character name when he describes "the enduring mystery that is *Hamlet*/Hamlet."[103] This book is about what happens when the textual mystery of Shakespeare encounters the archival ambitions of modern information culture. It is an encounter in which the desire to archive and master all the world's data collides with cultural materials that seem to be inexhaustibly complex, yet teasingly knowable. The Shakespearean archive is therefore just another name for one of the structuring contradictions at the heart of modernity: to remember the past is to change it.

---

[102] Frye, *Educated Imagination*, p. 12. For Frye's 1989 joint keynote to the Association for Computing in the Humanities and the Association for Literary and Linguistic Computing, see "Literary and Mechanical Models."
[103] Werstine, "Textual Mystery," p. 2.

2 | Leaves of brass: Shakespeare and the idea of the archive

TITUS. [C]ome, I will go get a leaf of brass
And with a gad of steel will write these words,
And lay it by. The angry northern wind
Will blow these sands like Sibyl's leaves abroad,
And where's our lesson then? Boy, what say you?

Titus Andronicus, 4.1.101–5

Nothing lasts. Even the works of the great Shakespeare will disappear when the universe burns out – not such a terrible thought, of course, when it comes to a play like *Titus Andronicus*, but what about the others?

Woody Allen, "The Condemned," p. 21

Visitors entering the Thomas Fisher Rare Book Library at the University of Toronto, like visitors to similar libraries the world over, are greeted by a bust of Shakespeare. The selection of this one author from among myriad other possibilities makes a kind of sense given the role that modernity has accorded to Shakespeare as a secular patron saint of libraries, books, reading, and print culture.[1] Indeed, Shakespeare is one of the very few authors to have an entire library dedicated to him, his period, and his legacy, in the form of the Folger Shakespeare Library, whose symbolic location next to the Library of Congress and not far from the Smithsonians on the Washington Mall reinforce Shakespeare's role in American cultural identity. Generally, Shakespeare's iconographic presence may reinforce the integrity of a library, but the patronage relationship works both ways: libraries also reinforce Shakespeare's integrity by serving as heterotopias where all aspects of Shakespeare come together as a symbolic and material whole, compensating for the indeterminacy of so much of the

---

[1] See Taylor, *Reinventing Shakespeare*, pp. 87–94 and 197–9, and Bristol's chapter "The Function of the Archive," in *Shakespeare's America*, pp. 62–90.

Shakespeare canon and the inaccessibility of origins in the form of Shakespeare's authorial manuscripts.[2]

Libraries embody the dream of inscriptive permanence, where scattered Sibylline leaves may be brought together and accorded the permanence of writing in brass (even *Titus Andronicus*, whose unique surviving copy of the 1594 first quarto is preserved at the Folger). The connections between Shakespeare and archives, on the other hand, are less clear. Despite the metaphorical interchangeability of archives and libraries in popular discourse, they are distinct kinds of institutions with very different origins and natures.[3] Libraries generally house published material, while archives generally house unique unpublished records. Furthermore, most modern libraries (with the exception of rare book libraries) contain material that is meant to circulate in the wider world, while archives house the records of an organization or individual that are no longer in active use, and must be read *in situ* in the absence of facsimile surrogates. Above all, archives carry a specific preservational mandate, which they fulfill by serving as receiving institutions, inheriting records directly from their makers (or posthumously from the makers' estates), and, through a process of appraisal, preserving records judged to hold enduring value.[4] Although libraries play an important preservational role as well, especially deposit libraries, archives are the institutions whose day-to-day function is to hold the line against the attrition of time, saving records that would otherwise be lost.

Understanding the full range of meanings of the word *archive* is key to this book's goal of exploring the prehistory of digital Shakespeare. This chapter considers how poststructuralists and archivists (and some scholars

---

[2] On the concept of the heterotopia, a type of space in which many social and temporal aspects of a society accumulate, see Foucault, "Of Other Spaces."

[3] My comments in this paragraph notwithstanding, scholars and professionals in archives, libraries, and museums have in recent years explored the convergences between these types of cultural heritage institution. Also, as any archival researcher knows, archives may contain stray books or artifacts that normally belong in other kinds of institutions, and archives themselves are often found within libraries and museums – the main building for the Smithsonian's National American History Museum, for example, also houses next door to each other its Archives Center and the Dibner Library for the History of Science and Technology. On convergence, see Given and McTavish, "What's Old Is New Again," and Waibel and Erway, "Think Globally, Act Locally."

[4] On archives and preservation, see Cloonan, "Preserving Records." For accounts of the history of archival thought accessible to non-specialists, see Cook, "Past Is Prologue," and Ridener, *Polders to Postmodernism*.

who are both) have expanded and delimited that range of meanings. The fantasy of the perfect archive permeates Shakespeare studies, not least because the documentary traces of Shakespeare's working life are so elusive. The problem of Shakespeare's empty archive reveals itself in controversial cases of surviving records that call into question the abstract structures that order Shakespeare's text, canon, and biography. The most well-known example is the debate over the identification of Shakespeare as Hand D in the *Sir Thomas More* manuscript, whose positive attribution would add a new play to the canon – or already has, considering its inclusion in the Arden Shakespeare series – and provide a unique glimpse into the working documents of Shakespeare as a journeyman playwright collaborating with his peers.[5] The *Sir Thomas More* manuscript teases us with the scenario of having access to the kinds of documentary riches that survive from modern writers: notebooks; drafts; revisions; correspondence with publishers, readers, reviewers, literary agents, and other writers – all documents normally associated not with editions or libraries but with archives. Except for the debated Shakespearean attribution of Hand D in *Sir Thomas More*, we have none of those archival documents for Shakespeare.

As evidence of the working realities of dramatic authorship, manuscripts can throw into sharp relief claims that literary executors made for authors, such as John Heminge and Henry Condell's well-known representation of Shakespeare's authorial habits in the First Folio: "His mind and hand went together: And what he thought he vttered with that easinesse, that wee haue scarse recieued from him a blot in his papers."[6] This trope of idealized inscription expands to include imaginary technologies of writing in the stationer Humphrey Moseley's epistle to readers in the 1647 folio collection of Francis Beaumont and John Fletcher's works:

What ever I have seene of Mr. *Fletchers* owne hand, is free from interlining; and his friends affirme he never writ any one thing twice: it seemes he had that rare felicity to prepare and perfect all first in his owne braine ... before he

---

[5] See Jowett, (ed.), *Sir Thomas More*. A distinction sometimes overlooked in the debate is that attributing the *text* of Hand D's additions is separate from the question of attributing the handwriting itself. Gabriel Egan summarizes the evidence to conclude that "whomever's the handwriting, Shakespeare is the author" of the Hand D material; *The Struggle for Shakespeare's Text*, p. 205.

[6] *Mr. William Shakespeares Comedies, Histories, & Tragedies* (London, 1623), sig. ᵖA3r.

committed one word to writing, and never touched pen till all was to stand as firme and immutable as if ingraven in Brasse or Marble.[7]

Both of these rhetorical gestures seek the same effect: to deflect interest in the material and temporal dimensions of authorship, with its blotted and interlined drafts, and in their place to erect a symbolic monument to the permanence and finality of an author's inscriptions. For Jonson, Shakespeare, and Beaumont and Fletcher, the most recognizable of those monuments took bibliographic form in folio collections, but archives stand as stubborn reminders that authorship is about more than books.

This chapter examines how the idea of the archive informs Shakespearean textual scholarship, both directly and indirectly, especially in its concerns with the relations of fragmentary material inscriptions to abstract wholes. My secondary purpose in this chapter is to use Shakespearean textual scholarship to triangulate two other domains that communicate all too infrequently, namely poststructural discussions of archives, on the one hand, and the scholarly literature of archivists, on the other. Ironically, the archive's metaphorical appeal has led many historians, literary scholars, and critical theorists to make the gesture of returning to the archive in their work, yet most stop short of engaging the scholarship of those who never left the archive – that is, archivists themselves. This chapter likewise revels in the metaphorical power of the archive, but not to the extent that it effaces actual archivists by accepting the archival metaphor as the last word on the matter.

In this regard, my purpose is similar to Kate Theimer's in a recent *Journal of Digital Humanities* article in which she diplomatically takes digital humanists to task for appropriating the word *archive* (especially in the names of projects such as the *William Blake Archive* and the *Shakespeare Quartos Archive*) while neglecting decades' worth of archival concepts and practices that have given the word its meaning and force.[8] Theimer carefully avoids any disciplinary territoriality with regard to the term, but still makes a strong argument for understanding the multidisciplinary resonances of words like *archive*. However, the perspective offered in Theimer's article is that of the professional archivist, rooted in stable vocabulary and longstanding definitions, which

[7] Humphrey Moseley, "The Stationer to the Readers," in Beaumont and Fletcher, *Comedies and Tragedies*, sig. A4v.
[8] Theimer, "Archives in Context."

tends not to focus on recent theoretical developments in archives, an area of tremendous intellectual energy in the past decade. Even so, as Theimer's article makes clear, it is one thing to consider *the archive* as a resonant symbol in the cultural imagination, and another to consider *archiving* as a day-to-day activity carried out by professionals who reflect upon their practice. My goal in this chapter is to show that those worlds are not so far apart.

The question I wish to consider is not *what is an archive?* (or who has the authority to define it), but *what constitutes archival understanding?* Putting the question this way allows us to consider how archival thinking manifests itself in different forms across traditional domain boundaries. For example, Shakespeare editing has traditionally been considered a literary activity, one that seeks to recover traces of literary and dramatic practice discernable through printed texts. However, one could also characterize aspects of Shakespeare editing as conjectural forms of archival arrangement, in that textual critics and bibliographers attempt to reconstruct the normal operations of organizations or businesses (namely Shakespeare's playing companies, publishers, the Stationers' Company, the Master of Revels' office, and others) through the documents generated by their day-to-day transactions.[9] Modern archives were originally conceived as repositories to preserve the records generated by the quotidian life of an increasingly bureaucratic society, especially the records of governments, businesses, and other organizations that have fallen out of current use. Sometimes the originating contexts of records are well documented, sometimes not. In the latter cases, archivists often do the forensic work of arrangement to reconstruct those organizational contexts, just as Shakespeare editors conjecturally reconstruct the documents that printers used in the typesetting of plays.

The biggest difference between archival and editorial theory lies in their origins and purposes. Editorial theory through most of its history has focused on individual authors, while archival theory originated in the record-keeping practices not of individuals, but of public institutions, businesses, and other large organizations. As Cook and Schwartz point out, "there is a basic dichotomy of archives being, on the one

---

[9] *Archival arrangement* refers to the active intervention of archivists in a fonds, or group of records, to restore the original order of their creation, when necessary, in cases of suspected disruption or reordering. For a definition and history of the concept, see Yeo, "Debates About Description," pp. 91–4.

hand, heritage places with documentary records that embody historical
memory and humanist culture, and archives being, on the other hand,
bureaucratic by-products that encompass administrative evidence and
public accountabilities."[10] Recently, archival theorists such as Heather
MacNeil and Andrew Prescott have illuminated what Prescott calls "the
textuality of the archive" by bringing elements of textual scholarship to
bear upon questions shared by editors, historians, and archivists alike,
which converge in topics like authenticity, archival description, and the
relationships among work, document, and text.[11] As MacNeil describes
in her article considering the archivist as editor, "The traditional textual
critic's efforts to restore a text as closely as possible to its original,
authentic form mirrors the archivist's efforts to identify and represent
the original order of a body of records through arrangement."[12]
This chapter will examine that mirroring of archival and editorial
thinking from the other side of the glass, as it were, and consider how
Shakespearean textual scholarship sometimes functions as archiving by
another name, just as archivists can be more like editors than either
discipline tends to realize.

Shakespearean inscriptions

The lynchpin idea that ties archival and editorial perspectives together is
inscription. It is a term with many uses and definitions. Paul Ricoeur, for
one, defines inscription as "the fixation of oral expressions of discourse
by a material support" but distinguishes inscriptions from ordinary
writing by emphasizing their status as "external marks adopted as the
basis and intermediary for *the work of memory*."[13] Memory performs
cultural work, but memory also requires work in the form of material
mediation, and it is this doubled sense of "the work of memory" that
invests inscriptions with their symbolic power. Archivists have a unique
perspective on the materiality of memory as textual work, and archiving
as a formal practice is premised on the knowability of an inscription's
origins and authenticity: the moment of a record's creation that constitutes what archivists call the *archival bond*, which defines its

---

[10] Cook and Schwartz, "(Postmodern) Theory," p. 181.
[11] Prescott, "Textuality of the Archive," and MacNeil, "Picking Our Text," and
"Archivalterity."
[12] MacNeil, "Picking Our Text," p. 269.
[13] Ricoeur, *Memory, History, Forgetting*, p. 147, emphasis added.

relationship both to its originating authority and to other records born into the same functional context.[14] Margaret Hedstrom describes the importance of inscriptions in constituting these relationships for archivists, both symbolically and practically: "the material manifestation of a record comes to be through an act of recording or inscription. The form of the inscription can be anything that is within the social, cultural, political, and technological means and imaginations of the time and place when it occurs."[15] These records may originate with relatively isolated individuals, such as working literary authors, or with individuals working within networks of correspondence and document-sharing (like other kinds of working literary authors).

While archivists like Hedstrom recognize the symbolic power of inscriptions, that theme has been developed more fully by media historians such as Friedrich Kittler and Lisa Gitelman, who argue that the symbolic force of inscriptions is inseparable from their materiality.[16] Indeed the one derives from the other, as Gitelman points out: "Unlike radio signals, for instance, inscriptions are stable and savable ... The difference seems obvious, but it is important to note that the stability and savability of inscriptions are qualities that arise socially as well as perceptually."[17] An example that Shakespeareans know all too well comes from the puritan William Prynne, who in 1633 expressed outrage that folio volumes of plays "are now new-printed in farre better paper" than most Bibles – his choice of the words "printed *in*" signalling (and expecting from the reader) an awareness of the inscriptive nature of letterpress printing, which bites into paper rather than simply depositing ink on it, unlike modern offset printing.[18] Prynne understood the material symbolism of

[14] On the concept of the archival bond and its basis in the field of diplomatics, see Duranti, "Archival Bond," pp. 215–16. Yeo offers a different view of the concept in "Conceptual Fonds," p. 63, n. 62.

[15] Hedstrom, "Archives, Memory, and Interfaces," p. 25.

[16] On the concept of inscription in media studies and critical theory, see Kittler, *Discourse Networks* and *Gramophone, Film, Typewriter*; Gitelman, *Scripts, Grooves*, and *Always Already New*; Hayles, *Writing Machines*, p. 24; Latour, *Science in Action*, pp. 68–9; Kirschenbaum, *Mechanisms*; Lastra's chapter "Inscriptions and Simulations: The Imagination of Technology" in his *Sound Technology*, pp. 16–60; and Galey, "Tablets of the Law."

[17] Gitelman, *Always Already New*, p. 6. These ideas will be of particular importance to the discussion of sound technologies in Chapter 5.

[18] On letterpress printing as inscription, see Bringhurst, *Elements of Typographic Style*, p. 138. This topic also receives substantial discussion in Chapter 4, and in my article "Tablets of the Law."

literary inscriptions and their substrates, and might even have agreed, in his own way, with Gitelman and Hedstrom on their socially constructed nature. Indeed, for Prynne the persuasive power of material forms was exactly the problem.

Shakespeare and his contemporaries made strategic use of the symbolic power of inscriptions, especially in the literary motif of writing in brass. As a supposedly permanent substrate like marble, leaves of brass – like the one Titus prompts young Lucius to imagine – served as an imaginative medium for what Roger Chartier calls "the manifold relationship between inscription and erasure, between the durable record and the ephemeral text" that has preoccupied early modern authors and postmodern theorists alike.[19] Shakespeare makes several references to brass as a substrate, sometimes connoting permanence – as in Camillo's conviction that "Nor brass, nor stone, nor parchment bears not one [historical exemplar of vindicated regicide]" (*The Winter's Tale* 1.2.361) – and sometimes connoting the vulnerability of even the strongest worldly substrates to time and mortality, as in Sonnet 65's opening plea for beauty's fragility:

> Since brass, nor stone, nor earth, nor boundless sea,
> But sad mortality o'ersways their power.

Time and again, early modern writers emphasize the durability of brass as an inscriptive medium only to subvert it, even in contexts such as the prefatory material of the Shakespeare First Folio, a material context that would seem to elicit only assertions of permanence. Yet Leonard Digges devalues all other forms of inscription in order to praise the book as archive, claiming in his encomium to Shakespeare that

> *when that stone* [of Shakespeare's tomb] *is rent,*
> *And Time dissolues thy* Stratford *Moniment,*
> *Here we aliue shall view thee still. This Booke,*
> *When* Brasse *and Marble fade, shall make thee looke*
> *Fresh to all Ages.*[20]

Ben Jonson makes much the same point in the famous image-text diptych that opens the volume, in which he asserts that the brass-

---

[19] Chartier, *Inscription and Erasure*, p. vii.   [20] F1, sig. πB1.

engraved frontispiece portrait is an unsuitable medium to register Shakespeare's wit:

> the Print would then surpasse
> All, that was euer writ in brasse.[21]

Running through these examples one detects a carefully managed tension between inscribed leaves of brass and printed leaves of paper, yet the availability of the term *leaf* in early modern English to describe both kinds of writing surfaces also implies a unity of purpose as technologies of memory.[22]

Heminge, Condell, and Moseley certainly understood the benefits of setting up some notion of an archival bond in the minds of potential purchasers of their folio collections. Those books will occupy the next chapter, but first it is worth taking stock of the imaginative power of inscriptions that precedes and underwrites the making of books as monuments. The cultural enshrinement of Shakespeare's text and memory seems to generate what Eric Ketelaar has called "archival temples" on a scale not shared by any other secular writing.[23] Similarly, Michael Bristol has described how this monumentalizing tendency took the form of the research library, especially in the United States – a phenomenon explained partly by Anthony James West's account of the mass migration of First Folios across the Atlantic in the first decades of the twentieth century.[24] It is no surprise that archives should double as monuments for modern authors whose personal papers have survived; Shakespeare's manuscripts have not, but, strangely, Shakespeare sometimes lends authenticity to the idea of archiving itself.

One of the world's most iconic archives, the National Archives Building in Washington DC, does not monumentalize Shakespeare so much as recruit him to monumentalize its own mission. Figure 2.1

---

[21] F1, sig. ᵖA1v. The Jonson–Droeshout example receives further discussion in the next chapter; see pp. 84–6.

[22] See *OED*, "leaf" *n.*[1], def. II.7.a and II.10.a–b.

[23] Ketelaar, "Archival Temples." See also the discussion of Pierre Nora's notion of *lieux de mémoire* in this book's Introduction, p. 5, as well as Brown and Davis-Brown, "Making of Memory."

[24] Bristol, *Shakespeare's America*, p. 63. For details on the great Folio migration from England to America, which was also largely a migration from private collections to public institutions, see West, *Shakespeare First Folio*, vol. I, pp. 29–51 and 141.

Figure 2.1 Statue outside the National Archives Building, Washington DC.

shows one of two statues guarding the research entrance on the building's north side, a man holding a closed book representing The Past, and a woman holding an open book representing The Future (pictured). The Future's pedestal bears the inscription "WHAT IS PAST IS PROLOGUE" (in roman capitals) from *The Tempest*.[25] A related gesture toward the intimate links between documents and the past's imagining of the future was made when the building's corner-stone was laid by Herbert Hoover in 1933. Inside the cornerstone were placed a number of documents, including a Bible, copies of the public acts authorizing the building's construction, autographed engravings of President Hoover and the Secretary of the Treasury, letterhead of the office of the architect, the day's program of ceremonies, copies of each of Washington's daily newspapers, and copies of the United States Constitution and Declaration of Independence. All these symbols are designed to work together: the Shakespeare text inscribed on the outside of the National Archives emphasizes the continuity of culture and authority, underwritten by the institutional documents placed in the cornerstone, where they perform an imaginative merging with the material of the building itself. Yet, as with any text, this archival temple is not entirely self-consistent in its meanings, either. It seems a curious choice to include duplicates of the Constitution and Declaration of Independence in the cornerstone, considering that the building was purpose-built to house their originals. This archival temple, built to celebrate original documents and the national origins they embody, contains in its own cornerstone two tributes to the power of copying.

The National Archives Building thus embodies Prescott's notion of the textuality of archives in the most literal and symbolic ways imaginable. However, it is also in the nature of texts to change in transmission, whatever their monumental forms may assert to the contrary. The Shakespeare inscription on the National Archives is a case in point, in that it errs ever so slightly from the text of *The Tempest* that it quotes, whose only authoritative source is the First Folio. Figure 2.2 shows a detail of the National Archives inscription with the Folio text below it.

---

[25] The inscription refers to *The Tempest*, 2.1.258, but see below.

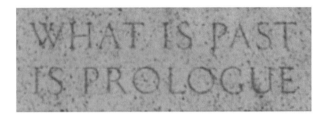

Figure 2.2

Leaving aside the obvious differences in media between stone and paper, and between building and book, I would draw attention first to a grammatical variant: the expansion of "what's" into "WHAT IS." Marjorie Garber, noticing a pattern of misquotation of this phrase here and elsewhere (including Oliver Stone's film *JFK*), attributes the invisible formalizing of the Folio's language to the notion that "Shakespeare, a figure of high seriousness, is apparently not supposed to speak in something as undignified – or as supposedly modern – as a contraction."[26] There is also a typographical variant in the form of the Folio's capitalization of "Prologue," a distinction lost in the phrase's conversion to capitals. In the Folio, capitalizing "Prologue" serves to personify the word's referent as a type of dramatic role. An early modern prologue could just as easily be an actor on a stage, introducing a play, as it could be part of a book – though the latter meaning is likely to be the one that would occur to passers-by on Pennsylvania Avenue. In the Folio, then, the Prologue in "what's past is Prologue" is an actor, history is a drama, and all the world's a stage. These typographical signals are lost in the monumentalizing of Shakespeare's text to serve a different kind of history.

The phrase from *The Tempest* that authorizes the historical mission of the National Archives also provides the title for one of the foundational accounts of archival theory and practice: "What Is Past Is Prologue: A History of Archival Ideas Since 1898, and the Future Paradigm Shift," published by archivist Terry Cook in 1997 and still regularly cited by scholars and assigned to students as one of the most important recent works of archival theory.[27] Like the National Archives

---

[26] Garber, *Profiling Shakespeare*, pp. 284–5.   [27] Cook, "Past Is Prologue."

Building's architects, Cook uses the text of Shakespeare to articulate the relationship between records, memory, and the archival enterprise: "as Shakespeare discerned, 'what is past is prologue.' Before archivists as a profession can write their own prologue for the next century, they need to understand better their own past."[28] In a similar vein, another article co-written by Cook and Joan Schwartz on archives and postmodernism takes as an epigraph *As You Like It*'s oft-quoted lines "All the world's a stage / And all the men and women merely players" (paired with Elvis Presley's reference to the same Shakespearean conceit in "Are You Lonesome Tonight") to thematize their argument that archiving constitutes a kind of postmodern performance, with archivists, like actors, as co-creators of meaning, not just custodians or conduits of it.[29]

Their conclusion takes the comparison of archiving to Shakespearean performance even further, in an argument no less striking for its relevance to editing:

Thinkers about archives need of course to keep their feet on the floor-boards of the archival stage. They need to show that the "postmodernisms" they advocate are not some ivory-tower debate by self-indulgent academics, but a vital, living concern for all archivists in the performance of their daily work. The postmodern script is not something written never to be performed, but rather to be performed continually. While no two performances can (or should) ever be the same, as no two Hamlets are ever the same (even by the same actor), the script for "thinking archives" needs to become a shared dynamic resonating in the daily work of "doing archives." Shakespeare said, "The play's the thing," the actual acting out of the script. Our immediate task, then, is to ask: what script are we following?[30]

Cook and Schwartz go on to identify some of the "scripts" that archivists have been performing over the history of their profession, embodied in field-defining writings such as the so-called Dutch Manual of 1898, and the works of Hilary Jenkinson and Theodore Schellenberg in the twentieth century.[31] Cook and Schwartz's characterization of the entire archival

---

[28] Cook, "Past Is Prologue," p. 19.
[29] Cook and Schwartz, "From (Postmodern) Theory," p. 171.
[30] Cook and Schwartz, "From (Postmodern) Theory," pp. 183–4.
[31] Cook and Schwartz list the major discipline-defining works of archival science as Jean Mabillon, *De re diplomatica* (1681); S. Muller, J. A. Feith, and R. Fruin, *Handleiding voor het Ordenen en Beschrijven van Archieven* (1898), known informally as the Dutch Manual and translated as *Manual for the Arrangement and Description of Archives* (see entry for Muller in Bibliography); Hilary Jenkinson, *A Manual of Archive Administration* (1922);

profession as being like a performance of *Hamlet* provides a remarkable example of the broader cultural phenomenon with which this book is concerned, namely the enlisting of Shakespeare to help information workers in different periods to think through problems of preservation, loss, and informatic complexity. Worth noting, as well, is Cook and Schwartz's implicit understanding that Shakespearean performance embodies the disseminative qualities they also associate with postmodernism, in which meaning – whether of a play or a profession – remains open to refashioning by the agents of its performance.

Schwarz and Cook's concerns about the power of archivists align closely with concerns about the interventions of editors expressed by Leah Marcus and other advocates of unediting, who developed their methods of critically reading the interventions of editors in relation to Shakespeare and other early modern authors.[32] The two fields even have parallel authority figures whose theories dominated the twentieth century, Fredson Bowers and Hilary Jenkinson, and whose positivist tenets have been challenged in recent years.[33] However, these intellectual lines have remained mostly parallel over the past two decades with few direct intersections, despite their strong similarities.

The discussion that follows will attempt to bridge between the worlds of archiving via Shakespeare, whose texts provided many of the prototypical problems upon which twentieth-century editing honed its methods. That body of editorial theory has seen many of its longstanding orthodoxies overturned in recent years, especially the primacy of authorial intentions, the unquestioned nature of certain types of dramatic documents, and the distinction between categorically good and bad Shakespeare playtexts. With these changes in editorial theory has come a general acknowledgment of the editors themselves as agents in the transmission of texts, still bound by principles of rigour and evidence,

---

Eugenio Casanova, *Archivistica* (1928); Theodore Schellenberg, *Modern Archives: Principles and Techniques* (1956) and *The Management of Archives* (1965). Cook's own "Past Is Prologue" could reasonably be added to this list to represent the postmodern turn in archival theory.

[32] Textual and archival scholarship share ancestry through the centuries-old disciplines of diplomatics and paleography, and through figures such as Jean Mabillon. As David Greetham describes, Mabillon was one of the crucial early modern scholars "whose work on identifying forgeries gradually began to turn the practice of diplomatics into the critical attitudes of paleography: that is, a competence in accurate transcription of ancient documents led the way for a critical evaluation of the scripts themselves"; *Textual Scholarship*, p. 318. On unediting see the Introduction, n. 22.

[33] See n. 40 below.

but no longer insulated from their decisions by the scientific detachment to which positivist New Bibliographers aspired. Shakespeare has been at the centre of these changes in editorial theory ever since the controversial Oxford Shakespeare edition of the 1980s. At the same time, archivists have been undergoing a parallel reevaluation of their field's orthodoxies, largely influenced by the body of ideas that literary editors usually call poststructuralism (referring to the language-focused work of Saussure, Barthes, Derrida, and others), and that archivists tend to call postmodernism. Archivists, like editors, were once regarded as dispassionate custodians of records, intervening in their historical trajectories only to nudge them away from oblivion. Like editors, too, archivists have spent the last decade reevaluating their role as historical and textual agents.

Archives and archivists focus attention on those agents in ways that bibliography and digital humanities – at least in their more conservative, purist forms – can easily neglect. To a positivist textual scholar like Fredson Bowers, a manifest error like the misquotation of *The Tempest* may exemplify what happens to texts in the hands of fallible human agents, but ultimately matters only as a problem to be solved. As Bowers himself said of textual error, "Only a practicing textual critic and bibliographer knows the remorseless corrupting influence that eats away at a text during the course of its transmission ... One can no more permit 'just a little corruption' to pass unheeded in the transmission of our literary heritage than 'just a little sin' was possible in Eden."[34] One wonders if Bowers, during his many years at the nearby University of Virginia, ever walked down Pennsylvania Avenue and noticed the error on one of America's chief temples to cultural heritage, perhaps imagining himself setting out from the Folger on a midnight editing mission with hammer and chisel. Others might resign themselves to the idea that recontextualization is the way of all text, especially Shakespearean phrases such as "the play's the thing," whose original context in *Hamlet* holds a rather different meaning from the one Schwartz and Cook present in the quotation above.[35] The same is true of "what's past is Prologue" – a phrase spoken not by *The Tempest*'s presiding magus, Prospero, but by the play's villain, Antonio, as he

---

[34] Bowers, *Textual and Literary Criticism*, p. 8. This quotation receives more detailed discussion in Chapter 6; see pp. 230–1.

[35] The phrase in context reads "The play's the thing / Wherein I'll catch the conscience of the King" (*Hamlet*, 2.2.606–7).

persuades Sebastian to kill his brother Alonso and usurp the throne of Naples. Casual visitors to the National Archives Building might be surprised to learn that the building thus bears an exhortation to murder a rightful king – making it a grimly fitting epigraph for Stone's *JFK* after all.

As Bowers knew all too well, the phenomenon of textual error not only creates new meanings, but also propagates them, as in Terry Cook's article title and unreferenced quotation from the play, which evidently quotes the National Archives Building rather than any Shakespeare edition.[36] In other words, both the National Archives Building and one of the foundational publications in archival theory carry out their work under the inscription of a Shakespeare text that has undergone "transformission," as Randall McLeod terms it.[37] The paradox at work here is very much of a piece with Shakespeare's tangled textual history, as an institution dedicated to the preservation of texts actually changes one in the transfer to a new material context, and does so in the very act of signalling its dedication to cultural heritage. This is the paradox at the heart of archiving: to preserve a text is to change it.

Poststructuralist conceptions of the archive

To understand how that paradox has fed the poststructuralist fascination with archives over the past two decades, consider an episode that Andrew Murphy recounts from the archival research that went into his landmark study *Shakespeare in Print*. After calling up some of the publisher Macmillan's archival materials held at British Library, Murphy realized that

the process used by the company in the nineteenth century for mechanically making copies of its outgoing correspondence was imperfect, with the result that some volumes of Macmillan letters held by the British Library now consist entirely of blank pages. The experience of having fastidious librarians deliver neatly bound blank books to one's desk in the rarefied atmosphere of the British Library manuscript reading room is not without its own peculiar charm, but one cannot help registering a sense of genuine loss also.[38]

---

[36] Cook, "Past Is Prologue," p. 34.
[37] McLeod, "Information on Information," p. 246.
[38] Murphy, *Shakespeare in Print*, pp. 10–11.

Murphy's account of his own *Raiders of the Lost Ark* moment – analogous to the film's climax, when the Ark of the Covenant is opened only to reveal that the Tablets of the Law have crumbled into dust – exemplifies the preservational challenges routinely faced by archivists. However, his anecdote also captures the connections between inscriptions, materiality, and institutionalized forms of memory that poststructuralists regard as the most important aspects of archives. The Macmillan records' imperfect mechanical reproduction, which professional archivists might regard as a practical problem to be solved, becomes in poststructural theory an emblem for the normal conditions of memory – personal, social, and institutional. In Murphy's example, the material failure of a publishing company's institutional memory takes on a new meaning as a present absence, especially in juxtaposition to the care with which the blank books are treated by the "fastidious librarians." His anecdote, while grounded in the real, also captures poststructuralism's imagined space of the archive, where information carries on a secret life of its own, supposedly changing and reorganizing itself when no one is looking.

As I mentioned in this book's Introduction, the word *archive* does not mean the same thing to all disciplines. Those differences register linguistically as well as conceptually, as Cook describes, with "The 'archive' (singular) usually engaged by [non-archivists] ... as a metaphoric symbol, as representation of identity, or as the recorded memory production of some person or group or culture."[39] Yet as Cook rightly laments, non-archivists often fail to account for the history of archives themselves as institutions shaped by concepts, theories, and practices native to the archival profession, all of which may shape researchers' experiences as much as the assumptions they bring with them into the archives. The non-archivists that Cook has in mind here are mainly historians (he is writing in the *Canadian Historical Review*), but one could extend the category of those who use *the archive* (singular) to critical theorists, literary scholars, anthropologists, media scholars, and any other branches of the humanities and social sciences that have been influenced by Derrida's or Foucault's writings on the archive.[40] For example,

[39] Cook, "Foreign Country," p. 498. On the disciplinary relationships between archivists and historians, see also Blouin and Rosenberg, *Processing the Past*, and Ketelaar, "Writing on Archiving Machines."

[40] For a literature review on this topic, see Manoff, "Theories of the Archive." The principal collections of scholarly work responding to Derrida's and Foucault's

consider the language of an introduction to a special issue of *English Studies in Canada* on the archive written by literary scholars Michael O'Driscoll and Ted Bishop: "The archive, we now easily recognize, takes a variety of institutional forms, including record repositories, museums, and libraries, but the term also accounts for all manner of inscription: monographs, photographs, film and video, databases, blogs, email, websites, monuments, paintings, and architectures, to offer just a partial list."[41] This assertion of the breadth of *the archive*'s referent may stretch the term beyond practical usefulness, and exemplifies the poststructuralist discourse that prompted Cook's call for rapprochement between archival theory written by archivists, on the one hand, and the theorizing of archives by scholars outside the profession, on the other.[42] That (re)encounter between fields would surely involve some diplomatic correction of the terminological elasticity of poststructuralists, but there is more to the relationship; many prominent archival theorists have shown that poststructural thinking about archives can productively unsettle assumptions about memory, technology, and power.[43] In this section I will draw primarily from Derrida's *Archive Fever* to articulate three concepts – the *substrate*, *archiviolithism*, and *consignation* – which will later prove helpful in understanding the Shakespearean archive and the connections between editorial and archival theory.

conceptions of the archive are: two special issues of *History of the Human Sciences*, 11.4 (1998) and 12.2 (1999); Voss and Werner (eds.), *Toward a Poetics of the Archive*, special issue of *Studies in the Literary Imagination*, 32.1 (1999); *The Postmodern Archives*, special issue of *Archivaria*, 51 (2001); Comay (ed.), *Lost in the Archives* (2002); Hamilton, *et al.* (eds.), *Refiguring the Archive*; Schwartz and Cook (eds.), *Archives, Records, and Power*, special issue of *Archival Science*, 2.1–2 (2002); and O'Driscoll and Bishop (eds.), *The Event of the Archive*, special issue of *English Studies in Canada*, 30.1 (2004). For a more recent example of Foucault's notion of the archive applied within a digital humanities context, see Parikka, "Archives in Media Theory."

41 O'Driscoll and Bishop, "Archiving 'Archiving,'" p. 4.
42 See the discussion of Paul Eggert's related critique of broad uses of *the archive* in the Introduction, p. 13, as well as Steedman, *Dust*. An example of bridge-building between these worlds was a recent conference at Yale University, "Beyond the Text: Literary Archives in the 21st Century," sponsored by the Beinecke Rare Book and Manuscript Library, 26–7 April 2013.
43 To let one example stand for many, see Verne Harris's discussions of Derrida, archives, and pre- and post-apartheid South Africa in *Archives and Justice* and his contributions to Hamilton, *et al.* (eds.), *Refiguring the Archive*.

Derrida's *Archive Fever* provides the touchstone for most critics who use the term *archive* in its doubled sense of institution and metaphor. The metaphorical slippage he exploits has not gone uncriticized, and *Archive Fever* all too often remains the extent of non-archivists' reading on the topic, but the book has also had an energizing effect within archival studies.[44] Derrida begins his meditation on the archives of psychoanalysis with the etymology of the word *archive*, which derives from the Greek *arkheion*: "initially a house, a domicile, an address, the residence of the superior magistrates, the *archons*, those who commanded ... On account of their publicly recognized authority, it is at their home, in that *place* which is their house (private house, family house, or employee's house), that official documents are filed."[45] In his account of the original archival temples, Derrida also notes the dual role of the archons: "They do not only ensure the physical security of what is deposited and of the substrate. They are also accorded the hermeneutic right and competence. They have the power to interpret the archives ... Even in their guardianship or their hermeneutic tradition, the archives could do neither without substrate nor without residence."[46] These powers of inclusion and exclusion have become the primary theme of poststructuralist discussions of archives. Within textual studies, the archival links between authority and authenticity have received their most pointed questioning by David Greetham in a chapter on "The Cultural Poetics of Archival Exclusion."[47] Greetham points out that "to a future culture, it may be more likely that the bibliographical ephemera – the ticket stubs and laundry lists, the jottings on the backs of envelopes – will appear more valuable as evidence than the self-evident monuments we have chosen to represent us."[48] Even the records that organizations like Macmillan intended to preserve do not reach the

---

[44] Derrida's unempirical approach to archives is an object of criticism in Steedman's *Dust*; see p. 68. On the different meanings of the term *memory* in relation to archiving, see Brothman, "The Past that Archives Keep."

[45] Derrida, *Archive Fever*, p. 2, emphasis in original. Many critics situate their use of *archive* by quoting Derrida on its etymology; see, for example, O'Driscoll and Bishop, "Archiving 'Archiving,'" p. 5, and Steedman, *Dust*, p. 1. Voss and Werner include a full-page dictionary excerpt for *archive* as verb and noun on the page preceding their table of contents in *Poetics of the Archive*.

[46] Derrida, *Archive Fever*, p. 2.

[47] Greetham, "Who's In, Who's Out: The Cultural Poetics of Archival Exclusion," in *Pleasures of Contamination*, pp. 117–51.

[48] Greetham, *Pleasures of Contamination*, pp. 132–3.

present in the forms their originators intended, as Murphy discovered. His story serves as reminder that archives are constituted as much by their gaps and exclusions as by the principles of responsible record-keeping.

Murphy's story also highlights the importance of substrates as surfaces that receive and preserve inscriptions. The importance of substrates is always practical and symbolic at the same time. Derrida characterizes the archive, from its very origins, as a composite system, one made up of the *archon*'s house itself – its walls, doors, and guards – along with the system of interpretation and entitlement that makes the documents "speak the law."[49] For Derrida and other critics writing in recent years on memory, inscription, and the material substrates that bind them together, the image that has captured the composite nature of archives like no other is Freud's 1925 "Note Upon the Mystic Writing Pad," which finds a model for memory in the design of a children's toy: the *Wunderblock* or Mystic Writing Pad. The toy permits one to write on a wax substrate with a stylus, but with a plastic layer in between that can be lifted to erase the visible marks – though, crucially for Freud and Derrida, the inscriptions on the wax substrate remain even after the surface layer has been erased. Inexhaustible capacity united with total recall: the Mystic Writing Pad has it both ways.

Derrida's reading of Freud's reading of this device has resulted in the Mystic Writing Pad becoming an iconic representation of memory in the form of an archival yet erasable technology, with the device's rhythm of inscription and erasure serving to literalize and externalize processes that invisibly mold personal and social memory.[50] Freud states that external substrates can either receive temporary information with infinite repetition (like chalk and slate) or store limited amounts of information as permanent inscriptions (like ink and paper) but, crucially, they cannot do both. Compared to human memory, mnemonic technologies are always ambivalent given that, as Freud asserts, "our mental apparatus accomplishes precisely what they cannot: it has an unlimited receptive capacity for new perceptions and nevertheless lays down permanent – even though not unalterable – memory-traces of them."[51] In this way, a composite archival technology such as the

[49] Derrida, *Archive Fever*, p. 2. See also the tripartite definition of archives quoted in the Introduction, p. 15.
[50] Spieker, *The Big Archive*, p. 21, and Elsaesser, "Technical Media."
[51] Freud, "Mystic Writing-Pad," p. 228.

Mystic Writing Pad challenges the simplistic view of memory technologies as straightforward extensions of human capacities, and, by extension, of digital computers merely as tools.

Another challenge to instrumentalist notions of memory technologies takes the form of what Derrida terms *archiviolithism*, a kind of structural forgetting that shadows memory technologies, like the Freudian death-drive. Freud expresses this idea in a comment on the Mystic Writing Pad's inability to provide a perfect record of everything: "once the writing has been erased, the Mystic Pad cannot 'reproduce' it from within; it would be a mystic pad indeed if, like our memory, it could accomplish that."[52] For Freud, the mind is the model archive but, unlike the Mystic Writing Pad, the wax tablet of the subconscious does not allow for efficient and accurate information retrieval. Fantastic idealizations of archives, as imaginary compensations for the real failures of information management, depend upon the "mystic" qualities attributed to substrates. Yet the fantasy that human memory could perfectly record and recall all informatic traces is undermined by the realization that such a prodigious natural archive is outside our conscious scope.

Derrida's fascination with the Mystic Writing Pad in *Archive Fever* (and decades earlier, in "Freud and the Scene of Writing") suggests a related contradiction at the heart of Freud's concept of memory as inscription, in that the mental archive is a powerful mechanism for recording impressions, but it does not create a record as such, at least not one that can be made to reproduce what it records.[53] Therefore, an archive properly speaking must always be somewhat outside the self, having what Derrida calls "a certain exteriority" that preserves it from the amnesic, "archiviolithic force" of forgetfulness: the informatic death-drive.[54] Thus, there is a measure of nostalgia and loss at the heart of any memory technology given that its purpose is inevitably compensatory. A consequence that textual scholars and digital humanists must live with today is that any investment in mnemonic supplements is shadowed by a simultaneous distrust and idealization of human memory.

Inscriptions thus owe their symbolic power to this archiviolithic anxiety that attends all material writing, as well as all technological supplements to

---

[52] Freud, "Mystic Writing-Pad," p. 230.
[53] Derrida, "Freud and the Scene of Writing," pp. 199–200, 221–9, and *passim*.
[54] Derrida, *Archive Fever*, p. 11, emphasis removed.

memory. What ties Freud's inscriptive model of memory to the information culture around him in the early twentieth century – and to ours today –
is the problem of volume, and the realization that memory can exceed the
scale of the human. Derrida groups the volume-managing functions of
"unification, of identification, [and] of classification"[55] under the more
abstract principle of *consignation*: "By consignation, we do not only
mean, in the ordinary sense of the word, the act of assigning residence or
of entrusting so as to put into reserve (to consign, to deposit), in a place and
on a substrate, but here the act of *con*signing by *gathering together signs*"
under a transcendent order.[56] Consignation is the systematizing impulse,
the desire to regularize everything in a given archive, to protect the contents
from heterogeneity, irregularity, and other forms of internal disorder. It is
the impossible perspective which, like Jorge Luis Borges's aleph, views all
the elements of the archive as a unified whole, and "aims to coordinate a
single corpus, in a system or a synchrony in which all the elements
articulate the unity of an ideal configuration."[57] Early modernists will
recognize in this description the encyclopedic tradition inherited from
the Renaissance and the Enlightenment, along with its intellectual bag-
gage. As Hilary Clark describes, "The idea that prior to organization,
knowledge is a dishevelled heap of fragments and odd facts, haunts
the encyclopedic enterprise ... This mass of data, then, like noise in
information theory, is the ground against which complex orders and
information become perceptible."[58]

As cultural historians such as Thomas Richards have shown, actual
practices of encyclopedic knowledge management in the nineteenth
century tended to reverse the ideal progress of knowledge described
above by Clark: the consignation of records within an archive often
preceded and ultimately overran their integration into the governing
episteme, however encyclopedic its scope. As Richards explains with
regard to the knowledge-management practices of the British Empire
at its apex, the civil servants in the Foreign Office and the various

---

[55] Derrida, *Archive Fever*, p. 3.
[56] Derrida, *Archive Fever*, p. 3, emphasis in original.
[57] Derrida, *Archive Fever*, p. 3, and Borges, "The Aleph." See also Ketelaar,
    "Archival Temples," p. 237; Harris, *Archives and Justice*, pp. 42–3; and Eggert,
    "Brought to Book," p. 12, n. 15.
[58] Clark, "Encyclopedic Discourse," p. 99; see also Blair, *Too Much to Know*,
    pp. 168–72.

departments charged with managing the world's largest empire were simply unable to keep up with the mass of incoming records:

These people were painfully aware of the gaps in their knowledge and did their best to fill them in. The filler they liked best was information. From all over the globe the British collected information about the countries they were adding to their map. They surveyed and they mapped. They took censuses, produced statistics. They made vast lists of birds.[59]

Michael O'Driscoll gives us useful terms for this type of shift in archival resource-allocation: on the one hand, *epistemic management*, "the management of ideal knowledge," is the defensive posture of encyclo-pedists; on the other, *textual management*, "the management of mate-rial texts," is the strategy of those who seek, conjecture, or sometimes impose order at the level of documents.[60] Textual management, as O'Driscoll puts it, "recognizes and privileges the sheer materiality of the text and, through the manipulation and juxtaposition of documen-tary materials, seeks to situate itself advantageously within the space of the archive."[61] To apply O'Driscoll's terms to the situation described by Richards, the crisis of the Imperial archive is epistemic management's inevitable displacement by its other, given that the former "is charged with the organization of knowledge and seemingly elides or evaporates what are actually overwhelming quantities of material inscriptions."[62] But epistemic management, "the transcendence of the archive," cannot budge the mass of "material documents on which it is dependent," especially when that mass is augmented on the scale of empire.[63] By contrast, Richards's "vast lists of birds" exemplify the strategy – or compulsion – of textual management. Lists, as basic information structures, can seem to assert a measure of control over phenomena, though every list also exists in tension with the world it attempts to manage (as we shall see with regard to the catalogue of plays in the Shakespeare First Folio in the next chapter).

Poststructuralist concepts like epistemic and textual management, as well as inscription, archiviolithism, and consignation, provide a vocabulary for discussing aspects of archives that are not always foremost in archivists' own engagements with poststructuralism,

[59] Richards, *Imperial Archive*, p. 3.
[60] O'Driscoll, "Derrida, Foucault," p. 288.
[61] O'Driscoll, "Derrida, Foucault," p. 289.
[62] O'Driscoll, "Derrida, Foucault," p. 288.   [63] *Ibid.*

which understandably tend to focus on power and authority. My concern here has been to draw out aspects of poststructuralist conceptions of the archive that illuminate the symbolic and practical functions of inscription technologies, like the new media experiments we will examine in subsequent chapters. The link between materiality and power runs through all of these ideas, especially in situations like Murphy's encounter with Macmillan's blank record books, in which the large-scale institutional character of archives depends upon material properties of mechanical reproduction. The imperfect Macmillan company records show archiviolithism at work, especially in Murphy's contextualization of his story as disquietingly typical of the realities of archival research. Modernity depends on the notion that governments, corporations, and other forms of institutionalized power retain control over their documentary existences, inscribing their identities, as it were, on leaves of brass.[64]

Textual scholarship has made its own investments in that narrative, as Tom Stoppard satirizes in his play *The Invention of Love*, in which a fictional version of the New Bibliographer Alfred Pollard raises a toast to the British Museum Library as "the aggregate of human progress made stackable."[65] Stoppard's wonderful phrase captures the illusion of epistemic manageability offered by books, with the corresponding unwieldiness of archival records and their sometimes unmanageable texts serving as counterpoint. Derrida's reading of Freud in *Archive Fever* has also helped fuel recent interest in the technologizing of memory throughout the humanities, and with it a renewed interest in memory and writing technologies in Shakespeare's time. One of the most influential examples is an article by Peter Stallybrass, Roger Chartier, J. Franklin Mowrey, and Heather Wolfe on "Hamlet's Tables and the Technologies of Writing in Renaissance England."[66] Their description of early modern wax table books like the ones Hamlet references as a memory supplement ("My tables! Meet it is I set it down"; 1.5.107[67]) are remarkably akin to Freud's Mystic Writing Pad: "To the extent that

---

[64] See MacNeil, "Trusting Records."   [65] Stoppard, *Invention of Love*, p. 72.
[66] Stallybrass, *et al.*, "Hamlet's Tables"; see also Chartier, *Inscription and Erasure*, pp. 22–5, and Galey, "Tablets of the Law." For an overview of wax tablets as a writing technology, see Rouse and Rouse, "Wax Tablets." For an overview of writing technologies in relation to the arts of memory, see Whitehead, *Memory*, pp. 15–49.
[67] Thompson and Taylor (eds.), *Hamlet* (based on the 1623 First Folio text).

memory works like a table-book, it implies forgetfulness as much as remembrance," a tension that works within what they call the play's "opposition ... between technologies of permanence and technologies of erasure."[68] The bibliographic research of Stallybrass, Chartier, Mowrey, and Wolfe shows how poststructuralist questioning of modernity's narratives of inscription as power leads naturally to the empirical analysis of the substrates that make inscription possible.

For this reason, I do not share Paul Eggert's fear that the influence of Derrida's *Archive Fever* in textual studies comes "at the cost of further depriviliging the material archive by shifting the fundamental locus of explanatory power elsewhere."[69] Leaving aside the question of why "the material archive" and the work done there deserve special privilege in the first place, the example of archival theory written *by* archivists shows that Derrida's line of inquiry, when pursued with a healthy interdisciplinary breadth, leads right back into paper archives. Indeed, such lines of inquiry often lead into the physical particulars of the records that reside in these discursively overdetermined spaces – these aggregates of human progress made stackable. (None can call themselves poststructuralists who do not understand the properties of paper.) Such composite perspectives on memory technologies are called for by the composite nature of archives themselves.

Archival and editorial theory

Although poststructural theorists and those influenced by them have generated new and valuable ways of thinking about archives, Terry Cook is right in pointing out that their work tends to suffer from a major omission: the scholarly literature of archivists themselves. As Margaret Hedstrom warned in 1991, and as Kate Theimer emphasized recently in a digital humanities context, many uses of the term *archive* happen to neglect the basic mission of archivists: in Hedstrom's words, "to understand information in its context, to identify what is valuable, or to retain records and make them accessible as long as they have value."[70] Hedstrom notes with some alarm (and a hint of territoriality)

---

[68] Stallybrass, *et al.*, "Hamlet's Tables," pp. 414–15.
[69] Eggert, "Brought to Book," p. 12.
[70] Hedstrom, "Electronic Incunabula," p. 336; see also Theimer, "Archives in Context."

that "archivists have literally lost control over the definition of *archive*."[71] That redefinition of the term by other fields led to collections of articles on poststructural conceptions of archives by literary scholars, historians, and other non-archivists, notably in special issues of *History of the Human Sciences, Studies in the Literary Imagination, Alphabet City,* and *English Studies in Canada.*[72] Much of the exciting work in these collections is animated by the poststructural conceptions of archives discussed in the preceding section. However, even though these collections deal directly with the nature of archives, not just the archive as metaphor, almost none of the contributors engage directly with archival concepts and scholarship.[73] Even Greetham, a textual scholar who can hardly be accused of narrow disciplinary thinking, manages to write a detailed, insightful, and well-referenced article on what archivists would recognize as archival appraisal without citing a single archivist or using the term *archival appraisal.*[74] The voice of the archives profession is almost entirely silenced in these works – ironic given the poststructuralist emphasis on the marginalizing effects of archives themselves, and the need to recover voices silenced by institutional power. My intention is to address this blind spot by examining how archivists have grappled with a fundamental idea: that archiving in any form is always more than metaphor, and depends upon the ability, as Hedstrom puts it, to "understand information in its context."

Privileging the deeply contextual nature of information is a value that archivists share with textual scholars. There are remarkable parallels between both fields in their hybrid focus on the relationship of

---

[71] Hedstrom, "Electronic Incunabula," p. 336, italics in original.
[72] See note 40, above.
[73] For notable exceptions among the articles in these collections see Ernst, "Archival Action," and Lahusen, "Archival Journey." Some of the articles in these collections engage archival thinking indirectly via the history of archives and librarianship; see Brown and Davis-Brown, "Making of Memory," and Patrick Joyce, "Liberal Archive." Other works by non-archivists who have engaged the scholarly literature of archives directly include Spieker, *The Big Archive,* and Codebò, *Narrating from the Archive.*
[74] The Society of American Archivists' online glossary defines archival appraisal as "the process of determining whether records and other materials have permanent (archival) value" and notes, "The basis of appraisal decisions may include a number of factors, including the records' provenance and content, their authenticity and reliability, their order and completeness, their condition and costs to preserve them, and their intrinsic value" (www2.archivists.org/glossary/terms/a/appraisal/).

documents, materiality, and meaning, and their commitment to preserving the materials on which historical understanding is based. Among textual scholars, that latter imperative has tended to take the form of scholarly editions and facsimiles, which has prompted at least one archivist, Heather MacNeil, to ask in turn how the work of archiving is more like editing than either field realizes. I will turn to her work on the disciplinary parallels below, but must first acknowledge the differences between the fields – differences that are key to this book's argument that Shakespeare's textual afterlives have been shaped significantly by textual agents besides editors, especially in their relations to the writing technologies and power structures that have preoccupied poststructural considerations of the archive.

Archival theory's relatively recent turn toward understanding the records generated by individuals, such as authors, outside organizational contexts may strike literary scholars as surprising, especially given the long history of literary archives as foundational scholarly resources.[75] However, this theoretical latency makes sense considering that archives originated to preserve records generated by the day-to-day operations of organizations, whereas scholarly editing tends to focus on the exceptional: literary or historical texts of unusual cultural significance, often defined by canons that set certain authors and works apart. In particular, the ordinariness of archival records in relation to the contexts of their creation has required a distinction between circulating and non-circulating records: in an organization, circulating records (those which still have work to do) are held in a registry, while non-circulating records (those of interest primarily for historical purposes) enter the archives, though typically only after a process of archival appraisal to determine which records are worth preserving. Sven Spieker, though not an archivist himself, draws upon this distinction in his account of modernity and memory, which marks his work as a salutary exception to the pattern of non-archivists failing to engage archival theory. As Spieker relates,

The registry is crucial . . . not only because its name evokes registration, the idea of producing an analogue recording of ongoing activities, but also because it represents the middle element in a triad that has had a formative influence on what we have come to define as modern: the office, where records are produced; the registry, where they are kept as long as they circulate; and the archive itself,

---

[75] See Hobbs, "Reenvisioning the Personal"; Douglas and MacNeil, "Arranging the Self"; and Douglas, *Archiving Authors*.

where they are stored in perpetuity. In altered form, this triad returns in the Freudian psychic apparatus – modernism's most formidable archive gadget – where its separate elements connote different mnemonic functions.[76]

In Spieker's characterization of this foundational archival concept, the assumed relationships between office, registry, and archive are more than elements in a theory; they are also reflective of modernity's picture of memory, whether psychological or institutional. As we shall see, those structures also reproduced themselves in the New Bibliography's theories about the archival nature of Shakespeare's playhouse.

Chief among archival theory's foundational ideas is the meta-concept of *provenance*, which reflects archivists' fundamental goal of accounting for the deep contextuality of recorded information. The concept of archival provenance – as distinct from the similar concept of provenance used by book historians and others who deal with the histories of artifacts – articulates that contextuality through two sub-principles, as described by Jennifer Douglas and MacNeil: *respect des fonds*, a principle dictating "that the records of a person, family, or corporate body be kept together and not intermingled with the records of other creators"; and *original order*, a principle dictating "that records be preserved in the order given to them by the entity that created them."[77] Original order and *respect des fonds* are sometimes referred to as the inward and outward dimensions of the principle of provenance, a dualism that reflects archivists' concern for records' relations to the world around them, and for the patterns of order discernable within.[78] As Terry Eastwood describes, "Understanding the meaning of any individual document depends on knowing its relationship with the entity that produced it, the purposes the entity pursues, the entity's manner of pursuing its purposes, the purpose the document serves, and its place in the scheme the entity devises for its documents."[79] This fabric of purposes materialized in a set of documents forms a whole that archivists tend to call a *fonds*; once identified, the resulting goal for archivists, according to Eastwood, was "to carry that whole forward in time." The

---

[76] Spieker, *The Big Archive*, p. 21.
[77] Douglas and MacNeil, "Arranging the Self," p. 27. For more detail on the history of these concepts, see Ridener, *Polders to Postmodernism*, pp. 32–4, 37–8, and *passim*.
[78] See Horsman, "Taming the Elephant," p. 51.
[79] Eastwood, "A Constructed Realm."

parallels to textual and literary theory are worth noting here, especially the similarity between *respect des fonds* and Foucault's author function.[80] Both the archival and the literary conceptions of an organic wholeness as the ground of textual production have a practical benefit: they serve to bestow a functional unity on groups of documents, allowing institutions to organize them into unities like the work, the authorial canon, and the fonds.

Archivists, like literary theorists, have also criticized the deceptive sense of homogeneity these unities can bestow, and have noted the constructedness of the boundaries of any given fonds.[81] As Douglas and MacNeil describe, "The principles ... presume the existence of an affinity between abstract wholes and material parts; the concept of fonds communicates a sense of wholeness to something that physically exists only in fragments."[82] Their phrasing echoes Derrida's notion of consignation, through which he describes how archives create systems "in which all of the elements articulate the unity of an ideal configuration."[83] Although archival records do indeed have original contexts of production like those of books, archivists have recently broadened the concept of provenance to account for influences beyond single, originary moments. Tom Nesmith redefines provenance as "the social and technical processes of ... records' inscription, transmission, contextualization, and interpretation which account for [their] existence, characteristics, and continuing history."[84] Nesmith's approach to provenance evokes McKenzie's sociology of texts in its pluralist conception of agency and meaning in textual production.[85]

MacNeil has explored the affinities between archival and textual studies more than any other scholar on either side. As she describes, "textual criticism aims to restore a literary text as closely as possible to its original, authentic form, while archival arrangement seeks to reconstruct the 'authentic,' meaning original, order of a body of records."[86]

---

[80] Foucault, "What Is an Author?".

[81] As Geoffrey Yeo and others have demonstrated, the concept of the fonds is much debated in archival theory at present; see Yeo, "Conceptual Fonds."

[82] Douglas and MacNeil, "Arranging the Self," p. 27.

[83] Derrida, *Archive Fever*, p. 3.   [84] Nesmith, "Still Fuzzy," p. 146.

[85] For example, see McKenzie's discussion of *Citizen Kane* and archives in *Bibliography and the Sociology of Texts*, pp. 64–76, which also ends on a Shakespearean note with reference to Prospero's library and drowned book.

[86] MacNeil, "Archivalterity," p. 3.

Other parallels follow from this in her analysis, including the similarity between the critical apparatus of an edition and the archival description of a fonds, both of which frame the meaning of their objects and, more fundamentally, work to establish trust between reader and document.[87] For MacNeil, one of the consequences of this parallel for archivists is that archival description could take on the self-reflexive attributes of scholarly editions, especially those in the traditions of historicist editing and versioning, given their elevation of material contexts and multiple versions, rather than eclectic editing, which synthesizes different authorities into single editions.

It is the concept of authenticity, however, that coordinates the primary connections between the fields. As MacNeil argues, "In both fields, originality and authenticity are closely tied to the identification and stabilization of final authorial intentions."[88] Adapting Joseph Grigely's notion of textualterity, along with the post-New Bibliographical editorial theory of McKenzie and McGann, MacNeil adapts for archiving the basic premise of poststructural textual theory that "literary, artistic, and architectural works . . . are in a continuous state of becoming as they age, are resituated, recontextualized, reissued and restored."[89] As MacNeil argues, echoing Grigely, McKenzie, and numerous other textual scholars, "alterity – textual change and difference – is as integral to the meaning and authenticity of a cultural text as the final intentions of the artist or author" – an idea that MacNeil recasts as "archivalterity" when applied to archival fonds and records.[90] Acknowledging archivalterity is important for archivists as agents who, like editors, intervene in the materials they curate. Archivists following the conventional wisdom of their profession would, like editors, occasionally have to intervene to correct errors or restore lost materials, sometimes risking the effacement of some historical traces as they attempt to preserve others. Even supposedly straightforward archival practices like description and arrangement have been argued to be interventions of a sort: constructions of authenticity as opposed to a positivist application of rationality leading to truth.[91]

---

[87] MacNeil, "Picking Our Text," p. 269.
[88] MacNeil, "Archivalterity," p. 3; see also Mak, "Uses of Authenticity."
[89] MacNeil, "Archivalterity," p. 9; see also Grigely, *Textualterity*.
[90] MacNeil, "Archivalterity," pp. 9 and 14.
[91] On postmodern approaches to archival description, see Duff and Harris, "Stories and Names."

As MacNeil describes, the analogy between archiving and editing runs deeper than methods and metaphors, with the connections being fundamentally epistemological. Noting that many scholarly editions are abstractions derived from many sources, she argues that "both traditional textual critics and archivists are concerned with the relationship between material parts and imaginary wholes."[92] This observation goes to the heart of Shakespearean textual scholarship over the past century, and captures the New Bibliographers' remarkable capacity to build forensic investigation into a systematic account of all textual transmission. MacNeil's observation, when applied to Shakespearean textual scholarship, also highlights the paradoxical role of Shakespeare's absent manuscripts as the paradigmatic textual problem around which twentieth-century bibliography was built.

The Shakespeare editor as archivist

Considering the archivist as editor is only one side of the equation, however; what about the editor as archivist? In asking this, I should make clear that I differentiate the question from that of the editor (or bibliographer, or book historian) as a researcher *within* archives, even though many editors are no strangers to archival research. Instead, I am interested in the ways editors have functioned like archivists in employing the kinds of archival concepts described above, even if by other names. For example, in light of the discussion of original order and the importance of this much-debated concept, one might regard the debate over the sequencing of the individual *Canterbury Tales*, whose surviving manuscripts yield evidence for multiple, conflicting orders of tales, as no less an archival problem than an editorial one. The interpretive stakes of the different orders would be familiar to archivists, whose sensitivity to context would call attention to the literary consequences of different sub-groupings and juxtapositions within the *Tales* as a conjectured whole. Shakespeare's plays provide even more opportunities to consider editors as archivists, given that Shakespeare pursued his dramatic composition within the business context of playing companies, whose day-to-day functional documents became literary monuments in retrospect. To what extent are Shakespeare editors dealing

---

[92] MacNeil, "Picking Our Text," p. 270.

with the results of archival decisions in the past, and acting like archivists when they untangle those decisions?

For example, textual scholars could learn from the debate over archival description, especially the power of names and categories to shape interpretation.[93] That is hardly a radical idea in a field that has spent the past two decades questioning bibliographical categories with names like *bad quartos* – a term which at least splits no hairs about its pejorativeness. But archival theory calls textual scholars to do more than simply watch their language; archivists' critique of their own discipline often exposes the unexamined value systems that are built out of words. The same kind of inquiry is visible in John Jowett's questioning of the very naming of what the New Bibliographers called *playbooks* and *prompt books*:

> If we think of a "book-keeper" who annotates a "playbook," we will develop an image of that document having a documentary, even archival function. If, instead, we refer to a "prompter" who maintains a "prompt book," the implication is that the text in the manuscript has a more immediate connection with the play as spoken and performed on the stage.[94]

Jowett is thinking very much like an archivist here, not just as a user of archives, when he presents the naming of types of records as not merely a terminological quibble but a way of defining the relationships between documents and the contexts in which they originate. This is what Schwartz and Cook mean when they refer to "the heavy layers of intervention and meaning coded into the records by their creators and by archivists long before any box is opened in the research room."[95]

The larger point here is that the New Bibliographers, like archivists, were thinking not simply of terms and categories, but of whole systems of documentary production and preservation in the early modern theatres. From them Shakespeare editors inherited a model of textual production, one that depended on the hypothetical reconstruction of documents that have been lost, or may never have existed, but a model that nonetheless established what archivists might recognize as principles of provenance

---

[93] See Duff and Harris, "Stories and Names."
[94] Jowett, *Shakespeare and Text*, p. 35.
[95] Schwartz and Cook, "Modern Memory," p. 6.

for early modern dramatic texts.[96] A key part of this model was the notion of Shakespeare's theatre not only as an "inscription engine" (to borrow Adrian Johns's term for the scientific laboratory as envisioned by Bruno Latour), but also as an archive itself.[97]

An important conclusion of Paul Werstine's recent study of the evidence for the bibliographic categories of prompt books and foul papers is that New Bibliographical theory has never properly worked through W. W. Greg's assumption that the early modern playhouse was also an archive for Shakespeare's and others' foul papers, ensuring their availability as copy for the printing of plays, sometimes after an interval of years or decades. As supporting evidence for this hypothesis, Greg offers a scribal note in a manuscript copy of the play *Bonduca* made by the King's Men's bookkeeper, Edward Knight, in which Knight (like a good archivist making a transcription) intervenes in response to a gap in the textual record: the absence of two scenes and part of a third from his exemplar's fifth act provokes Knight to note that "the booke where by it was first Acted from is lost: and this hath beene transcrib'd from the fowle papers of the Authors wᶜh were found."[98] One cannot help but think of Knight's encounter with the gap in the document at that moment as indicative of life in the archives, much like Murphy's account of the blank Macmillan account books, or Carolyn Steedman's admonition that no historian should be surprised when an archivist returns a call-slip with the explanation, "destroyed by enemy action during the Second World War."[99] The forms of theory we have been considering here – poststructural, archival, and editorial – are all preoccupied in different ways with such absences.

Greg apparently could not rest content with gaps in the archive, and on the basis of Knight's annotation builds an hypothesis about how the playhouse functioned as a system: "The inference is that these [foul papers] had been preserved in the archives of the company, perhaps in view of just such an accident. The company may also have thought it prudent to keep in their own hands all existing copies of a play

---

[96] This questioning of categories for dramatic documents has been led primarily by Werstine; see his "Narratives," "Post-Theory Problems," and *Playhouse Manuscripts*.

[97] Johns, *Nature of the Book*, p. 13.

[98] Quoted in Werstine, *Playhouse Manuscripts*, p. 13; italics and erasure omitted.

[99] Steedman, *Dust*, p. 68.

they purchased in order to safeguard themselves against dishonesty."[100] Greg goes on a few pages later to attribute more archival motivations to the playing company, building a narrative of an archival bond:

If the author handed over his foul papers for transcription, they were sometimes at any rate preserved in case of accident to the prompt-book; and even if he prepared his own fair copy it is possible that the company demanded the production of foul papers as a precaution against underhanded dealing, though this is little more than a conjecture … Thus it is possible that the company would have in its archives at least one autograph copy of any play in its repertory. We have the word of Heminge and Condell that the King's men possessed some of Shakespeare's own manuscripts, including foul papers.[101]

The consequence, Greg goes on to claim, is that there is "nothing fantastic in the suggestion that if the sharers authorized an edition of one of their plays it might be printed from a manuscript in the author's own handwriting." My purpose is not to judge whether Greg was right or wrong in this hypothesis about the theatre as archive – although his evidence was weak, as Werstine has pointed out.[102] Rather, the slide from conjecture into certainty in these quotations from Greg shows how rational systems are underpinned by faith in the power of inscription.

What is at stake here is the question of wholeness in our picture of the past, and in its representation in editions. Greg's example leads us back to Julia Flanders's question about the relation between archives and editions (quoted briefly in the Introduction and here with more context):

The desire to increase readerly access to primary data, paired with a now frequent questioning of the nature of the editor's role, impels the electronic edition increasingly towards inclusiveness as a way of avoiding editorial intervention … [W]hat pressure does the term "archive" … put on the conceptualization of the "edition"?

These terms seem to pull in opposite directions, and must do so as long as we think of them in terms of mutual inadequacy: the archive as a failure to provide an editorial synthesis; the edition as a failure to provide access to all the evidence.[103]

As Flanders argues, archives and editions need not be antithetical structures of knowledge: "the more we work with both, and the more

---

[100] Greg, *Editorial Problem*, p. 27.   [101] Greg, *Editorial Problem*, pp. 33–4.
[102] Werstine, *Playhouse Manuscripts*, pp. 31–2 and 99–100.
[103] Flanders, "Body Encoded," p. 136.

indigenous they become to the electronic world, the more . . . it will be useful to see them as converging."[104] The shifting and multiple meanings of the word *archive*, some of which we have surveyed in this chapter, serve as a reminder that the meaning of *edition* is also a moving target, subject to cultural and technological changes even long before our own era of digital archives. The chapters that follow will explore the ramifications of Flanders's question throughout the long history of Shakespeare and new media, where the contest between synthesis and exhaustiveness has been fought time and again. As we shall see in subsequent chapters, digital media are not the first to offer the prospect of having Shakespeare both ways.

There is something of Hilary Clark's "dishevelled heap of fragments" (quoted above) hovering behind Flanders's description of the way digital humanists regard archives as repositories of everything, with the heap of fragments becoming both threat and opportunity at once. For example, Peter Donaldson's *Shakespeare Electronic Archive* is one of a number of large digital projects begun soon after the rise of the Web that deliberately adopted the word *archive* rather than *edition* or *library*. As Donaldson describes, the project gathers together a multitude of inscriptions, including "the early folio and quarto editions, the literally hundreds of complete editions and the much greater number of editions of single works published since the seventeenth century, a vast body of critical and interpretive literature, a small library of sources and supposed sources, records of theatrical productions, including playbills, promptbooks, reviews, and other materials."[105]

To this already daunting list Donaldson adds Shakespearean works of visual art, films, photographs, sound recordings, and other records of performance. A key aspect of the project is the unbreakable link between vast archives and vulnerable inscriptions. Donaldson makes this link clear in his closing analysis of the debate over an apparent variant in *The Tempest*, when Ferdinand says that "So rare a wondered father and a [wise/wife] / Makes this place paradise" (4.1.123–4). A compositor would normally set the long-s form of the letter *s* in the middle of a word like *wise*, meaning that the words *wiſe* and *wife* would be almost graphically indistinguishable in early modern typography, despite their very different meanings in context.[106] The examination of

[104] *Ibid.*   [105] Donaldson, "Digital Archive," p. 173.
[106] See Jowett's summary of the debate in *Shakespeare and Text*, pp. 26–9.

multiple copies of the First Folio was the only way to verify whether the compositor had originally set an "f" whose crossbar had worn down during printing, such that "wife" began to look like "wiſe" in successive copies. In this case, the presence or absence of barely a millimeter of ink determines an interpretive question about the play, but requires the entire apparatus of the Folger Shakespeare Library and potentially Donaldson's digital archive to settle.

These instances of minute contested inscriptions serve as reminders that archives are about small things, easily lost and easily forgotten, the seeking of which can escalate into a cultural preoccupation and symbolic struggle against forgetting. By the turn of the twenty-first century, it seemed as though the word *archive* had wound its way through history and language just in time to capture the thrill of massive digital projects. The word served especially well for projects that actually came to fruition, like the *Shakespeare Electronic Archive*. My interest is in the surplus meaning the word *archive* brought with it, such that the archive could become an imaginative interface to match Donaldson's digital interfaces. But an interface to what? The rhetorical power of the word *archive* in these contexts lies in its capacity to bracket the very question, enabling Shakespeareans to imagine an abstract totality of information and documents glimpsed through discrete parts.

Some would argue that the presentation of all the evidence in a case like the wife-versus-wise example, as opposed to a summary and verdict delivered by an editor, makes the difference between a digital edition and a digital archive.[107] However, practicing archivists might question whether digital humanists have an accurate understanding of archives if they consider them as a model for "avoiding editorial intervention," or as neutral repositories of "all the evidence" or even "data" – these being the names that Flanders puts to some of their assumptions.[108] What archives normally contain are fonds (or series in the Australian tradition) made up of records, which, as this chapter has shown, may be just as constructed and partial as the materials that editors wrestle into shape. (I am not imputing this misunderstanding to Flanders, whose quotation above summarizes widespread perceptions in the digital humanities community as of the late 1990s.) The textuality of

---

[107] See the discussion of Massai's conception of digital editions versus digital archives in Chapter 1, pp. 15–16.

[108] Flanders, "Body Encoded," p. 136.

archives, as Prescott argues, calls into question any positivist approaches to the documentary materials of history: "Insofar as those traces are overwhelmingly textual, our relationship with the past is constantly mediated by the limitations and uncertainties of the texts which survive. Our investigation of the past is an exploration of those very uncertainties and ambiguities."[109] Or, as Randall McLeod puts the same idea, with characteristic typographical subversion, "The struggle for tne text *is* the text."[110] What this means for digital humanists, Shakespeare editors, and others concerned with practical, project-oriented scholarship is that there is no avoiding the thorny questions raised by postmodernism.

Titus's conceit of writing on leaves of brass only to see his words scattered like Sibyl's leaves before the wind captures archivists' concerns about the immutability and authenticity that modernity tends to attribute to documents. In all the examples presented in this chapter, the trope of writing in brass symbolically collapses the gap between inscribing and archiving, making those acts one and the same. The actual practice of archiving, however, is less about custodianship of immutable leaves of brass than it is about chasing after scattered Sibylline leaves, and wrestling with the conflicting meanings introduced by time and chance. Sam Schoenbaum likewise invoked this image in his preface to *William Shakespeare: a Documentary Life*: "Time scattered the Shakespeare papers like leaves before the wind, destroying a number (how many we cannot say), but tucking some safely away in odd corners, and preserving others under the kindly dust of the muniments room."[111] Loss may seem like the prevailing condition of the Shakespearean archive, but only if one's focus is limited to the spectral authority of manuscripts as the fount (or fonds) from which all authenticity springs. As Schoenbaum's work demontrates, the Shakespearean archive is not entirely empty, and sometimes the Sybilline winds can be agents of preservation, even more than leaves of brass.

---

[109] Prescott, "Textuality of the Archive," p. 34.
[110] McLeod, "Information on Information," p. 279, emphasis in original.
[111] Schoenbaum, *A Documentary Life*, p. xi.

3 | *The archive and the book: information architectures from Folio to variorum*

Trust in the text begins with the form of the book. As we saw in the previous chapter, archives build their own form of trust through the textuality of monuments, which manages the tensions between preservation and loss that influence the understanding of archives, from their discursive framing to their physical instantiation in stone. This chapter considers the flip side of the textuality of monuments: the monumentality of texts. The 1623 Shakespeare First Folio in particular functions as an inherited archive of playtexts, about half of which would not have survived if the Folio had not existed. Ben Jonson underscores this monumental function of the book, as a material object transmuted into memory, in his encomium to Shakespeare in the Folio's prefatory materials ("Thou art a Moniment, without a tombe"), and John Milton develops the theme in his own prefatory poem to the 1632 Second Folio when he writes that Shakespeare needs no "starre-ypointing Pyramid" because he has "in our wonder and astonishment" built himself "a lasting monument."[1] In both poems the book points beyond itself, reminding the reader that the graspable codex only seems to be a bounded whole. David Scott Kastan takes up the same idea centuries later in his reading of Van Dyck's 1632 portrait of John Suckling turning the leaf of a Shakespeare Folio. As Kastan points out, the Shakespeare book in the portrait functions metonymically, creating associations between material objects and idealized abstractions, including authorship, performance, and literary prestige.[2] Books and buildings alike can generate the illusion that they are self-sufficient, contained between covers or walls. Yet the overshadowing figure of the archive troubles that sense of containment – especially in the centuries after Suckling's time, as the works of Shakespeare became layered

---

[1] F1, sig. πA4r; F2, sig. πA5r. On the homonym *tomb/tome*, see de Grazia, *Shakespeare Verbatim*, pp. 35–7, and Lanier, "Encryptions."
[2] Kastan, *Shakespeare and the Book*, pp. 11–13.

with commentary and emendations that accompanied them through their literary afterlives. In this chapter I will consider how the idea of the archive crosses into the field of book history, in which context I argue that books may be considered archival when they take on a specifically preservational mandate, and when they struggle – sometimes visibly on their pages – with the threats of forgetting and loss.

Books do not always win that struggle, and the history of Shakespeare and the book offers revealing instances of cracks in the information architectures of monumental books. The term *information architecture* entered the language in the mid-1970s thanks to Richard Saul Wurman, who needed a term that acknowledged the role of designers as more than mere decorators, but rather as creators of the deep systems of interpretation and meaning-making that subtend all human artifacts and shape the experiences of those who use them. As Wurman and Joel Katz remark in one of the earliest publications on the topic,

The visual communication of information is particularly fortuitous for both artist and audience when it takes place in the environment it is communicating information about. It is such a situation where visual translation (in the form of a map or diagram) and the sensory, visual reality (the environment) can be simultaneously experienced ... [I]t is in such circumstances where we can be made aware of things we have taught ourselves to see without really seeing, as the congruence of the experience and the graphic hits us.[3]

These are potent ideas to apply to books. The visual and spatial bias in Wurman and Katz's language may seem to frame information architecture as antithetical to the textual character of books, but the perspective makes sense if we think of books as designed objects, and of texts as spaces, rather than simply of books as containers for words. As practitioners of the book arts can attest, books have information architectures just as all designed objects and systems do. Wurman, as a practicing architect, might have thought first about information architecture as a guide to designing libraries, not books, but typographers and book designers have developed their own bibliographic version of information architecture, much of it anticipating Wurman's ideas by many decades, even centuries, though it has gone by other names.[4]

---

[3] Wurman and Katz, "Beyond Graphics," p. 40. For a more recent discussion, see Wurman, "Introduction."

[4] See Tschichold, *New Typography* and *Form of the Book*, and Bringhurst, *Elements of Typographic Style*. For another discussion of information architecture

Information architectures can model experience in any form, but as Johanna Drucker points out, "the models of these structures are often invisible"; her examples name some architectural models of information systems whose effects are often felt as much as seen:

An alphabetical ordering is a model. So is a tree structure, with its vocabulary of parent–child relationships and distinct assumptions about hierarchy. Matrices, lattices, one-to-many and one-to-one relationships, the ability to "cross-walk" information from one structure to another, to disseminate it with various functionalities for use by broadly varied communities, or to restrict its forms so that it forces a community to think differently – these are all potent features of information architecture.[5]

Yet as Drucker emphasizes, the values of transparency and ease of use that dominate the discourse of information architecture are just that: values, which reflect cultural investments rather than transcendental truths. The Shakespearean archive is yet another kind of cultural investment with technological manifestations, and in this chapter we will consider how the idea of the archive shapes and unsettles the form of the book.

Kastan, Margreta de Grazia, and others have established that Shakespeare's cultural apotheosis through the form of the book was not inevitable, but rather a managed process that unfolded over time, influenced by publishers, editors, readers, and other agents involved in what D. F. McKenzie called the sociology of texts.[6] My purpose here is to further unsettle the naturalness of Shakespeare's relationship with the book, and to illustrate how the idea of the Shakespearean archive, as an imagined totality of transmissible texts, has shaped and, in turn, been shaped by the form of the book. As book historians have shown, the form of the book is always in motion despite cultural preoccupations with books as islands of fixity in a mutable world. One of the most surprising but welcome effects of digital textuality upon book design has been the mainstream embrace of bibliographic experimentation, popularized through works such as Mark Z. Danielewski's *House of Leaves* and Jonathan Safran Foer's *Tree of Codes*, which exploit defamiliarizing effects usually associated with artists' books.[7] As these

within a book history context, see Galey, Bath, Niles, and Cunningham, "Architectures of the Book."
[5] Drucker, *SpecLab*, p. 16.   [6] See McKenzie, *Bibliography*.
[7] See Drucker, *Artists' Books*.

examples show, it would be a mistake to think of experimentation with interfaces as an exclusively digital pursuit.

Shakespeare's texts have prompted similar book-based experiments in editorial presentation, such as Stephen Booth's facing-page critical edition/facsimile of the *Sonnets*, Michael Warren's unbound leaves of *The Complete King Lear*, Jesús Tronch-Pérez's *A Synoptic Hamlet*, and Bernice Kliman's synoptic print and electronic edition, *The Enfolded Hamlet*. Even Charlton Hinman's facsimile edition of the 1623 Shakespeare First Folio can be called an experimental book in that it allows researchers to work with a version of the Folio that does not exist in any single surviving copy, but represents a composite of the best pages in terms of correctness and print clarity, reproduced as a synthesis of different copies. In this chapter, I will attempt to see the book with different eyes, and to recognize, as Hinman and these other editors have, that no book stands alone. All books materialize parts of networks of information that can never be represented in their totality, only imagined. To unpack that argument, this chapter will juxtapose an obvious example of Shakespeare and bookishness, the 1623 First Folio, with a less obvious one, the New Variorum Shakespeare (NVS) editions begun by Horace Howard Furness in the late nineteenth century.[8] Both examples were information experiments in their own times, and their early prototyping stages reveal how their creators imagined and struggled with an emerging Shakespearean information architecture.

These two examples will also illustrate how the distinction between *epistemic management* and *textual management*, as proposed by Michael O'Driscoll and discussed in the previous chapter, define the two poles of responses to Shakespearean information overload.[9] The 1623 First Folio was in many ways a project in epistemic management in that it constructed the very conditions by which its referent, the Shakespearean dramatic corpus, could be known by its readers. The heavy lifting in this work of constructing was performed largely by the Folio's paratextual front matter, whose function, as de Grazia

---

[8] A note on usage: I capitalize *Variorum* when specifically referring to the series of Furness's editions and its modern continuation by the Modern Language Association. I leave the word uncapitalized when referring to other Shakespeare variorums and the variorum format generally. I tend to use *New Variorum* for Furness's editions and *NVS* for the MLA editions, if only because spelling out the word *New* seems a bit incongruous now that we are 140 years into the project.

[9] See Chapter 2, p. 63.

describes it, "was not to document an existing reality [involving Shakespeare as a dramatic author] but to constitute one retrospectively. The language of the preliminaries works performatively rather than referentially, simultaneously speaking and effecting."[10] This is a fundamentally different strategy from textual management, which, according to O'Driscoll, "recognizes and privileges the sheer materiality of the text and, through the manipulation and juxtaposition of documentary materials, seeks to situate itself advantageously within the space of the archive."[11] Textual management, as we shall see, was Furness's solution as both a reading strategy, undertaken with the Philadelphia Shakespeare Society, and a material practice, which Furness undertook as an information experimenter armed with scissors, glue, and disposable copies of Shakespeare editions. Both strategies may be pursued as paths to hermeneutic deliverance from the temporal materiality of books, as the final section of this chapter will examine, yet both paths also lead unavoidably though the dark basement of the Shakespearean archive.

Shakespeare's book, the book's Shakespeare: the 1623 First Folio

The 1623 collection *Mr. William Shakespeares Comedies, Histories, & Tragedies*, now known as the Shakespeare First Folio, bears consideration as an experiment in a new medium, especially when placed alongside the other experiments considered in this book. The First Folio was only the second book to collect an English dramatist's plays together in the folio format, following Ben Jonson's 1616 *Workes*, though Shakespeare's folio did not follow Jonson's controversial model of mixing plays with poems as forms equally worthy of collection in a prestigious format. The Shakespeare First Folio was, however, the first posthumous collection of an English dramatist's plays in folio, Shakespeare having died seven years before its publication. In this sense, the Folio is less Shakespeare's book than it is the book's Shakespeare.[12] The role of the Folio's design in the transmission and reception of Shakespeare has thus been a matter of consequence to

---

[10] De Grazia, *Shakespeare Verbatim*, p. 41.
[11] O'Driscoll, "Derrida, Foucault," p. 289.
[12] On the mutual construction of books and authors, see Chartier and Stallybrass, "What Is a Book?"

Shakespeareans, from the moment of the Folio's publication through to the rise of book history and materialist approaches to literature in recent years (much of which builds on the foundational bibliographic studies of the Folio earlier in the twentieth century).[13] My purpose here is to imagine the Folio as it coalesced toward that moment of publication, and to use bibliographical evidence to understand the book's prototype stages, as its creators were wrestling with the form that the Folio's information architecture would take.

Shakespeareans have inherited the Folio as a monumental product of these efforts, but bibliographic analysis of the many surviving copies has revealed glimpses of the Folio as process, through which we can recover a partial picture of the decisions its creators were making. The most well-known case is the decision to proceed with the Folio project without Shakespeare's play *Troilus and Cressida*, for which permission to print was acquired by the Folio syndicate late in the project, after parts of the volume were already being printed on the apparent assumption that *Troilus and Cressida* would be quietly omitted. The result is that *Troilus and Cressida* now stands as a bibliographical disturbance in the volume, sending minor ripples through its information architecture in the form of pagination errors and other inconsistencies.[14] (We shall return to some of those ripples below.)

The paratexts of books are especially sensitive to the consequences of changes during the printing process, and the Folio's preliminaries and other paratexts register those changes in ways that cast new light on the Folio as a project in epistemic management. If trust in the text begins with the form of the book, as I argue throughout this chapter, the form of the Folio as a book may seem surprisingly fluid given the concerted efforts of its creators to impose fixity on the ways future generations would come to know Shakespeare. The Folio's paratexts exert influence over the editorial policies, cultural convictions, and even vocabularies

---

[13] See Hinman, *Printing and Proof-Reading*; Blayney, introduction to the second edition of *The First Folio of Shakespeare: The Norton Facsimile*, pp. xxvii–xxxiv; West, *Shakespeare First Folio*, vols. I and II; de Grazia, *Shakespeare Verbatim*; Marcus, *Puzzling Shakespeare*, pp. 2–25; and Burt and Yates, *What's the Worst*, pp. 1–4.

[14] For accounts of *Troilus and Cressida*'s printing in the Folio, see Jowett, Shakespeare and Text, pp. 46–68, and Hinman's introduction to the first edition of the Norton Folio facsimile, xxv (reprinted in the second edition, edited by Blayney). See also Hinman, *Printing and Proof-Reading*, vol. I, pp. 27–8, and vol. II, pp. 526–9.

of Shakespeareans, yet they do so from a position of conflicted author-ity. That conflict extends beyond matters of hermeneutics to the very structure of the Folio as a cultural artifact assimilated into modern information architectures. For example, the Through Line Number (TLN) system devised by Charlton Hinman for the Norton Folio fac-simile, which has since become an indispensable referencing system for Shakespeare scholars, excludes the Folio front matter along with other non-dramatic print elements.[15] If the TLN system furthers the tendency to abstract the Folio texts from the book itself, making Folio playtexts subject to a universal reference system, it also creates blind spots in the field of addressable objects, permitting certain elements to drop out of the resulting structure of information. Yet the Norton facsimile also depends on the Folio paratext to compensate for an omission of its own, in that anyone wishing to look up a given play in the facsimile, as opposed to a given TLN or signature, must rely on the Folio's own Catalogue and pagination.

The Folio opens with a paratextual challenge to the reader to recon-cile the conflicting imperatives of two media, text and image, in the form of the Droeshout engraving of Shakespeare's portrait and Jonson's poem on the facing page:

> To the Reader.
> This Figure, that thou here seest put,
> It was for gentle Shakespeare cut,
> Wherein the Grauer had a strife
> with Nature, to out-doo the life:
> O, could he but have drawne his wit
> As well in brasse, as he hath hit
> His face; the Print would then surpasse
> All, that was ever writ in brasse.
> But, since he cannot, Reader, looke
> Not on his Picture, but his Booke.   B. I.[16]

(Figure 3.1 shows the portrait and facing poem as they appear in the 1862 facsimile made by the Royal Ordnance Survey, which will receive detailed discussion in the next chapter.) As if offering a challenge to

---

[15] On the TLN system's exclusions, see Berger, "The New Historicism and the Editing of English Renaissance Texts," p. 196; and Greetham, *Pleasures of Contamination*, 62–3.

[16] F1, sig. πA1v.

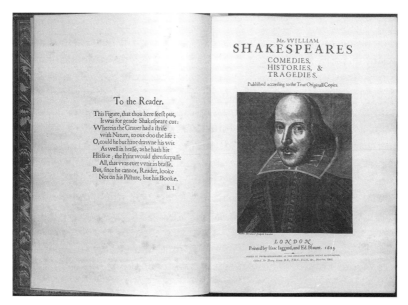

Figure 3.1 The 1623 First Folio's title page and facing poem as they appear in the Royal Ordnance Survey's facsimile (1862).

digitization projects *avant la lettre*, the poem warns of the infidelity of images to what they represent by asserting a set of unstable oppositions: between the agent ("the Grauer") and object of representation ("Nature"); between media of mechanical regularity ("Print") and of artisanal creativity (the engraver's "brasse" plate); between inward "wit" and outward "face"; and, most of all, between image and text, with the latter displacing the former: "Reader, looke / Not on his Picture, but his Booke." The Folio's pairing of Jonson's poem and Shakespeare's image also holds several lessons for thinking about digital information architectures. First, the Folio here thematizes the imbalance between text and image that has characterized humanities computing since its beginnings in the middle of the twentieth century, in which tools and theories have been biased toward text to the neglect of images (at least until recently).[17] Also, the poem's placement before the Folio's title page challenges the logic of structural divisions that one finds in the documented models of descriptive bibliography and the

[17] See Kirschenbaum (ed.), *Image-Based Humanities Computing*.

Text Encoding Initiative Guidelines, which formalize scholarly assumptions about materials that might otherwise remain tacit. When digital facsimiles show the book page by page, following the structural logic of screens, they fail to represent the expressive form of the codex, in which the opening, not the individual page, provides the unit of viewing.[18] The Folio thus opens with a semiotic gesture that only a codex book can make, as the verso of one leaf gestures across the opening to the recto of another. Crucially, Jonson also enjoins the reader to make a bodily gesture inherent to the codex: the turning of a leaf, thereby leaving the picture behind and moving on to the reading of Shakespeare's book.

Peter Stallybrass makes matters worse for the supposed self-identicality of the book when he points out that the title-page leaf, bearing the most iconic image of Shakespeare the author, holds the ironic distinction of being the most hybrid and least physically integral part of the Folio.[19] The leaf's text was probably printed first on a normal letterpress, leaving the space for Shakespeare's portrait blank. The portrait itself would have been printed in a second process, from a copper plate on a rolling press, and in the establishment of Droeshout the engraver, not Jaggard the printer. Furthermore, the title-page leaf was not part of a full sheet, and therefore has no conjugate leaf, making it relatively easy to insert into the Folio's preliminary gathering. As Erin Blake and Kathleen Lynch put it, "the half-sheet engraved-and-letterpress title page is a free agent, easily substituted and shuffled into new sequences of pages," whose extractability makes its survival in so many original copies so remarkable.[20] Stallybrass emphasizes an unsettling conclusion of their research: that the most iconic part of the Folio's symbolic and bibliographic architecture is also its least physically integral. In apparent contradiction to the Folio's claims to monumentality – and to its later reception as such – the Folio's makers appear to have been deft, even comfortable in dealing with a

---

[18] On the expressive form of the book, see McKenzie's first chapter in *Bibliography*. For an artist's take on this binary between text and image, see Wade, "Droeshout's First Folio Shakespeare." Wade's image is reproduced in McKenzie, *Bibliography*, p. 30.

[19] Peter Stallybrass, "Why and How: A Conversation About Teaching Book History," roundtable with Anne Coldiron, *Teaching Book History*, Folger Institute Workshop, Folger Shakespeare Library, Washington DC, 13 December 2012; see also Blake and Lynch, "Looke on his Picture."

[20] Blake and Lynch, "Looke on his Picture," p. 31.

remarkable degree of bibliographic fluidity. The received form of the book, like the architectural façade of the US National Archives building (discussed in the previous chapter), thus imposes a sense of inevitability upon materials whose internal organization – conceptual and physical – betrays its contingency from its very beginnings.

In considering the Folio as an early project in Shakespearean information architecture, it is also worth considering its architects and the roles they may have played in the book's formation. One of the great open questions in the history of the Folio is the precise nature of the roles played by John Heminge and Henry Condell, two colleagues of Shakespeare's in the King's Men and the named authors of the Folio's much-debated epistle "To the great Variety of Readers." Were these two functioning as what we would recognize as editors, exercising all the powers of intervention that the name implies? Were they instead closer to archivists, making faithful transcriptions of private papers over which they had custody? Or, do these modern terms give us adequate language to describe what Heminge and Condell considered themselves to be doing when they collaborated with the printers William and Isaac Jaggard and the other members of the syndicate that published the Folio? Heminge and Condell's own description of their role is worth quoting at length:

It had beene a thing, we confesse, worthie to haue bene wished, that the Author himselfe had liu'd to haue set forth, and ouerseen his owne writings; But since it hath bin ordain'd otherwise, and he by death departed from that right, we pray you do not envie his Friends, the office of their care, and paine, to haue collected & published them; and so to haue publish'd them, as where (before) you were abus'd with diuerse stolne, and surreptitious copies, maimed, and deformed by the frauds and stealthes of iniurious impostors, that expos'd them: euen those, are now offered to your view cur'd, and perfect of their limbes; and all the rest, absolute in their numbers, as he conceiued the[m].[21]

Thus one of the most frustratingly vague passages in Shakespearean editorial history, and the beginning of what Stephen Greenblatt has termed "the dream of the master text" (to which we will return below).[22] Among the questions at stake in this passage are Heminge and Condell's level of access to some kind of company archive (as

---

[21] F1, sig. πA3r.
[22] Greenblatt, "The Dream of the Master Text," in Greenblatt, Cohen, Howard, and Maus (eds.), *Norton Shakespeare*, pp. 65–76.

discussed in Chapter 2), their standards in the selection of copy, and their exhaustiveness in assembling Shakespeare's canon.

This passage has also come to typify the problem of historical distance between modern editors and the earliest custodians of Shakespeare's dramatic corpus. The language of the epistle permeates Shakespeare scholarship in much the same way as Shakespearean expressions permeate modern English. It has even migrated into other discourses about textual transmission, as when McKenzie uses the phrase "maimed and deformed" to describe the texts of New Zealand's Treaty of Waitangi.[23] Yet the uncertainty over the passage's meaning is also inescapable. John Dover Wilson, writing of "The Task of Heminge and Condell" in 1923, appears to make a case for regarding Heminge and Condell as editors based on the language of their epistle: "These words were, I believe, carefully chosen ... The terms 'editor' and 'edit' were unknown at this period, but the function was well expressed by the phrase 'to set forth and oversee.'"[24] However, Dover Wilson was writing at a time when the meaning of editing was being redefined by the emerging New Bibliography, and is also quick to downplay an editorial presence of any kind in the Folio by adjusting Heminge and Condell's supposed editorial function into something more archival: "Heminge and Condell were not 'editors,' as has been commonly supposed, but merely 'gatherers' or 'collectors' of copy for the printers."[25] Heminge and Condell, for their part, apply at least three verbs to describe their roles ("collected ... published ... offered") but only one noun: "Friends."[26]

Keeping the themes of monumentality and information architecture in mind, we should note another assertion that Heminge and Condell appear to be making in their epistle: that the Folio gathers together the entire corpus of Shakespeare's dramatic works, "absolute in their numbers" – an ambiguous phrase that may imply that there are no omissions in the playtexts, or in the Shakespearean dramatic corpus represented in the Folio (or both).[27] The phrase is inaccurate either way, as Heminge and Condell must have known. The most glaring omission in the Folio, if we take it as an archive of Shakespeare the author, not just Shakespeare

---

[23] McKenzie, *Bibliography*, p. 126.   [24] Wilson, "Task," p. 54.   [25] *Ibid.*

[26] On the different interpretations of Heminge and Condell's role, see Murphy, *Shakespeare in Print*, pp. 41–2 and 48–9; Egan, *The Struggle for Shakespeare's Text*, pp. 13–15; and Erne, *Shakespeare as Literary Dramatist*, pp. 148–50.

[27] On the meanings of the word "numbers" in Milton's sonnet on Shakespeare, many of which are relevant to this context, see the introduction to Chapter 6.

the dramatist, is the absence of Shakespeare's poetry: the narrative poems "Venus and Adonis" and "The Rape of Lucrece," as well as the sonnets and shorter poetic works, which were not gathered into a single edition of Shakespeare until Edmund Malone's in 1790. The omission of poetry would make sense if Heminge, Condell, and their collaborators considered the Folio to be a monument to Shakespeare's dramatic authorship specifically, though Jonson's *Works* of 1616 would have offered a model for a folio collection that joined poems with plays (admittedly with the latter recast as dramatic poems).

In any case, the Folio's own table of contents undercuts the claims to completeness made by Heminge and Condell just a few pages beforehand. This list of plays (see Figure 3.2) is the first graphical depiction of the Shakespearean dramatic canon, incomplete though it may seem today when contrasted with the contents of any single-volume complete works. Even so, in the 1623 Catalogue we can already see what would become the traditional division into comedies, histories, and tragedies, though later periods would introduce other structuring categories such as problem plays and romances. We could call this Catalogue page a visualization in the modern digital sense, given that it makes visible something – Shakespeare's dramatic canon – that would not be visible otherwise. An archival perspective alert to questions of original order and arrangement might also note that the order of the plays on the Catalogue page has nothing to do with their chronological place in Shakespeare's dramatic career: the history plays are ordered by reign, like sections in a history book, and the first play in the Catalogue happens to be the comedy *The Tempest*, one of Shakespeare's last plays (and therefore perhaps most familiar to potential buyers). Douglas Lanier makes these points when he describes the Folio as an incomplete translation of Shakespeare's dramatic corpus into book form, caught between the imperatives of transmitted text and ephemeral performance, and notes that "this is a volume which – perhaps unconsciously, perhaps strategically – has it both ways."[28]

But as with almost any canon, archive, or encyclopedic structure, some fugitive piece of information seems always to escape. In this case, the play *Troilus and Cressida* has no entry in this table of contents, even though the play appears in the Folio between *Henry VIII* and *Coriolanus*. It appears that the owner of the right to copy *Troilus and Cressida*, Henry

---

[28] Lanier, "Encryptions," p. 229.

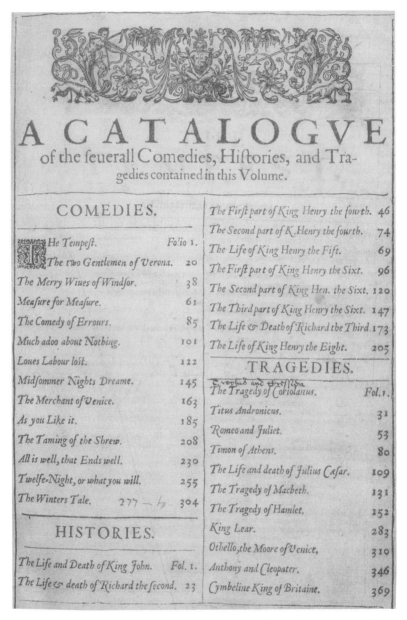

Figure 3.2 The 1623 First Folio catalogue page with manuscript corrections.

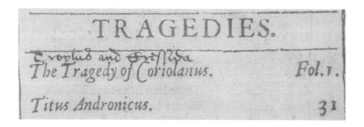

Walley, objected to its planned inclusion in the Folio, and although those objections were somehow overcome, the play's temporarily uncertain status affected the Folio's manufacture.[29] Evidently the sheets that included the Catalogue were printed before *Troilus*'s status was secured, but were never corrected, and then were bound together with corrected states according to normal practice in early modern printing.[30] *Troilus and Cressida* therefore occupies a kind of null space in the Folio, between the last history and the first tragedy. A consequence is that a blind spot appears in the encyclopedic vision the Catalogue represents. One seventeenth-century reader repaired the blind spot by adding a manuscript correction, as shown in the Figure 3.2 detail above, such that *Troilus and Cressida*'s title appears in the correct position.[31] (In the same copy, a different hand has also corrected the erroneous page number given for *The Winter's Tale*.) This correction exemplifies the overlap of print and manuscript cultures that Randall McLeod and David McKitterick emphasize when they point out that early modern printed books were regularly subject to manuscript correction by readers.[32] The Shakespearean archive represented by the Folio's "Catalogue" thus transmits its cultural heritage imperfectly, and with the necessary intervention of inscribing agents other than the author.[33]

---

[29] I use *right to copy* here as distinct from *copyright*; on the crucial difference between these concepts, see Blayney, "Publication of Playbooks," pp. 394–5 and 398–9.

[30] See note 14 above.

[31] This copy of F1 is owned by the State Library of New South Wales (no. 192 in West's census), which has generously allowed the *Internet Shakespeare Editions* (ISE) to publish images of their pages online. A digital facsimile may be viewed at internetshakespeare.uvic.ca/Library/facsimile/book/SLNSW_F1.

[32] See McLeod, "Information on Information," and McKitterick's chapter "A House of Errors," in *Print, Manuscript and the Search for Order*, pp. 97–138.

[33] While the effect of the Folio's erroneous Catalogue is preserved in the Norton facsimile (edited by Blayney), it is likely to be lost in an electronic facsimile of the

Archival interfaces such as the First Folio thus create material sites where the work of epistemic management may be carried out. Printed books register traces of that work differently from archival entities such as fonds and collections, but they elicit the same questions about authenticity and its role in stabilizing the relationship of fragments to imagined wholes. Epistemic management, as distinct from textual management, achieves this stability by regulating how that whole might be imagined, as opposed to reconfiguring the fragments in different ways. The bibliographical disturbances that historians of the book have noticed in the Folio, and especially in its paratexts, may be read as traces of epistemic management in the way they retrospectively construct Shakespeare as an author and as textual corpus while seeming merely to document his dramatic career, as de Grazia has observed.[34]

Books like the Folio stage-manage their archival functions carefully to achieve the illusion of naturalness, such that a constructed notion of the book still stands as the form against which all other media of preservation and transmission are measured. Angus Phillips, in a discussion of the future of the book claims that "you may not have the equipment to play a vinyl record from the 1960s or an 8-track from the 1970s, but you can still pick up Shakespeare's First Folio and read it"[35] – an assertion which depends on our overlooking the book itself as an interface, not to mention the carefully controlled conditions under which one may encounter a First Folio in a rare book library. As we have seen, what we call *the* Folio is anything but stable and unitary: no two surviving copies are typographically identical throughout (if one includes inking errors); some copies survive only in fragments, or with missing or damaged leaves (in some cases replaced by facsimiles); and important parts of Shakespeare's corpus are silently omitted from the Folio, with *Troilus and Cressida* nearly meeting the same fate despite Heminge and Condell's claims to completeness.[36] In this sense, any given copy, fragment, or disbound leaf of the Folio is not so much a

---

Folio, given the importance of addressability in digital media. The electronic table of contents for the ISE facsimile of the First Folio corrects both the *Troilus and Cressida* and *Winter's Tale* errors: ise.uvic.ca/Library/facsimile/overview/book/ F1.html.

[34] De Grazia, *Shakespeare Verbatim*, p. 41.

[35] Phillips, "Does the Book Have a Future?," p. 557.

[36] On the states of surviving copies of the Folio, see West, *Shakespeare First Folio*, vol. II. West and Rasmussen have collated press variants in all surviving copies of the folio; see their *Descriptive Catalogue*, Appendix 1, pp. 875–82.

single product of print culture as an instance of an ongoing textual and material process – one that kept on going into later centuries.

The surviving copies of Shakespeare Folios serve as reminders that books archive traces of their quotidian lives all the time. Book historians and other scholars have noted the presence of foreign objects, or impressions left by them, in Folios, including hair, eyeglasses, and scissors.[37] The copy of the First Folio in my university's Thomas Fisher Rare Book Library contains the imprint of a rose that some long-forgotten reader pressed between the leaves of *Cymbeline*, hence its informal name "The Rosebud Copy" – a serendipitous linguistic link to *Citizen Kane*, with its images of the singular, desired object lost among stacks of collected artifacts.[38] If the Suckling portrait as interpreted by Kastan represents the Shakespeare book entering the world, these artifacts and their impressions show the world entering the book. That happens sometimes by accident, and sometimes through the kinds of capricious agency (such as that of a doodling child[39]) by which we are reminded that books are incomplete artifacts unless they reach the hands of readers. Reader marginalia in Shakespeare Folios, too, has become a rich area of study as book historians have called attention to the value of copy-specific aspects of books. The example of the Folio with readers' corrections of the Catalogue page discussed above, when regarded in this light, shows a reader's awareness not only of a larger Shakespearean archive of plays whose graphical representation on the printed page required manuscript correction, but also of the connection between the Shakespearean archive and his or her own material instantiation of it. That unknown reader's impulse to fill in the missing bit of Shakespearean information – to complete the imperfect whole – would become amplified on the scale of industrial print culture by the end of the nineteenth century.

---

[37] See Blayney's Folger Shakespeare Library exhibition catalogue, *The First Folio of Shakespeare*, pp. 32–3.

[38] The Fisher copy is no. 191 in West's census. See also the Fisher copy's entry in West and Rasmussen (eds.), *Descriptive Catalogue*, pp. 770–1.

[39] West's *New Worldwide Census* notes annotations in copies of the Folios, one of the most unusual cases being that of West no. 136, held by the Folger Shakespeare Library (Folger no. 78). This copy bears doodles made by a child in the eighteenth century, including drawings of houses and a fireplace. The Folger website quotes Gail Kern Paster's observation that "This book, now so valued by collectors, was once valued ... as a surface for scribbling" (*First Folio No. 78: A Child's Shakespeare*; www.folger.edu/template.cfm?cid=3361).

Reading with scissors: prototyping the New Variorum Shakespeare

I made a mighty Variorum *Hamlet*, cutting out the notes of five or six editions, besides the Variorum of 1821, and pasting them on a page with a little rivulet of text. 'Twas a ponderous book ... eight or nine inches thick – I took great delight in burning it some years ago.

Horace Howard Furness, letter to W. J. Rolfe (January 28, 1900)[40]

The preceding section considered Shakespeare's First Folio as an archival book which, in the view of some, carries Shakespeare's plays through the passage of time and material transmission unaltered from their first moments of inscription. The final section will explore that view in detail, but first it will be useful to consider the antitype to this image of a history-proof textual archive in the form of the New Variorum – a series of editions whose copious notes and appendices attach the weight of history to Shakespeare's text. As archival books of a different sort, New Variorum editions represent the history of a Shakespearean text as an unwieldy collection of multitudinous records, facts, arguments, suppositions, and errors, amounting to what current NVS co-general editor Richard Knowles has called "the memories of the profession."[41] Like most critics, de Grazia locates the genesis of the Shakespeare variorum in Samuel Johnson's *Proposals for a New Edition of Shakespeare* of 1756, which proposed the application of the variorum format to Shakespeare, to be realized nearly ten years later in Johnson's edition of 1765. As de Grazia points out, Johnson's model represented "a new respect for the editorial and critical claims of others," and did so by reprinting all significant prior commentary, leaving the reader to judge their merits.[42] However, Johnson, like most of the other eighteenth-century variorum editors, occupied the dual roles of commentator on the Shakespeare text and curator of prior commentary. As curator, Johnson affixed names to others' annotations, but, as commentator, he left his own notes unsigned. Thus, notes de Grazia, "his emendations, synonyms, and paraphrases possessed a transitional status, neither quite Shakespeare's nor quite his own."[43]

---

[40] Furness, *Letters*, vol. II, pp. 54–5.
[41] Knowles, "Variorum Commentary," p. 42.
[42] De Grazia, *Shakespeare Verbatim*, p. 209.
[43] De Grazia, *Shakespeare Verbatim*, p. 212–13.

The boundary between archive and archivist is never absolute, and the negotiation of that boundary unfolded on the pages of a succession of books from the First Folio up to Furness's own Variorum.

Furness's *New* Variorum was named to distinguish it from the Malone–Boswell variorum printed in 1821, which in turn was meant to supersede several eighteenth-century editions that experimented with Shakespeare and the variorum format, most notably those of Lewis Theobald in 1733, as well as Samuel Johnson in 1765, Johnson with George Steevens in 1773, and Edmund Malone in 1790.[44] These editors, in turn, were looking back to classical editions of Horace and Virgil when they first applied the variorum format to Shakespeare. The term *variorum* comes from the Latin phrase *cum notis variorum* (meaning "with the notes of various commentators") that would appear on the title pages of editions of classical authors. For eighteenth-century editors and printers to publish Shakespeare editions in this manner was to claim that Shakespeare deserved the status of a classic, and to rank his works within the larger inherited archive of Western culture.

By the time Furness began work on his New Variorum in the middle of the nineteenth century, an accumulated volume of Shakespeare commentary, criticism, and emendations had grown like suburbs around the paratexts already present in the folios and quartos. For this reason alone, digital Shakespeare editors today follow in Furness's footsteps more than any other editor's. Furness may receive less attention than Malone in terms of editorial theory and history, yet more than any other editor before or since, Furness's career exemplifies a response to the perceived burden of too much Shakespearean information. In material terms, that response was twofold: the edited volumes of the New Variorum

---

[44] There is no consensus as to which edition represents the first Shakespeare variorum. According to Philip Brockbank, "Under one convention the editions of 1773 [Johnson and Steevens, ed.], 1778 [Johnson and Steevens, ed.], and 1785 [Johnson, Steevens, and Reed, ed.] are referred to as Variorum; but under another, slightly more appropriate, Reed's editions of 1803 and 1813 are called the First and Second Variorum, and Boswell's [edition of 1821] the Third" ("Shakespearean Scholarship," p. 723). The notation system in modern NVS editions agrees with the latter scheme as described by Brockbank, beginning each of the sigla for these editions with a lower-case letter v, but with the addition of Steevens and Reed's edition of 1793. A. R. Braunmuller cautiously pushes the first variorum back to Johnson's edition of 1765, with the qualifications that the edition represents a "crypto-variorum format" ("Shakespeares Various," p. 9). Knowles goes back to Theobald as the beginning of the Shakespeare variorum tradition ("Variorum Commentary," p. 38).

series and the Shakespeariana collecting project that went hand in hand with the editing, eventually becoming the Horace Howard Furness Memorial Library at the University of Pennsylvania.[45]

However, as Thomas Richards's study *The Imperial Archive* demonstrates on a larger scale, accumulating a massive archive on a subject is one thing, but knowing its contents is quite another. Although Furness has been studied as part of the Shakespearean book-collecting culture of the nineteenth and early twentieth centuries, his mission as Variorum editor sets him apart, as Michael Bristol notes, in that it resulted in his collection becoming "a working library, rather than an accumulation of rare objects."[46] In contrast to, say, Henry Clay Folger – nicknamed "Forty Folio Folger" for his aggressive collecting – Furness's ultimate objective was not to get books into his library, but to render his library as a book. Behind that library stood the more shadowy figure of the Shakespearean archive, as the imagined and unattainable totality of Shakespeare scholarship that Furness perceived as a burdensome inheritance. My interest here is in the book's function as an archival interface to these imagined totalities of information, both real and imagined.

Furness's New Variorum editions have their roots in the group readings and discussions of the Philadelphia Shakespeare Society in the 1860s and 70s, which tended to focus on what we would now call the reception history of Shakespeare.[47] Their literary interests required the handling of large volumes of reference material in physical form, including previous editions of Shakespeare, books and articles about his work, and books dealing with Shakespeare's sources and contemporaries. Even in 1866, when Furness began work in earnest on the first New Variorum edition, *Romeo and Juliet*, there was an overwhelming mass of inherited material, much of it redundant and in need of textual management. As Furness relates in a retrospective letter in *Shakespeariana* in 1888,

Every member [of the Philadelphia Shakespeare Society] had a copy of the variorum of 1821, which we fondly believed had gathered under each play all

[45] On the formation of this collection, see Bristol, *Shakespeare's America*, pp. 64–70, and Traister, "Furness Memorial Library."
[46] Bristol, *Shakespeare's America*, p. 65.
[47] For a discussion of the New Shakespeare Society contextualized within a broader analysis of modernism and the rise of professional Shakespeare studies, see Grady, *Modernist Shakespeare*, pp. 43–7.

Shakespearean lore worth preserving down to that date. What had been added since that year was scattered in many different editions, and in number-less volumes dispersed over the whole domain of literature. To gather these stray items of criticism was real toil, real but necessary if we did not wish our labour over the text to be in vain. It constantly happened – remember it was before the days of Booth's "Reprint," Staunton's "Photolithograph," Ashbee's Facsimiles of the Quartos, or of the Cambridge Shakespeare – … that we spent a whole evening over a difficult passage (and as we were all members of the Bar they were battles royal) only to find that the whole question had been discussed and settled by learned men elsewhere. Hence it dawned on us that if we were to pursue our studies with any of the ardor of original research we should exactly know all that had been said or suggested by our predecessors.[48]

The technological milestones in this account are worth noting. Furness refers to Lionel Booth's type reprint of the First Folio (1862–4), which attempted to reproduce typographical idiosyncrasies of the original; to Howard Staunton's photolithographic facsimile of 1866; and to William Ashbee's series of forty-seven early quarto facsimiles (1861–71), in which individual letters were hand-traced to create lithographic plates.[49] Furness had great confidence, Philip Brockbank notes, in "the new techniques of reproduction, collating the four quartos from Ashbee's facsimiles, and the First Folio from Staunton's photolitho-graph" for his edition of *Romeo and Juliet*, and new technologies of reproduction enabled the work of textual management like never before (as the next chapter will explore in more detail).[50]

Furness's project may be a nineteenth-century update of the Enlightenment encyclopedism that motivated Malone, but it also reflects the specifically late Victorian tendency to gather massive amounts of data to assuage anxieties over the lack of genuine

---

[48] Horace Howard Furness, *et al.*, "How Did You Become a Shakespeare Student?," pp. 439–40.
[49] On these three projects, see Murphy, *Shakespeare in Print*, pp. 192–4. On the Cambridge Shakespeare (1863–6), edited by George Clark and William Aldis Wright, see Murphy, pp. 202–6, and Chapter 7 of this book.
[50] Brockbank, "Shakespearean Scholarship," p. 726. One could locate Furness within the same tendency to regard technology as an intervening change that Joseph Loewenstein sees in the early twentieth-century New Bibliography, and that F. P. Wilson sees in regard to the study of dramatic manuscripts later in the century. See Loewenstein, *Author's Due*, especially chapters 1 and 8; and F. P. Wilson, *Shakespeare and the New Bibliography*, p. 50.

understanding, as the British Empire's information-gathering bodies experienced in their encounters with colonial others such as India and Tibet.[51] As L. C. Knights describes in terms that invite comparison with the present, Shakespeare scholarship in the nineteenth century "progressed by *accumulation* rather than a process of growth or development from a centre."[52] That tendency materialized in the form of Furness's editions as books. Furness's typically modest description of these books in an 1872 letter as "my unworthy, bulky, overgrown, and obese Variorum" ironically contrasts with their publisher's construction of them as affordable luxury commodities in the late nineteenth- and early twentieth-century book trade.[53]

One publisher's advertisement calls attention to the material features of the New Variorum volumes, expressed as a list of selling points set off in ornamental type: "In large 8vo Volumes. Superfine Toned Paper. Fine Cloth. Uncut Edges. Gilt Top."[54] The Furness collection at the University of Pennsylvania also includes blank dummy volumes created for salesmen to show off the quality of the paper and binding, presumably to reach the market segment that regarded books mainly as furniture.[55] Flipping through one of these blank New Variorum volumes gives one the odd experience of a Shakespeare edition as an empty archive, a sensation akin perhaps to Andrew Murphy's account of finding Macmillan's self-erasing records (discussed in Chapter 2; see pp. 56–7). The blankness of those dummy New Variorum pages gives no hint as to the struggle to represent an unwieldy totality of information upon them. Yet hints of that struggle come through in the language of the same advertisement quoted above, which notes that each New Variorum offers, "On the same page with the text, a collation of the ancient copies, folio and quarto, and of the majority of modern critical editions." The importance of the page as an archival interface is emphasized as well in the next selling point: "The notes (also on the

---

[51] See Richards, *Imperial Archive*, p. 3, and his chapter "Archive and Utopia," pp. 11–44, which deals with the surveying of India and Tibet.

[52] Knights, "Shakespeare and Shakespeareans," p. 79, emphasis in original. On Furness's Shakespeare collecting in a Victorian context, see Traister, "Furness Memorial Library," pp. 62–3.

[53] Furness, *Letters*, vol. I, p. 177.   [54] *Furness Family Papers*, box 46.

[55] University of Pennsylvania, Rare Book and Manuscript Library, Furness Collection, call no. 90 1871F v.1 dummy. I am grateful to Peter Stallybrass for alerting me to this book.

same page with the text) of all the editors whose texts are collated, together with other notes, emendations and conjectures, and comments *from all sources accessible to the editor and deemed worthy of preservation*" (emphasis added). This last phrase acknowledges the inescapable contingencies and exclusions that condition variorum editing and reading alike, and even makes omission of information a selling point in its appeal to editorial judgment. The final selling point in this ad makes the interface challenges of textual management even clearer, especially in the increasingly international context of nineteenth-century Shakespeare scholarship:

In an appendix will be found reprints of those early quartos which are so unlike the received text as to preclude the possibility, within the restricted limits of footnotes, of giving an intelligible record of their collation with other editions. Also, criticisms and illustrations from English, German, and French sources, too voluminous to be incorporated in the commentary on the same page with the text.

Here we can see the publisher's acknowledgment of what happens when the imagined totality of the Shakespearean archive must be wrenched into the shape of the book. Yet there is also a subtextual appeal to the pleasures of plenitude, as potential buyers are invited to indulge their encyclopedic desire to own, if not necessarily to read, their very own Shakespearean archive. To Furness and the Philadelphia Shakespeare Society, the New Variorum editions represented an attempt to manage this archive, and to rationalize it spatially on the page of the Shakespeare text itself.

As with the 1623 First Folio, the prototype stages of the New Variorum reveal struggles with the representation of the Shakespearean archive in book form. The editions were a technical challenge from the beginning, as Furness's origin story indicates. Oddly enough, the catalyst for the New Variorum's first publication may not have been Shakespeare's cultural prestige, or even the marketability of Shakespeare's name, but rather the daunting informatic complexity of the Variorum editions as printed books and publishing ventures. As Furness's grandson mentions in his edition of Furness's letters, the Philadelphia company J. B. Lippincott took on the project not primarily out of any particular enthusiasm for selling Shakespeare editions, but "because they desired to send a volume of theirs to compete for the medal offered by the Division of Printing in the [1873]

Vienna Exposition."[56] The New Variorum's editorial scope and typographic complexity amounted to a publishing achievement in 1873 almost on a par with Teena Rochfort Smith's *Four-Text Hamlet* a few years later, and the NVS *Romeo and Juliet* received an honourable mention (though not a medal) in the Division of Publishers of Educational Books.[57] Furness and Lippincott may have had different motives for pursuing the project, but both regarded themselves as undertaking feats of information management, whose materialization in book form tested the capacities of scholarship, information management, and nineteenth-century printing all alike. This theme of Shakespeare as a proving-ground for new information technologies and practices will resurface many times in subsequent chapters.

Furness's editions took shape through a succession of prototype stages, including the cut-and-paste *Hamlet* volume, mentioned in the epigraph above, that Furness apparently took such great delight in burning. However, one can get a sense of Furness's textual labours thanks to the collection of his annotated editions and workbooks at the University of Pennsylvania library, which includes what appears to be a surviving sibling of the "ponderous book" that met the same fate as *Citizen Kane*'s Rosebud. This huge, battered *Hamlet* workbook is made up of blank pages with snippets of Shakespeare text and commentary taken from other editions and pasted onto the same page – a material record of how Furness read with scissors in hand, making a new edition of his own by cutting and pasting.[58] Furness's textual collation process also leaves a material trace in the form of heavily annotated copies of prior editions, especially the 1863–6 Cambridge editions. Through a complex but systematic set of annotations, including

---

[56] Furness, *Letters*, vol. I, p. 161. See also Furness's letter to Rolfe (28 January 1900); *Letters*, vol. II, p. 55.
[57] Murphy, *Shakespeare in Print*, p. 158.
[58] *Furness Family Papers*, box 21. This remarkable volume also archives traces of past research on it. An unsigned typewritten note tucked into the front quotes the letter to Rolfe quoted in my epigraph above, and speculates that this may be the volume that Furness mentions, which somehow went unburnt after all. However, a handwritten note signed "William Woodson, November, 1970" refutes this by pointing out that Furness's source text in this workbook was Karl Elze's 1857 edition, not the 1821 Malone–Boswell edition that Furness must have used for the first New Variorum *Hamlet*. Typical of archives, the workbook also contains a seemingly random third item in the form of an unidentified newspaper clipping of a story dated 26 March 1903, on how a University of Iowa junior law court found Hamlet guilty of manslaughter in the death of Claudius.

pasted-in slips of paper (an image of which appears on this book's cover), Furness constructed the textual apparatus that would eventually be condensed into the New Variorum's textual notes. Yet translating the information synthesized in these workbooks into print was no easy task, either. In preparing the first New Variorum volume, *Romeo and Juliet* in 1870, Furness evidently went through a number of "experimental proofs" (as Murphy describes them) which Lippincott provided Furness in the initial stages as they worked through "different layouts, styles, and combinations of type size."[59] Furness wrote afterward that "eight times did I remodel the first twenty pages of that volume [*Romeo and Juliet*]."[60] All these efforts show that the New Variorum was a project in Shakespearean interface design as well as information management. These several stages could be considered private prototypes, and we could add a public prototype in the form of the NVS *Romeo and Juliet* volume(s) that went to Vienna in 1873, in the sense that its contextualization within an industrial exhibition would have made it more than just a book on a shelf.

A particularly interesting public prototype of the first New Variorum edition appeared in the form of a prospectus published by Lippincott in 1870.[61] This small unbound pamphlet contains a two-page announcement and description of the series signed by the publisher, followed by a reprint of Furness's six-page defense against accusations of piracy levelled by William Aldis Wright in *The Athenaeum* earlier in the year (about which more below), followed by sample pages of *Romeo and Juliet*'s Prologue and seven lines of Sampson and Gregory's opening exchange, followed by one last essential item of paratext, a blank subscription form for the volume, soliciting pre-publication sales at a price "not to exceed $10 per copy." From a purely editorial perspective, the prospectus might seem no more than an inconsequential bit of Shakespearean ephemera, but to a book historian these few unbound leaves reveal a confluence of the different imperatives at work in the New Variorum as a publishing project.

---

[59] Murphy, *Shakespeare in Print*, p. 156.
[60] Furness in a letter to Clement Mansfield Ingleby, 6 August 1871, quoted in Gibson, *Philadelphia Shakespeare Story*, p. 61.
[61] Untitled prospectus for the New Variorum Shakespeare edition of *Romeo and Juliet* (Philadelphia: J. B. Lippincott, 1870). All references to the prospectus here are to the copy held by the Folger Shakespeare Library, call no. PR2752.P8 C6 Cage no. 42.

The centrepiece of the prospectus is ostensibly the sample of New Variorum pages, which, like a modern technology demo, was calculated to impress not only by its content but also, even primarily, by the visual force of its interface. Readers of Shakespeare editions would have seen something fairly novel in the now-familiar three-level *mise-en-page* that comprises playtext (sometimes barely a "rivulet," as Furness laments in the epigraph above), collation notes, and commentary notes, with the lower two layers organized in two columns. The English editor Howard Staunton had introduced the three-layer page to his series of Shakespeare editions published between 1857 and 1860, probably derived from Richard Bentley's 1711 edition of Horace, though Furness's critical apparatus was on another scale entirely.[62] For the Variorum's earliest readers, the closest points of visual reference would have been variorum editions of classical authors, along with the algebraic collation note format of the Cambridge Shakespeare published just a few years before. Versions of this basic tripartite layout have now become the norm for scholarly Shakespeare editions thanks to the Arden, Cambridge, and Oxford series, but it is easy to forget that readers of this prospectus in 1870 would have been presented with something relatively new: an interface to spatialize the Shakespearean archive on the page, and with the same sense of visual empowerment that digital Shakespeare editions strive to inspire today. In the prospectus's emphasis on the New Variorum's visual integration of playtext, collation notes, and commentary within the space of the page, we can see a bibliographic version of Wurman and Katz's notion that an information architecture is most effective when it coincides spatially with "the environment it is communicating information about."[63] It should be no surprise, then, that the final page of the New Variorum interface appears across the opening from a more well-established type of bibliographic interactivity: a blank form asking the reader for money.[64]

In addition to the economic, informatic, and typographic imperatives that converge in these pages, the prospectus also reflects a scholarly conflict over Furness's proposed re-use of the playtext and collation

---

[62] See Braunmuller, "Shakespeares Various," pp. 8, 11, and 14, n. 24.

[63] Wurman and Katz, "Beyond Graphics," p. 40. See p. 79.

[64] On the pricing of the New Variorum and Furness's later complaints about publishing and book prices, see Murphy, *Shakespeare in Print*, p. 158.

notes from the Cambridge editions of 1863–6, edited by George Clarke and William Aldis Wright. In early 1870 Furness found himself defending against Wright's accusation that he was committing a kind of piracy in his plan (announced in January in *Notes and Queries*) to reuse the Cambridge texts and collation notes as the basis of his Variorum editions. In *The Athenaeum* of 29 January 1870, Wright expressed his displeasure with this plan, and especially with what he regarded as Furness's misrepresentation of his and Clarke's editorial labours, taking his case to the highly visible forum of *The Athenaeum*. This prompted Furness to rethink his plans for the Cambridge text and notes, and the six-page defense in the prospectus reprints a letter to that effect which Furness published in *The Athenaeum* on 19 March.[65] The matter was settled amicably in a few more public and private exchanges, and Furness and Wright proved themselves exceptions to the legacy of feuding Shakespeare editors by maintaining an epistolary friendship that lasted many years.[66]

Paradoxically, the debate turned on the question of the intellectual property rights of an editor, as manifested in the *editor*'s representation of another *author*'s works and textual history. In other words, it was a debate about the originality of a representation. In the years prior to international copyright, and in an era of widespread American piracy of British publications, the only intellectual property rights that Wright could assert were moral ones, though Furness appears to have taken them just as seriously in his conduct toward Wright.[67] Indeed it appears that Furness abandoned his controversial plan for the Cambridge texts and notes almost immediately. Wright quotes what must be an earlier prospectus in his *Notes and Queries* article dated 20 January: "The prospectus states: 'The text will be that of the Cambridge editors, and to the textual notes of that edition will be added … various readings'" from a long list of scholarly editors.[68] The Folger copy of the prospectus,

---

[65] Unsigned notice titled "The Cambridge Shakespeare," *The Athenaeum*, no. 2212 (19 March 1870), pp. 388–9.

[66] For a detailed account of the dispute see Gibson, *Philadelphia Shakespeare Story*, pp. 61–8. For a record of Furness's half of his epistolary relationship with Wright, see Furness, *Letters*, vol. I, pp. 159–97.

[67] On the nineteenth-century American appropriation of Shakespeare generally, and of Shakespeare editions specifically, see Murphy's chapter "American Editions," in *Shakespeare in Print*, pp. 142–66.

[68] William Aldis Wright, "The Cambridge Shakespeare," *The Athenaeum*, no. 2205 (29 January 1870), p. 161.

which I have been discussing here, dates the publisher's announcement as
"Feb. 1870" and begins instead with what must be a revision: "The
TEXT of this Edition will be formed upon the principle of following,
where various readings occur, such readings as have been adopted by a
majority of the ablest Editors."[69] (Obviously the addition of Furness's
response to Wright would be another difference between this prospectus
and the one Wright saw.) With the New Variorum *Othello* in 1886,
Furness abandoned his characteristically ambitious – and perhaps hastily
conceived – editorial policy for the playtexts. But it is worth pausing to
note Furness's proto-digital thinking here: the editorial strategy he gives
in the prospectus could be read as a kind of aspirational crowdsourcing to
the masses of prior editors, wherein consensus decided the readings. It is
just as notable that the eventual alternative both to the crowdsourcing
approach and to the interoperability approach (i.e. using someone else's
text) was to fall back on the arbitrary stability of the First Folio. Furness is
frank about this arbitrariness in the preface to the New Variorum
Othello, and argues,

Even if a remedy [to Shakespeare's textual complexity] be proposed which by
all is acknowledged to be efficacious, it is not enough for the student that he
should know the remedy; he must see the ailment. Let the ailment, therefore,
appear in all its severity in the text, and let the remedies be exhibited in the
notes; by this means we may make a text for ourselves, and thus made, it
will … speak to us with more power than were it made for us by the wisest
editor.[70]

Thus, within the space of a few years, Furness's editorial policy progressed through three proto-digital strategies: interoperable open data
(which turned out not to be so open after all); crowdsourcing, at least of
a historical kind; and a forerunner of unediting and digital archives, as
the quotation above indicates.[71] As it turned out, the New Variorum
absorbed the monumental function of the Folio, yet also built a layer of
readerly agency into its own archival interface.

Variants sometimes register competing imperatives in textual production, as Furness and Wright well knew, and it is remarkable that this
prospectus for an edition *of* Shakespeare succumbs to the same textual

---

[69] New Variorum prospectus, p. 1; see n. 61 above.
[70] Furness, preface to *Othello*, p. vi.
[71] On digital archives verses editions of Shakespeare, see the discussion of Sonia
Massai's definition of the terms in the Introduction, p. 16.

condition *in* Shakespeare that it seeks to stabilize. Even the textual notes themselves, as mechanisms to track variation, vary in their syntax and content between the February prospectus and the complete edition of *Romeo and Juliet* published the following year.[72] These small changes, along with minor changes in the punctuation and layout of the playtext, testify to Furness's earlier comment about his ongoing tinkering with the edition's form – its interface – as well as its content. That seemingly endless toil of scholarly labour, eventually provoking Furness's incendiary reaction described in the epigraph above, testifies to the complexity of the Shakespearean archive as editors attempted to wrestle its totality into bookish form in the late nineteenth century. Michael Bristol suggests that however much we might desire to rationalize "the history and the dispersal of the text through a complete archive of its variants," it remains impossible to make one book the archive of another: as Bristol argues, "such an archive cannot itself take the form of a printed edition, since any determinate edition instantiates the very problem the archive is supposed to overcome, that is, the concretization of a historically determinate set of editorial decisions."[73]

The history of Shakespearean information experiments and prototypes discussed throughout this book may also be understood as responses of various kinds to the aporia Bristol identifies: books are insufficient forms for mapping bibliographic complexity.[74] Having no digital alternative to the book form available to him, Furness's editorial strategy took the form of textual management, which O'Driscoll characterizes as the "manipulation and juxtaposition of documentary materials," and which reflects Furness's era of bureaucratic modernity far better than the more radical strategy of epistemic management – that is, the reorientation of the Shakespearean corpus itself as a knowable object.[75] However, as we shall see, both the Folio and the Variorum have played their parts in a long-running project of epistemic management

---

[72] The commentary notes remain essentially unchanged. I have not been able to examine other copies of this prospectus, but it would be interesting to know if other versions show other variants.

[73] Bristol, *Shakespeare's America*, p. 101. See Loewenstein's analysis of the reactions to Sidney Lee's First Folio facsimile of 1902, in which he sees similar questions at stake; *Author's Due*, pp. 255–62.

[74] See McGann, "The Rationale of Hypertext," in *Radiant Textuality*, pp. 53–74.

[75] O'Driscoll, "Derrida, Foucault," p. 289.

to establish a text of Shakespeare that would transcend all historical forms of information architecture.

Dreams of the master text

One of the legacies of the Shakespeare Folio and Variorum alike was to lend material form to different strains of Shakespearean archive fever. While the 1623 First Folio stakes its authenticity on an archival recovery project, the Shakespeare Variorum finds the truth of its text in the cumulative labours of prior editors and commentators, all faithfully recorded and arranged. The difference between these forms of authenticity was understood by Edward Capell, whose 1768 edition of the plays was the first to attempt a truly systematic and exhaustive collation of all the editions that preceded it. At one point in Capell's introduction he speaks of himself in the third person:

> The editor now before you . . . possess'd himself of the other modern editions, the folio's, and as many quarto's [*sic*] as could presently be procur'd . . . Thus furnish'd, he fell immediately to collation . . . first of moderns and moderns, then of moderns with ancients, and afterwards of ancients with others more ancient: 'till, at the last, a ray of light broke forth upon him, by which he hoped to find his way through the wilderness of these editions into that fair country the Poet's real habitation.[76]

Capell casts his encyclopedic labours in almost biblical language of deliverance, in which the temporal work of information management leads to a promised land where editor finds atonement with poet. From this encyclopedic work the truth emerges for Capell, as he goes on to relate: "He [i.e. Capell] had not proceeded far in his collation, before he saw cause to come to this resolution – to stick invariably to the old editions (that is, the best of them) which hold now the place of manuscripts, no scrap of the Author's writing having the luck to come down to us."[77] However, the absence of Shakespeare's manuscripts makes such invariability difficult in any editorial policy, and Capell cannot even complete his sentence without admitting exceptions, such as needing to discern "the best" of the old editions, and the need for emendation even of the best texts. Capell's vivid image of an apocalyptic release

---

[76] Capell (ed.), *Comedies, Histories, and Tragedies*, vol. I, pp. 19–20.
[77] Capell (ed.), *Comedies, Histories, and Tragedies*, vol. I, p. 20.

from the amassed history of the Shakespeare texts would be echoed two decades later in Edmond Malone's preface to his Shakespeare variorum of 1790 (discussed in the Introduction): "When our poet's entire library shall have been discovered, and the fables of all his plays traced to their original source, when every temporary allusion shall have been pointed out, and every obscurity elucidated, then, and not till then, let the accumulation of notes be complained of."[78] Both of these prophetic declarations by key eighteenth-century Shakespeare editors testify to the conceptual shift from editorial labour as poetic insight and reasoned intervention to editing as the finding and collating of documents.

The vision of textual deliverance that Capell describes has been named "The Dream of the Master Text" by Stephen Greenblatt, who introduces the classroom-oriented *Norton Shakespeare* with an extended editorial *caveat lector* under that title. In an uncharacteristic move for an editor of a single-volume edition of Shakespeare's works, Greenblatt takes a step back and offers an excursion into editorial theory and the texts' cultural history:

> The words on the page should ideally give the reader unmediated access to the astonishing forge of imaginative power that was the mind of the dramatist. Those words welled up from the genius of the great artist, and if the world were not an imperfect place, they would have been set down exactly as he conceived them and transmitted to each of us as a precious inheritance.[79]

The self-consciously speculative mode of wishful thinking is notable here, partly because it provides a way for Greenblatt to articulate archival desires – his own and his readers' – *as* desires, externalizing and naming them without extinguishing them. Dreaming of the master text is an editorial trope that runs throughout Shakespearean textual studies, and Greenblatt is far from alone in his evocation of the regretful tone of Heminge and Condell – even to the point of echoing their language ("as he conceiued the[m]"). W. W. Greg, for instance, follows his exhaustive analysis in *The Editorial Problem in Shakespeare* with the following speculative excursion in a mode similar to Greenblatt's, this time speaking in the language of Heminge and Condell:

---

[78] Malone (ed.), *Plays and Poems*, vol. I, part I, pp. lvi; see pp. 1–2.
[79] Greenblatt, "The Dream of the Master Text," in Greenblatt, *et al.* (eds.), *Norton Shakespeare*, p. 71.

If [Shakespeare] had enjoyed a longer evening of leisure, who can say what might not have happened? Did he sometimes dream in his garden at Stratford of a great volume of his plays, such as his friend Jonson was busy preparing? and did he go so far as to talk over the idea with his old colleagues when they visited him in those last peaceful days? "It had been a thing, we confess, worthy to have been wished, that the author himself had *lived* to have set forth and overseen his own writings; but since it hath been ordained otherwise, and he *by death* departed from that right …" [quoted from Heminge and Condell's epistle] Is this merely rhetorical regret, or is it a hint of a project actually discussed? We can never know. Only we can say that had the dream come true the editorial problem in Shakespeare might have been very different from what it is.[80]

The "dream" that Greg imagines can only be glimpsed through the evidence of the Folio as a book and its related publishing records; what the book actually monumentalizes, however, amounts to loss as much as preservation.

Knowing that the editorial problem in Shakespeare was real, Greg and the New Bibliographers in effect unbound the Folio by abstracting each text from the book and treating each play as a discrete textual unit to be edited on its own terms, using methods appropriate to the kinds of documents they inferred to stand behind the printed text (authorial foul papers, scribal transcripts, prompt books, previous printings possibly with playhouse annotations, and combinations of these; several of these categories are still matters of intense debate). Yet the dream of the master text dies hard, and Folio texts of Shakespeare are often made to bear a burden of uniform accuracy and authority disproportionate to the presumable heterogeneity of their sources and circumstances of production. The result is that the plays contained in the Folio have functioned in certain reception traditions as though they were a single textual unit equivalent to the codicological unit of the Folio itself. In other words, contrary to the New Bibliographical method of making an allegedly informed guess about a given Folio play's underlying copy – on an individual basis, play by play – there is nonetheless a widespread

---

[80] Greg, *Editorial Problem*, p. 157, emphasis in original. Lukas Erne offers a more optimistic reading of Heminge and Condell than Greg, interpreting them to mean that Shakespeare would have been present; Erne, *Literary Dramatist*, p. 99. See also Murphy's reading of the same passage from Greg in *Shakespeare in Print*, p. 203.

desire to inherit the Folio as a perfect archive, unified in its faithful transmission of texts.

That desire elevates the Folio from imperfect book to sublime archive, and emboldens some readers to invest its texts with authority right down to the placement of commas. This tendency manifests in a range of textual practices usually regarded as marginal to scholarly editing. One tradition, called the "Folio method," interprets the First Folio as though it were Shakespeare's typescript, preserving his exact intentions in all aspects of typography, punctuation, and lineation.[81] The Folio method takes bibliographic form in the Applause First Folio Editions of single-volume plays, "Prepared & Annotated" by Neil Freeman. These books ask to be read like "musical scores" in their representation of the Shakespeare text, as Anthony Dawson puts it in his critique of the series.[82] The Applause editions' threefold rationale, as stated in the general introduction to all the plays, seems at first glance similar to that of a scholarly transcription, old-spelling text, or facsimile: (1) to "show the reader what the First Folio ... set down on paper, rather than what modern editions think ought to have been set down"; (2) to make clear to readers and actors "some of the information the original readers might have garnered from F1"; and (3) to place both Folio readings and their common editorial emendations in proximity, so readers can see where and how modern texts depart from the Folio.[83] Oddly, the phrasing of the first objective is not *what Shakespeare actually wrote*, as it is so often put, but what the Folio "set down" as though the book had written itself.[84] Freeman's third editorial goal of putting Folio (and sometimes quarto) readings in proximity with significant emendations echoes some of the Shakespeare Variorum's information architecture – including its usefulness to actors and dramaturges – but there remains the difference that, for Freeman,

---

[81] The closest that any advocate of the Folio method comes to a bibliographically aware defense of the approach is Weingust, *Acting from Shakespeare's First Folio*. However, Weingust's defense is based on a flawed understanding of basic facts of bibliography and editing; for a critique of Weingust and Freeman, see Kidnie, *Shakespeare and the Problem of Adaptation*, pp. 145–7.

[82] Dawson, "Imaginary Text," p. 148.

[83] Freeman (ed.), *Taming of the Shrew*, p. vii.

[84] On the iconic idea of "what Shakespeare wrote," see pp. 210–11, and Steven Urkowitz's ironic use of the phrase in "'Well-sayd olde Mole,'" p. 41.

Shakespeare seems to have served as ghostly compositor and proof-reader for his own posthumous Folio.

Like any other editor, Freeman must reckon with the obvious misprints that may occur in any text, and he does so revealingly, in a way that privileges the folio format as a codicological unit. The Applause general introduction is prefaced by an explanation of the terms *folio* and *quarto* for the lay reader, and a short summary of each of the folio printings from F1 to F4. In each case, Freeman cites scholarly opinion on the relative authority of the F1–4 texts, noting the scant authority of F2 and the high degree of correction in F4. Despite his stated antipathy toward editors, Freeman becomes one when faced with obvious misprints such as "wh?ch" in *Twelfth Night* or "speeh" in *Romeo and Juliet*. The corrections must come from somewhere, as Freeman acknowledges: "If there are no alternative contemporary texts (a Quarto version of the play) or if no modification was made by any of the later Folios ... then the F1 printing will be set as is, no matter how peculiar, and the modern correction footnoted." What is remarkable here, especially in the light of the book as an archival interface, is that in Freeman's thinking format alone determines textual authority. There is no distinguishing between the relative authority of quarto texts, or between the folios, despite his earlier acknowledgment that they are not all the same. Freeman also makes a troubling distinction here between folio texts and "modern" texts, and it is not clear where modernity begins in his editorial model – presumably sometime between F4, printed in 1685, and Nicholas Rowe's first multivolume edition of 1709. However much F4 might deserve to be considered a modern edition, with emendations based on as much apparent thought and research as Rowe's or any of his successors', its format, layout, and perpetuation of the F1 paratext place it in direct line of succession to inherit Shakespearean authority. Presumably it would not be so if F4's editor were named.[85]

The Folio method's fetishizing of authorship through typography has no bibliographical validity, and whatever theatrical merit it provokes probably owes more to the talents of the actors, directors, and dramaturges than to the authority of their scripts. As Dawson says of the Applause editions, "such books ... give a sense of being in direct

---

[85] On the Fourth Folio's putative modernity, see Black and Shaaber, *Seventeenth-Century Editors*, pp. 58–66.

communication with some quasi-mystical and deeply authoritative voice from the past, indeed with Shakespeare himself," but at the expense of any understanding of the complex realities of textual production.[86] (Not all actors misunderstand Shakespeare's textual history in this way; Declan Donnellan, for example, rightly notes that accidentals in Shakespeare's texts may reflect the printers' rather than the author's preferences, and proposes an acting exercise involving the depunctuation of passages to explore breathing patterns – in effect, the opposite of the Folio method.[87]) However marginal the Folio method may seem, it stands as one of the most pronounced and systematized responses to the perception of Shakespearean information overload. The Folio method authorizes readers to sweep away all prior commentary and textual scholarship on Shakespeare and, thus unburdened, find their own form of interpretive deliverance.

Some critics feel that the Shakespeare Variorum represents a parallel kind of failure to stabilize the Shakespeare text. Neil Rhodes and Jonathan Sawday compare monumental editions like variorums to the legacy of now-decaying "tunnels, railways, bridges, and sewerage systems" left over from the late Victorian fever for building civic infrastructure.[88] Variorums, in Rhodes and Sawday's terms, stand as "monuments to a belief in the stability of the printed word, and the possibility of freezing, for all time, that which has been thought and said," amounting to no more than what they call "an admission of failure, a recognition that there is no last word in textual matters." They appear not to have considered Furness's own unediting strategy for the New Variorum text, as quoted above, but even NVS editor Maurice Hunt acknowledges that "for many postmodernists, variorum editions represent a hallmark of obsolete modernism, that of the freezing of meaning in a static form that challenges time's flux ... By their massive size and daunting apparatus, they lend the appearance of finishedness to an enterprise that can never be finished."[89] Rhodes and Sawday's infrastructure analogy is an apt one for digitization, considering that the Internet itself is left-over infrastructure from a previous era, the Cold War, designed to support a communications system that could work

---

[86] Dawson, "Imaginary Text," p. 148.
[87] Donnellan, *Actor and the Target*, pp. 255–8.
[88] Rhodes and Sawday (eds.), *Renaissance Computer*, p. 11.
[89] Hunt, "New Variorum Shakespeares," p. 62.

even after a nuclear attack had torn it to tatters. (As Bruce Sterling has pointed out, the brilliance of the Internet is that it was designed to work in tatters as its normal condition.[90]) However, Hunt disputes the characterization of the variorum format as what McGann calls "the still point in the turning world of texts, a text which would arrest, and even reverse, the processes of textual change and corruption."[91] Such a dim view of the NVS would relegate the editions to what Hunt calls the "tomes/tombs" of an "obsolete modernism."[92] However, Hunt also contends that the variorum structure anticipates postmodernist approaches in its copious textual apparatus, which conveys the heterogeneity of the Shakespeare text more than any other kind of edition. (Any reader unpersuaded by Hunt's argument is well advised to spend time with the Furness workbooks in the University of Pennsylvania special collections; the cut-and-paste physicality of these books vividly materializes Furness's engagement with the postmodern qualities of bricolage, pastiche, and incompleteness in his editorial labours.)

The essential difference between an NVS edition and a critical edition is that a critical edition is selective, providing only the most salient points of commentary for a reader, whereas a Variorum is comprehensive, providing a synthesis of the text's cultural history and reception. Rhodes and Sawday's critique seems less applicable to NVS editions than to critical editions, especially those infused with the positivism of Bowers. The original context of McGann's monumental "still point in a turning world" image is worth revisiting, considering that the target of his critique is the critical edition, not the Variorum:

What is especially important for us to see about the critical edition is its aspiration to transcend the historical exigencies to which all texts are subject. A critical edition is a kind of text which does not seek to reproduce a particular past text, but rather to reconstitute for the reader, in a single text, the entire history of the work as it has emerged into the present. To the scholar's eye, *the critical edition is the still point in the turning world of texts, a text which would arrest, and even reverse, the processes of textual change and corruption.*[93]

[90] See www.library.yale.edu/div/instruct/internet/history.htm.
[91] McGann, *Critique*, p. 93; quoted in Hunt, "New Variorum Shakespeares," p. 62.
[92] Hunt, "New Variorum Shakespeares," p. 62.
[93] McGann, *Critique*, p. 93, emphasis added.

The sense of an "entire history of [a] work" recoverable in the form of an edition motivated Furness's first efforts toward variorum editing, but by our own time, on the other side of the New Bibliography, that desire has naturalized itself in the form of the critical edition.

Unlike in most critical editions, however, authorship undergoes a kind of fragmentation in the NVS apparatus, which shows better than any other kind of edition that what we call a Shakespearean playtext bears the traces of many agents. Shakespeare may be chief among them, but never the sole agent of literary production when we allow that even the setting of type involves the shaping of meaning, not just its pure transmission through an idealized communications channel. To critics who subscribe to Barthes's argument about the death of the author (and the corresponding birth of the reader, in the complete formulation), the NVS offers, in Hunt's words, "the best opportunity to learn how the playwright's text has become destabilized, undercut, distorted, and even on occasion wished out of existence by major revisions, omissions, and improvements, some of which produce poetically superior readings through a new kind of collaboration."[94]

For example, we can parse the note to one of the NVS *Winter's Tale*'s most difficult cruxes as a list of improvements with proper names attached.[95] Here is a set of emended versions of the Folio's perplexing line "Affection? thy Intention stabs the Center" (1.2.138), reconstructed from the NVS edition's textual note (printed here in the note's reading order, not chronological order):

NICHOLAS ROWE: Imagination! Thou dost stab to th'Center.
EDWARD CAPELL: Affection, thy intention stabs to the center.
HOWARD STAUNTON: Affection thy intention stabs the centre?
STYAN THIRLBY: Affection! thy invention stabs the centre:
SAMUEL JOHNSON &
  GEORGE STEEVENS: Affection! thy intention stabs the center.

Notice that the name WILLIAM SHAKESPEARE appears nowhere in this list, not even in conjunction with the Folio reading that appears in the edition's playtext. Shakespeare's name appears on the spine of the book, but, paradoxically, working within the information architecture

---

[94] Hunt, "New Variorum Shakespeares," p. 64; see Barthes, "Death of the Author," p. 148.
[95] Turner, *et al.* (eds.), *The Winter's Tale*.

of the NVS apparatus it is impossible to attribute text in any explicit way to Shakespeare. The apparatus permits an editor to assert, in effect, "Styan Thirlby wrote this" but not "William Shakespeare wrote this." This is because the modern NVS's playtext is not subject to the editorial functions we would expect from a critical editor, such as emendation, modernization, and selection of a base text according to text-critical principles, and its value derives not from any efforts to mediate between readers and authoritative Shakespeare texts, but rather from the play-text's function as an index for commentary and textual notes. These qualities of the NVS textual note structure serve as a synecdoche for the Variorum as a whole. While some views of the Folio would infuse every comma and dash with a presiding Shakespearean *genius loci*, the NVS playtext empties itself of any authorial pretext and becomes pure refer-ent, something merely to coordinate line numbers and references. The Shakespeare text presented in the Variorum provides the structure of an archive, not the essence of an author, thus inverting the epistemic strategy of the First Folio itself as discussed earlier in this chapter.

Barthes famously describes the reader as the real focus of a text's multiplicity: "The reader is the space on which all the quotations that make up a writing are inscribed without any of them being lost; a text's unity lies not in its origin but in its destination."[96] Just as archives exist for the future, not the past, so are Variorums about destinations, not origins. The Variorum's approach to readership reflects a qualification that Barthes makes about readers: "this destination cannot any longer be personal: the reader is without history, biography, psychology; he is simply that *someone* who holds together in a single field all the traces by which the written text is constituted."[97] The experience of reading Variorum commentary straight through, as opposed to consulting parts of it, reveals the impossibility of a reader who could be considered a "single field" of understanding that coordinates what Barthes calls "*all* the traces" and "*all* quotations" (emphasis added). The Variorum does not reconstitute this total field within its readers because, in a manner of speaking, it is an unreadable book in the sense that it cannot be received as a totality. A master text implies a master reader, yet Hunt may be right in calling Variorums postmodern, if we think of the volumes' postmodernity in the same vein as Joyce's *Ulysses*. Joyce's encyclopedic novel seems to

---

[96] Barthes, "Death of the Author," p. 148.
[97] Barthes, "Death of the Author," p. 148, emphasis in original.

call forth the subjectivity of an ideal reader, one capable of perceiving every joke, allusion, cross-reference, and detail of Joyce's schemata, yet the very same encyclopedism renders such a subjectivity unattainable due to sheer scale. (Did Joyce himself remember his novel as a totality, in every detail, even after its publication?) The modern Variorum similarly hints at the idea of the encyclopedic reader who perceives the Shakespearean universe in a grain of sand, and just as readily shows this to be an impossible perspective. The dream of the master text is a solitary dream, yet a postmodern reader is one who never reads alone.

All these themes converge in an 1894 photograph of Furness reading a book in his private Shakespeare library, alone and yet surrounded by information (Figure 3.3). Barthes's reader may have been without history, biography, or psychology, but these are the very dimensions that book historians look for in scenes of reading like this one. We can measure the historical distance between the Folio and New Variorum, as books and as information architectures, by contrasting this photograph with Van Dyck's 1632 portrait of Sir John Suckling, which

Figure 3.3 Horace Howard Furness in his private library at Lindenshade, *c*.1891.

Kastan unpacks for its metonymic equation of Shakespeare with the form of the book. In Suckling's time Shakespeare could be represented by a single book labelled with his name, an illusion of bibliographic equivalence between author and book that ceased to be sustainable by the late nineteenth century. For the benefit of the camera, Furness has selected one book from a multitude, which stands in for the unrepresentable whole of the library. But this is not just a space of reading; it is also a space of writing and editing, and specifically of annotating, cutting, and pasting. Furness appears here as an editor who has organized the contents of this archive into single Variorum volumes, just like the volume he holds in his hands. Also, like Suckling in the painting, and like the reader of the First Folio who obeys the injunction of Jonson's title-page poem, Furness appears to be turning the page: the iconic gesture of bodily engagement with the codex book.

As a representation of textual labour, the photograph also calls for a double-vision on the viewer's part: on one hand we see an independently wealthy nineteenth-century Shakespeare collector, secure within his treasure-trove of Shakespeariana; at the same time, we see a Shakespeare editor, sitting comfortably as a learned amateur archivist amongst records that he has spent years gathering, appraising, and describing for the sake of some imagined future use. It is a posed photo with calculated effects, but what is the relationship between the wealth of material held in this space and the reader in the middle of it all? This is an image of mastery over volumes of information, but certain contextual details also make this a figure for information's material vulnerability. As Furness noted in a letter to Wright on the danger fire posed to books, his library was made "all of brick, iron, with cement floor and asbestos ceiling, and an iron door which closes automatically in case of fire."[98] Furness also links the architecture of his private library to the hermeneutics of Shakespeare research when he mentions in a letter from 1902 that "as for the Sonnets, Shakespeare (as I think) no more unlocked his heart in them than he unlocked my fireproof [library]."[99] As an inheritor of Malone's epistemology,

---

[98] Furness, *Letters*, vol. II, p. 57. In the same letter to Wright at Cambridge University (4 March 1900), Furness mentions a fire that ravaged the Lippincott offices and writes, "It makes me shudder to think of that MS. of Milton [held at Trinity College], and how ruthlessly flames would eat it up." See also Gibson, *Philadelphia Shakespeare*, p. 241.

[99] Letter to W. J. Rolfe, February 1902, Furness, *Letters*, vol. II, p. 84.

Furness looks for truth not in biography revealed through poetry, but in the encyclopedic labour of information management: the labour of document-collecting and of page-turning, conducted safely behind fire-proof walls.

As we shall see in the next chapters, rather than being superseded by new technologies, the book's distinctive materiality reasserts itself in ways that trouble idealized narratives of technological remediation.[100] This tendency manifests itself, like a *memento mori*, in the centre of the photograph of Furness. Because of the long exposure required for the photograph, the book Furness holds becomes the one thing in the picture that is out of focus, presumably because he was moving the book and turning pages while the camera's shutter remained open. (For a higher-resolution image, see the version of Traister's "The Furness Memorial Library" posted at respository.upenn.edu/library-papers/ 13.) This photograph, in addition to visualizing the book as physically vulnerable, also visualizes it as a mobile object, one whose very mobility becomes visible thanks to photography's ability to record the accidental. The book in motion, in the hands of a reader, stands in contrast to the surrounding books at rest: information in transmission versus information held in potentiality. That blurred image of reading in the midst of a static, photographed collection captures the doubleness of the Shakespeare text caught between the information architectures of the edition and the archive, and of the body and the book.

---

[100] See James Lastra's critique of the reduction of photography to "the camera's 'click,'" in *Sound Technology*, pp. 12–13, and the discussion in the next chapter, p. 120.

4 | The counterfeit presentments of Victorian photography

Memory and Oblivion, like Day and Night, and indeed like all other Contradictions in this strange dualistic Life of ours, are necessary for each other's existence: Oblivion is the dark page, whereon Memory writes her light-beam characters, and makes them legible; were it all light, nothing could be read there, any more than if it all were darkness.

Thomas Carlyle, "On History Again" (1833)[1]

Roland Barthes thought it paradoxical that the nineteenth century should be the one to invent both Photography and History (whose establishment as social institutions he signals with capital letters). As he describes in *Camera Lucida*, "Earlier societies managed so that memory, the substitute for life, was eternal . . . this was the Monument. But by making the (mortal) Photograph into the general and somehow natural witness of 'what has been,' modern society has renounced the Monument."[2] This chapter considers what happens when books as bibliographic monuments (as discussed in the preceding chapter) become objects of photographic representation within the context of what Richard Terdiman calls the Victorian crisis of memory, which resulted from the realization that memory was more artificial than natural, and therefore subject to techno-logical mediation and even manipulation.[3] Thomas Carlyle's interchange-ably photographic and bibliographic metaphor from his 1833 essay "On History Again" resonates with Joseph Niépce and Louis Daguerre's first experiments with paper photography, which were underway around the same time in France, but his proto-photographic metaphor for memory evokes other meanings as well when considered in retrospect.[4] Carlyle's

---

[1] Carlyle, "On History Again," p. 109.   [2] Barthes, *Camera Lucida*, p. 93.
[3] Terdiman, *Present Past*, p. 31. See also the Introduction, p. 20.
[4] It is also possible that Carlyle could be alluding to Thomas Wedgewood's attempts to capture images in a *camera obscura* thirty years before. On Carlyle's other technological metaphor for memory and history, the palimpsestic manuscript, and its relation to Derrida's ideas about writing and erasure, see Flint, *Visual Imagination*, pp. 165–6.

imagery of light imprinting memories onto a substrate alludes to the old convention of memory as manuscript writing, but also anticipates the language that William Henry Fox Talbot would use in the first photographically illustrated book, *The Pencil of Nature*, published between 1844 and 1846. As if he foresaw modern inscription technologies like optical disc burners, Carlyle's description of writing in light on a material substrate captures the dual fantasy and anxiety of the archive in his century and in our own.

With the development of photography through the decades of the Victorian period, the camera increasingly became a technology through which the nineteenth century's preoccupation with preserving the past could be articulated. As we have considered elsewhere throughout this book, Shakespeare's texts play a conflicted role as what Pierre Nora calls *lieux de mémoire* in the degree of cultural work they are required to perform, given their status as flawed and fragmentary vehicles of English cultural heritage that constitute one of literature's greatest bibliographical and editorial problems.[5] The nineteenth century was the first great age of facsimiles and other forms of documentary reproduction, and the rise of the photographic facsimile in the mid- to late nineteenth century parallels the more recent rise of digitization projects such as *Early English Books Online* (EEBO).[6] Ironically, many of the recent criticisms of EEBO – that its images distort the features of pages and the scale of books as objects; that it misleadingly represents single copies of books as representatives for all copies; that many of its represented books simply leave things out and get things wrong – point to effects of photography that fascinated technologists and readers alike in the Victorian period, namely the photograph's capacity to capture the

---

[5] Nora, *Realms of Memory*, vol. I, p. 1.
[6] This chapter focuses specifically on Shakespeare, but a broader history of photographic facsimiles may be found in McKitterick's chapter "The Arrival of Photography," *Old Books*, pp. 114–38. For a reading of Talbot in relation to digital imaging and visual art, see Burnett, "A Scene in a Digital Library." One might argue that the Victorian photographic counterpart to the torrent of digitized Shakespeare texts in the late twentieth century took the form not only of facsimile reproductions of books, but also of nostalgic author portraits. Helen Groth notes the "astonishing output" of Shakespeare-related photographs, "with volumes devoted to Shakespeare and his birthplace far outnumbering all others"; *Victorian Photography and Literary Nostalgia*, p. 36.

accidental, the contingent, and the imperfect.[7] However, as Bonnie Mak demonstrates in "Archaeology of a Digitization," a bibliographical case study of EEBO's remediation of microfilm and other layers of old technical infrastructure, it is worthwhile to regard technologies for representing history *as* historical artifacts themselves. In the same spirit, this chapter explores how Shakespeare's texts took part in a symbolic economy of preservation and loss in the middle of the nineteenth century that prefigures modern digitization, and looks specifically at how Shakespeare came to be read through the camera eye.

The early photography of books has been covered in bibliographical manuals such as Philip Gaskell's *New Introduction to Bibliography*, which tells the story of the camera and the book in technological terms, but the cultural and epistemological dimensions of that relationship are in need of further exploration by textual scholars. The perspective of textual scholarship has a great deal to offer the history of media, especially approaches such as media archaeology, which seek to challenge received narratives that too easily essentialize new media. For example, film historian James Lastra calls attention to the error of reducing photography to "the camera's 'click'"; as he points out, "The apparent punctuality and singularity of the gesture of button-pushing, so familiar to us all, may lead us to think of 'photography' as a phenomenon based on a particular device – the camera – and a particular act – pointing and shooting."[8] Lastra echoes the book historian's and bibliographer's emphasis on the entanglement of technology and human agency when he argues that "the various processes embodied in the camera entail mixtures of quite distinct developments in chemistry, optics, mechanics, printing, and so on. It should also be clear that the act of button-pushing distracts from the equally important acts of ... staging (even if we apparently choose not to stage), narrativizing, developing, printing, and presenting to the beholder."[9] This approach accords well with D. F. McKenzie's sociology of texts, but histories of photographic book facsimiles – like triumphalist claims for mass digitization projects in the present – often overlook the social

---

[7] For a representative sample of bibliographically minded criticism of EEBO, see Gadd, "Use and Misuse"; Mak, *How the Page Matters*, pp. 62–71, and "Archaeology of a Digitization"; Werner, "Material Book Culture"; and Kichuk, "Metamorphosis." See also the fascinating collection of EEBO errors at Whitney Trettien's blog: facsimilefail.tumblr.com.

[8] Lastra, *Sound Technology*, p. 12.   [9] *Ibid.*

and interpretive contexts of new visual media. Telling the story of the technology alone is not enough, and ideological keywords like *content* and *access* fall short of the material specificity that our vocabulary needs.

Given the long-running metaphorical traffic between bodies and books since the early modern period, what was the nature of the archive that photography created for books?[10] Part of the answer might be the now-familiar Foucauldian thesis that regimes of surveillance produce, rather than repress, a kind of corporeal truth in observed bodies, which I would extend to photographed books.[11] The book under the lens exhibits not just materiality but specifically corporeality, subject to allegedly infallible tests akin to Othello's "ocular proof" (3.3.365). To early modernists the corporeality of books is nothing new, from the thoroughly anthropomorphic terms of hand-press printing (*spine*, *skeleton*, *head*, *foot*, *beard*, and so on), to the infamous prefatory epistle to the 1570 edition of *The Tragidie of Ferrex and Porrex* (or *Gorboduc*), which genders an earlier unauthorized edition as a wanton, ravished textual corpus.[12] What changes with Victorian photography, however, is the representational logic of instrumental realism and its archival practices rooted in the preservation and organization of material documents. As Allan Sekula argues, "The central artifact of this system is not the camera but the filing cabinet."[13] Inscribed within this emerging episteme, the available meaning of any given book as an object changed, in a sense, because its possible relations to other books and to the act of looking had also changed.

This chapter takes up these questions by considering how Shakespeare's quartos and folios became some of the first books to be reproduced photographically in the middle of the nineteenth century.

---

[10] See Stallybrass, "Books and Scrolls"; Goldberg, *Writing Matter*; and Masten, *Textual Intercourse*.

[11] See Foucault, *Discipline and Punish*.

[12] John Day's epistle, "The P[rinter] to the Reader," describes how the printer of the 1565 edition of *Gorboduc* "put it forth exceedingly corrupted: even as if by meanes of a broker for hire, he should have entised into his house a faire maide and done her villanie, and after all to bescratched her face, torne her apparell, berayed and disfigured her, and thrust her out of dores dishonested. In such plight after long wandering she came at length home to the sight of her frendes who scant knew her but by a few tokens and markes remayning"; Norton and Sackville, *The Tragidie of Ferrex and Porrex* (London, 1570), sig. A2r.

[13] Sekula, "The Body and the Archive," pp. 7 and 16.

In 1858 John Payne Collier oversaw the reproduction of the Duke of Devonshire's copy of the first quarto of *Hamlet* using photolithography, and in 1861 the Royal Ordnance Survey began photographing the Dryden copy of the First Folio in a project that would lead to Howard Staunton's facsimile of 1866. These Shakespearean photographic experiments prefigure the recent turn to image-based computing in humanities computing, and demonstrate that very early in the camera's history, it became a tool not just for the artist, but also for the literary editor and bibliophile.[14] In this chapter I will consider these two facsimile projects as case studies, but will turn first to the question of what it meant to read a photograph and related visual media in the nineteenth century.

Learning to read photographs with Shakespeare

An 1856 advertisement for the London Stereoscopic Company (see Figure 4.1) depicts a Victorian household being guided by Shakespeare in their encounter with a new optical technology, the stereoscope, and with a new mode of vision in the form of three-dimensional photorealism.[15] The ad appropriates a familiar line from *Hamlet* –"Seems Madam! Nay, it IS!" – complete with quotation marks, italicized title, and banderole to establish the textual origin of the citation. However, the ad brings together a number of media; not only the quoted text of *Hamlet* and the stereoscope itself, but also the engraved image, along with the serialized publication in which the ad appears (one of the first published serial parts of Dickens's *Little Dorrit*), and, most of all, the memory of the reader who is expected to recognize and recontextualize this fragment from *Hamlet*. The ad thus demonstrates both the multimedia environment in which Victorians found themselves and the assumptions that the makers of those early media made about their viewers. This chapter deals with the various dynamics captured in this image, in which the Victorians, like users of

---

[14] See Kirschenbaum (ed.), *Image-Based Humanities Computing*, especially his Introduction, pp. 3–6; see also Terras, *Digital Images*.

[15] This particular example would have been encountered by the first readers of Dickens's *Little Dorrit*, as it appears on the first page of an early issue of the novel's first run of serial parts (no. 4, March 1856; from a copy held by the Thomas Fisher Rare Book Library, University of Toronto, call no. D-10 2109). I am grateful to Albert Masters for bringing this example to my attention.

Figure 4.1 *Hamlet* quoted in a stereoscope advertisement appearing in one of the first serial parts of Charles Dickens's *Little Dorrit* (1856).

digital resources in the present, were learning to read emergent forms of realism through new media – especially photography – which coexisted with competing modes such as painting. My particular interest in this chapter has to do with the representational stakes between "seems" and "IS!" in the relation of copies to originals. In one of Shakespeare's own stagings of the interpretation of images, Hamlet apparently produces a pair of images (possibly miniatures) of his father and uncle, and enjoins his mother to "Look here upon this picture, and on this, / The counterfeit presentment of two brothers" (3.4.51–2).[16] The question I wish to consider is how the early photographic facsimile, along with the medium of photography itself, embodies the trope of the counterfeit presentment, substituting itself for its predecessor, but with a difference.

As we shall see in this chapter's other examples, encountering Shakespeare in these unusual media contexts – as opposed to more familiar contexts such as the pages of Victorian editions, or the stage, or paintings – prompts questions about how Shakespeare and the media in question affect each other's interpretation. In the ad, Hamlet's line is transplanted from its original context in the play, where he protests the intractability of his grief to his mother (1.2.76), and seems oddly out of place in relation to the image, in which mixed company in a middle- or upper-class domestic setting peer through a stereoscope like a parlor game. What voice speaks the line of Shakespeare here? Is the man standing on the right supposed to be quoting *Hamlet* to the woman looking through the stereoscope, perhaps as an ironic response to a comment about the three-dimensional effect produced by the two stereoscopic images? (As one of the press blurbs below expostulates, "The *two* become *one*, and produce effects unknown to Art.") Or does the text of Shakespeare speak here in a more abstract way, a disembodied voice from the world of books and theatre, endorsing a new optical medium with an even greater claim on reality? How much imaginative surplus does this seemingly offhand quotation carry, considering that the quotation links two sets of domestic relationships? The harmonious scene pictured in the ad sits uncomfortably next to the court scene it quotes from *Hamlet*, which evokes the incest, murder, and inter- and intra-familial power struggles that have put the times out of joint. Would readers have recognized an intertextual frisson that amplified the thrill

---

[16] On Shakespeare's pattern of thematic and linguistic doubling (hendiadys) in *Hamlet*, see Kermode, *Shakespeare's Language*, pp. 100–13.

of wonder at the stereoscope, giving a literary inflection to the desire for a new consumer technology? The interpretive complexity that comes with Shakespeare in this and other examples of Victorian new media can just as easily complicate cultural reception as stabilize it.

In response to the long-running critical project to connect photography and modernity, following Barthes, Sekula, and Susan Sontag, I ask in this chapter what difference it makes when the photographic subjects are not bodies or scenes, but books. Shakespeare helped stage the encounter with new optical media, and the eyes of the viewers represented in this image were the ones that eventually read Shakespeare through the mediation of the camera and the photo-facsimile. However, histories of photography have largely overlooked the crucial transition in which the camera began to reproduce complete documents and books to be used as resources, as distinct from scenic depictions of books as objects. This under-recognized dimension of photography forms part of the prehistory of digitization in the way it unites evidentiary and preservational ways of looking: photographs of books enable readers to see with new, mechanically enhanced vision, but they also inscribe observed objects (including documents) into an emerging visual order of reality, in which objects become real once they can be recorded.

Strictly technological or bibliographical accounts of photography can overlook the wealth of analysis that Victorianists and others have produced on nineteenth-century photography's cultural history, which connects topics ranging from crime and surveillance,[17] to book illustration and the graphic arts,[18] to documentary and literary realism,[19] to science and medical imaging.[20] Of particular importance for my purposes is Sekula's article "The Body and the Archive," which traces the rise of photography as a technology of instrumental realism in the late Victorian period, becoming what he calls "both an *object* and

---

[17] See Sekula, "The Body and the Archive," and Green-Lewis, *Framing the Victorians*.

[18] See Carol Armstrong, *Scenes in a Library*; Jussim, *Visual Communication and the Graphic Arts*; and Crary, *Techniques of the Observer*.

[19] See Green-Lewis, *Framing the Victorians*; Nancy Armstrong, *Fiction in the Age of Photography*; and Novak, *Realism, Photography, and Nineteenth-Century Fiction*.

[20] See Daston and Galison, *Objectivity*, and Tucker, *Nature Exposed*.

means of bibliographic rationalization" by which the archive of all possible documents was ordered.[21] Between 1880 and 1910, argues Sekula, this conflicted technology had become so integrated with state-wide archival ambitions and practices – in the same vein as Thomas Richards's characterization of the imperial archive (discussed in this book's Introduction)[22] – that "photographic archives were seen as central to a bewildering range of empirical disciplines, ranging from art history to military intelligence."[23] Sekula and other scholars of this period have tended to focus on the new economies of social power at work in these technologies and cultural formations, usually locating that power in its effects upon bodies, like the subjects of police photographs, or upon the natural world as apprehended by science.[24] However, as Lorraine Daston and Peter Galison demonstrate, photography's takeup by the natural and social sciences leads inevitably back to its origins with Talbot and Daguerre as an art form, one thought to replace drawing and engraving with the beauty of indexical signs – that is, of the phenomenological records of things themselves.[25] In many domains, early photography blurred the lines between technology and art, and between tool and technique – though the permeability of such categories has also become the norm in the book arts and digital humanities alike.

Talbot's *Pencil of Nature* demonstrates how the photograph entered the cultural imagination via the book. His catalogue of new forms of vision joins photographs with the form of the book, combining media but also guiding the reader's interpretation of the media themselves, much like the stereoscope ad discussed above. As Carol Armstrong points out, *The Pencil of Nature* serves as a general commentary on

---

[21] Sekula, "The Body and the Archive," pp. 7 and 57, emphasis in original.
[22] Richards, *Imperial Archive.*   [23] Sekula, "The Body and the Archive," p. 56.
[24] On optical technologies of objectivity in the nineteenth century, see Daston and Galison, *Objectivity*; Tucker, *Nature Exposed*; and Jonathan Smith, *Charles Darwin.*
[25] Daston and Galison, *Objectivity*, p. 130. See also Young, "*Hamlet* and Nineteenth-Century Photography," p. 261. In some ways early photography was also continuous with painting, in that retouching photographs by hand was not uncommon – though the practice was much debated among scientists; see Daston and Galison, *Objectivity*, pp. 115–90. There is evidence that photolithographed book facsimiles were sometimes retouched, which I have discussed in "Dizzying the Arithmetic of Memory," ¶11–12; see also Parrott, "Errors and Omissions."

books, not just photography, and also comments upon earlier biblio-graphic forms in two images.[26] Plate VIII, titled "A Scene in a Library," depicts shelves of books (see Figure 4.2); the following plate, titled "Fac-simile of an Old Printed Page," offers what may be the first complete photographic reproduction of a single document, a deed written in Norman French (see Figure 4.3). As Armstrong suggests of the latter plate, it "asserts at one and the same time its closeness to the original and its status as not-the-original ... it ruptures the book's unity; it is proximate to what it records, but not quite the thing itself."[27] The representational tensions Armstrong notes, which will be familiar to modern eyes trained on digital images, are nonetheless smoothed over in Talbot's caption to the plate: "To the Antiquarian this application of the photographic art seems destined to be of great advantage."[28] History proved him right, and photolithography became the basis of a fundamental shift in the reproduction of texts.

However, it is important to consider how that history unfolded – that is, how we arrived at a point, long prior to digital screens, where we could look at an image of a page reproduced by a camera and consider it unremarkable. Part of the importance of *The Pencil of Nature* for the prehistory of digitization is that photographic reproduction of books began with a gesture toward utility. Yet when one looks at Talbot's images, one can imagine how strange they must have seemed to Victorian eyes. In the representation of books on the shelf, they were seeing familiar objects represented in a way they had never seen before. In the representation of the Norman deed, they were seeing an unfa-miliar object from their own distant past, one they might never have laid eyes upon but for this new technology. In retrospect, one can see in these images two of the parameters of digitization projects today: making rare materials newly accessible, and mediating familiar objects in ways that make them newly strange to our eyes. In this respect, the repro-duced Norman deed exists on a continuum with digital projects like *Early English Books Online*, the *Shakespeare Quartos Archive*, and others.

As this chapter will show by the end, the history of photolithography, while forming part of the prehistory of digitization in terms of questions of authenticity, is also the history of letterpress printing's displacement

[26] Carol Armstrong, *Scenes in a Library*, pp. 107–78.
[27] Carol Armstrong, *Scenes in a Library*, p. 151.   [28] Talbot, *Pencil of Nature*, n.p.

Figure 4.2 Plate titled "A Scene in a Library" from William Henry Fox Talbot, *The Pencil of Nature* (1844–6).

by the camera. Andrew Prescott suggests that "In approaching the digital age, we can learn a great deal from examining how our Victorian colleagues first explored the possibilities of photography."[29] Prescott's discussion of early photographic facsimiles of documents such as *Domesday Book* and the Utrecht Psalter emphasizes the question of trust, specifically the uneven development of trust in photography to give faithful reproductions of historical documents.[30] The photograph allegedly offers what Barthes calls "a certain but fugitive testimony," and its legacy in the form of other technologies, such as photocopies and digital images, has prompted textual scholars such as G. Thomas Tanselle and Bonnie Mak to warn readers against unquestioning trust in facsimiles of any kind, from photocopies to the digital images

[29] Prescott, *Representing Texts*, p. 10.
[30] Barthes, *Camera Lucida*, p. 93. On the question of trust, see Terras's discussion of "The Truth of Images" and the history of manipulated photographs in *Digital Images*, pp. 194–8.

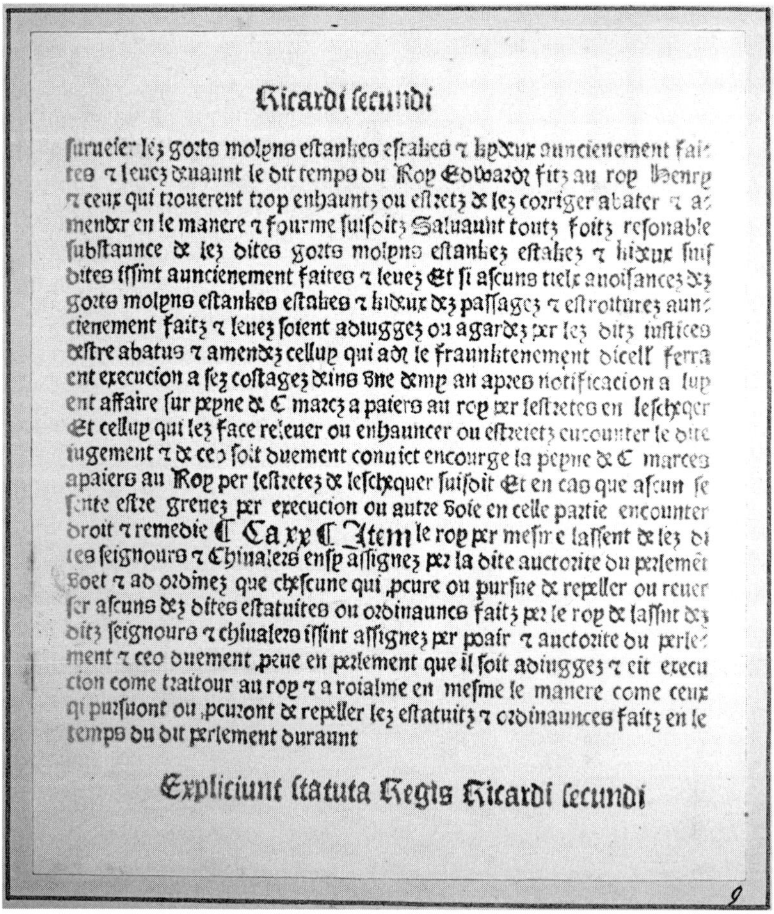
Ricardi secundi

furueier lez gorts molyns estankes estabes ꝛ kydeux auncienement faites ꝛ leuez deuaunt le dit temps du Roy Edward fitz au roy Henry
ꝛ ceux qui trouerent trop enhauntz ou estretz de lez corriger abater ꝛ a-
mender en le manere ꝛ fourme suisoitz Saluaunt toutz foitz resonable
substaunce de lez dites gorts molyns estankez estakez ꝛ kidaux sins
dites issint auncienement faites ꝛ leuez Et si ascuns tielx anoisancez dez
gorts molyns estankes estakes ꝛ kideux dez passagez ꝛ estroiturez auncienement faitz ꝛ leuez soient adiuggez ou agardez per lez ditz iustices
destre abatus ꝛ amendez celluy qui ad le fraunktenement dicell ferra
ent execucion a sez costagez deins vne demy an apres notificacion a luy
ent affaire sur peyne de C marcz a paiers au roy per lestretes en lescheqer
Et celluy qui lez face releuer ou enhauncer ou estreitz encounter le dite
iugement ꝛ de ceo soit duement conuict encourge la peyne de C marces
apaiers au Roy per lestretez de lescheqer suisoit Et en cas que ascun se
sente estre grenez per execucion ou autre voie en celle partie encounter
droit ꝛ remedie ¶ Ca xx ¶ Item le roy per mesme lassent de lez dites seignours ꝛ Chiualers ensy assignez per la dite auctorite du parlemēt
voet ꝛ ad ordinez que chescune qui pcure ou pursue de repeller ou reuer-
ser ascuns dez dites estatuites ou ordinaunces faitz per le roy de lassent dez
ditz seignours ꝛ chiualers issint assignez per poair ꝛ auctorite du parlement ꝛ ceo duement preue en parlement que il soit adiuggez ꝛ eit execucion come traitour au roy ꝛ a roialme en mesme le manere come ceux
qi pursuont ou pcuront de repeller lez estatuitz ꝛ ordinaunces faitz en le
temps du dit parlement duraunt

Expliciunt statuta Regis Ricardi secundi

Figure 4.3 Plate titled "A Fac-similie of an Old Printed Page" from William Henry Fox Talbot, *The Pencil of Nature* (1844–6).

on EEBO.[31] As Tanselle puts it, "The essential fact … is that every reproduction is a new document, with characteristics of its own, and no artifact can be a substitute for another artifact."[32] The technology of photography, once it was combined with the mass-reproduction techniques of lithography (in which a photograph could be transferred to a

[31] Tanselle, "Reproductions and Scholarship," pp. 25–54. Bonnie Mak discusses EEBO in her chapter on "The Digital Page," in *How the Page Matters*, pp. 62–71, and in her forthcoming article "Archaeology of a Digitization."

[32] Tanselle, "Reproductions and Scholarship," pp. 33–4.

substrate and reprinted from it en masse), resulted in the substitution of photolithographed books for their printed originals, sometimes illicitly. Abhijit Gupta writes of firms in Taiwan and Hong Kong that would dump photolithographed piracies into the later colonial Indian book trade: "If a book composed of letterpress was thus reproduced on a good quality machine, it was virtually indistinguishable from the real thing, and only an expert would be able to tell them apart."[33]

Shakespeare provides an illuminating set of materials to test questions of authenticity given that early reception of Shakespearean facsimiles inspired surprisingly high levels of trust, motivated by the desire to see the Shakespearean archive with the technologically enhanced vision that the new optical media seemed to promise. "Seems ... Nay, it IS!" could serve as the truth-claim made for nearly all early photographic applications, yet Shakespeare's own bibliographic archive, the 1623 First Folio, begins by destabilizing the relation between an image and its referent, as the preceding chapter showed in its discussion of Jonson's poem paired with the Droeshout title-page engraving. In the encounter with that image (Figure 3.1, p. 85), the Folio's reader is at once drawn into and admonished against making the kind of erroneous substitution of which Hamlet accuses Gertrude in the closet scene, when presented with images of her former and current husbands. Hamlet's own act of image collation and concern with the veracity of portraits anticipates the kind of scrutiny to which Shakespeare's own picture would be subjected, in disobedience to Jonson's injunction thundering in the index of Shakespeare's most recognizable book. Just as the whole Folio title page has become the part of that book most often detached and circulated through mechanical reproduction, so has the Droeshout image come to be examined with an intensity approaching the forensic. Witness the level of scholarly and general interest in the Sanders portrait, represented in the 2002 collection *Shakespeare's Face*.[34] "Dead and collected" is how Alexander Leggatt describes the Droeshout portrait, contrasting it with the livelier mid-career Shakespeare allegedly pictured in the Sanders portrait.[35]

---

[33] Gupta, "We Can List You," p. 80. On "the criminal part of facsimiles" and their nefarious history as fake first editions in the rare book trade, see McKitterick, "Old Faces and New Acquaintances," p. 164.

[34] Nolen (ed.), *Shakespeare's Face*.

[35] Alexander Leggatt, "The Man Who Will Not Meet Your Eyes," in Nolen (ed.), *Shakespeare's Face*, p. 281.

Marjorie Garber, in the same volume, discusses an 1875 book offering a phrenological examination of the Shakespearean cranium pictured in the Droeshout and other portraits.[36] Leah Marcus comments elsewhere on the Droeshout engraving's unconventional lack of ornamentation, which sets it apart from authorial frontispieces of its own time, and perhaps also inures itself to modern eyes by presenting Shakespeare as a proto-modern himself, as though the engraving were an early instance of photorealism.[37] Whatever 1623 readers made of the Droeshout engraving, modern eyes have scrutinized it like a mugshot.

Shakespeare's most recognized portrait thus embodies one of the prevailing themes running through recent scholarship on early photography: the optical and epistemic power that the photograph exerted over the body. Sekula and Jennifer Green-Lewis in particular explore the "new juridical photographic realism" that invested police photographs with power to inscribe bodies within archives of surveillance data.[38] Prominent in the history of photography we receive from Victorianist literary and cultural studies are figures such as Alphonse Bertillon, who in the 1880s was the first modern systematizer of criminal identification using biometrics, and Francis Galton, the founder of eugenics, who in the same period experimented with composite photographs to identify the abstract physiognomy of the "criminal type."[39] Galton's epistemic strategy was to erase difference until only the residue of truth remained. By layering multiple semi-transparent photographs of criminals' faces over one another, Galton hoped that the essential character of the criminal type would show through. (It didn't.)

In 1885 the same experiment was attempted with several of Shakespeare's portraits by Walter Rogers Furness (son of New Variorum Shakespeare editor Horace Howard Furness, discussed in Chapter 3), who published a short limited-run octavo titled *Composite Photography Applied to the Portraits of Shakespeare*.[40] In search of Shakespeare's

---

[36] Marjorie Garber, "Looking the Part," in Nolen (ed.), *Shakespeare's Face*, pp. 160–4. Jonathan P. Lamb explored similar territory in his paper "Shakespeare's Giant Head" for the 2012 Society for Textual Scholarship conference in Austin, Texas.

[37] Marcus, *Puzzling Shakespeare*, pp. 2–3.

[38] The phrase is Sekula's, from "The Body and the Archive," p. 5.

[39] Sekula, "The Body and the Archive," pp. 18–19.

[40] Walter Rogers Furness, *Composite Photography*. The title page notes "fifty copies printed."

true likeness, the junior Furness gathered seven photographs of portraits thought to have authority (including the Chandos, Droeshout, and Ashbourne) plus photographs of Shakespeare's death mask and bust on the Stratford Monument. Sorting these images into left- and right-facing portraits, Furness's book reproduces them individually and in three different composites. Figure 4.4 shows the composite photograph of the

Figure 4.4 Composite photograph of various portraits of Shakespeare (1885).

Chandos, Droeshout, Jansen, Felton, and Stratford portraits, and the Stratford bust. A reviewer of the experiment in *Shakespeariana* comments that "One would suppose that combining so many portraits, one on top of the other, would produce nothing but a hopeless confusion of lines. Yet such is not the case . . . the nose, mouth, eyes, eyebrows, and moustache are perfect. The expression, however, is different from that of any of the portraits of which it is composed."[41] The reviewer seems to have understood how Galton's approach anticipates big data in the plural sense, by which aggregates and composites reveal patterns not perceptible in instances. Whether this composite reveals Shakespeare's true face, or offers other biographical revelations such as Shakespeare's alleged Catholicism or unusual cranial capacity, I shall leave to readers to discern for themselves.

This composite photograph may tell us next to nothing about Shakespeare, but it reveals far more about its makers. As a new media experiment, it suggests a desire to find the singular truth among differences, and inflects that desire through the still-evolving technology of the camera. As Furness says in his introduction, after referencing Galton's 1883 *Inquiries into Human Faculty and Its Development*, a composite photograph is "the final photograph obtained from the exposure to the same sensitized plate of a series of human faces. A photograph thus 'composed' presents, according to Mr Galton's ingenious theory, the face typical of the group."[42] The approach is oddly parallel to his father's proposed and quickly abandoned editorial policy for the New Variorum Shakespeare (discussed in the preceding Chapter 3, see pp. 102–4) of determining the playtext by accepting the most commonly adopted variants and emendations. Like the contours of Shakespeare's physiognomy, Shakespeare's truest text would come forth by the force of quantity and consistency, with variants fading away into indistinctness – though still collated in an apparatus, which for the junior Furness took the form of the individual portrait photographs also included in the book. Like Teena Rochfort Smith's contemporaneous experiment in typographical variation (discussed in the Introduction), the composite photographs attempt to archive variants

---

[41] J. Parker Norris, "Composite Portraits of Shakespeare," *Shakespeariana*, 21.2 (September 1885), pp. 449–50.

[42] Walter Rogers Furness, *Composite Photography*, p. 3. See Galton, *Inquiries into Human Faculty*.

within a single system, yet its wholeness is threatened by its own com-plexity – just as Rochfort Smith's *Four-Text Hamlet* was defeated in 1883 by the printer's inability to keep up with her typographical encod-ing. As the junior Furness hints in his comment about exposing a series of images on the "same sensitized plate," he imagined photography as providing an ideal substrate, coordinating change and permanence alike within the same system, as Freud would imagine with the Mystic Writing Pad a few decades later (see pp. 60–1). Yet variation haunts this system, as the book's reviewer reveals when he remarks that "The various collars and costumes can all be faintly seen, and produce a very curious effect."[43] Historical and material differences linger in the composite like ghosts in a spirit photograph, making the image in Figure 4.4 less a portrait of Shakespeare than a mirror of the late nineteenth-century photographic imagination itself.

How then does Shakespeare's appearance in the earliest photo-graphic experiments anticipate the "crisis of faith in optical empiri-cism" that Sekula describes being sparked by the camera's use by police later in the Victorian period?[44] Like all forms of reading, scrutinizing an image forensically is not something that comes naturally; it must be learned, and the Victorians learned to look at photographs just as modern readers are now learning how to regard new digital media. Walter Rogers Furness, in the example above, clearly had much to learn about the non-indexical aspects of photography's relation to the real, especially in photographs of artistic works in other media. But are we so different? Important as it is to understand the impact of the new optical technologies upon modes of representation, it should be remembered that Shakespeare also had a significant reciprocal influ-ence on the way those technologies entered the cultural imagination. Subsequent chapters will consider how that same tendency manifests in our own digital texts, but the rest of this chapter explores how that learning processes for new media first began in the middle of the nineteenth century, with the mildly criminalized bodies of two Shakespeare books.

---

[43] J. Parker Norris, "Composite Portraits of Shakespeare," *Shakespeariana*, 21.2 (September 1885), pp. 450.
[44] Sekula, "The Body and the Archive," p. 57.

The first photo-facsimile: Collier's Q1 *Hamlet* (1858)

Readers of *The Photographic News* of 18 February 1859, especially those mindful of the plot of *Hamlet*, might have paused over the juxtapositioning of two notices, one printed below the other:

FACSIMILE "HAMLET" – A curious and interesting application of photography has been recently made, to the reproduction in facsimile of the margin copy of the first edition of Shakespeare's "Hamlet." This facsimile was liberally ordered, at the expense of the late Duke of Devonshire, for multiplication of the copy to the extent of forty examples, with a view to their circulation among the great libraries of the country, and those of a few favoured private individuals. The text was transferred by photography to stone, and Mr. Netherclift undertook to translate it from the stone to paper. As a facsimile each copy is perfect.

PHOTOGRAPHIC IDENTIFICATION OF A MURDERER. – On the 11th Nov., 1854, at Retiers, a man named Lefeuvre, a carpenter, shot and killed a woman whom he suspected of poisoning his dog. He immediately afterwards fled and was condemned to death, *par contumace*, on the 22nd May, 1855. A few days since, a man was arrested as a vagrant at Rodez, and as he refused to give his name, the aid of photography was called in, and a number of portraits of him were sent to different police stations. One of them happened to reach Retiers, and was soon recognized as the portrait of the murderer who had so long evaded justice.[45]

Given the connections between photography and surveillance noted above, it is a fitting coincidence that one of the first public notices of the first photographic book facsimile was printed next to a story that could have come straight from accounts of Bertillon's later criminological investigations – and which reads like a strange parody of *Hamlet*'s third and fourth acts, with modern transpositions of technology, geography, and gender. Juxtaposed with the sensational anecdote of the "Photographic Identification of a Murderer," the *Hamlet* notice generates a number of ironies, including the shared themes of surveillance, secrecy, revenge killing (possibly misdirected), flight, and the apprehension of a murderer whose identity must be confirmed by non-human agency. Further ironies become apparent when one considers the pseudo-criminal status of the first quarto of *Hamlet* (Q1) as what Laurie Maguire terms a *suspect text*, whose mugshot

---

[45] *The Photographic News*, 1.24 (18 February 1859), 286. The *Hamlet* notice is reprinted from *The Art-Journal*, vol. 4, new series (1858), 347.

hung for many years in the New Bibliography's rogues gallery of bad quartos. There is also the outright criminality of the *Hamlet* facsimile's instigator and overseer, John Payne Collier, who by 1859 was well established in his dual career as the Duke of Devonshire's librarian and a forger of early modern documents.[46] In this chance placement of notices in *The Photographic News*, the juridical and bibliographic modes of the emerging photographic episteme find themselves side by side and thematically entwined via *Hamlet*.

The facsimile that prompted the notice was the result of an experiment in photolithography undertaken by Collier and the lithographer Joseph Netherclift the year before. Forty copies were made for distribution by Collier on the Duke's behalf to various individuals and libraries in September of 1858.[47] (Figure 4.5 shows the title-page opening from the copy at the Folger Shakespeare Library, with a dedication in Collier's hand.) The idea of the photographic reproduction of documents for practical purposes was proposed by Talbot in relation to his "Fac-simile of an Old Printed Page," but the Collier Q1 *Hamlet* holds the distinction of being the first book to be reproduced *in toto* by a photographic process.[48] Philip Gaskell emphasizes this as a bibliographical event of great significance, commenting that "This facsimile and its twin [Collier's follow-up Q2 *Hamlet* facsimile in 1859] were remarkably

---

[46] On Q1 *Hamlet*'s textual legacy, see Maguire, *Shakespearean Suspect Texts*, and Lesser, *Hamlet After Q1*. On Collier, see Freeman and Freeman, *John Payne Collier*.

[47] Some of Collier's correspondence regarding these copies is held at the Folger Shakespeare Library, along with copies of the facsimiles. One copy, sent by Collier to W. Wardlaw Reid to make up for one that failed to arrive, was evidently made up from Collier's own corrected proofs (Folger call no. PR2807. A34 copy 4 Sh.Col.).

[48] This conclusion concurs with Philip Gaskell's *New Introduction to Bibliography*, pp. 270–71. Franklin B. Williams claims that James Orchard Halliwell-Phillips "experimented with simple photography; for instance, in 1857 he did *STC* 13073 [*The Famous Victories of Henry the Fifth*, 1617] in ten copies on photographic paper (surviving examples are too faded for use)"; "Photo-Facsimiles of *STC* Books," p. 112. Helmut Gernsheim's *History of Photography* calls the 1858 *Hamlet* "The second book to be illustrated by photolithography in Britain," the first being John Pouncy's *Dorsetshire Photographically Illustrated* in 1857 (p. 546). However, Gernsheim's word "illustrated" compares apples and oranges. The 1858 *Hamlet* facsimile takes first place if one observes the distinction between books illustrated by occasional photolithographic plates, like *The Pencil of Nature*, and books entirely reproduced by that method. See also McKitterick, *Old Books, New Technologies*, pp. 108–9.

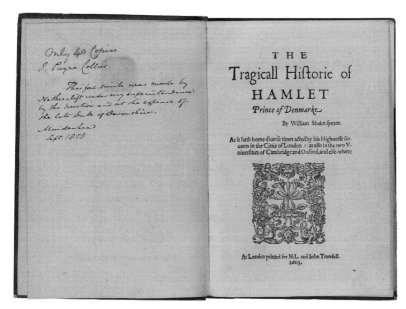

Figure 4.5 Title page with John Payne Collier's inscription from a copy of the Devonshire Q1 *Hamlet* facsimile (1858).

well done – there was little retouching, and the results are closer to the originals than were the Griggs–Furnivall photolitho facsimiles of the 1880s – and they were moreover the forerunners of a method of book production that was to challenge letterpress printing itself a hundred years later."[49] The prototyping of photography as a technology for modern book production begins, in practical terms, with Shakespeare.

However, other factors stand in the way of writing this event into any straightforward narrative of technological progress in service of cultural heritage. The first is the choice of material, given that Q1 *Hamlet* transmits Shakespeare's text in its most vexing form, thought to be derived from a source close to a theatrical version.[50] *Hamlet* holds the distinction

---

[49] Gaskell, *New Introduction*, pp. 270–1. On the facsimiles' distribution and surviving copies see Murphy, *Shakespeare in Print*, p. 445, n. 24.

[50] At the time of the facsimile's publication in 1858, a commenter in *The Athenaeum* describes the reproduced quarto as "a surreptitious impression ... made up of short-hand notes, &c. taken during the performance" and claims that Q2 "was printed to supersede it, but whether with the sanction of the author, or of the actors, must remain doubtful"; article signed "C.", "Our Weekly Gossip," *The Athenaeum*, no. 1619 (6 November 1858), p. 588.

of being the only play in the Shakespeare canon to have three authoritative source texts (Q1; Q2, printed in 1604–5; and F, the 1623 Folio); all
the other plays have no more than two sources to reconcile. Q1 *Hamlet*
has never fitted comfortably into any model constructed by textual scholars to explain it, including the much-debated bad quarto hypothesis. Q1's
puzzling departures from the F/Q2 texts (such as "Corambis" for
"Polonius," as well as "Rossencraft" and "Guilderstone") sit alongside
uncanny doubles of familiar lines ("To be, or not to be – ay, there's the
point"; 7.115) and scenes (the Ghost in the closet scene enters in his
nightgown, not armour [11.57.sd]), and yet are accompanied by some
apparently authoritative stage directions that modern *Hamlet* editors
have seen fit to use.[51] As Zachary Lesser and Peter Stallybrass describe
Q1's reputation among Shakespeareans, "the first quarto of *Hamlet* . . .
remains the unliterary acting version that, as a foil, sets off the literariness
of *Hamlet* to be discerned in Q2."[52] In retrospect, several decades of New
Bibliographical classification of Q1 as a memorially reconstructed bad
quarto have produced what Lesser and Stallybrass call "the odd result . . .
that this playbook seems not to be a book at all; it is only a dim
recollection of a performance through which we can glimpse the oral
culture of the Elizabethan playhouse. Q1 *Hamlet*, it seems, is not for
reading."[53] As a choice for a prototype for a new facsimile project even in
1858, its merits must have seemed more bibliographical than literary.

Furthermore, the first quarto of *Hamlet* stands as a belated addition
to the Shakespearean archive, having been discovered relatively late in
the play's editorial tradition. For the first two centuries of the play's
history, the first edition was thought to be the book now called Q2, until
1823 when what would become the Devonshire copy of Q1 was found
in a closet in Barton by Henry Bunbury, nephew of Shakespeare editor
Thomas Hanmer, who had evidently acquired the rare quarto bound
together with familiar Shakespeare plays.[54] Along with the first quarto
of *Titus Andronicus*, the unique surviving copy of which was discovered
only in 1904, Q1 *Hamlet* evokes the recovery narratives romanticized

[51] Quotations from Q1 are taken from Thompson and Taylor (eds.), *Hamlet: The Texts of 1603 and 1623*.
[52] Lesser and Stallybrass, "First Literary *Hamlet*," p. 372.
[53] Lesser and Stallybrass, "First Literary *Hamlet*," p. 379.
[54] See Bunbury's account of the discovery in his edition of the *Correspondence of Sir Thomas Hanmer*, p. 80, fn. Lesser indicates that evidence for Q1's provenance prior to Bunbury's discovery is inconclusive; see his forthcoming *Hamlet After Q1*, p. 5.

in *Raiders of the Lost Ark* and *Citizen Kane*, with the quarto surfacing as a historical artifact that changes the present's understanding of the past, like the Rosetta Stone (discovered by Napoleon's army in Egypt only two decades before Q1 *Hamlet* was found). The book reproduced in this first photographic experiment was therefore among the rarest books in the Devonshire library, one of only two known copies in the world in 1858, and to this day. In this sense, the facsimile symbolizes both preservation and loss at once, in that it safeguards a rare book whose very existence also reminds us of all the texts lost to history, and raises the possibility that other parts of Shakespeare's textual legacy may lie forgotten in closets.

Yet another of Q1's distinctions, the presence of sententiae marks to flag noteworthy passages for readers, works together with Q1's archival uniqueness and putative orality to make the Collier facsimile a remarkable crossroads of different memory technologies. Lesser and Stallybrass, following G. K. Hunter, point out that Q1 *Hamlet* "is the first play of Shakespeare's to be printed with what was rapidly becoming a distinguishing feature of plays for the learned or scholarly reader … sententiae or commonplaces that are pointed out to the reader, either by commas or inverted commas at the beginning of each line or by a change in font (usually from roman to italic)."[55] Readers of Q1 *Hamlet* – at least those with training to recognize the marks – thus received punctuational encouragement to inscribe specific lines and passages in their memories and commonplace books alike. The sententiae marks were therefore not merely typographical oddities; they linked the lines of the play to an early modern system of cultural memory, which connected the pages of the book to human judgments and memories, to educational systems to train those faculties, and to other books which serve as material substrates for this memory system. Q1 *Hamlet* thus materializes Carlyle's metaphor of memory's "light-beam characters" inscribed on a page, with the page of the book mirroring the page of the trained reader's memory. It is not clear whether Collier would have recognized these marks for what they were, but the power generally attributed to the camera is that it captures the phenomenal world independently from human cognition, as distinct from diplomatic

---

[55] Lesser and Stallybrass, "First Literary *Hamlet*," p. 376. On sententiae marks and their relation to quotation marks generally, see Estill, "Commonplace Markers and Quotation Marks."

reprints, which require editors to determine their texts character by character.[56] As James Lastra rightly objects, the essentialized moment of the "camera's click" tends to elide the many human choices at work in the making of a photograph, including framing and composition, but the example of the Q1 facsimile nonetheless shows how one does not need to comprehend an object's nature perfectly in order to photograph it.[57] (Indeed, that became photography's chief value for nineteenth-century science as an instrument of observation.) The subsequent editorial tradition of Q1 generally failed to reproduce the sententiae marks, as Lesser and Stallybrass point out, but the camera remembers indiscriminately even if it cannot understand.

Considering Q1's multiple relationships to systematized forms of memory, Collier could not have picked a more multivalent book for his prototype. The most remarkable aspect of the facsimile's creation, however, is the disquieting fact that its creator is now regarded as one of the nineteenth-century rare book trade's most accomplished forgers. Collier was the librarian for the sixth and seventh Dukes of Devonshire, whose library served as one of the nineteenth-century's foremost research centres for early modern books, and it was apparently Collier's ambition to reproduce all of the first quartos of Shakespeare's plays (though the seventh Duke of Devonshire was rather less supportive of the project than his predecessor).[58] Even while Collier's experiment was underway in 1858 he was fending off allegations that he had faked the marginalia in a copy of the Shakespeare Second Folio of 1632 known as the Perkins Folio. (Joseph Netherclift, the lithographer mentioned in *The Photographic News* notice quoted above, would later produce a facsimile, sans photography, of Collier's self-annotated and much-scrutinized Perkins Folio, and would be drawn into the controversy over its authenticity.[59]) There is no small irony, then, in his depiction in *The Athenaeum*'s column "Our Weekly

---

[56] Fredson Bowers notes this difference in his advocacy of title-page transcription over photographic reproduction as a way of training the bibliographic mind: transcription forces a descriptive bibliographer to decide what a particular mark means, while photography merely reproduces it. See Bowers, *Principles*, p. 136, and Galey, "Encoding as Editing as Reading."

[57] See Lastra, *Sound Technology*, pp. 12–13.

[58] Article signed "C.", "Our Weekly Gossip," *The Athenaeum*, no. 1619 (6 November 1858), p. 588.

[59] Freeman and Freeman, *John Payne Collier*, p. 719, n. 5.

Gossip," published as Collier was distributing the Q1 facsimile in September, 1858: "[the Collier Q1 facsimile] is, we believe, the first entire volume ever executed in lithography, and every line and letter has gone repeatedly under the inspection of Mr. Payne Collier, so that its accuracy, amounting almost to identity, cannot be doubted."[60] The controversy over the Perkins Folio, for which Collier is best known today, eventually ruined his reputation and sparked investigations into every aspect of his scholarship, revealing him to have been a prolific forger – and, to be fair, a genuinely talented one.

As mentioned above, Prescott has argued that digitization stands to learn by reflecting upon who was undertaking these Victorian facsimile projects, and why.[61] The example of Collier's facsimiles underscores his point. Should it surprise us that an early pioneer in the application of imaging technologies to rare books was also an expert in the construction of history via material interventions into documents? As M. T. Clanchy suggests, forgers "are best understood not as occasional deviants on the peripheries of legal practice, but as experts entrenched at the centre of literary and intellectual culture" who, by all means available to them, "re-created the past in an acceptable literate form."[62] Clanchy writes in the context of professional scribes in the twelfth century, but the same could be said of Collier in the nineteenth. Forgery has always been the art of the plausible.

Although the 1858 Collier facsimile and its reception exemplify the supposed power of photography to index reality, Collier's approach to the project also manipulates the representation of a bibliographic artifact by providing a hybrid of both surviving copies of Q1.[63] The Devonshire copy was missing its last leaf, supplied in the facsimile by an image from the British Library copy of Q1, which itself lacks its title leaf. In other words, the 1858 Q1 facsimile was not a simple photographic reproduction of a single document, like Talbot's "Fac-simile of an Old Printed Page." Instead, it offered a virtual reassembly of Q1, not unlike Charlton Hinman's use of photography and optical collation a

---

[60] Article signed "C.", "Our Weekly Gossip," *The Athenaeum*, no. 1610 (4 September 1858), p. 300.
[61] Prescott, *Representing Texts*, p. 10.
[62] Clanchy, *Memory to Written Record*, p. 320.
[63] McKitterick notes another intervention in the form of the restoration of running heads cropped during the binding of the originals; *Old Books*, pp. 108–9.

century later to virtually reconstruct the Folio in what he believed to be its most correct state, resulting in a facsimile that corresponds not to any surviving copy, but to the book as it should have been.[64] As *The Athenaeum*'s commentator emphasizes, having just noted the composite nature of the facsimile, "the book now about to be distributed is complete in every respect and gives a perfect representation of the original, even to the minutest point, line, or speck impressed by the antiquated types."[65] This remarkable statement of trust in representational fidelity appears in the same article as the claim for the facsimile's accuracy "amounting almost to identity," quoted earlier. Witness also *The Photographic News*'s closing assertion about the *Hamlet* project in the notice quoted above: "As a facsimile each copy is perfect" (which could also be a vague reference to Collier's virtual completion of the surviving Q1 copies). Similarly, an 1863 article in the rare book journal *The Philobiblion* asserts that, given the error rates of hand-traced or typeset reprints, "The only possible security against mistake appears to be photography. By the help of this invaluable agent ... it is practicable ... to obtain copies of any manuscript, or printed book, so closely resembling the original as almost to defy distinction."[66] As the Victorians were learning how to read photographs, one of the possible responses was faith in the photograph's indexical relation to the real, though Collier's facsimile could more accurately be described as having an indexical relation to the virtual.

For the New Bibliographers of the twentieth century, reproductive technologies facilitated crucial discoveries such as the identification of shared types and ornaments in the Pavier quartos. As Joseph Loewenstein describes, "The photograph and collotype not only satisfied an expanded bibliophile market, they also made possible what the type facsimiles of the old bibliophile author-societies could not: they fostered a cohort of far-flung academic investigators engaged in systematic typographic research and exhaustive investigation of press variants."[67] The photograph's potential as a medium that reveals new

---

[64] Hinman, *Printing and Proof-Reading*. See also Chapter 3, p. 81.
[65] Article signed "C.", "Our Weekly Gossip," *The Athenaeum*, no. 1610 (4 September 1858), p. 300.
[66] "Photo-lithographic fac-similes of the earliest authoritative texts of Shakespeare's works," *The Philobiblion*, 21 (1863), pp. 213–14, emphasis removed.
[67] Loewenstein, *Author's Due*, p. 260.

evidence also shows through in the relatively recent discovery – or rediscovery – of sententiae marks in Q1 *Hamlet* (discussed above), which exemplifies the value of making images of books, and not simply transcriptions, available on a broad scale.[68] Systematic research requires a network of trained eyes, as Loewenstein points out, to make sense of seemingly small details like the inverted commas marking Q1's notable lines. As McKenzie argues, "the material forms of books, the non-verbal elements of the typographic notations within them, the very disposition of space itself, have an expressive function in conveying meaning."[69] The example of Collier's Q1 facsimile, along with the First Folio facsimile I shall examine next, show that that McKenzie's "disposition of space" may be construed even more broadly than he perhaps intended. Photography, the technology that underlies the facsimiles where many now encounter those "non-verbal elements" like sententiae marks, changes the imaginable spatial relations within and among individual books.

Barthes touches upon the newly imaginable material relations between objects in *Camera Lucida*: "The photograph is literally an emanation of the referent. From a real body, which was there, proceed radiations which ultimately touch me, who am here; the duration of the transmission is insignificant; the photograph of the missing being, as [Susan Sontag] says, will touch me like the delayed rays of a star."[70] Over time, these possible relations were increasingly governed by the sense that material objects could be penetrated by patterns of information – a cultural perception that Katherine Hayles calls *virtuality*.[71] Books, like bodies under Galton's photographic gaze, exhibited their virtuality by radiating visual evidence that could be captured by the new optical technologies, and then systematically comprehended within an epistemic apparatus that formed a network of objects and observers. As we shall see, however, that network had its basis in the knowledge infrastructures of the imperial archive itself.

---

[68] Lesser and Stallybrass, "First Literary *Hamlet*"; see also Hunter, "Marking of Sententiae."
[69] McKenzie, *Bibliography and the Sociology of Texts*, p. 17.
[70] Barthes, *Camera Lucida*, pp. 80–1.
[71] See Hayles, *How We Became Posthuman*, pp. 13–14. This concept receives more detailed discussion in Chapter 6.

The Royal Ordnance Survey's First Folio facsimile (1862)

If the Q1 *Hamlet* facsimile of 1858 is the first book to be reproduced photographically, the First Folio follows close behind thanks to one of England's largest knowledge infrastructure projects, the Royal Ordnance Survey.[72] Their research on photographic reproduction of maps led them to make the surprising turn to the mapping of England's documentary archive in the early 1860s. Thanks to photographic research led by the director of the Ordnance Survey, Colonel Henry James, and acting on a directive from William Gladstone (then Chancellor of the Exchequer, later Prime Minister), the staff at the Survey's Southampton office found themselves the principal innovators of rare book facsimiles through the 1860s and into the early 70s. James is credited with inventing photozincography, a cost-effective process similar to photolithography but using zinc plates in place of stones.[73] The textual malleability of this new technology superseded the inscriptive permanence of engraving, and promised to keep pace with modernity itself. Yet photozincography had its genesis in the reproduction of texts. Colonel James's account of the invention describes his experimentation in winter of 1859 with an amateur etching given to him by a woman he met while holidaying on the Isle of Wight. From the unnamed woman's etching James turned to reproducing a "small Deed of the time of Edward I" as proof of concept. James continues,

> The day after this occurred, I was directed by the late Lord Herbert to meet him and the Chancellor of the Exchequer at the Treasury, on business connected with the Survey, and it was at this interview that Mr. Gladstone asked me if I knew of any process by which some of our ancient manuscripts in the Record Office could be copied. The experiment of the day before enabled me to answer at once in the affirmative; and as proof of our being able to do so, I had the small Deed of the time of Edward I., of which copies are bound up with my report of the year 1859, copied and printed by Photo-zincography, and this has led to our having to copy by this process "Domesday Book," or the Great Survey of William the Conqueror, which was written in the year 1086, at Winchester.[74]

---

[72] For a broader overview of the Ordnance Survey's facsimile projects and the role of photolithographic methods in printing and the book trade, see McKitterick, *Old Books*, pp. 122–6.

[73] See Gernsheim, *History of Photography*, p. 547.

[74] From James's preface to the first edition of the report by his colleague, A. de C. Scott, *On Photo-zincography*, as quoted in Wakeman, *Aspects of*

These initial experiments were as much about developing the technology as about preserving the documents, but the selection of material for technological prototypes has cultural significance: these are public performances of a new textual technology.

For its first photozincographic book reproduction, the Ordnance Survey chose to remediate the *Domesday Book* of its own medieval ancestor, William the Conqueror (completed in 1086 in two volumes, known as *Great Domesday* and *Little Domesday*). Beginning in 1861 with the section pertaining to Cornwall, the whole of *Domesday* was published in facsimile in thirty-five volumes, one for each county, over three years. Captain A. de C. Scott's introduction to the volume for Somersetshire emphasizes their care for the material book and the non-invasiveness of their photographic process: "In examining copies made by Photo-zincography, it must always be remembered that the original document is not even handled or touched by the copyist, each leaf of the book is placed in succession before the camera by the officer from the Public Record Office, in whose charge it constantly remains."[75] (This statement is perhaps disingenuous considering that both *Domesday* volumes had been disbound for photographing, to be rebound in 1869 by Robert Rivière.) The follow-up project to *Domesday Book* was no less than a magisterial four-volume photographic archive, *Facsimiles of National Manuscripts, from William the Conqueror to Queen Anne*, whose first volume advertised itself as "including the only perfect original copy of Magna Carta now extant" in fold-out pages, though reduced in size from the original.[76] Michael Twyman notes that the size reduction of *Magna Carta* represented an advance in facsimile technology, since it would have been exceedingly difficult to rescale an image using non-photographic means – another example, like Collier's hybrid facsimile, of photography's capacity to manipulate the objects of its representations.[77] This first *National Manuscripts* volume also included reproductions of Shakespeare's will and various documents of the Stationers' Company, and was followed by similar collections of national manuscripts for Scotland and Ireland, among other, smaller projects.

Victorian Lithography, p. 46. Copies of the report are now difficult to find, but Wakeman reprints the whole of James's preface to the first edition of *On Photo-zincography*. The second edition has a revised preface by James, which I quote below; see note 81.

[75] A. de C. Scott, Introduction to *Domesday Book*, n.p.

[76] *Facsimiles of National Manuscripts*, vol. I, Preface, n.p.

[77] Twyman, *Early Lithographed Books*, p. 250.

As McKitterick comments in a chapter on the Ordnance Survey's place within the history of photographic facsimiles, it is clear that from the beginning James "wished to make available to the public documents that were usually locked away from sight."[78] In this regard, James's project exemplifies one of the two imperatives of digitization that I mentioned at the outset, that of making rare materials newly accessible. That tendency led them to Shakespeare in 1861 while the *Domesday* project was underway, when the Ordnance Survey undertook their first photographic facsimile of a printed book, the Dryden copy of the First Folio.[79] They were guided in this choice by noted chess player and Shakespearean editor Howard Staunton, who was involved with a number of projects to reproduce Shakespeare documents. The Ordnance Survey never did produce a complete Folio facsimile, and Staunton took the project to other publishers who used the Ordnance Survey's techniques to make a complete Folio facsimile in 1866, but not before the Survey had produced a prototype containing the front matter through to the end of *A Midsummer Night's Dream*.[80]

---

[78] McKitterick, *Old Books*, p. 124.

[79] The follow-up to this project would be *Shakespeare's Sonnets, Reproduced in Facsimile by the New Process of Photo-zincography in use at Her Majesty's Ordnance Survey Office* (London: L. Reeve, 1862); see also McKitterick, *Old Books*, p. 125. It appears that Edward Dowden (quoted below) owned a copy, now held by the Folger Shakespeare Library (call no. PR2848 1862 Sh.Col.).

[80] Twyman *Early Lithographed Books*, p. 250. Twyman says of the 1866 Staunton facsimile, "A close look at the volume shows that it was printed from stone rather than metal plates. The whole undertaking has to be seen as a tremendous technical and organizational achievement bearing in mind the infant state of photolithography at the time. It cannot have been easy to reproduce effectively the poor presswork of the original seventeenth-century letterpress printing and to cope with the curvature of the pages ... As an artefact, it looks rather grander than the original from which it was reproduced" (pp. 252–3). The Folger Shakespeare Library holds a copy of the facsimile with Staunton's proof corrections, whose extent and detail reveal the high degree of care he took with the reproduction (call no. Folio PR2752 1866n copy 4 Sh.Col.). As if anticipating the flaws in EEBO pointed out by Sarah Werner, among others (see her article "Material Book Culture," and the sources cited in note 7 above), one of Staunton's most common corrections throughout the proof volume is "speck," but many annotations are not purely corrections, and reveal Staunton taking the opportunity afforded by the proofreading to flag and think through problems of early modern typography. For example, at one point in *The Merchant of Venice* (p. 170 in the comedies, going by the Folio's pagination) Lorenzo says to Salino "my affaires haue mad: you wait"; Staunton has written the word "made" in the margin, along with "what does this mean?" On Staunton's facsimile see also Murphy, *Shakespeare in Print*, pp. 192–3.

As with the example of the New Variorum prospectus, which included sample pages of Horace Howard Furness's 1870 edition of *Romeo and Juliet* (discussed in the previous chapter, pp. 101–2), the Royal Ordnance Survey's Folio facsimile prototype became known first through promotional materials. A report written by Scott and prefaced by James, titled *On Photo-zincography*, was published in 1862 (with subsequent reprints), and did much to legitimize the technique in the eyes of the government and the public.[81] Scott's report is a remarkable document in Victorian new media and the construction and reception of new imaging technologies. Following James's preface, which gives a history of the photozincographic method and situates it in relation to similar discoveries by others, Scott gives a detailed sixteen-page explanation supplemented by three technical diagrams of the photographic apparatus. These materials all serve to validate Scott's frank assertion that "The advantages of Photo-zincography consist in its power of multiplication, combined with its photographic truth."[82] The remarkable part of the report, however, is the sequence of twelve full-page sample plates showing the range of what photozincography could reproduce. Like the set of photographic subjects of Talbot's *Pencil of Nature*, the samples in Scott's report modulate through a sequence of representational possibilities: the first page of *King John* from the 1623 First Folio; a page from *Domesday Book* pertaining to Hampshire; a manuscript indenture document; a political map of Dalston Parish in Cumberland; a topographical map of part of Yorkshire; two Piranesi engravings of antique vases (on separate plates); part of an engraving of a Raphael panel in the Vatican; an engraving of Raphael's unfinished painting *The Transfiguration*; a photograph of the Temple of Luxor at Thebes; a photograph of a street scene in Cairo; and a photograph of trees on the Southampton common. This varied but carefully chosen group of representable objects adds up to tell the story of "photographic truth," as Scott calls it, and like Comenius's illustrated children's book *Orbis Sensualium Pictus* from two centuries prior, presents the reader with an encyclopedic catalogue of the representable world in pictures.[83]

[81] Scott, *On Photo-zincography*. I have been unable to view a copy of the first edition, and throughout reference the copy of the second edition held by the New York Public Library.

[82] Scott, *On-Photozincography*, p. 16.

[83] On Comenius's mode of representation and the form of the book, see Galey, *et al.*, "Architectures of the Book," pp. 26–8.

Although space prevents me from unpacking the representation strategies at work in Scott's report (one imagines reading it with eyes keyed to the same things that Carol Armstrong sees in *The Pencil of Nature*), it is worth considering the significance of the First Folio image as the lead item among the sample plates. That significance was also important to the writer of an unsigned review of Scott's publication in *Mechanic's Magazine* in 1863:

One of the plates expressly demonstrates the capability of these sister processes [photozincography and photolithography] for the multiplication, with delicate minuteness, of rare printed works – it is a copy of a page of the folio Shakespeare of 1623, a work in course of reproduction at the Ordnance-office, by permission of the War Department, and at the instance of Howard Staunton, Esq., of the *Illustrated London News*. Nothing can possibly exceed the fidelity with which, in this instance, all the quaint peculiarities of typography, punctuation, and orthography, visible in the original, are reflected in the copy. An examination of this specimen alone will serve to demonstrate the exceeding value of the process to which it owes its origin.[84]

The writer seems to have taken a cue from the exuberant language of the report itself, whose caption to the Folio plate points out its "unerring accuracy," and which claims that all the examples represent the details of the originals "as truthfully [as] the reflections in a mirror" – a reference to a technology which, by the middle of the nineteenth century, had successfully effaced its own role as a medium.[85] The Folio also functions in this example to legitimate a new archival technology while at the same time asserting its own status as archivable cultural heritage, thus continuing its own project as a book that had been ongoing since at least 1623 (as discussed in Chapter 3).

Whether by intention or accident, the content of the Shakespeare example in Scott's pamphlet also participates in a narrative of authenticity, in that the page from *King John* happens to include the scene in

---

[84] *Mechanic's Magazine* (23 January 1863), pp. 53–4. In a subsequent issue, Colonel James clarifies that Staunton was not in fact working directly with the Southampton office on the Folio facsimile at this time (6 February 1863, p. 105). Staunton himself answers in the following issue, claiming to have invested time and money in getting the Southampton office's Folio project underway, but then "having been denied permission to exercise personal supervision of the work, which is essential to its accuracy," which led him to withdraw from the Royal Ordnance Survey project (13 February 1863, p. 126).

[85] Scott, *On-Photozincography*, p. [ix].

which Falconbridge the Bastard presents his claim to legitimacy while standing beside his brother. As the Bastard asks of the king, in the "quaint peculiarities of typography, punctuation, and orthography, visible in the original" on the sample plate,

> Compare our faces, and be Iudge your selfe
> If old Sir *Robert* did beget vs both,
> And were our father, and this sonne like him.[86]

Like the closet scene in *Hamlet*, this scene enacts the tropes of the counterfeit presentment and the visual scrutiny of near-duplicates, but with the difference that the Bastard invites viewers to undertake the specifically bibliographical task of comparing two copies of an absent original to establish a family stemma. It is possible, of course, that *King John* was chosen because the play appears roughly halfway through the Folio, at a point where the sample copy might have been easiest to lay flat, but my argument throughout this book is that the content chosen for prototypes and tech demos participates in their meaning-making even if by accident – and the integration of the accidental into orders of meaning is one of the particular innovations claimed for photography since Talbot. (This theme will reappear in relation to Alexander Graham Bell's and Thomas Edison's selections from *Hamlet* and *Richard III*, respectively, in the next chapter.)

The hyper-accurate photographic technology so celebrated for its fidelity also permitted new forms of intervention. In a similar way to Collier's reconstruction of a virtual copy of Q1 *Hamlet* by combining photographic images, James and the Ordnance Survey project took this constructivist tendency even further by making a reciprocal intervention into the material history of the Folio. The Ordnance Survey prototype contains no introduction or other added text, but James and his colleagues leave their mark in one place: the Folio's own title-page imprint (see Figure 4.6). To the more famous names of Jaggard and Blount, James added his own and that of the new technology that enabled the reproduction: "COPIED BY PHOTO-ZINCOGRAPHY AT THE ORDNANCE SURVEY OFFICE SOUTHAMPTON, *Col. Sir Henry James R.E., F.R.S., F.G.S., &c., Director,* 1862." James's addition offers the somewhat playful implication that the history of the book is still ongoing – perhaps with future imprints to be added by

---

[86] Scott, *On-Photozincography*, plate 4; *King John*, 1.1.79–81.

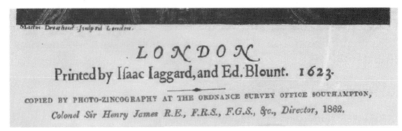

Figure 4.6 Detail of Figure 3.1, showing modified publisher's imprint as it appears in the Royal Ordnance Survey's facsimile of the Shakespeare First Folio (1862).

technologists yet unknown.[87] This addition also begins what appears to have been a tradition of tongue-in-cheek imprints and colophons added by James and his team to some of their facsimiles. Jonson's instruction on the Folio's facing page to "look not on [Shakespeare's] Picture, but his Booke" takes on new meaning when one reads it in the Ordnance Survey facsimile, whose modified title page embodies the technological changes that would transform books in the next century.

It is hard to imagine a modern scholarly digitization project permitting such indulgence by its technical staff, or indeed to imagine information professionals wanting to leave their mark on the Folio's title page, like adding one's own signature on the Mona Lisa. Professional standards, like those laid out in Terras's *Digital Images for the Information Professional* and the guidelines of the Text Encoding Initiative, use metadata and tagging techniques to maintain an inviolable boundary between the objects and agents of digital representation. Yet James and his colleagues violate that boundary with purposive playfulness, literally writing themselves into the bibliographical history of England's documentary heritage in a way that asserts the power of their new technology both to preserve and to alter. (It is a tradition that persists into the era of mass digitization, though perhaps less self-consciously, in the form of

---

[87] The Ordnance Survey exhibits a similar playfulness with the material book in its reproduction of T. J. Bailey's *Ordinum sacrorum in Ecclesia Anglicana defensio*; according to Wakeman, an inserted colophon reads, "*Registro consecrationis Archiepiscopi Parkeri ... photozincographice expresso ...* 1870"; quoted in Wakeman, *Aspects of Victorian Lithography*, p. 57. For a modern counterpart, see the title page of Williams and Lazzuri (eds.), *Foliomania!*, a Folger Shakespeare Library exhibition catalogue that playfully modernizes the First Folio title page.

digitized volumes found on Google Books and the Internet Archive that carry superimposed imprints such as "Digitized by Google" and "Digitized by Microsoft ®".) By contrast, Collier left no record of his assembly of photographic images into a virtual copy of Q1 *Hamlet*, at least in the copies I have examined; aside from his handwritten dedications of individual copies, the Q1 page images seem to speak for themselves. James's more radical approach may well be the more honest of the two: the fanciful imprint may be his single editorial moment of visibility in the facsimile, in the absence of an editorial preface or apparatus, but he takes that opportunity to signal his representational power over the supposedly neutral image. In any case, this chapter's Folio and Q1 facsimile examples, when placed together, show that the expression "the camera never lies" (quoted by Terras to be disproven by her several examples of modern photographic manipulation) is less accurate than the notion that the camera produces a different kind of truth.[88]

However, the perceived instrumental realism of these facsimiles – which, as I have argued, belies their underlying constructivist approaches to representation – had consequences for Shakespearean literary interpretation. For example, a story on Staunton's Folio facsimile in *The Philobiblion* in 1863 laments the inaccuracy of reprints of the Folio and quarto texts, as well as the increasing financial barriers to owning an original copy of these books, yet also contextualizes these problems within a basic textual dilemma:

> These texts [the Folio and quartos] are the only authorities we possess for the words of Shakespeare; and, hurriedly and negligently as they were permitted to appear, *deformed* as they are by typographical and other imperfections, it is to these ancient copies that every reader desirous of fully understanding this transcendent author must first devote his days and nights.[89]

Notable in this statement is the reappearance of Heminge and Condell's language of supersession of previous modes of textual reproduction, denigrating some or all of the quartos as "maimed and deformed."[90] The latter word echoes in *The Philobiblion* writer's language, just as Heminge and Condell's other memorable phrase, "stolne and surreptitious," echoes in an earlier *Athenaeum* writer's description of Q1 *Hamlet* as "a

---

[88] Terras, *Digital Images*, p. 195.
[89] Unsigned article, *The Philobiblion* (September 1863), p. 213, emphasis added.
[90] On Heminge and Condell's statement and the difficulty of interpreting it, see Chapter 3, pp. 87–9.

surreptitious impression."[91] The language of supersession continues in the *Philobiblion* article (some of which we have already considered above):

to meet the ever-growing demand for Shakespeare's early texts, the costly and painful process of tracing every page has latterly been adopted in the case of a few of the quarto plays, and with some success. Even this plan, however, though much less liable to error than reprinting, is by no means infallible. The only possible security against mistake appears to be *photography*. By the help of this invaluable agent, and with an ingenious process of transferring the subject from the collodion negative to zinc or stone, it is practicable, as is shown in the wonderful fac-simile of *Domesday-Book*... so closely resembling the original as almost to defy distinction.[92]

Here, as in the responses to the Collier facsimile, one can see a rhetoric of copies and originals in which the nearly unreproducible material details of the originals take on a new importance, even as the new technologies seem able to collapse the distinction.

This desire for a medium that could convincingly simulate transparency made its way into literary interpretation as facsimiles became part of the Shakespearean landscape of the late Victorian period. Here is a response from Edward Dowden in an 1880 review of several of the Griggs–Furnivall photolithographs of Shakespeare quartos:

A student of Shakespeare's text who possesses the first folio and the quartos may defy the race of commentators and conjecturers; he has the materials for forming an opinion before his own eyes. Such a recurrence to the original sources stimulates the feelings and makes demand on the judgment ... It has been possible to work – and that with no sense of distrust – with one's eye upon a page of Mr. Staunton's *facsimile* or Booth's admirable reprint.[93]

Dowden updates Jonson's injunction from the Folio – look not on Shakespeare's books, but on pictures of his books – with the difference that the affordances of Victorian technology changed what looking meant. That desire to find truth in the corporeality of the text would iterate over a century later in the unediting movement, from which the

[91] Article signed "C.", "Our Weekly Gossip," p. 588; see also note 50 above.
[92] Unsigned article, *The Philobiblion* (September 1863), p. 214, italics in original.
[93] Edward Dowden, review of four Griggs–Furnivall Shakespeare quarto facsimiles, *The Academy*, no. 441 (16 October 1880), p. 270, italics in original.

rationale for image-based digital archives drew considerable strength in the 1990s, as it does today.[94]

In his reassertion of the primacy of the material book, Dowden also alludes to the archive of commentary and emendation that has accumulated around the Shakespeare text, and that itself had found material expression in the New Variorum Shakespeare editions begun by Horace Howard Furness in 1871 (discussed in Chapter 3). The photographic facsimile may have served, in Dowden's eyes, as a kind of anti-variorum in its relation to scholarly commentary, but both kinds of editions could be regarded as expressions of the late Victorian archival fantasies that Victorianists like Thomas Richards have illuminated in other contexts, as what he calls "the collectively imagined junction of all that was known or knowable, a fantastic representation of an epistemological master pattern."[95] The photographic facsimile and the variorum, despite their contrasting natures, are parts of the same Victorian infrastructure for knowledge about Shakespeare. Indeed, the nineteenth-century variorum has been compared to the now-decaying Victorian civic infrastructure of bridges, roads, railways, tunnels, and sewer systems.[96] What I would emphasize in this particular prehistory of the present is the way Shakespeare fits into this larger infrastructure. With the Ordnance Survey, we have an institution of imperial and civic infrastructure developing new technologies for reproducing texts, and looking back to an English documentary archive for texts to reproduce. Documents such as *Domesday Book*, *Magna Carta*, and the Shakespeare First Folio constitute an imagined archive just as much as any physical collection of artifacts. They represent what Pierre Nora calls the crystallization of memory as *lieux de mémoire*, having been invested with the symbolic aura of cultural heritage.[97] This nineteenth-century intersection of the camera and the archive – Sekula's file cabinet metaphor writ large, on the scale of empire – prefigures the intersections of libraries and large-scale digitization initiatives in our own time.

---

[94] See Marcus, *Unediting the Renaissance*, and Egan's chapter on "Materialism, Unediting, and Version-Editing, 1990–1999," in *The Struggle for Shakespeare's Text*, pp. 190–206.

[95] Richards, *Imperial Archive*, p. 11.

[96] Rhodes and Sawday (eds.), *Renaissance Computer*, p. 11.

[97] Nora, *Realms of Memory*, vol. I, pp. 1 and 14. See the discussion of Nora in the Introduction, p. 5.

The digital legacy of Victorian photography

William Morris has predicted that typography will cease to exist during the next century, and he may be right in his forecast. I see it threatened by the camera, the etching fluid, and by the (at present) harmless and inoffensive "typewriter," in the keyboard of which lies the germ of something much greater in the future.

    Robert Coupland Harding, "Concerning Fashion and Taste" (1895)[98]

Photographic reproductions of books – as distinct from scenic depictions such as Talbot's "Scene in a Library" – connect the Shakespearean archive with the photograph's conflicted status as both an imitator of and substitute for prior modes of representation like painting and type facsimiles. In that difference lies the most valuable lesson these facsimiles hold for us: not just the fact that Shakespeare texts were present at the inception of the new technologies, but specifically the ways photography was used. James's and Collier's facsimile projects, along with Michael Warren's *Complete King Lear* and more recent digital experiments, use the camera to model and manipulate what they represent. In other words, they use the camera to edit. Here one can find part of the answer to Julia Flanders's question quoted in this book's introduction, "what pressure does the term 'archive' ... put on the conceptualization of the 'edition'?"[99] The archival and editorial imperatives co-exist within these experiments, serving as a reminder that we are not the first generation to negotiate the divided nature of new media. For the Victorians, as for us, technologies of memory are at once a guarantor of fidelity to the past and a means for intervening in it materially, leaving us with the paradox that to preserve a text is to change it.

The camera, like the telephone and phonograph (both the subject of the next chapter), was one of the technologies through which Victorians

---

[98] Harding, "Concerning Fashion and Taste," p. 488. See also McKenzie, "'What's Past is Prologue,'" p. 273. McKenzie misattributes this quotation to an 1894 issue of Harding's magazine, *Typo* (vol. 8, 27 January), though the Harding essay in *Typo* that McKenzie evidently had in mind, titled "A Hundred Years Hence," deals similarly with Morris's prediction about typography and makes for fascinating reading in its own right. A digitized version is available from the *New Zealand Electronic Text Centre*: nzetc.victoria.ac.nz/tm/scholarly/tei-Har08Typo.html.
[99] Flanders, "The Body Encoded," p. 136. See pp. 4 and 74–5.

imagined the future and reconfigured the past. Our own anxieties about the death of the book are anything but a historical exception, and it is useful to consider how photolithography represents an earlier death of the book – that is, of the book as Victorians knew it at the time. On this point, McKenzie cites the uncanny prophecy made by New Zealand printer and typographer Robert Coupland Harding in 1894 (quoted in the epigraph above). As McKenzie points out, Harding was more of a prophet than he could have known in his statement about the dual promise and threat of the typewriter and its descendants, in that he anticipates what McKenzie calls "the prodigality of texts escaping the definitive forms of print."[100] Like Carlyle, with his proto-digital metaphor of writing in light, Harding in his prophecy imagined our present with uncanny prescience. In an essay titled "A Hundred Years Hence," published in Harding's own *Typo* magazine in 1895, he speculates about the kinds of books that will exist in 1993, and notes the rapid succession of technologies in his own time:

Shorthand is displacing the old writing character; the type-writer is dislodging caligraphy; every branch of printing save type-composition is performed at terrific speed; and the compositor, picking his types one by one, is distanced by every other department. In the writer's apprentice-days all types were cast singly in the hand-mould – now there are many printers who have never seen a hand-cast type.[101]

"In fact, the machines have come," Harding goes on to say, and proceeds to chronicle the effects of familiar devices of the machine-press era such as the Linotype and Monotype, as well as the Thorne composing machine, which discriminates between individual types "with more than human precision."[102] Together with these printing technologies, Harding also marvels at the potential effects of the multiple telegraph and camera, and accurately predicts that "The suggestion that a pile of thousands of sheets will be printed from type-written or other copy by a single electric flash is by no means an incredible one."[103] Harding managed to discern the shape of things to come, and it is notable that his foresight depended not on idealistic references to Gutenberg galaxies but on detailed technical knowledge of printing, writing, and the full history of their transformations.

---

[100] McKenzie, "'What's Past Is Prologue,'" p. 273.
[101] Harding, "A Hundred Years Hence," p. 1.   [102] *Ibid.*   [103] *Ibid.*

Harding's prophecy about the camera replacing letterpress printing came true in the 1950s, decades before the personal computer allegedly began to hasten the death of the book. The letterpress book was an extinct form by the end of the mid-century – at least for most purposes beyond fine printing – having been replaced by various forms of photo-offset printing, in which the printed page remains two-dimensional and never receives the inscriptive bite of type. Robert Bringhurst describes this transition from letterpress to offset printing as a kind of loss; as he puts it, "A book produced by [letterpress] is a folding inscription, a flexible structure in low relief. The black light of the text *shines out from within* a well-printed letterpress page."[104] Long before personal computing sparked new speculation about the death of the book at the hands of other media, the book was already completing a long transition, which one might describe as the death of one kind of book. Although this chapter has focused on early photography for its analogues to digitization, it has also described some of the technological bases for considering the modern book as the product of the camera as much as the Gutenberg press.

That leaves us with an unsettling conclusion about the origin stories we tell about the printed book as a technology. *The Pencil of Nature* is widely recognized as the first book to be illustrated by photography, but the less glamorous Collier Q1 *Hamlet* facsimile stands as a crucial lost ancestor of the present: not simply the first photographic facsimile, but also the first instance of modern photo-offset printing of a complete book – indeed, of a book that could only be called complete through the intervention of photography, as we have seen. Laments and celebrations alike for technological change often invoke Gutenberg's name as the single point of origin for the printed book, but in doing so they overlook the crucial transitional period described in this chapter, without which the modern book could not have come into being.[105] The vast majority of books that readers encounter today bear less technological resemblance to the letterpress books of Gutenberg and other early printers than they do to Collier's humble facsimile, reproduced not by letterpress but by photography in combination with lithographic offset printing.

[104] Bringhurst, *Elements of Typographic Style*, p. 138, emphasis in original.
[105] Adrian Johns critiques that position in other ways in *Nature of the Book*; see his chapter "Faust and the Pirates: The Cultural Construction of the Printing Revolution," pp. 324–79.

Harding clearly understood this, but he might not have realized the consequence that Collier's Q1 facsimile holds for the cultural history of print: that the Q1 *Hamlet* facsimile was the first book to be made using the methods that would displace letterpress printing by the middle of the next century. In other words, the book's technological modernity begins not with Gutenberg's Bible, but with Shakespeare – and it begins surreptitiously, in the form of a forger's facsimile of the bad quarto of *Hamlet*.

5 | Inventing Shakespeare's voice: early sound transmission and recording

The wire sang on overhead with dying falls and melodious rises that invited him to follow; while above the wire rode the stars in their courses, the low nocturne of the former seeming to be the voices of those stars,

> Still quiring to the young-eyed cherubim.

Recalling himself from these reflections Somerset decided to follow the lead of the wire. It was not the first time during his present tour that he had found his way at night by the help of these musical threads which the post-office authorities had erected all over the country for quite another purpose than to guide belated travellers.

Thomas Hardy, *A Laodicean* (1881)[1]

At the beginning of Thomas Hardy's media-obsessed 1881 novel, a young architect finds himself wandering at nightfall in the Wessex countryside until he picks up the strange humming of a telegraph wire, at which moment he naturally thinks of Shakespeare. The architect's decision to follow the wire to its terminus at the castle of his future employer (and eventual bride) sets the plot of *A Laodicean* in motion, and hints at the novel's theme of modernity's imperfect reckoning with the inherited past. The same theme runs through this chapter, which examines the apparent naturalness of invoking Shakespeare in relation to the recording and transmission of sound. In this passage, Hardy's image of telegraph wires as singing "musical threads" takes part in the general project of metaphorical intelligibility that was needed for new media in the late nineteenth century. Hardy references Shakespeare twice in describing the telegraph and information transmission: the wire's singing with "dying falls" alludes to Orsino's words in praise of music in the opening lines of *Twelfth Night* (1.1.4), and the inset quotation comes from Lorenzo's image of the stars emitting the music

---

[1] Hardy, *A Laodicean*, pp. 16–17. I am grateful to Fiona Coll for introducing me to this novel.

of the spheres, as he looks at the night sky with Jessica in *The Merchant of Venice* (5.1.60–2). The "low nocturne" of the telegraph's hum replaces the audible order of the Ptolemaic universe in Hardy's modernizing of Shakespeare's image, though the Shakespearean reference also serves to naturalize the presence of a new technology and its infrastructure on the landscape. However, as the typographical interruption of the inset quotation also hints, the presence of Shakespeare texts in early encounters with sound technologies can also be disruptive, calling attention to what Randall McLeod calls information's transformission.[2]

The telephone, like the telegraph before it, raised the particular challenge of representing information in its invisible yet material forms. As we shall see, that challenge was shared by technologists, journalists, actors, poets, and novelists all alike. The dynamic between Shakespeare and technology, along with the emergent problem of representing the elusive materiality of a new phenomenon called information, also runs through the emergent genre of the nineteenth-century tech demo. It is a genre, past and present, that depends upon the thrill of the new, and upon a sense of the future erupting into the present under the guiding hand of the scientific inventor. That relation between audience, inventor, and technological artifact is usually routed through the prototype, as a kind of unfinished yet portentous object of apprehension and curiosity. Many textual scholars and media historians have been looking back to sound technology's earliest prototyping periods in recognition of what Lisa Gitelman calls the value of "the novelty years, transitional states, and identity crises of different media."[3] Considering the telephone and the computer in their prototypical forms, before they solidified into *the* telephone and *the* computer, serves to dislodge the technological essentialism that besets discussions of digital media in the present.

To restate this book's premise, it matters when technologists use Shakespeare to test, demonstrate, and authenticate new media prototypes, even though claims for the appeal of new media usually rest on their ability to represent nearly anything. A confident assertion of content-neutrality often underpins progress-driven histories of technology, in which materials like literary texts become passive content to be

---

[2] See the discussion of Randall McLeod's portmanteau term *transformission* in Chapter 2, p. 56.
[3] Gitelman, *Always Already New*, p. 1.

remediated by the active agents in the equation, the new media themselves. My interest throughout this book is in how cultural materials push back, mutually shaping the media (and the avatars of those media) which seek to appropriate them into technological progress narratives. It is also my premise that the interactions between humans, texts, and machines become nowhere more fraught than in new media's appropriation of Shakespeare in their formative stages. To reproduce or transmit Shakespeare texts through a new medium is to engage with some of the most textually and ontologically complex material in the Western literary tradition, considering not only Shakespeare's editorial history but also its relation to performance, which has never been a matter of simple derivation. Shakespeare is not the only English writer with an immensely complex textual tradition, but what I have termed the Shakespearean archive takes shape when that textual complexity interacts with the imperatives of cultural heritage, which privilege authenticity, wholeness, and transmissibility. This is why one finds Shakespeare involved in so many technological versions of what Pierre Nora calls *lieux de mémoire*, or material and symbolic sites where, as he puts it, "memory is crystallized."[4] Only the Bible can rank alongside Shakespeare as such a powerful confluence of cultural imperatives and material intractabilities; one cannot say the same for, say, Charles Dickens or nineteenth-century newspapers, fascinating as they are in their own contexts, and important as scholarship on them continues to be.[5] Shakespeare's texts therefore make a difference in the meaning of new media as cultural events, even in Shakespeare's paradoxical interchangeability with other forms of information.

Where the preceding chapter explored that difference with regard to photography and Victorian visual culture, this chapter is concerned specifically with sound and its emerging technologies, both of transmission (the telephone) and recording (the phonograph). As with photography, Shakespeare was present at some of sound technology's formative moments in ways that condition the meaning of those technologies and of Shakespeare alike in the cultural imagination. This chapter focuses on the work of Alexander Graham Bell and Thomas

---

[4] Nora, *Realms of Memory*, vol. I, p. 1.

[5] On the comparison between Shakespeare and the Bible in this context, see DeCook and Galey's Introduction to *Shakespeare, the Bible, and the Form of the Book*, and the chapters in that collection.

Edison, both of whom came to define the identity of the inventor, and both of whom happened to be devotees of Shakespeare. Edison, for one, boarded with actors, attended Shakespeare performances, occasionally imitated Richard III during his early career as a telegraph operator in Cincinnati, and is said to have refined his telegraphic hand and ear by practicing on Shakespeare plays.[6] Bell, likewise, was exposed to Shakespearean speeches from an early age thanks to his father, the famous elocutionist Alexander Melville Bell, who lectured many times on Shakespeare's plays. This chapter considers their recruitment of Shakespeare in the prototyping and exhibition stages of various aspects of their work, and focuses especially on three of their inventions: Bell's telephone in 1876–8; Edison's kinetophone in 1913; and Bell's graphophone, developed in the early 1880s but rediscovered in the archives in 1937 and again in 2010. Rather than attempting to sketch a general history of Shakespeare and sound technology, this chapter continues this book's strategy of reading specific scenes from the Shakespearean archive that illustrate the complex relationships between Shakespeare, media, and information.[7]

Preceding chapters tended to focus on artifacts; in this chapter, however, the arrival of sound technology means that we must reckon with the tech demo as a special genre of performance, in which the artifact is but one actor. As in performance criticism of Shakespeare, events are difficult to reconstitute through documentary evidence and impossible to recapture entirely, just as they are impossible to experience in totality from any single human perspective. Aural media also remind us that events cannot be reduced to any one kind of sensory experience, even though the visual tends to be information culture's dominant register of experience, then as now. For that reason, I have resisted the temptation to use the term *media spectacle* to describe the instances of technological theatricalism analyzed here, even though researchers such as Carolyn Marvin have shown how spectacular new media could be in the late nineteenth and early twentieth centuries.[8] (As a thought experiment, when reading the accounts of listening audiences in this chapter,

---

[6] Israel, *Edison*, pp. 28–9; *Papers of Thomas A. Edison*, vol. I, pp. 16 and 22, n. 45.

[7] Histories of Shakespeare and sound recording may be found in Lanier, "Shakespeare on the Record," and Buchanan, *Shakespeare on Silent Film*.

[8] See Marvin, *When Old Technologies Were New*, especially her chapter "Dazzling the Multitude: Original Media Spectacles," pp. 152–90.

imagine what those people were doing with their eyes as they strained to hear – especially those sitting in theatres and music halls, where they were used to having their gaze directed by the performers.) I have instead settled on the somewhat less satisfying term *tech demo*, colloquial abbreviation and all, partly for its relative sensory neutrality and partly for its seeming anachronism. However, by the end of this chapter I hope that any sense of anachronism will be proved illusory, considering that Shakespearean tech demos of over a century ago helped create a genre in which digital humanists perform today.

"I see a voice": inscribing sounds, voicing inscriptions

As an aural counterpoint to the *Hamlet*-quoting stereoscope ad from 1856 discussed in the preceding chapter (see Figure 4.1), consider the 1908 National Phonograph Company ad shown in Figure 5.1, in which a multiracial group of servants and masters happily shares the aural experience of recorded music – a scene of social and racial concord epitomized by the quasi-Shakespearean caption, "One touch of harmony makes the whole world kin."[9] Like the recontextualization of Hamlet's "Seems Madam! Nay, it IS!" in the stereoscope ad, this oft-quoted line from *Troilus and Cressida* also means something rather different in context when spoken by Shakespeare's own advertising expert, Ulysses, to persuade the truculent Achilles to leave his tent and rejoin the Greek forces besieging Troy. Ulysses' appeal to Achilles' vanity plays upon a cynical valorization of newness that corresponds with new media's reception in 1908 as well as the present:

> One touch of nature makes the whole world kin –
> That all with one consent praise new-born gauds,
> Though they are made and moulded of things past,
> And give to dust that is a little gilt
> More laud than gilt o'er-dusted.   (*Troilus and Cressida* 3.3.169–73)

As in the Hardy epigraph above, the new media context both evokes and changes the meaning of the original, here with "harmony" silently displacing the word "nature" in the original context. It is a telling substitution, considering that "harmony" is a property of the

---

[9] As printed in *McClure's Magazine*, 31.1 (May 1908), p. 17. For Gitelman's reading of the same ad, see *Scripts, Grooves*, pp. 137–8.

"One touch of harmony makes the whole world kin."

THE Phonograph would never have become the great popular entertainer it is but for Edison. He made it desirable by making it good; he made it popular by making it inexpensive.

The EDISON PHONOGRAPH

has brought within reach of all, entertainm⟨ nt which formerly only people of means could afford. It has even displaced more expensive amusements in homes where expense is not considered.

Figure 5.1 Detail of a National Phonograph Company advertisement (1908), captioned with a paraphrase from *Troilus and Cressida*, "One touch of harmony makes the whole world kin."

machine's recorded music, while "nature" in Ulysses' speech is a governing property of humans – though it supposedly governed them differently in the racially polarized America of 1908. Recontextualized within the racialized social schema of the phonograph ad, the fragment of Ulysses' larger speech serves both to recruit literature, putting the words of Shakespeare at the service of the National Phonograph Company, and to trouble the ad's representation of social history, as the displaced word "nature" waits in the wings to question the hierarchies that the ad both erases and enforces. In its Shakespearean gesture of bridging social difference through shared media experience, the ad implicitly re-emphasizes the divisions that would again take effect once the music stopped.

Ads like this are recognizably part of the visual culture of the early twentieth century, but cultural historians and media archaeologists have recently been working to show that the nineteenth and early twentieth centuries had aural cultures as well. John Picker's *Victorian Soundscapes*, for example, seeks to "turn the Victorian gaze on its ear" by linking the study of Victorian science and technology to "literary and cultural representations of sound, voice, and hearing."[10] In a more trenchant critique of technological determinism that evokes Wolfgang Ernst's approach to media archaeology, Jonathan Sterne argues for a cultural history of sound reproduction that rejects the impact narratives in which technologies are depicted as self-contained and autonomous agents from their moments of origin. As Sterne claims, "Such narratives cast technologies themselves as primary agents of historical change: technological deification is the religion behind claims like 'the telephone changed the way we do business,' 'the phonograph changed the way we listen to music.'"[11] These impact-narrative truisms echo in the discourse surrounding digital humanities today, much of which breathlessly repeats variants of the phrase "the computer has changed the way humanists think and work." Given that cultural historians of sound have been working through complex questions of determinism, materiality, and technological change in their field for many years prior to the latest rise of the digital humanities, what can their approaches teach us about the long history of literary texts and new media? What difference does the content of early experiences of sound technology make to the ways they were received and understood, especially when that content was material like Shakespeare's *Hamlet*, whose supernatural themes complicate the "technological deification" that Sterne identifies? These questions will lurk in the background noise as we consider various scenes of various sound technologies' earliest appearances, along with Shakespeare's role in shaping their meaning (and vice versa).

---

[10] Picker, *Victorian Soundscapes*, p. 7. Cf. Lastra's aim of reintroducing "'sound' into modernity and modernity into 'sound,'" in *Sound Technology*, p. 4.
[11] Sterne, *Audible Past*, p. 7.

One factor that complicates any cultural history of sound is the idea of inscription as a link between the technical and symbolic function of media, which we have already considered in relation to Shakespeare and archives (see Chapter 2). Cultural historians of media have also emphasized the importance of inscription in understanding both the material properties of new media and their cultural representations, which do not always align.[12] Katherine Hayles defines inscriptive media as any technology that can "initiate material changes that can be read as marks," which she takes to include letter-press and photo-offset books as well as digital computers.[13] Gitelman nuances this definition with the distinction that "Unlike radio signals ... inscriptions are stable and savable."[14] As Gitelman's example of radio waves suggests, patterned disturbances in air pressure or the electromagnetic spectrum may not qualify as readable marks. Hayles also argues for inscription's importance as a cultural trope, asserting that "the materiality of inscription thoroughly interpenetrates the represented world," and her point is borne out by the struggle to render sound as inscription in nineteenth-century media.[15]

Bell's father, Alexander Melville Bell, wrestled with the problem in his elocutionary work, and devised an elaborate writing system that he called Visible Speech, intended to guide deaf speakers in their pronunciation and to encourage them to abandon signing.[16] A section of "Illustrative Readings" in one of Melville Bell's several promotional pamphlets renders several Shakespearean passages as Visible Speech, beginning with a soliloquy from *Hamlet* (Figure 5.2).[17] This 1886 pamphlet shows a remarkably early translation of Shakespeare text into a new encoding system, though in this case the code was intended not for machine processing but for a human learning to enunciate words with little or no aural feedback. The choice of Hamlet's "What a piece of work is man" speech to lead off the examples may have been deliberate,

---

[12] See, pp. 46–56. [13] Hayles, *Writing Machines*, p. 24.

[14] Gitelman, *Always Already New*, p. 6. [15] Hayles, *Writing Machines*, p. 130.

[16] Jennifer Esmail deals with the conflicted legacy of Bell's work with the deaf in *Reading Victorian Deafness*. For her discussion of Visible Speech specifically, see pp. 183–4. Esmail reproduces an image from an 1867 Melville Bell pamphlet showing Portia's "quality of mercy" speech from *The Merchant of Venice* (4.1.181–202) depicted in Visible Speech, which the pamphlet claims "as pronounced in the time of Shakespeare." See also Lepore's chapter on visible speech in *A Is for American*, pp. 162–86.

[17] Alexander Melville Bell, *English Line-Writing*, p. 30. A digitized version is available at www.archive.org/details/englishlinewriti00bell.

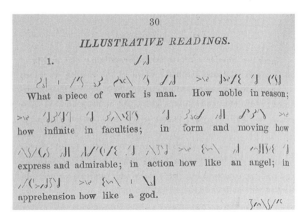

Figure 5.2 Lines of *Hamlet* rendered as Visible Speech in Alexander Melville Bell's pamphlet *English Line-Writing: A New, Simple, and Exact System of Phonetics* (1886).

considering its optimistic representation of human capacities (provided it is taken without irony). The selection of Shakespearean set-pieces mixed with other literary passages not only adds another layer of orality to the complex relationship between Shakespearean stages and pages, but also locates that orality specifically within the bodies of deaf people, whose precise movements were to be disciplined by Visible Speech.

Shakespeare provided a helpful imaginative framing of the process of rendering sound as inscription and vice versa.[18] At least two witnesses of early sound technology demos seized upon Bottom's moment of synesthesia in the final act of *A Midsummer Night's Dream*, in which Bottom acts the part of Pyramus seeking his lover on the other side of the wall: "I see a voice. Now will I to the chink / To spy and I can hear my Thisbe's face" (5.1.191–2). Bottom's comic mismatching of senses and phenomena served to express the paradox of inscribable sounds and soundable inscriptions for a *Boston Daily Advertiser* reporter, who prefaced a story about a Visible Speech lecture in 1874 with the quotation "I see a voice."[19] Similarly, an 1875 *Boston Evening Transcript*

[18] Richard Menke similarly emphasizes literary texts as agents in the formation of Victorian information culture; see Menke, *Telegraphic Realism*, pp. 3–5.

[19] From a handwritten transcription of an article attributed to the *Boston Daily Advertiser* (10 April 1874); *Bell Family Papers*, box 403, folder titled "'Visible Speech' Lecture Before Boston Society of the Arts, April 1874." References to

story about Bell's early sound-wave visualization system, the phonautograph, makes the same Shakespearean allusion to describe its impression of the device:

Until lately, one did not expect, except it be in "a midsummer night's dream," to see a sound. But now we have changed all that ... [Bell] displayed upon a large camera the very air ripples or sound waves produced in sounding various words and letters as registered upon a glass surface treated with a coating of lampblack by means of a pencil operated by the reverberating human ear-drum.[20]

The phonautograph, unlike Visible Speech, depended upon the disembodiment of speech in the most literal way, even to the extent of incorporating a human cadaver's ear into the system.[21] These *Midsummer Night's Dream* references, juxtaposed with the Shakespearean "Illustrative Readings" for Visible Speech, together define the multiple relationships between Shakespeare and technology that this chapter will explore. Shakespeare served as exemplary content for new aural media, but also as an imaginative framework through which the changing relationships between sound and inscription might be understood.[22]

items in the Library of Congress's *Alexander Graham Bell Family Papers, 1834–1974* collection are given throughout under the short title *Bell Family Papers*, with box number and folder name, as well as original publication information (where available) in the case of newspaper clippings and other published materials included in the collection. A digitized portion of the collection and a finding aid may be found at www.loc.gov/collection/alexander-graham-bell-papers/. I am grateful to the staff at the Library of Congress Manuscript Reading Room, Madison Building, for their assistance with these materials.

[20] Reprinted in *The Silent World* (15 February 1875); *Bell Family Papers*, box 403, folder titled "Visualization of Vibrations of Speech, Salem, Mass, Jan 19, 1875."

[21] On the phonautograph, see Sterne, *The Audible Past*, pp. 52–6; and Esmail's chapter "'Finding the Shapes of Sounds': Prosthetic Technology, Speech, and Victorian Deafness," in *Reading Victorian Deafness*, pp. 163–91.

[22] The phrase "I see a voice" also furnishes the title of Jonathan Rée's 1999 book, subtitled *Deafness, Language and the Senses – a Philosophical History*, which deals with Shakespeare and Visible Speech (pp. 258–65) and reproduces a figure from Joshua Steele's 1775 *Essay Towards Establishing the Melody and Measure of Speech* that represents those qualities in Hamlet's "To be, or not to be" soliloquy using modified musical notation (p. 256). See also Esmail's discussion of Kate Field's "Pen Photographs" of Charles Dickens's public readings, and Field's reference to Bottom's line when she wishes for a means of synesthetically visualizing speech; Esmail, *Reading Victorian Deafness*, p. 100.

Accounts of the development of sound technologies often describe scenes of the inventors straining to make out messages amid silence or noise. With the telephone, those test messages often amounted to ordinary speech acts, such as "Do you understand what I say?" or the famous first telephonic transmission, "Mr. Watson – come here – I want to see you," sent by Bell to his assistant Thomas Watson in the telephone's first expression of bodily absence and desire.[23] An example of this kind of prototypical telephonic exchange is recounted as an exhibit in an 1880 telephone patent case, in an exchange that occurred during prototyping in October, 1876, according to Bell's lab notes:

BELL TO WATSON.　　– If you understand what I say, say something to me.

WATSON TO BELL.　　– It is (decidedly) the best I ever saw.

BELL TO WATSON.　　– It is the best *I* ever heard.

WATSON TO BELL.　　– Success at last has (*attended*) our efforts.

BELL TO WATSON.

> "Let us then be up and doing,
>> With a heart for any fate.
> Still untiring, still pursuing,
>> Learn to labor and to wait."[24]

Bell caps off the telephonic test with poetry, in this case the final stanza from Henry Wadsworth Longfellow's "A Psalm of Life." In moments like this a stanza of poetry becomes ontologically layered. In one sense, the stanza's status as a shared cultural reference serves to naturalize its utterance as a speech act, despite its seeming incongruousness in this scientific test (and, later, legal testimony). In a different sense, poetry becomes just another sequence of sound waves to be converted into electrical signals and back again, transmitted through an information system utterly indifferent to content. (A definition which, notably, works only when the humans are not considered part of the information system.) In yet another sense, this transmitted poem remains very much a poem in the typographical form it takes in the court testimony, in which the transcriber of Bell's notebook has made sure to reproduce

---

[23] See Bruce, *Bell*, pp. 181–2.

[24] *Telephone Suits*, part II, p. 84, italics in original. I am unable to tell what the italics and parentheses mean in this transcript; they could indicate notes on delivery, or the transcriber's interpolations, or one of each.

bibliographic codes such as lineation, indentation, and capitalization. Typographic intervention into the representation of sound is also visible in the italicized "*I*" in Bell's correction of Watson, where Bell emphasizes hearing over seeing.

Similarly, Bell's paper for the American Academy of Arts and Sciences on 10 May 1876, highlights the value of recognizable cultural texts as test content:

> Familiar quotations, such as, "To be, or not to be; that is the question." "A horse, a horse, my kingdom for a horse." "What hath God wrought," &c., were generally understood after a few repetitions. The effects were not sufficiently distinct to admit of sustained conversation through the wire. Indeed, as a general rule, the articulation was unintelligible, excepting when familiar sentences were employed.[25]

Bell continues to describe how their tests moved from these recognizable quotations – which, notably, included not just Shakespeare but also the famous inaugural phrase sent by telegraph, "What hath God wrought" – on to the basic linguistic components of speech. However, as in the Longfellow example, the dramatic effects of surprise, triggered by variances in reception quality, also become part of the experimental process in this example, with changes in the state of the technological system registering as aural experiences of literature. As Bell goes on to describe, "Occasionally . . . a sentence would come out with such startling distinctness as to render it difficult to believe that the speaker was not close at hand." Modern listeners can experience similar moments of recognition thanks to recent recovery and digitization efforts by the Smithsonian National American History Museum and the Lawrence Berkeley National Laboratory, who have been working with early graphophone recordings deposited with the Smithsonian by Bell's Volta Laboratory in the 1880s. Their earliest deposited record includes the spoken lines "There are more things in heaven and earth, Horatio, / Than are dreamed of in our philosophy" (*Hamlet* 1.5.168–9), and another contains several lines of Hamlet's "To be, or not to be" soliloquy (3.1.58–90). Both may be heard at the website *FirstSounds.org*, and will receive more detailed discussion below. As in other examples, there is no small irony in the choice of the first *Hamlet* quotation to signify successful transmission, given that it is often slightly misquoted in similar contexts

---

[25] Alexander Graham Bell, "Researches in Telephony," p. 8.

(see below), with "your philosophy" appearing in at least one case (which happens to match the allegedly corrupt Q1 text) as well as the erroneous plural "philosophies." However, the point may be that it functions successfully as a Shakespeare quotation even when inaccurate, just as "play it again, Sam" calls to mind *Casablanca* even though no character speaks that exact phrase in the film.

Like Bell, Edison occasionally used Shakespeare as test material for prototyping and publicizing his inventions. For example, Gitelman indicates that during the prototyping in 1875 and 1876 of what Edison called an electric pen – a device for transmitting writing over electrical wires, like a fax machine from the 1990s – Edison and his associates would repeatedly test the device using the opening speech from *Richard III*, beginning with the line "Now is the winter of our discontent" (see Figure 5.3).[26] For Edison and his assistants, these lines served as an equivalent to the phrase *hello world* for programmers today: traditional words whose appearance as output signals at least one little victory, and would iterate many times throughout the development process. Gitelman mentions that some of this text even shows up in the illustrations for the patent, and emphasizes that it matters that Edison used Shakespeare for these tests; as she points out, "Edison selected Shakespeare randomly perhaps, electing the first line of his favorite play out of myriad possibilities, but the phrase appropriately became his 'Eureka!' implying a nowness, an emphatic present, as stencils made with the electric pen got better and better as the device was improved."[27] The ironies of using Richard's words to signify fidelity to originals and legitimacy in lines of succession may or may not have been lost on Edison, who apparently made habitual use of these lines as test material throughout his career.[28] A *New York Daily Graphic* article of the

---

[26] Gitelman, *Scripts, Grooves*, pp. 161–2. This and many other notebooks may be viewed at Rutgers University's online *Thomas A. Edison Papers Project*: edison. rutgers.edu/NamesSearch/SingleDoc.php3?DocId=NE1676255. The project's online newsletter, *The Edisonian*, has gathered links to several documents showing Edison's use of *Richard*. I am grateful to Paul Israel, the project's director and general editor, for supplying Figure 5.3.

[27] Gitelman, *Scripts, Grooves*, p. 162.

[28] A telephone demo conducted by Edison and his assistant, Charles Batchelor, in 1878 (as Bell's own telephone demos were achieving great success) included the recitation of the *Richard III* opening, coupled with the ubiquitous "Mary had a little lamb" (*Papers of Thomas A. Edison*, vol. IV, p. 102, n. 2.). For a discussion of *Richard III*'s connections to media, and particularly of media allegories in Richard Loncraine's 1995 film version starring Ian MacKellan, see Donaldson, "Cinema and the Kingdom of Death."

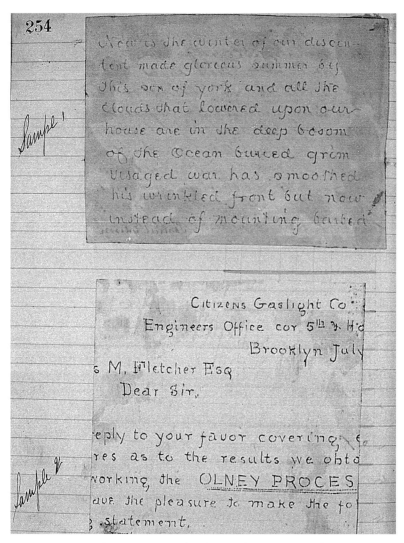

Figure 5.3 Two electric pen samples from Edison's notebooks, showing the opening lines of *Richard III* and a business letter.

same year describes a phonograph demonstration at Edison's Menlo Park laboratory, where the great inventor reportedly took requests:

"What'll you have next?" asks Edison. "Shakespeare," replies THE GRAPHIC. And the inventor gives this to the [recording] machine in a solemn tone:

"Now is the winter of our discontent
Made glorious summer by this son of York;
And all the clouds that lower'd upon our house
In the deep bosom of the ocean buried!"

It was returned [by the phonograph upon playback] in a tone of voice and accentuation almost melancholy, the declamation being quite tragic. The word "lowered" was mispronounced as it had been at first, to rhyme with "board" instead of "showered," and many characteristics of the voice were preserved.[29]

Inscription and iteration are key tropes in this demo, as in the electric pen's prototyping, but here the reporter also comments on two elements that will echo throughout other examples in this chapter: the easy transmissibility of variance and error (i.e. the supposed mispronunciation of "lowered"); and the transformative effects of mediation upon performance, with the tragic tone of the speaker not only "preserved" by the recording, but now attributable to the speaking machine itself. Edison understood transformission, and put it to work.

The experiences of the inventors, their assistants, and the occasional invited witness to these scenarios soon became the experiences of audiences at public tech demos. Recognition became a stock effect of the public performances of new media, whose exhibitors drew upon a range of literary and other examples to delight and amaze heterogeneous audiences. As Gitelman describes with reference to Edison phonograph demos, "In making their selections for recording and playback, exhibitors made incongruous associations between well-known lines from both Shakespeare and Mother Goose, between talented musicians and hacks ... between animal and baby noises and the articulate sounds of speech. Audiences could ... participate together in the enactment of cultural hierarchy."[30] As we shall see, Edison and Bell both knew how

---

[29] William Croffut, "The Papa of the Phonograph: An Afternoon with Edison, the Inventor of the Talking Machines," *New York Daily Graphic* (2 April 1878), reprinted in *Papers of Thomas A. Edison*, vol. IV, pp. 217–18. In this story, the Shakespeare was preceded by playback of some ordinary conversation and utterances in other languages and dialects; it was followed by a few lines from Thomas Gray's "Elegy Written in a Country Church-Yard" ("The path of glory leads but to the grave") and an anecdote about Edison having recorded a barking dog a few days before.

[30] Gitelman, *Always Already New*, p. 35; on specific instances of mixing Shakespeare and Mother Goose in exhibitions, see p. 33.

to recruit Shakespeare into the emerging genre of the public tech demo – though, as ever, Shakespeare's recontextualized works made meanings of their own.

Performing *Hamlet* with Alexander Graham Bell

Hamlet, more than any other of Shakespeare's plays, has become a strange attractor for discussions of media archaeology, especially those concerned with memory, inscription, transmission, and, oddly enough, the telephone.[31] Richard Burt and Julian Yates offer a recent example in their reading of *Hamlet*'s telephonic messages and dropped calls, drawing on Avital Ronell's experimental and provocative account in *The Telephone Book: Technology – Schizophrenia – Electric Speech*; as Ronell puts it, "To be, or not to be" became "the telephone's most sacredly repeated declamation before an audience" and marks "the interstice between ghostly conjuration and the voice of the other."[32] *Hamlet*'s preoccupation with communication and liminality provides an imaginative framing for experiments with the telephone as a new medium, in which the heroic figure of the inventor, in command of an uncanny new technology, compels distant ghosts to speak. Alexander Graham Bell may have been attracted to *Hamlet*'s "To be, or not to be" speech as test material in his telephone demos for these or other reasons, but it was a consequential choice in any case, as Douglas Lanier argues: "Bell's choice of Hamlet's soliloquy, with its focus on bodily presence and absence and its concerns about the unpredictabilities of the hereafter, uncannily anticipates issues that haunt audio reproduction in general and the phonographic recording of Shakespeare in particular."[33] This section explores these themes through archival records of Bell's demos, and considers how *Hamlet* became an uncanny presence in the earliest networks of the transmitted human voice.

Bell and Shakespeare shared an early crucial moment on stage together at the 1876 Centennial Exhibition in Philadelphia on 25 June, in a demonstration of Bell's telephone prototype that would later prove decisive in the invention's history. Various first-hand

---

[31] On inscription and erasure in *Hamlet*, see Stallybrass *et al.*, "Hamlet's Tables"; Ayers, "Reading, Writing, and *Hamlet*"; and Galey, "Tablets of the Law."

[32] Ronell, *The Telephone Book*, p. 283; see also pp. 283–5, and Burt and Yates, *What's the Worst*, pp. 23–6.

[33] Lanier, "Shakespeare on the Record," p. 415.

accounts of the event can be found in the Bell Family Papers at the Library of Congress, which includes both private letters and newspaper clippings, and in the published record of a telephone patent case that began in 1878, in which several of the participants in the Philadelphia demo gave testimony.[34] Most accounts depict Bell as the underdog at the event, receiving a marginal exhibition space in contrast to his competitor, Elisha Gray, who was exhibiting his telegraph in the same building. Apparently Bell's invention might have gone unnoticed without the intervention of Dom Pedro, the Emperor of Brazil, whose party had been touring the exhibits along with a panel of the Exhibition's judges headed by Sir William Thompson (later Lord Kelvin). The Emperor, who had met Bell on a previous occasion, took an interest in Bell and steered the judges' party toward his telephone exhibit, where they heard, among other things, lines from *Hamlet* spoken through the telephone.

Thompson recounted his experience of Bell's demonstration in an address to the British Association in Glasgow a few months later:

In the Canadian department I heard "To be or not to be ... there's the rub," through an electric telegraph wire; but, scorning monosyllables, the electric articulation rose to higher flights, and gave me passages taken at random from the New York newspapers: – " S.S. Cox has arrived" (I failed to make out the S.S. Cox); "The City of New York," "Senator Morton," "The Senate has resolved to print a thousand extra copies;" "The Americans in London have resolved to celebrate the coming 4th of July." All this my own ears heard, spoken to me with unmistakable distinctness by the thin circular disc armature of just such another little electro-magnet as this which I hold in my hand ... This, the greatest by far of all the marvels of the electric telegraph, is due to a young countryman of our own, Mr. Graham Bell.[35]

---

[34] For a full account, see Bruce, *Bell*, pp. 188–98. The published records of the patent case are cited here under *Telephone Suits*.

[35] Sir William Thompson, address to the British Association, Glasgow, p. 427, first ellipses in original. Count du Moncel, in an account of the event published just three years after, quotes a slightly different though perhaps more eloquent version of Thompson's opening line: "in the Canadian department I heard 'To be or not to be? There's the rub,' uttered through a telegraphic wire, and its pronunciation by electricity only made the rallying tone of the monosyllables more emphatic"; du Moncel, *The Telephone*, pp. 36–7. Noting the "translative leaps of memory recall" that may account for the divergent accounts, Avital Ronell points out that "the telephone has begun to produce telephonic effects by the sheer fact of its existence" (*Telephone Book*, p. 285).

As a public face of Victorian science himself, Kelvin speaks before the British Association as a witness before a jury, dispelling doubts about the new technology with the evidence of his senses. Thompson's own report as head of the Exhibition's panel of judges stresses the experiential weight of his evidence: "I need scarcely say I was astonished and delighted; so were others . . . who witnessed the experiments and verified with their own ears the electric transmission of speech."[36] His report concludes,

perhaps the greatest marvel hitherto achieved by the electric telegraph, has been achieved by appliances of quite a homespun and rudimentary character. With somewhat more advanced plans, and more powerful apparatus, we may confidently expect that Mr. Bell will give us the means of making voice and spoken words audible through the electric wire to an ear hundreds of miles distant.[37]

For Thompson, this was a technology with a future. His prediction would prove true in short order, and Bell's fortunes improved dramatically following the 1876 Philadelphia Exhibition demo.

Key to this scientific narrative is the presence of Shakespearean content among the aural proof chosen by Bell to convince the receiver of the message's validity. The uncanny experience of hearing Shakespeare's words through a strange new medium was a calculated effect, one significantly coupled with hearing extracts from a newspaper, the most familiar late-nineteenth century medium for disposable information. Bell's demo in Philadelphia thus appears to distinguish Shakespeare from information while deftly drawing an equivalence between them as content for the same medium. As Douglas Lanier suggests with regard to this episode, "perhaps, too, [Bell] wanted to show his audience the invention's capacity for transmitting messages more weighty than nursery rhymes, conventional speeches and popular songs."[38] As the reasoning went, if the telephone can faithfully transmit the best that has been thought and said in English literature – which also

---

[36] Sir William Thompson, "Report on Awards, Group XXV., Centennial Exhibition . . . Alexander Graham Bell, Salem, Mass., US," reprinted in *Telephone Suits*, part II, p. 35. See also Silvanus P. Thompson, *Life of William Thompson*, vol. II, p. 671.

[37] *Telephone Suits*, part II, p. 35. Thompson was later called upon to testify to these events in another patent challenge; his testimony of 24 January 1882, was reprinted in part in Jones, "A Review," pp. 296–7.

[38] Lanier, "Shakespeare on the Record," p. 415.

has the virtue of sounding familiar, and is easy to pick up through a low-fidelity medium – surely it will be serviceable enough for everyday use. In Bell's demonstration, the very words of Shakespeare embodied connectivity.

The Shakespeare text also helped the participants in the Philadelphia Exposition demo play up the theatricality of the event. For example, Elisha Gray, who had joined the party, recounted what he witnessed in his testimony for a patent suit a few years later:

> The Emperor had just been using the receiving instrument, and as he took it down from his ear and started away to the transmitting end, he said, "To be or not to be." From this I took the cue as to what was being recited at the transmitting end. I listened intently for some moments, hearing a very faint, ghostly, ringing sort of a sound; but finally, I thought I caught the words, "Aye, there's the rub." I turned to the audience, repeating these words, and they cheered.[39]

Gray's account reveals that he was aware of the audience as such, and knew his part. Contemporary newspaper accounts also highlight the theatricality of Bell's demonstration, usually with Thompson and especially the Emperor of Brazil cast in the roles of witnesses. One account, attributed in the article to Bell himself, reads like the successful presentation of a gift in a royal court:

> [Dom Pedro] took me by the arm and spoke most enthusiastically about my telephone work, which rather opened the eyes of the judges, tired though they were with the day's strain. When he took one end of the line and I took the other and began to repeat Shakespeare to him in the best dramatic style at my command, and "To be or not to be" whizzed into the ear of the venerable Emperor, my victory was complete.[40]

This story casts Bell as an actor, and attributes his "victory" to a mix of technological achievement, royal graciousness, and dramatic performance. Another account emphasizes the Emperor's role as an actor in this piece of technology theatre:

> Mr. Bell placed his royal friend at the receiving end of the line. At the other end he took up his own position and spoke into the transmitter the query, "Is it to be

---

[39] Elisha Gray, "Deposition of Elisha Gray," in *Telephone Suits*, part I, p. 138.

[40] Undated article titled "Bell's Electric Toy" from an unidentified newspaper; *Bell Family Papers*, box 321, folder titled "United States International Exhibition, Philadelphia, 1876."

or not to be?" The startled monarch gave a spring, exclaiming, "My God! it speaks!" and shouted back the prophetic response, "It is to be! It is to be!" That moment decided the fate, fame, and fortune of Alexander Graham Bell.[41]

One suspects a certain amount of poetic license in these versions of events. However, the point here is not the fidelity of the account to the event, but the ways these contemporary accounts invite their readers to imagine the event, with *Hamlet* serving as a kind of script to stage the encounter with new media. The Emperor of Brazil, as depicted in the second story, echoes Hamlet's shock at finally hearing the voice of the Ghost in his encounter on the battlements ("it speaks!"), and even answers the Shakespearean existential question in his own words ("It is to be!"). Even Gray, an engineer giving testimony in a legal deposition, resorts to the imaginative word "ghostly" to describe the sound of a voice coming through the noise.

Jonathan Sterne emphasizes that a medium cannot be reduced to any specific device, such as the one Bell exhibited in Philadelphia; rather, Sterne argues, "a medium is a network of repeatable relations."[42] For the telephone, that repeatability of relations grew from late 1876 through 1878 as Bell took his invention on tour through the eastern United States and then to England, where he performed demonstrations for the public on the stages of theatres and music halls, often including *Hamlet* among his aural samples.[43] A sequel to the Philadelphia episode was reported in the *London Times* of January 16, 1878 as a private performance for Queen Victoria and members of her household given at Osborne House on the Isle of Wight on two days prior, with a telephonic connection to nearby Osborne Cottage, the home of the Queen's private secretary.[44] The demo included a performance by the American journalist and actor Kate Field, who happened to be making a

---

[41] Article titled "The Bell Telephone," from an unidentified Olathe, Kansas newspaper dated 13 September 1894, and noted as a reprint from the *Deaf-Mute's Journal* of 23 August; *Bell Family Papers*, box 321, folder titled "United States International Exhibition, Philadelphia, 1876."

[42] Sterne, *Audible Past*, p. 210.

[43] For a general account of Bell's telephone lecture tour, see Rhodes, *Beginnings of Telephony*, pp. 40–3.

[44] "The Telephone at Court," *London Times* (16 January 1878). See also Scharnhorst, *Kate Field*, pp. 125–30. Picker describes a more elaborate program for the event, including a long-distance connection to an orchestra, and reproduces a depiction of Bell's demo for the Queen from a yellowback railway novel cover; see *Victorian Soundscapes*, pp. 101, 103.

pilgrimage to Stratford-upon-Avon a few months earlier, and was subsequently recruited by Bell to help promote the telephone in England. Field sang songs including "Kathleen Mavourneen" and "Comin' Thro' the Rye," as well as an Irish folk song not mentioned in the *London Times* story, which her biographer Gary Scharnhorst believes was motivated by Field's Irish Republican sympathies.[45] Shakespearean material played a large role in the form of the "Cuckoo Song" from *Love's Labour's Lost* and Rosalind's Epilogue from *As You Like It*. Rosalind's repeated reference to gender and embodiment in the Epilogue ("If I were a woman I would kiss as many of you as had beards that pleased me, complexions that liked me, and breaths that I defied not" [5.4.212–15]) would certainly have called attention to the disembodiment of Field's performing voice, much as Lanier has suggested with regard to Hamlet's soliloquy in Philadelphia. The power dynamics would also have been fascinating to observe, given that an independent American actress was speaking in the voice of Shakespeare's strongest heroine, asking the audience's sanction for the performance that went before. Rosalind conjures that response from a divided audience, speaking first to the women and then to the men, herself a palimpsest of genders and identities by the end of the play.[46] The telephone's ostensible power was to overcome distance, but as Bell's Shakespearean intertexts reveal, the telephone also served to make strange the subjectivities involved in performing and listening.

Figure 5.4 shows scenes from a more typical telephone demo as depicted on the cover of *Scientific American* for 31 March 1877.[47] In

---

[45] Scharnhorst, *Kate Field*, pp. 128.

[46] Field published *The History of Bell's Telephone* in 1878, one of the invention's earliest accounts, and according to Scharnhorst promoted Bell's telephone with remarkable perspicacity. Not long after the demo for the Queen, Field arranged for a telephonic performance to be included as an interlude during a benefit for the Shakespeare Memorial at Stratford on 22 May 1878. As a playbill for the event describes the interlude (sandwiched in the program between scenes from *As You Like It* and *The Merchant of Venice*), "For the first time in England, Shakespearean airs will be played several miles away on the Telephone Harp . . . and will be conveyed electrically to The Gaiety Theatre. Musical fire will be produced, by means of Geisler Tubes." Remarkably, she apparently managed to secure a telegraphic connection between the theatre in London and Shakespeare's home in Stratford (though reportedly with mixed results). For details, including a reproduction of the playbill, see Scharnhorst, *Kate Field*, pp. 131–3.

[47] "The Telephone," *Scientific American*, 36.13, new series (31 March 1877), pp. 191, 200. For similar newspaper depictions of Bell demos, see *The Daily*

PROFESSOR A. GRAHAM BELL'S TELEPHONE.—Fig. 1.

Figure 5.4 Bell's telephone demo in Salem, MA, with remote participants calling in from Boston. Detail of the front page of *Scientific American* (31 March 1877).

the lower panel, we see Bell with an audience in Salem, Massachusetts, communicating live with Boston as shown in the panel above. Bell and his invention are literally on stage, and audience, actor, and recording

Graphic (6 March 1877); *Bell Family Papers*, box 402, folder titled "Essex Institute, Salem, Mass, Feb 1877."

journalist alike understand this to be a performance. Props are visible as well, including the telephone itself and an easel, which in the *Scientific American* image appears to visualize different signal patterns.[48] These public performances were semi-improvised but still guided by a script. To let one example stand for many, the Plymouth *Western Morning News* of 22 August 1877, gives this account of a performance in England:

Professor Bell's illustration of the telephone was the finest and most successful that has eve[r] been given in this country. He gave a succinct history of the "evolution" of this marvellous instrument, commencing by experiment on the human ear, and leading up to the present marvellous invention. The illustrations not only included speaking and singing, but for the first time in this country the transmission of organ playing ... The notes of "God Save the Queen" were immediately audible throughout the room. The great marvel was the perfect manner in which the harmonic chords were transmitted, seeing that the telephone contains only one vibrating plate ... The notes of a cornet ... were distinctly audible all over the room, and when Mr. H[?] [at the] Post-office shouted "Auld lang syne" into the ... large telephone there, its strains were heard by most of those present. The declamation of "To or not to be" [*sic*] was similarly effective."[49]

As we can see, the telephone demo itself would take on a rhythm of exchanged messages – banter about local weather might follow strains of "God Save the Queen" or "Auld Lang Syne," or lines from *Hamlet* – punctuated by communal acts of listening and recognizing together as an audience. (The equivalent of the telephone game, in which a message is whispered from person to person to see how it mutates, seems to have taken place here, too, in the story's misquotation of Shakespeare's most well-known phrase.)

Sometimes Bell would switch the sounds around to speakers located in different parts of the hall to thrill the audience. As a witness comments in a later *Scientific American* article, writing about a demo in New York City wired up with an organist in Yonkers, "It is a most bewildering sensation to hear a song faintly emitted first from a box on

---

[48] The signal patterns on Bell's visual aids are represented in greater detail in an illustration for *The Daily Graphic* of 6 March 1877; *Bell Family Papers*, box 402, folder titled "Essex Institute, Salem, Mass, Feb 1877."

[49] "The Telephone. – Professor Bell Explains His Discovery," *Western Morning News* (22 August 1877); *Bell Family Papers*, box 402, folder titled "Lecture for British Association for Advancement of Science, August 21, 1877."

the stage, then from another suspended overhead, and finally from a third across the room, as the operator switches the current from one telephone to another."[50] The effect appears to have been similar to one sometimes used for the Ghost's disembodied injunction to "swear" in *Hamlet*'s first act (and also anticipates the quadrophonic experiments in *musique concrète* that Pink Floyd would exploit nearly a century later in their early concert tours). Some newspaper accounts of the demos emphasize the uncanniness of the new medium, and one in particular, from the *Boston Daily Advertiser* of 5 May 1877, invokes the language of *Hamlet* to express the strangeness of the technological encounter with voices from beyond: "'There are more things in heaven and earth, Horatio, than are dreamt of in your philosophy,' and Horatio would have accepted it without question had he been in Music hall [*sic*] last evening to hear the experiments on the telephone by Professor A. Graham Bell and his assistants. The weirdness and novelty were something never before felt in Boston." The "weirdness and novelty" of this demo evidently prompted the writer of the story, perhaps unconsciously, to repeatedly echo *Hamlet*'s theme of communication with the hereafter:

an attempt was made to see if Mr. Watson, speaking without the battery [from Providence], could be heard by the audience. All listened, and the ghost-like inquiry came from over the right shoulder, over the left and mid-air overhead, "Do you understand what I say? Do you understand what I say?" They all did, and laughed heartily to think they could.[51]

Here we see an early instance of the trope linking disembodied and mediatized voices to the supernatural, at which Gray hinted in his description of "ghostly" sounds on the line (and which Jeffery Sconce traces throughout media history in his book *Haunted Media*). In the newspaper story's imagery, there is something of Hamlet and Horatio's encounter with the Ghost on the battlements, as the audience strains to make out messages from beyond. "It was hard to tell where the sound ceased and the silence began," notes the *Boston Daily Advertiser*, evoking imagery perfectly suited to the battlements scene and the

---

[50] "The Speaking Telephone in New York," *Scientific American*, 36.23 [new series] (9 June 1877), p. 351.
[51] "The Telephone," *Boston Daily Advertiser* (5 May 1877), italics removed; *Bell Family Papers*, box 402, folder titled "Boston, April, May, 1877."

hurried interview with Old Hamlet's ghost: "its end was as uncertain as the line between daylight and darkness."

Shakespeare thus performed a kind of cultural work within Bell's demos, rendering the wondrous intelligible and the intelligible wondrous. The effect depended upon Shakespeare's juxtapositioning with other texts, and in demos like the ones at Boston, Salem, New York City, and Plymouth, a snippet of poetry from Shakespeare or Tennyson would be mixed with familiar airs such as "Old Lang Syne," "Yankee Doodle," "God Save the Queen," "Nearer My God to Thee," "Home Sweet Home," "Hold the Fort," and – in the case of a cornet player with a sense of irony, performing in Somerville, Massachussetts, for the audience in Boston – the aptly chosen popular song "Thou Art So Near and Yet So Far."[52] These transmissible cultural texts served as a leavening agent, mixing the strange with the familiar. Bell's demos also staged a convergence of media as well as content, featuring not only the telephone itself at centre stage, but also a blend of the traditional performance genres of scientific lecture and music-hall revue, as well as the now-familiar visual medium of projected slides. As one reporter notes of the Boston demo, Bell's lectures were supplemented by "sketches thrown by a stereopticon ... upon a screen just in front of the great organ [i.e. the telephone]."[53] (In another ironic foreshadowing, several reporters

---

[52] The reporter for a *Boston Sunday Times* story of 6 May 1877 ("Science and Sensation," discussed in more detail below), remarks upon the contextual humour of "Thou art so near and yet so far," apparently a puckish afterthought immediately following the serious and patriotic "Hail Columbia." Bell evidently adapted some of his choices to his setting. For example, an unidentified newspaper clipping describing a demo on 25 October 1877, for the Philosophical Society of Bradford, England, mentions that audiences heard lines from Tennyson's poem "The Brook": "For men may come, and men may go, / But I go on for ever"; *Bell Family Papers*, box 402, folder titled "Telephone; Address, Bradford, England, Oct. 25, 1877."

[53] "The Telephone," *Boston Daily Advertiser* (5 May 1877). It appears that audiences, if not Bell himself, saw in these slides an analogy between the progression of the telephone over time and the stages of Darwinian evolution. The Plymouth *Western Morning News* story quoted above mentions the "evolution" of the telephone in quotation marks, and the *Boston Daily Advertiser* story makes the link explicit: "No less than nineteen of these sketches were given in the first part of the lecture, and the gradual growth of the instrument was shown in the same way as the doctrine of evolution is set forth by pictures beginning in bioplasm and culminating in man." On the role of physiological aesthetics in the public takeup of evolutionary theories, see Jonathan Smith, *Charles Darwin*.

anticipate complaints about PowerPoint by complaining of too many slides, burdened with too much technical detail.)

The Boston demo of 4 May 1877 was one of the most ambitious in its gathering-together of multiple information streams, in that Bell connected his Boston audience via telephone to two distant locations: Somerville, with Watson and the ironic cornet player; and Providence, Rhode Island, where a locally performing tenor named Brignoli had been persuaded to sing into the telephone. Figure 5.5 adds yet another mode of representation to the multi-media nature of the event, in the form of a *Boston Sunday Times* reporter's cartoon showing an impression of the transmission of information, visible in the distance-bridging wire carrying musical notes which then pour out of the receiving device. Note that this is a cartoon, unlike the *Scientific American* illustration, which was drawn in that periodical's usual mode of technical realism. Both the *Scientific American* cover and the *Boston Sunday Times* attempt to make visible what was invisible to the distant participants, and to represent the (nearly) unrepresentable whole of the telephone demo as both event and technical system. Where *Scientific American* uses juxtaposition to make the scenario intelligible, the Boston cartoonist uses abstraction, surrealism, and a touch of humour. The *Boston Sunday Times* is also a different kind of periodical from *Scientific American*, which adds to the cartoon's temporal immediacy: this is an image of informational transmission over a new medium as imagined by a journalist probably encountering the telephone for the first time. Reporters reached for familiar analogies to describe Bell's ability to switch the incoming and outgoing sound between the Somerville and Providence channels; the *Boston Daily Advertiser* compares Bell's action to the switching on of a gas light, while the story that goes with this image exclaims, "Switching off songs, coming over a sixty mile wire, just as steam cars are switched on a railroad! What are we coming to?"[54]

This image showed the shape of things to come, as the reporter intuited. In particular, the musical notes racing down the wire and tumbling onto the stage evoke the atomization of information that became a dominant trope between the late nineteenth century and the present – and which bedevilled twentieth-century information theorists'

---

[54] "The Telephone," *Boston Daily Advertiser* (5 May 1877); "Science and Sensation," *Boston Sunday Times* (6 May 1877).

Figure 5.5 Cartoon depicting a telephone link between Boston and Providence, from Bell's demo in Boston as depicted in the *Boston Sunday Times* (6 May 1877).

attempts to explain information mathematically, as the next chapter will consider.[55] However, keeping the textual transmission of Shakespeare in mind, it is worth remembering that musical note

---

[55] See also Katherine Hayles's discussion of virtuality and materiality in *How We Become Posthuman*, pp.13–14 and *passim*.

symbols lose their original meaning when abstracted from the notation of a musical staff, just as Shakespeare quotations change in their meaning when they become bits of recontextualized information that circulate apart from their plays. (Recall the examples of "One touch of harmony makes the whole world kin" from *Troilus and Cressida*, discussed above, and *Hamlet*'s "Seems Madam! Nay, it IS!" from the stereoscope ad discussed in the preceding chapter.) The wire itself matters in this cartoon, too, given that most of Bell's telephone demos emphasized the different kinds of information the medium could carry. Taken as an abstract emblem of Bell's demos generally, the wire depicted here carried telegraphic signals, music, conversation, and occasionally some text from *Hamlet*. What is being pictured here is the idea of information in one of its formative moments – and specifically the idea of information as substance – as atomized material stuff that could spill onto the stage, as it seems poised to do in the cartoon.[56]

The late twentieth-century version of this trope may be found in the 1990s vogue for book covers that essentialize information as binary code or as a cascade of digital symbols, like the data-rain images from the *Matrix* films. The *Boston Sunday Times* cartoonist picked up on the need to make new media metaphorically intelligible to audiences, for which Bell, Edison, Thomas Hardy and so many other experimenters and technologists exploited Shakespeare's familiarity, cultural authority, and supposed transmissibility. But a paradox emerges in Bell's demos, and especially in this image of information as a flow of interchangeable and therefore meaningless notes. (The next chapter considers how information theory defines information by its power to disambiguate meanings in a communications context; as Gregory Bateson puts it, a bit of information is a "difference which makes a difference."[57]) Shakespeare's texts, once implicated in this kind of new media performance, matter in their specificity and transmissibility in supposedly content-neutral information systems. Yet, as Richard Menke points out with regard to the telephone's relative ordinariness when it became fictionalized in the 1890s, by that time "Random newspaper passages outsoar 'to be or not to be' [referring to Thompson's account of Bell's 1876 demo]" and even from its debut "the telephone

---

[56] On the history of the idea of information, see Nunberg, "Farewell to the Information Age."

[57] Gregory Bateson, *Ecology of Mind*, p. 315. See pp. 209–10.

seemed to align with daily discourse rather than with transcendent literature."[58] The quotations and bits of information that happened to be Shakespeare could just as easily have been something else – a notice of the arrival of the SS Cox, perhaps – and the pleasure of recognizing Shakespeare through the static depends upon the very trope of interchangeability that downplays Shakespeare's uniqueness. As Burt and Yates describe in relation to Thompson's account of the Bell's Philadelphia demo, the telephone "rewires the infrastructure that translates words from place to place ... You may need to endure the static, but still the telephone beats the newspaper and its clippings, transmitting the voice across that distance while all those static clippings remain yet to be clipped, or sit inside envelopes on this or that liner, which may or may never arrive – what was its name again?"[59] Put another way, in Bell's demos Shakespeare's texts become data, but merely data. That paradox is one that digital humanists have inherited today, and its history will unfold throughout the remaining chapters.

Performing *Julius Caesar* with Thomas Edison

We have already considered Edison's use of Shakespeare with regard to the electric pen and phonograph, but a lesser-known episode in Edison's career depends upon a more elaborate use of Shakespeare. Beginning in the 1890s, the kinetophone (later merged with the kinetoscope) was Edison's attempt to synchronize moving pictures with recorded sound, anticipating the talkies that would not become established in Hollywood until the release of *The Jazz Singer* in 1927. Mindful, perhaps, of the number of silent Shakespeare films that had already appeared, Edison filmed a scene from *Julius Caesar* for a kinetophone demo in 1913, enlisting Shakespeare's stage as a place to show off his technological union of sound and vision. Shakespeare had already been established as a silent film sub-genre by 1913. His linguistically rich plays might seem like an unlikely choice for a silent film, but audiences in the early twentieth century might have seen a number of wordless Shakespearean scenes on film, beginning with an 1899 film based on Herbert Beerbohm Tree's production of *King John*. The Vitagraph company in particular worked to establish Shakespeare as a cultural

[58] Menke, "Medium is the Media," p. 213.
[59] Burt and Yates, *What's the Worst*, p. 25.

commodity to be experienced through silent film, producing or import-
ing more than thirty-six Shakespearean films between 1908 and 1913,
and programmatically linking the emerging medium's respectability to
Shakespeare's.[60]

However, Shakespeare was more than just a source of cultural capital
in early films; Shakespeare on silent film staged a collision of seemingly
antagonistic media. As Judith Buchanan points out: "[drama] imagina-
tively evokes the image through the suggestive power of the word,
[while film] does not just erode the power of the word by the privileging
of the image, but all but evicts those words from its playing space."[61]
Even from silent Shakespeare's beginnings in the 1899 *King John*,
questions of text and performance call attention to the transformission
of Shakespeare through new media. For example, Tree's one-minute
scene plays on themes of remediation in a number of ways, partly by
depicting a symbolic act of writing – King John's signing of *Magna
Carta* – and partly by making this represented act of inscription an
intervention itself into the text of Shakespeare's play: Shakespeare
omitted the signing of *Magna Carta* from his life of King John (just as
he omitted Robin Hood). As Michael Best puts it, "hence the inaugural
attempt to put Shakespeare on screen embodied the unending dialectical
struggle between film directors and the Shakespeare text."[62] Writing
may have been substituted for speaking in the 1899 *King John*, but there
is evidence that Shakespeare was also present in early experiments to
synchronize moving image with recorded sound, including the duel
scene in a 1900 film of *Hamlet* starring Sarah Bernhardt, and Edison's
1903 film *The Seven Ages of Man* (based on Jaques's set-piece from *As
You Like It*).[63]

Accounts of two of Edison's kinetophone demos in 1913 provide a
glimpse of audiences' encounters with new media as a vehicle for
Shakespeare performance – and, reciprocally, with Shakespeare as a
vehicle for new media. In late 1912 and early 1913, Edison had made

[60] Urrichio and Pearson, *Reframing Culture*, p. 68. Their chapter "Literary
Qualities: Shakespeare and Dante" provides a thorough overview of Vitagraph's
recruitment of Shakespeare and other literary sources.
[61] Buchanan, *Shakespeare on Silent Film*, p. 5.
[62] internetshakespeare.uvic.ca/Theater/production/recorded/238.
[63] Buchanan, *Shakespeare on Silent Film*, p. 15, n. 35. Research on Edison's *Seven
Ages of Man* appears to be scarce, but see Rothwell and Melzer, *Shakespeare on
Screen*, p. 33.

sufficient progress on the kinetophone to warrant bringing reporters to
a demo in his lab in West Orange, New Jersey, thereby generating buzz
for an upcoming run of kinetophone exhibitions in theatres in
Manhattan and Brooklyn. As with the Bell telephone demos, journalists
found themselves serving as witnesses to technological advancement
and the triumph of invention. A *New York Times* story by one of those
reporters opens with a verdict: "Talking motion pictures are at last a
reality . . . After many years of experimentation Mr. Edison has at last
perfected a machine synchronizing the motion picture and the phonograph."[64] The story goes on to describe the demo footage shown to the
assembly by Edison himself, which included a lecturer (on film) explaining the technology that was producing the effect, followed by scenes of
familiar objects emitting familiar sounds, such as china being broken,
dogs barking, and horns and whistles blowing: in short, a catalogue of
objects and their phenomenological traces, much like that of Talbot's
Pencil of Nature seventy years earlier.[65] Also, like Talbot's "Fac-simile
of an Old Printed Page," the kinetophone demo film went on to
expound the technology's documentary capacity and historical potential, arguing that it could record the speeches of statesmen and other
figures for posterity.

The demo film switched representational modes a third time, again
echoing Talbot by claiming for itself the status of an artistic medium. As
the *New York Times* story reports, "The next reel showed the miser
scene from [Robert Planquette's operetta] the 'Chimes of Normandie,'
and in turn the Miserere from [Giuseppe Verdi's opera] 'Trovatore,' the
quarrel between Brutus and Cassius from 'Julius Caesar,' a comedy
sketch entitled 'The Politician,' and two others, 'Her Redemption' and
'Dick, the Highwayman.'" By now this type of media jumble of high
and low, serious and comic, should be no surprise. As Gitelman has
commented with regard to the mixing of Shakespeare and Mother Goose
in the gramophone demos of earlier years, audiences were participating in
the enactment of a cultural hierarchy.[66] Synchronized sound enacted

---

[64] "Edison's Pictures Talk and Perform," *New York Times* (4 January 1913),
p. 7.

[65] An incomplete version of this film is available at www.youtube.com/watch?
v=uRqQhUQTaUc. On Talbot's *Pencil of Nature* as a catalogue of
photographically representable objects, see Carol Armstrong's chapter on Talbot
in *Scenes from a Library*, pp. 107–78, as well as pp. 126–9 above.

[66] Gitelman, *Always Already New*, p. 35. See p. 172 above.

cultural hierarchies by traversing them effortlessly, such that the *Times* reporter comments in particular on this encyclopedic effect of the medium: "In light and grand opera, in comedy and serious drama, the movements of the actors and singers were marked by the realism of the present-day stage."[67]

The force of new media Shakespeare performance (to borrow W. B. Worthen's term) comes through in particular detail in a photographically illustrated account of the next in Edison's succession of kinetophone demos, written by one Bailey Millard for *Technical World Magazine*, and with special focus on the demo's *Julius Caesar* sequence.[68] Millard's prosaic account emphasizes affect far more than most of the other contemporary reports we have been considering, beginning with his opening reference to the social spectrum of gathered witnesses within the space of the theatre: "We sat in the dark, chilly dress circle of a New York theatre one morning, a dozen of us, including a master mechanic, a few vaudeville actors, and three or four men of the press, waiting for the first stage rehearsal of a kinetophone play."[69] The *Julius Caesar* portion of the demo serves to frame most of Millard's account, providing a rare degree of insight into a witness's experience of a Shakespearean technology demo, and is worth quoting at some length. The demo begins with one of Shakespeare's works emerging from the machine, almost literally:

The machine began to sputter and the light to flicker fitfully, after a fashion painful to weak eyes, on the white curtain above the middle of the stage . . . Forth upon the screen in front of us strode Brutus and Cassius, eyeing each other with looks of scorn. The two old Romans paused. Cassius bent his manly brow and made a stately gesture. Then his lips parted and moved and out of his mouth came in clear, distinct bass tones, these words:

> "That you have wronged me doth appear in this:
> You have condemned and noted Lucius Pella
> Of taking bribes here of the Sardians.
> Wherein, my letters, praying on his side,
> Because I knew the man, were slighted off."

[67] "Edison's Pictures Talk and Perform," *New York Times* (4 January 1913), p. 7.
[68] Worthen, *Modern Performance*, pp. 3–4.
[69] Millard, "Pictures that Talk," p. 16.

To the thrill of anticipation succeeded the thrill of surprised delight. Surprised? Yes; because not only was here the vivid, swaying, gesturing, picture of a man talking, but he was talking in the even, natural, albeit somewhat stilted, tones of that familiar Cassius whom I had seen strutting the boards in this very scene time and time again in years of play-going. In other words, though I had expected realism, I had not expected any such realism as this.[70]

Millard describes the phenomenology of witnessing, via Shakespeare, the sensory realism of the new medium, registered in details such as the swaying and gesturing of bodies and the tonal qualities of voices. Even the reproduction of traditional scene blocking makes an impression on Millard: "While they talked and their voices rang through the empty auditorium, the two tragedians changed places that stage tradition might be conserved."[71] But where Bell's audiences experienced Edisonian eureka-moments with the recognition of spoken Shakespearean text – Bell's own word for them is "quotations"[72] – Millard's eureka-moment is less textual, more theatrical: he recognizes the medium's ability to transmit Shakespeare not as text but as performance.

One can detect Millard's willingness to participate in the drama for which he has been recruited, and it is worth recalling that by 1913 Edison and his associates were masters of the genre of the public tech demo. Indeed, the effects this demo seems calculated to produce, especially the sense of delight in blurring the line between recording and live performance, would become central to Edison's famous phonograph "tone tests" in the same period, in which audiences were challenged to discern the difference between a live singer and phonograph, both of whom performed for their delight from behind concealment on the stages of music halls.[73] As if appreciating a newfound liveness in drama – produced, paradoxically, by the fact of recording it[74] – Millard enthuses about the synchrony between sound and action,

---

[70] Millard, "Pictures that Talk," pp. 16–17.
[71] Millard, "Pictures that Talk," p. 17.
[72] Bell, "Researches in Telephony," p. 8; see above, pp. 169–70.
[73] On Edison's tone tests, see Emily Thompson, "Machines, Music, and the Quest for Fidelity."
[74] As Philip Auslander argues, "the very concept of live performance presupposes that of reproduction – that the live can exist only *within* an economy of reproduction"; *Liveness*, p. 57; emphasis in original.

word and gesture: Cassius extends his "itching palm" as he rebukes Brutus's accusation of accepting bribes (4.2.64); Brutus's reference to the ides of March is met by the sound and sight of Cassius blowing through his teeth in derision. Millard continues:

And so the ancient quarrel ran on, the two Romans swinging their hands as their speeches became more passionate, while their voices rang out boldly so that they could easily have been heard in the top gallery. As their lip movements slowed, the tones slowed with them. I am quite sure that the keenest lip-reader would not have detected any lack of synchronism between the labial and the enunciatory performance.[75]

This description hints at Edison's rationale for choosing this particular scene, in which interpersonal dialogue and a rising sense of conflict combine nicely with stage business and linguistic references to embodiment. It is a scene that modulates through a range of performance nuances – ideal for a new media demo seeking to emphasize the range of representable phenomena.

Edison's tactical use of *Julius Caesar* thus had to walk a fine line, balancing the goals of theatrical realism and representational transparency with the need to call attention to the operation of the medium itself. It seems to have worked perfectly on Millard:

The illusion was complete. In fact it was the kind of illusion that makes one forget its existence. It was far better than the work of any ventriloquist I have ever heard. One accepted the effect without thought of how it was produced. Only during the brief pauses did it occur to the auditor that a concealed talking machine was at work behind the screen as a component part of a complete mechanism that concurrently produced the moving imagery, the play of the lips and the resounding vocables.[76]

Throughout his account, and here in particular, Millard merges the role of scientific witness with that of discerning Shakespearean playgoer.[77] His language echoes the familiar genre of theatrical reportage, as though he were reviewing a live performance of *Julius Caesar*. What is

---

[75] Millard, "Pictures that Talk," pp. 17–18.
[76] Millard, "Pictures that Talk," p. 18.
[77] On the function of witnessing in the history of science, see Shapin and Schaffer, *Leviathan and the Air-Pump*, pp. 55–60. Of particular relevance to the kinetophone demo is their discussion of "virtual witnessing" (pp. 60–5), exemplified in Millard's published article, and their discussion of controlled spaces for witnessing experiments (pp. 335–6), exemplified in Edison's theatre.

most remarkable is that at no point does he refer to the technology itself as speaking, as many other early witnesses of the telephone and gramophone tended to do. For Millard, it was not the kinetophone speaking but Brutus and Cassius.[78]

Finally, the fleeting mention of silence in Millard's account is also significant, in that it reveals the operation of the machine behind the illusion. Presumably, during those pauses between utterances in *Julius Caesar* – those white spaces in the text that performance unfolds – Millard and the audience could hear the whirring of the kinetophone and film projector, perhaps the hum of the lamps, even the shuffling of the operators. It is in these moments, too, that Millard intuits the presence not just of a single device but of a system, "a complete mechanism" as he calls it, whose boundaries are not altogether clear. However, like the titular *Wizard of Oz* (published in 1900, adapted in a number of silent films, and eventually becoming a feature-length showcase for Technicolor in 1939) Millard knows that the audience should pay no attention to the mechanism behind the curtain – placed there by another wizard, the one from Menlo Park. Here, and increasingly in the examples and chapters to follow, we find evidence for one of Walter Benjamin's most important insights about technological modernity: "The equipment-free aspect of reality . . . has become the height of artifice."[79] For Edison and his inheritors, the feat of technological transparency became the real performance.

Noise and desire: transmitting Shakespeare into the twentieth century

> The first wax recording ever made of a human voice turned out today to be a quotation from Shakespeare.
>
> *New York Times* (27 October 1937)[80]

In the preceding examples of Shakespeare's appearance in aural media we have considered dimensions such as distance, embodiment, and performance. This concluding section adds preservation to that list of subtopics,

---

[78] Ironically, despite the warm reception the kinetophone received from Millard and the *New York Times*, it appears to have been taken off-market soon after; see Ball, *Shakespeare on Silent Film*, pp. 162–3.

[79] Benjamin, "Work of Art," pp. 233.

[80] "Original Wax Record, Made by Bell, Is Heard at Smithsonian After 56 Years," *New York Times* (28 October 1937), p. 8.

and in so doing explores the twentieth-century afterlives of nineteenth-century recordings. In 1937, a staged collision of Shakespeare's techno-logical past and present took place at the Smithsonian Institution in Washington DC. The occasion was the opening of a box containing a prototype phonograph and documentation that had been deposited with the Smithsonian in 1881 by Bell and two partners, his cousin Chichester Bell and Charles Tainter, as insurance against any patent challenge from the famously litigious Edison. The deposited prototype was never required as evidence, and so remained sealed in the Smithsonian's archives until 27 October 1937, when it was reopened as a matter of historical interest in the presence of Bell's daughters and great-grandson. The event took place under the auspices of the Dictaphone Corporation, whose office recording machines were based on Bell's patents, and who therefore had an interest in Bell's legacy. The box opened at the Smithsonian was believed to be the first surviving sound recording, in which Shakespeare's *Hamlet* furnished the words that Bell and his partners selected to authenticate both the technology's value and their claim to it.[81]

The *New York Times* article quoted above reports that auditors at the Smithsonian heard the following when the recording was played again in 1937:

T-r-a – T-r-a – There are more things in heaven and earth, Horatio, than are dreamed of in your philosophy – T-r-a. I am a gramophone and my mother was a phonograph.[82]

---

[81] Two caveats must be observed here. First, we now know that the earliest surviving recorded sound is not Shakespeare but the French folk song "Au Claire de la Lune," recorded on paper as a "phonautogram" by Édouard-Léon Scott in 1860; see www.firstsounds.org/sounds/scott.php. However, since Scott's recording resulted from an experiment in visualizing sound waves, one could argue that the Bell cylinder is the first recording made with the intention of being replayable. Second, sound historians Oliver Read and Walter L. Welch question whether the apparatus required for playback was available on the occasion, and suggest the text attributed to the recording might have come from the transcription on a card affixed to the graphophone with sealing wax; see Read and Welch, *From Tin Foil to Stereo*, pp. 28 and 31. However, the event as it actually occurred at the Smithsonian is less important for my purposes than how it was represented in popular media, through which it became part of the cultural history of recording.

[82] "Original Wax Record, Made by Bell, Is Heard at Smithsonian After 56 Years," *New York Times* (28 October 1937), p. 8.

As one of Bell's daughters was quoted as explaining, "It's the sort of thing father would have said … He was fond of quoting Shakespeare and he would have liked the little joke about the graphophone that came at the end."[83] The joke is a reference to the origin of Bell's graphophone research, which began in the adaptation and improvement of Edison's phonograph (hence the reversal of syllables in Bell's name for his device, and the fear of a patent challenge). A number of documents were sealed with the prototype in its metal box, including pages from *The New York Herald* and *The National Republican* to authenticate the date of deposit, and an attestation signed by Tainter and the two Bells giving details of the recording's creation in front of other witnesses (mostly Bell family members) on 25 September 1881, and confirming the words of the recording – even including the "T-r-a" sounds.[84] There was some confusion over whose voice is recorded on the cylinder, and the enclosed testimonial does not specify, though a subsequent newspaper story claims that Tainter later confirmed the voice to be Alexander Melville Bell's.[85] The overlay of actors and identities in this mini-drama is actually quite complex: Bell's own father speaks in the voice of Hamlet, which immediately morphs into the supposed voice of the machine itself, lending it not just human subjectivity, but that of the literary character who, more than any other, defines the modern subject in contemplation of itself. The recording thus enacts an incomplete performance of *Hamlet* that weaves the machine itself into the play's themes of communication with the dead; as Horatio says of the Ghost, "it … did address / Itself to motion like as it would speak" – a voice from the grave enjoined to speak to establish legitimate descent, with the part of Claudius implicitly falling to Edison in this little adaptation.

This episode has re-entered the cultural history of sound recording recently as part of the Smithsonian's efforts to recover this and other early sound recordings – a topic that I will defer until Chapter 7, which

---

[83] *Ibid.* Those trilling sounds are rather more dramatic than their transcription suggests. They can be heard with the rest of the recording at *FirstSounds.org*; see note 81 above.

[84] Smithsonian catalogue no. 312122, Volta Laboratory Deposit, box 3. I am grateful to Carlene Stephens of the Smithsonian National American History Museum for confirming the contents of the box and providing a transcription. See also *Bell Family Papers*, box 287, folder titled "Tainter, Charles Sumner."

[85] Leonard H. Engel, "Alexander Melville Bell's Voice on 'Graphophone' Record," *Sarasota Herald-Tribune* (27 November 1937).

deals with Shakespeare and digital preservation more broadly. Another kind of cultural text generated by the 1937 reopening of the graphophone took the form of a Dictaphone advertisement that ran in magazines such as *Newsweek*, *National Geographic*, and *Electronics World*. I quote at length a version that appeared in a 1943 issue of *Time* under the title "The voice that was buried for 56 years":

> "There are more things in heaven and earth, Horatio, than are dreamed of in our philosophies."
>
> That passage from Hamlet was spoken to the original "graphophone" invented in 1881 … It was recorded on a wax cylinder, which was sealed in a metal box. For over half a century, that box reposed in a dark vault at the Smithsonian Institution, Washington.
>
> In 1937, in the presence of representatives of the inventors, the box was opened and the first practical sound recording was replayed. Every word was heard plainly … and precisely as it had been spoken 56 years before!
>
> During the busy years bridged by those two events, thousands of Dictaphone dictating machines, developed from the original Bell and Tainter Graphophone patent, had gone into service in business offices around the world. Coming as the first challenge to an out-moded system of dictation which had endured since the days of the Greeks and Romans, Dictaphone saved time and effort – expedited the flow of work – made executives the *masters* rather than the *slaves* of daily routine.[86]

This advertisement serves to draw out the symbolic importance of encoding and decoding of material inscriptions in this media spectacle, and of Shakespeare as the object of those encoding and decoding processes. The wax inscriptions and the Shakespeare text invest each other with a certain power to authenticate each other, all in the service of an advertising narrative that subordinates the history of writing and labour to technological progress. The ad's appeal to Shakespeare as a transmissible text, and as recovered artifact, plays on desires that attend all technologies that mediate cultural materials: to feel under our feet a secure bridge between historical events; to feel our present confirmed by our past.

In the early twenty-first century, a very different response to those desires took the form of a sound installation and performance piece titled *Horatio Oratorio*, composed and performed by Aleksander

---

[86] Advertisement in *Time Magazine*, 49.21 (24 May 1943), p. 57, emphasis and ellipses in original.

Kolkowski, Frederico Reuben, and Sebastian Lexer, which used sounds from the same source along with other early recordings.[87] It was performed most recently in Edinburgh in 2011, as part of a multi-work concert called *Palæophonics* that explored the archaeology of recorded sound through performance.[88] The *Palæophonics* website echoes many of the themes of the present chapter in its description of *Horatio Oratorio*:

> An installation and performance exploring the early history of recorded sound, based on the first recorded utterances and music transcribed onto metal and wax and reproduced by styli, diaphragms and horns. The era of recorded sound as tangible material, has been supplanted by the digital file, *Horatio Oratorio* sings of the transformation of sound into object and its return into the ether [*sic*]. Edison phonographs, gramophones and mechanical instruments are combined with state-of-the-art electronics in a unique liaison between the contemporary and the obsolete.
>
> The installation creates a soundscape that reaches back in time, with fragments of archival material played alongside newly created sounds, all heard through recording and reproduction technologies of the past. The live music is derived from computer-aided analysis of two main sources: An 1881 graphophone-recorded Hamlet quotation and cylinders containing Handel's oratorio Israel in Egypt from 1888 – the earliest surviving recordings of live music, together with other historical recordings from the late 1800s.[89]

Video of a 2008 London performance is available online, showing Kolkowski on stage moving among an array of early gramophones and other sound devices, occasionally cranking them to keep them running, changing records, and adding new sound to the soundscape with a hybrid violin/phonograph.[90] *Horatio Oratorio* thus uses the 1881 Bell recording of Shakespeare to achieve a very different effect from the Dictaphone ad, in this case revelling in the pastness of the technology in a "liaison between the contemporary and the obsolete," as the website puts it. The progress narrative that sustained

---

[87] Kolkowski served as the sound artist-in-residence for the London Science Museum in 2012, recording numerous musicians and artists on the inscriptive medium of wax cylinders, and posting them in an online archive: *Phonographies: A Wax Cylinder Archive, Recorded and Curated by Aleks Kolkowski*, www.phonographies.org.

[88] The concert took place at the George Square Theatre in Edinburgh on 27 May 2011.

[89] palaeophonics.co.uk/72-2.

[90] See www.youtube.com/watch?v=G778Prw6-C0 and www.youtube.com/watch?v=mTvSq4iWmEg.

technological thinking in 1943 had become more complicated by the early twenty-first century, and recordings like Bell's were no longer mere milestones to measure the present's distance from the receding past. Rather, a work like *Horatio Oratorio* suggests that present and past media are implicit in one another, and become entangled through recorded cultural texts by Shakespeare, Handel, and others that blur the boundary between inscription and ephemeral vibration.

Preservation calls attention to the present as much as to the past. When Bell and his colleagues made their recording in 1881, they clearly intended it to have an afterlife, albeit mainly a legal one within the short-term horizon of patent litigation. By 1937 it had long outlived its legal function, and had become instead a time capsule, serving at once to emphasize and bridge the distance between past and present. By 1943 and the Dictaphone ad, Hamlet's words served to legitimate a recording technology and its underlying corporate progress narrative. By 2011 and *Horatio Oratorio*'s performance in Edinburgh, the recording became part of an artistic reconsideration of technological archive fever, as Kolkowski quotes Derrida on his website: "We are en mal d'archive: in need of archives ... It is to have a compulsive, repetitive, and nostalgic desire for the archive, an irrepressible desire to return to the origin, a homesickness, a nostalgia for the return to the most archaic place of absolute commencement."[91] (As Chapter 7 will show, this archive fever regarding the Bell recording would also become bound up with digital preservation.) Between 1881 and now, the metal box in a Smithsonian vault containing recorded words from *Hamlet* had become a materialization of the Shakespearean archive in the most vivid sense, evoking technological afterlives just as Shakespeare's play explored human ones.

As we can see in the succession of examples discussed in this chapter, late nineteenth- and early twentieth-century audiences became increasingly attuned to the performative nature of new audio media, bearing out Lanier's argument that recorded Shakespeare is its own kind of interpretive reinvention, not simply a derivative of the literary text.[92] As Katherine Rowe puts it, the use of Shakespeare as "launch content" for new media of all kinds "provides continuity and a standard against

[91] Derrida, *Archive Fever*, p. 91; as quoted on www.phonographies.org/about/introduction-2.
[92] Lanier, "Shakespeare on the Record," p. 416.

which to measure technological innovation. If the words emerging from Bell's [1876 Philadelphia] Centennial transmitter can be recognized as Shakespeare's, the technology has passed a symbolic threshold, conveying meaningful language, not just noise."[93] Yet noise remains the spectre at the banquet in these demos, and holds a fascination of its own that grew throughout the twentieth century, as media historians such as Friedrich Kittler and Jussi Parikka have shown.[94] Certainly by the time of *Horatio Oratorio* in the first decade of the twenty-first century, there was a sense that transmitting, recording, and performing Shakespeare in new (and renewed) media was about more than simply celebrating technological progress or artistic transcendence; mediatized Shakespeare enacted fundamental desires and anxieties regarding transmission and loss, inflected through new aural media. (Glen Campbell's 1968 song "Wichita Lineman," which could serve as a modern counterpart to this chapter's opening Thomas Hardy epigraph, manages to distill that century-old contest between noise and desire into three minutes of eerie poignancy.)

Early sound technologies involve strange juxtapositions, as Bell's and Edison's first audiences experienced in those early tech demos. The scenes from the prehistory of digitization recounted above seem at times to take on the qualities of steampunk science-fiction: Queen Victoria, Lord Kelvin, and the Emperor of Brazil straining to hear a disembodied voice speak Shakespearean lines over a telegraph wire; Edison, the Wizard of Menlo Park, using *Julius Caesar* to orchestrate a public media spectacle like his namesake in *The Wizard of Oz*; even the recovery of Bell's dictaphone prototype from the Smithsonian vaults in 1937 has a certain *Raiders of the Lost Ark* flavour, evoking the final scenes of the film (set in the same location, Washington DC, around the same year).

Affect matters. It was key to the early understanding of these technologies as they entered the cultural imagination, and it is no less part of how we understand them now, even when read through the scholarly lenses of media archaeology, book history, and textual studies. The next chapter deals with the transition of Shakespearean text from inscriptions into machine-readable code, an ontological shift that requires us to look back as much as forward. Just as Bailey Millard must have noticed the sound of Edison's kinetophone in the quiet moments

---

[93] Rowe, "Media History," p. 306.
[94] See Kittler, *Gramophone, Film, Typewriter*, and Parikka, "Mapping Noise."

between utterances, so must cultural historians of media attend to the mechanisms of new technologies that cannot be reduced to visual spectacles or abstractions of code; as Gitelman puts it succinctly, "Cultural history must also include the squeaks and noises of change."[95] As the next chapter will show, the fields of bibliography, electronic computing, cybernetics, and information theory – all of which developed in parallel in the middle of the twentieth century – inherited the preoccupations of the nineteenth. Noise and desire would become mixed together with Shakespeare's texts in new ways, challenging the image of smooth, noiseless modernity so often associated with idealistic representations of digital computing. After the noise of nineteenth-century new media, the rest is anything but silence, and Shakespeare's invented voice still sings in the wire.

---

[95] Gitelman, *Always Already New*, p. 84. See also Kirschenbaum's deliberate use of the seemingly obsolete word *mechanisms* in his book of the same title.

6 | Networks of deep impression: Shakespeare and the modern invention of information

Thou in our wonder and astonishment
Hast built thy selfe a lasting Monument:
For whils't to th'shame of slow-endevouring Art
Thy easie numbers flow, and that each part,
Hath from the leaves of thy unvalued Booke,
Those Delphicke Lines with deepe Impression tooke
Then thou our fancy of her selfe bereaving,
Dost make us Marble with too much conceiving

John Milton, dedicatory sonnet in the
Shakespeare Second Folio (1632)[1]

I would like to think that Milton somehow knew he was writing about computing when he wrote his encomium to Shakespeare. Since the advent of digital textuality, Milton's words have acquired significance he could not have foreseen. The word "numbers" in particular gathers together several meanings: numbers as the metrical units of Shakespeare's verse (*OED* "number" *n.* def. 17a); numbers as musical signs of order in the melodic, harmonic, and rhythmic qualities of Shakespeare's poetry (def. 17b, 14a, 14b); numbers more generally as objects in a collection that may be enumerated in a totality, in the manner that John Heminge and Henry Condell (inaccurately) describe the First Folio plays as being "absolute in their numbers"[2]; the numbers of Shakespeare's sonnets, which we use along with first lines as identifiers; the Old Testament book of Numbers, which deals with a census (the same type of event that led to one of the first pre-electronic computers[3]); and numbers as the type of data usually

---

[1] F2, sig. ᵖA5r. [2] F1, sig. ᵖA3r.
[3] The counting of America's 1880 census data was the impetus for one of the most influential pre-electronic computers, the Hollerith Tabulator; see Brian Winston, *Media, Technology*, p. 159.

associated with computation at its most essential – computers have their historical roots in the processing of numbers, not text. Milton also evokes a form of textual transmission familiar to anyone who uses a personal computer, that of making exact copies in an instant and on practically any scale. As anyone who has suffered major data loss can attest, modern computing forces upon us an equivalence between copying and preservation. Since a digital text's "deep impressions" are merely positively or negatively charged electrons on a magnetized disc surface – or the microscopic impressions laser etched into an optical disc – the devices we now associate with computing provoke a complex set of responses to preservation, largely in the absence of a single trusted substrate for digital archiving. In digital media, preserving data means keeping numbers flowing.

This chapter argues that Shakespeare's numbers flow with a difference in twentieth-century information culture. As we have seen in previous chapters, new media in the nineteenth and early twentieth centuries often shaped their emerging identities in relation to Shakespeare as transmissible content, remediating Shakespeare's texts in ways that made them recognizable and yet newly strange at the same time. By our own time, Shakespeare's texts have come to stand as both an ideal and a limit-case for the concept of information. That concept, in its modern guise, emerged from a late twentieth-century cultural formation that still dominates much current thinking about computing. Idealized as easily encoded, unproblematically transmissible data, Shakespeare's texts supposedly flow naturally into new digital forms of analysis, such that Shakespearean compatibility with digital media has become a truism. This chapter also marks a technological turn within the larger history recounted in this book: while the preceding chapters described new technologies for representing the texts of Shakespeare, this chapter brings us to the threshold of virtual, machine-*readable* Shakespeare texts, a theme that I also pursue in the next chapter in relation to the idea of digital data. However, electronic computing has a Cold War history that often gets left out of idealistic accounts of the digital humanities. Mid-twentieth-century encounters with the Shakespearean archive tested the boundaries between human and machine in ways that spanned surprisingly disparate knowledge domains, and yet defined the available meanings of the word *data* by the early twenty-first century.

The year 1949 was a crucial one for bibliography, information theory, and what we now call digital humanities. The postwar decades saw a boom in Renaissance editing and bibliography generally, and scholars used this period to theorize and codify editorial and biblio-graphical practices – the former in W. W. Greg's "Rationale of Copy Text" (first presented as a lecture in 1949) and the latter in the same year with Fredson Bowers's *Principles of Bibliographical Description.*[4] In these and other foundational works from the period, it becomes clear that the problems of Shakespeare's texts were central to the develop-ment of New Bibliographical thinking. But even as textual scholars used Shakespeare to theorize the ways literary texts bear the marks of their material transmission, so were information theorists such as Norbert Wiener, Claude Shannon, and Warren Weaver codifying the discipline now known as information science. Shannon and Weaver's 1949 book *The Mathematical Theory of Communication* proved as foundational to information science as Greg's and Bowers's works from the same year proved to bibliography.[5] To these formational events I would add another from 1949: the beginning of Jesuit scholar Roberto Busa's groundbreaking use of computers in his *Index Thomisticus*, a concord-ance to the works of Thomas Aquinas, the project generally credited with initiating the field of humanities computing. This chapter explores how the idea of the virtual Shakespeare text took shape within this historical confluence, as bibliography, information theory, and comput-ing converged on the same questions.

Although the term *virtual* has suffered much dilution in the theorizing of digital media and hypertext, N. Katherine Hayles provides a clear and useful definition: "Virtuality is the cultural perception that material objects are interpenetrated by information patterns."[6] Unlike many critics who invoke the term, she goes to great lengths to define and situate the idea of virtuality in relation to events such as the Macy Conferences on Cybernetics, held from 1946 to 1953. Even so, her descriptions of

---

[4] See Greg, "The Rationale of Copy-Text," in *Sir Walter Wilson Greg*, pp. 213–28, and Bowers, *Principles.*

[5] In the same year, Weaver published a summary for non-specialist readers as "The Mathematics of Communication" in *Scientific American.* Matthew G. Kirschenbaum notes the significance of these simultaneous publications in "Editing the Interface," pp. 19–20, n. 12, and *Mechanisms*, pp. 213–18.

[6] Hayles, *How We Became Posthuman*, pp. 13–14. On the semantic slippage of the word *virtual*, see also Flanders, "Body Encoded," pp. 27–8.

virtuality sound remarkably akin to the study of literary texts as the New Bibliographers conceived it. As Hayles puts it, "Seeing the world as an interplay between informational patterns and material objects is a historically specific construction that emerged in the wake of World War II."[7] If one were to replace the phrase "the world" with "literary texts" in this quotation, it would capture the mindset of the New Bibliography, especially in Greg's prewar definition of bibliography as "the science of the transmission of literary documents" and in the postwar turn to compositor analysis led by Fredson Bowers and Charlton Hinman.[8] Just as Milton's encomium evokes a particularly Shakespearean pattern of transmissible "easy numbers" flowing through the book and leaving deep impressions in other media, so was the New Bibliography determined to trace that flow of information back to its source.

The New Bibliographers' legacy continued but was contested, especially in the 1990s, when renewed interest in the materiality of texts coincided with the rise of the Web and what we now call the digital humanities. Some digital humanists, especially in the sub-field of text analysis, regarded digital tools as means to purge authorial transmissions of noise, while others more influenced by D. F. McKenzie, Jerome McGann, and Randall McLeod imagined digital editions that could represent nonauthorial interventions as meaningful in their own right.[9] As I have suggested in previous chapters, McLeod's portmanteau term "transformission" nicely captures the shift in thinking about the dual virtuality and materiality of texts since Greg (though one can detect in Greg's "Bibliography – An Apologia" a conflicted sympathy with the concerns of present-day textual materialists).[10] The metaphorical coincidences in Milton's sonnet, however anachronistic, anticipate

---

[7] Hayles, *How We Became Posthuman*, p. 14.

[8] Greg, "Bibliography – an Apologia," in *Sir Walter Wilson Greg*, pp. 135–57; see pp. 135, 137, 140, and 141.

[9] Representative examples may be found among the entries in the Blackwell *Companion to Digital Humanities*, edited by Susan Schreibman, Ray Siemens, and John Unsworth. Contrast the assumptions about nonauthorial agents in Hugh Craig's "Stylistic Analysis and Authorship Studies" (pp. 273–88) and John Burrows's "Textual Analysis" (pp. 323–47) with those in Martha Nell Smith's "Electronic Scholarly Editing" (pp. 306–22) and Johanna Drucker and Bethany Nowviskie's "Speculative Computing: Aesthetic Provocations in Humanities Computing" (pp. 431–47). For a more recent discussion of noise from the perspective of media archaeology, see Parikka, "Mapping Noise."

[10] McLeod, "Information upon Information," p. 246.

Shakespeare's twentieth-century role as a reference point for information theory, the epistemology that quietly governs the digital texts and tools that humanists work with today. Shakespeare represented ideal material for transmission and preservation, possessing complexity and cultural importance in equal measure.

That ideal is an unreachable one for some, and Shakespeare just as often becomes the limit case for imagining what information can do. W. B. Worthen, for example, objects that "the widespread assumption that Shakespeare's plays can mean the same thing as texts and as performances . . . is, in a sense, an 'information theory' understanding of text-and-performance arising from the iterative character of print: in this view, dramatic writing functions like encoded data, which can be properly (and identically) downloaded with the proper theatrical software."[11] Specifically, Worthen emphasizes that which escapes mechanical iteration: "To the extent that it clarifies the deep contextuality and contingency of performance meanings, drama seems not readily assimilable to 'information.'"[12] These are substantive objections, not to be taken lightly, but terms like "information theory" (in scare quotes) and "encoded data" should not be taken for granted either. Worthen's objection highlights the nuance in Hayles's definition of virtuality, which she qualifies as a *cultural perception*, not an innate quality or universal condition of information. Cultural perceptions are powerful, and it is essential to understand that information, as a concept, performs a kind of cultural work by means of its metaphorical mobility. As Willard McCarty suggests, "Having it is good. Being without it is bad. But its colourless, odourless, tasteless and elusive ubiquity makes the notion, however successful, exceedingly difficult to grasp critically – which fact should make us very suspicious."[13] Worthen voices that very suspicion with good reason when he objects to the quasi-scientific "sense that a photo carries the same 'information' whether it is displayed on [a] cellphone, laptop screen, in the newspaper, or in a gallery exhibition."[14] This is a notion that grates against the performance- and history-oriented approaches that have enlivened Shakespeare studies even as digital culture has been taking shape.

---

[11] Worthen, "Performing Shakespeare," p. 241.
[12] Worthen, "Performing Shakespeare," p. 240.
[13] McCarty, *Humanities Computing*, p. 110. See also Nunberg, "Farewell."
[14] Worthen, "Performing Shakespeare," p. 240.

Worthen and others who resist taking the mobility of information for granted would find support from present-day information studies, which has taken a materialist turn similar to that of textual studies. Information scholars such as Geoffrey Bowker, Ronald Day, Geoffrey Nunberg, David Levy, and Susan Leigh Star (among many others) have written extensively on the deeply contextual nature of information, especially the socio-cultural dimensions of its definition and use.[15] Day in particular has challenged the so-called "conduit metaphor" of information to which Worthen objects.[16] The present chapter's title signals its debt to Day's book *The Modern Invention of Information*, which contextualizes the idea of information within the political and philosophical upheavals of the twentieth century, and seeks to counteract the tendency of information culture not only to forget its history but to forget it has a history.[17]

As we head into a new generation of digital Shakespeare projects that mobilize the idea of information in various ways, it is worth taking account of our critical grasp on the idea, as well as the claims it makes on us. By understanding this crucial episode of computing's cultural history prior to the more familiar PC revolution, one can find new contexts for questions about Shakespeare and digital technologies of the present and future. How does the notion that Shakespeare's works are somehow exceptional in all of literature function in scientific knowledge domains which usually value generalizability over idiosyncrasy?[18] How does the perception of Shakespeare's printed texts as information patterns affect their reception and cultural meaning? How should we understand the interpenetration of texts and machines, given that most if not all of the Shakespeare text we have received is the product of a mechanical process? These questions all converge on the idea of the virtual Shakespeare text, an idea whose origins lie in the mid-twentieth century's formalizing and institutionalizing of the information culture

---

[15] See Nunberg, "Farewell," pp. 102–38; Bowker, *Memory Practices*, especially his chapter "The Empty Archive: Cybernetics and the 1960s," pp. 75–105; Bowker and Star, *Sorting Things Out*; Levy, *Scrolling Forward*; and Day, *Invention of Information*. See the discussion of archivists' commitment to understanding the contextuality of records and information in Chapter 2, pp. 65–9.

[16] Day, "Conduit Metaphor."

[17] Day, *Invention of Information*, p. 3. See the Introduction, p. 12.

[18] For a discussion of nomothetic versus idiographic perspectives on textuality, see Galey, "Human Presence," pp. 99–100 and 116–17.

that had been developing since the late Victorian period. This chapter explores the twentieth-century origins of the Shakespearean archive, first by examining some of the foundational ideas of information theory, and then by examining some historical and epistemological convergences between textual studies and the idea of information.

Reading Shakespeare with information theory

In this new theory the word information relates not so much to what you *do* say, as to what you *could* say. That is, information is a measure of your freedom of choice when you select a message... The two messages between which one must choose in such a selection can be anything one likes. One might be the King James version of the Bible, and the other might be "Yes."

Warren Weaver, "The Mathematics of Communication" (1949)[19]

Thou shalt commit adultery.

King James Bible (1631 misprint)[20]

⌐3yes3⌐ I said ⌐2yes2⌐ I will ⌐3[yes.] Yes.3⌐

James Joyce, *Ulysses* (synoptic edition)[21]

I have used the term *information theory* to refer to a field of study, but what exactly is the theory to which some humanities scholars have objected so categorically when applied to literature? This section summarizes information theory in its classical form, that of Claude Shannon's communications model as outlined in Warren Weaver's landmark essay, "The Mathematics of Communication." The model describes how a message travels from an information source to its destination, and how any changes resulting from the intervention of noise are subject to laws of probability. The components of the communications model, in sequence, are the *information source, transmitter, channel, receiver,* and *destination* (see Figure 6.1). As Weaver summarizes the theory, "The information source selects a desired message out of a set of possible messages ... The transmitter changes [encodes] this message into a signal which is sent over the communication channel to the receiver," at which point a reverse process

---

[19] Weaver, "Mathematics of Communication," p. 12.
[20] From the infamous version known as the Wicked Bible: *The Holy Bible Containing the Old Testament and the New* (London, 1631), Exodus 20.14. See also Norton, *Textual History*, pp. 95–6.
[21] Joyce, *Ulysses*, vol. III, p. 1726.

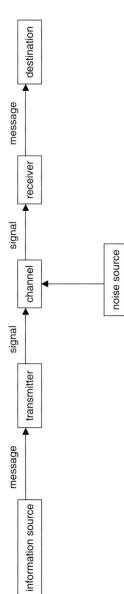

Figure 6.1 Shannon and Weaver's mathematical model of communication.

takes place in which "the receiver is a sort of inverse transmitter, changing the transmitted signal back into a message, and handing this message on to the destination."[22] The process may seem simple enough, but information theory identifies two areas where complexity intervenes. One is the communication channel, where the signal may change in ways the information source did not intend. According to Weaver, "These unwanted additions [to the signal] may be distortions of sound (in telephony, for example), or static (in radio) ... or errors in transmission (telegraphy or facsimile). All these changes in the signal may be called noise."[23] We shall return to this idea below.

Another area of complexity, and perhaps the most counterintuitive aspect of information theory, is the definition of information itself. The term *information* in information theory means something very different from everyday usage. In Shannon's model, information is not a thing, or a quality of things corresponding to *meaning* or *truth* or *accuracy*, but rather a measure of the disambiguation required to express an intelligible message. Gregory Bateson uses the example of writing systems:

An event or object such as the letter K in a given position in the text of a message *might* have been any other of the limited set of twenty-six letters in the English language. The actual letter excludes ... twenty-five alternatives. In comparison with an English letter, a Chinese ideograph would have excluded several thousand alternatives. We say, therefore, that the Chinese ideograph carries more information than the letter.[24]

As Weaver was often at pains to emphasize, "The concept of information applies not to the individual messages, as the concept of meaning would, but rather to the situation as a whole."[25] Information in this sense is thus a measurable quantity within a definable system, not an interpretive quality lurking within an individual text or artifact.

An example would be the well-known crux in Othello's final speech, in which he compares himself either to a "base Iudean" (according to the 1623 First Folio) or to a "base *Indian*" (according to the 1622 quarto). Much has been written on the meaning at stake in each variant, which may include Othello's acceptance or rejection of guilt for

[22] Weaver, "Mathematics of Communication," pp. 11–12; see also Shannon and Weaver, *The Mathematical Theory of Communication*.
[23] Weaver, "Mathematics of Communication," p. 12.
[24] Gregory Bateson, *Ecology of Mind*, p. 408, emphasis in original.
[25] Weaver, "Mathematics of Communication," p. 12.

becoming Iago's murderous dupe: in the one variant Othello may compare himself to the betrayer Judas; in the other, to a supposedly innocent and easily deceived Indian of the New World (or possibly the Far East). As Tom Davis points out in his discussion of this crux as an exemplary textual conundrum, "Other texts – computer programs, for instance, or bank statements – may similarly have momentous consequences attached to tiny items, but ... with literary texts ... you can never tell which word may be seized upon and installed as the core of an argument."[26] Textual critics have speculated that if the word *Indian* had appeared in the quarto copy in the early modern spelling *Indean*, the difference between the variants becomes a single letter, *n* or *u*.[27]

This is the kind of information encoding problem that can be understood from multiple perspectives. A computational text-analysis scholar, working under a paradigm inherited from information theory, might say that the quantifiable edit-distance between *Indean* and *Iudean* is 2 (step 1: delete *n*; step 2: insert *u*), and might then apply a similar analysis to the relative edit-distances of similarly contested cruxes in Shakespeare or broader corpora.[28] (How many significant cruxes hinge on variation of less than, say, two letters?) A bibliographer, working under a similar paradigm, might point out that a manuscript *u* can change to a typeset *n* through any of a number of mechanically constrained explanations: a compositor might read his copy incorrectly and reach for the wrong letter; he might read the copy correctly but set the right letter upside-down (or read it *in*correctly but set the *wrong* letter upside-down, resulting in an accidentally faithful setting of type); or, he might read the copy correctly, reach for the right letter, but nonetheless set the wrong letter because of what bibliographers call *foul case*, a scenario in which whoever worked with that case previously had incorrectly redistributed his used type back into their compartments.[29] However, if a bit of information is a "difference which

[26] Davis, "Monsters," p. 97.

[27] See Davis, "Monsters," pp. 97–8. References and analyses can also be found in Velz, "*Judean* and *Indian*," and Ranson, "Indian/Iudean."

[28] On the concept of edit-distance, see Butler, "Monkeying Around with Text," pp. 124–7.

[29] See R. B. McKerrow's discussion of these and other types of errors in *Introduction to Bibliography*, esp. pp. 255–8. He notes that turned letters are particularly difficult to explain as resulting simply from setting a type upside-down (pp. 257–8). Also worth noting, in the context of information theory, is his suggestion that foul-case errors will tend to produce nonsense, but misreadings of

makes a difference," in Bateson's famous definition, it is essential to understand what makes a difference in these contexts: to a bibliographer *n* or *u* is a mark made by a piece of metal type (usually, but not necessarily, with ink on it); but to a computational text analyst, these letters tend to be alphanumeric symbols displayed on a screen and manipulated in the computer's memory.[30] Both ways of thinking may be correct in their contexts, but that does not make them compatible.

If we expand the range of perspectives in this thought experiment, a paleographer might add to our consternation by pointing out that *n* and *u* may be identical graphic marks in early modern secretary hand. For example, what is the following word?

Based on its context, I can confidently assert this set of marks to mean "Inde" as in India, given that its manuscript source is a transcription of Langland's *Piers Plowman* made in 1531–2 by Sir Adrian Fortescue (the complete line reads "In Inde & in alysaundre in ermony & in spayne").[31] Note that the marks between the *I* and *d* could just as easily represent *u* as *n*. Now imagine that Shakespeare's dramatic manuscripts have been discovered, found to be written in a similar sixteenth-century secretary hand, and then published for the world in a diplomatic edition (an open-access digital edition, one hopes). Even if that edition attained the extraordinary level of detail of what Peter Robinson calls a "graphetic transcription" – that is, a transcription that records unique letter-forms, not just spellings – the editor and reader alike would still face the problem of disambiguating the message carried by this graphic signal,

copy will tend to produce words that make sense, even though they are not the author's (p. 258).

30 Gregory Bateson, *Ecology of Mind*, p. 315.

31 Bodleian MS Digby 145, f. 91r; reproduced by permission of The Bodleian Library, University of Oxford. I am grateful to Kathryn Kerby-Fulton for drawing this manuscript to my attention many years ago. For an analysis of Digby 145, a fascinating artifact in its own right, especially in terms of collaborative annotation, see Kerby-Fulton, "Women Readers."

with little help from the primary evidence itself.[32] The conclusion of this thought experiment may be deflating for those invested in the New Bibliographical search for a Shakespearean archive in the form of his dramatic manuscripts: even if Shakespeare rose from the grave like old Hamlet's ghost, wrote down the line from *Othello* exactly as it appeared in all his manuscripts, and silently handed the paper to our hypothetical gathering of specialists, none of them might be able to decode what Shakespeare actually wrote at the moment of inscription.

An information theorist hovering at the edges of this gathering of specialists might then point out that Shakespeare's inscription of the word in question (assuming he wrote in secretary hand, and spelled *Indian* as *Indean*) actually carries less information than the word in print: Shakespeare's handwriting might add ambiguity where print removes it, even if print replaces it with error. However, an information theory perspective would also attempt to take in the big picture in which the transmission of the text took place, with an eye to predicting and accounting for other instances of the same pattern of *Indean/Iudean* ambiguity in any medium. There is at least one instance introduced by digitization: the electronic text of Elizabeth Cary's play *The Tragedie of Mariam, the Faire Queene of Jewry* in ProQuest's Literature Online database. Act 2, scene 4, begins with the phrase "Well met *Indean* Lord," though the 1613 quarto clearly reads "*Iudean*," and the lord being well met here is clearly Judean (Salome's husband, Constabarbus).[33] Encoding ambiguity and error increase the probability that India and Judea switch places in other digitizations of early modern texts, as well. However, unlike the case of *The Tragedie of Mariam*, the Indean/Judean crux in *Othello* seems to me unresolvable on bibliographical evidence, even if Shakespeare's manuscripts were discovered tomorrow. The weight of interpretive plausibility for *both* the "Indian" and "Judean" options dooms Shakespeare emenders to settle for nudging the probability one way or the other, and dooms Shakespeare performers to making a creative choice rather than an appeal to textual authority (a situation which, according to Worthen, performance should embrace freely).[34]

Worth noting among these different perspectives is what they choose to disregard. Our hypothetical text-analysis scholar, for example,

---

[32] Robinson, "Is There a Text," p. 105.
[33] Cary, *Tragedie of Mariam*, sig. D2r.
[34] See Worthen, *Authority of Performance* and *Modern Performance*.

chooses to ignore the italics in the 1622 quarto variant, as does the information theorist (following Bateson, who deals with a twenty-six-letter alphabet, not the multitude of individual types which hand-press bibliographers often track).[35] The challenge presented by this and many other textual variants arises not from the interference of noise in transmission, which Shannon's theory prioritizes, but from the complexity of encoding presented by the materials themselves. All of our received Shakespeare texts, even the debated Hand D sections of the *Sir Thomas More* manuscript, reach us as products of a prior encoding process. This is an aspect of digitization that is dangerous to overlook, since doing so passes up the opportunity of using digital projects' design and encoding stages to understand cultural materials anew.

Another Shakespearean example serves to illustrate other aspects of Shannon's model. In his anti-Stratfordian excursus *Is Shakespeare Dead?* Mark Twain recounts how one Captain Ealer (on whose riverboat Twain apprenticed in his youth) would recite Shakespeare from memory in the wheelhouse, interlaced with running commentary on Twain's helmsmanship, such that "if we were in a risky and difficult piece of river an ignorant person couldn't have told, sometimes, which observations were Shakespeare's and which were Ealer's."[36] Recalling Ealer's jumbled recitation of a speech from *Macbeth*, Twain gives an example of two mixed messages, in which the language of the play slides in and out of the language of riverboat navigation:

What man dare, *I* dare!
Approach thou *what* are you laying in the leads for? what a hell of an idea! like the rugged ease her off a little, ease her off! rugged Russian bear, the armed rhinoceros or the *there* she goes! meet her, meet her! didn't you *know* she'd smell the reef if you crowded it like that? Hyrcan tiger; take any shape but that and my firm nerves she'll be in the *woods* the first you know! stop the starboard! come ahead strong on the larboard! back the starboard! ... *Now* then, you're all right; come ahead on the starboard; straighten up and go 'long, never tremble: or be alive again, and dare me to the desert *damnation* can't you keep her away from that greasy water? pull her down! snatch her! snatch her baldheaded! with thy sword; if trembling I inhabit then, lay in the leads! – no, only the starboard one, leave the other alone, protest me the baby

---

[35] Gregory Bateson, *Ecology of Mind*, p. 408.
[36] Twain, *Is Shakespeare Dead?*, p. 5.

of a girl. Hence horrible shadow! eight bells – that watchman's asleep again, I reckon, go down and call Brown yourself, unreal mockery, hence![37]

Captain Ealer fulfills Milton's prophecy of readers who monumentalize Shakespeare through the deep impressions of memory. According to Twain, Ealer "did not use the book, and did not need to; he knew his Shakespeare as well as Euclid ever knew his multiplication table."[38] Yet Twain himself falls short as the noise of the world intervenes; he laments, "it was a damage to me, because I have never since been able to read Shakespeare in a calm and sane way. I cannot rid it of his explosive interlardings, they break in everywhere."[39] This story captures the core concerns of information theory, including the "damage" Twain experiences as a result of the tangled messages and the command-and-control scenario as the wheelhouse crew, functioning as a single system, responds to results of its own actions ("ease her off!"; "*there* she goes!").

The Babel persisting in Twain's memory is an example of the Shakespeare text assimilating itself to the condition of information, and its comic effect depends upon the reader's impulse to disentangle the recognizably Shakespearean language – an impulse repeatedly frustrated by the ease with which the one message slips into the other, aided by the imperative phrasing which makes Twain himself into the ghost of Banquo by the end ("go down and call Brown yourself, unreal mockery, hence!"). The reader of this passage cannot help but relive the Shakespeare editor's eternal dilemma, compounded by Twain's implicit expectation that the original text of *Macbeth* should be deeply impressed in the reader's own memory. The whole text of the passage

---

[37] Twain, *Is Shakespeare Dead?*, pp. 5–6. The passage from *Macbeth* reads:

> What man dare, I dare.
> Approach thou like the ruggèd Russian bear,
> The armed rhinoceros, or th'Hyrcan tiger;
> Take any shape but that, and my firm nerves
> Shall never tremble. Or be alive again,
> And dare me to the desert with thy sword.
> If trembling I inhabit then, protest me
> The baby of a girl. Hence, horrible shadow,
> Unreal mock'ry, hence! (3.4.98–106)

[38] Twain, *Is Shakespeare Dead?*, p. 7.   [39] Twain, *Is Shakespeare Dead?*, pp. 6–7.

might be considered a signal, in Shannon's terms, but whether the recollected text of *Macbeth* or the navigational instructions are message or noise depends on what one considers important. The crux of Twain's joke is that each message can function as noise to the other, depending on one's perspective.

These examples also show that literary texts make for especially problematic messages, as they are themselves agents by virtue of their symbolic status within the communications model, not passive content: they can exert a ludic power over the reader to revise one's understanding of the very rules that would govern their encoding, transmission, and decoding. Weaver suggests information theory should be able to account for the transmission of the King James Bible and the single word *yes* with equal applicability, but overlooks that literary works are often active agents in thematizing their own material transmission. It misses the point to reduce, say, the famous last words of James Joyce's *Ulysses* – Molly Bloom's "yes I said yes I will Yes"[40] – to quantifiable information content, like an anti-aircraft gunner's "affirmative" in a radio message. The same is true of the King James Bible, which as an early modern book had its own complex printing history, and whose text did not stabilize until many years after its first publication in 1611.[41]

Yet it is that very reductionist tendency of information theory, and its continuing influence, which permits humanities computing technologies and methods to treat literary texts, as Jerome McGann puts it, "as if they were expository, as if their 'information' were indexable, as if the works were *not* made from zeugmas and puns, metaphors and intertexts, as if the textual structure were composed of self-identical elements."[42] In my *Ulysses* example, the simple word *yes* has considerable symbolic status as the final word in a literary text whose transmission was not only complex – to say the least – but also manipulated by its author to incorporate noise in the form of errors and accidents of textual encoding (similar to the so-called Wicked Bible's infamous error), into what Weaver might call its message.[43] The consequent visual complexity of Hans Walter Gabler's synoptic text, with its

[40] Joyce, *Ulysses*, p. 1727.   [41] See Norton, *Textual History*.
[42] McGann, *Radiant Textuality*, pp. 185–6, emphasis in original.
[43] On the paradoxical role of error in *Ulysses*, see Mahaffey, "Intentional Error." On the significance of Joyce's revisions to the final words, see Groden, *Ulysses in Focus*, pp. 25–6 and 198. Whether one considers "yes" to be the final word in the

elaborate system of typographic markup to indicate textual states, embodies McKenzie's point about the symbolic status of what Greg regarded as "arbitrary marks" (discussed below). Such graphical traces of authorial practice purport to track Joyce's easy numbers flowing (perhaps not so easily), but the textual problem in Shakespeare is defined by the absence of the manuscripts, annotated typescripts, and other documents that generate such complexity in the Joycean tradition. With Shakespeare and other literary texts, the editor's or encoder's desire to find informatic order sometimes produces it.

Defining information with Shakespeare

The only lecture by Turing that I attended was one he gave to the student mathematical society. It was entitled "On large numbers." Figuring in the lecture were the following large numbers M and N. A hypothetical bird flies, once each year, to the top of Mount Everest and removes one grain of "sand"; M is the number of seconds needed to level the mountain. The other number N was such that $1/N$ is the probability that "this piece of chalk will jump from my hand and write a line of Shakespeare on the board before falling to the ground." Turing had, of course, numerical estimates for M and N.

J. L. Britton, "Postscript," *Pure Mathematics* (1992)[44]

Despite the difficulty of reducing Shakespeare to a set of messages within an information system, early information theorists seemed oddly determined to make an example of him. Formative events like the Macy conferences embodied the spirit of what is now called interdisciplinarity, but information theory's origin and early takeup were decidedly on the scientific side of what C. P. Snow called the division of the two cultures, the arts and sciences.[45] Even so, Shakespeare appears

---

novel depends on how one regards the paratextual postscript "*Trieste-Zurich-Paris, / 1914–1921.*" printed just below in the 1922 Paris edition.

[44] In Turing, *Pure Mathematics*, p. xvii.

[45] See Snow, *Two Cultures*. There were early attempts on both sides to find common ground, though not always successfully. John Robinson Pierce's *Symbols, Signals, and Noise* (1961) has a chapter on "Information Theory and Art." Edward M. Jennings's 1970 edited collection, *Science and Literature*, reprints Weaver's essay "The Mathematics of Communication," pp. 13–27. In the same year John P. Sisk published an article titled "The Cybernetics of Othello," which examines Othello's decision-making patterns, but does not engage cybernetics as a field. Graham Bradshaw critiques the so-called conduit metaphor from a Shakespearean perspective in a 2005 article titled "Precious Nonsense and the Conduit Metaphor." A recent promising link between Shakespeare and the

in the theoretical discourse about information and computing from the beginning, even in one of the founding works of modern computing, mathematician Alan Turing's 1950 essay "Computing Machinery and Intelligence." This essay was one of the first serious scientific discussions of artificial intelligence, and proposes criteria for what has become known as the Turing test, a scenario in which a human judge converses with a hidden interlocutor who may be another human or a machine; if the judge cannot tell which is which, the machine has passed the test. Notably, Turing's article envisions this test partly in terms of a "sonnet-writing machine" that could simulate what he regards as an essentially human mode of communication.[46] Taking an example from Shakespeare's Sonnet 18 ("Shall I compare thee to a summer's day?"), he equates Shakespeare with an aspect of human communication that his audience would regard as exceeding the machine's capacity for modelling.

These very conditions materialized in an actual Turing test in 1991 at the Boston Computer Museum, in which ten human judges conversed via keyboard and screen with six artificial intelligence programs and four human confederates, with the confederates' and computers' iden-tities concealed. Shakespeare again showed up among the topics of conversation selected for the test, along with "dry martinis," "women's clothing," and other topics "of the sort appropriate for a cocktail party," as one of the referees recounts.[47] An episode of the public television series *Scientific American Frontiers* captured some of the conversations between the judges and a human confederate, Cynthia Clay, whose knowledge of Shakespearean matters such as the

worlds of information theory and programming may be found in Henry S. Turner's article "Life Science: Rude Mechanicals, Human Mortals, Posthuman Shakespeare" (2009). See also David Wellbery's more generalized conception of literature through information theory in his foreword to Friedrich Kittler's, *Discourse Networks*: "As soon as we conceive of literature as medially instantiated, then we must view its meaning as the product of a selection and rarefication. All media of transmission require a material channel, and the characteristic of every material channel is that, beyond – and, as it were, against – the information it carries, it produces noise and nonsense. What we call literature, in other words, stands in an essential (and again, historically variable) relation to a non-meaning, which it must exclude" (p. xiv).

[46] Turing, "Computing Machinery," p. 446. Cf. the note of alarm that Lester Asheim sounds in a 1955 article on the future of the book with regard to a scientist's claim that intelligent machines might eventually compose sonnets; Asheim, "New Problems in Plotting the Future of the Book," p. 287.

[47] Shieber, "Lessons," p. 72.

authorship complexities of *Pericles* unexpectedly reversed the dynamics of the Turing test: judges and audience members misidentified her as a computer.[48] As one audience member reasoned, "some of [Clay's] answers seemed too studied, as if they were somehow canned opinions that came from a large database"; similarly, a judge thought no human could command so much information about Shakespeare. The subtext of the episode is revealing. Clay's good-humoured but exasperated response – "People, go to school!" – highlights the ostensible status of Shakespeare information as a kind of public commons, like baseball statistics, but hints also at a decline in public knowledge of Shakespeare. By the time computing had advanced to the stage where a real Turing test was viable, a person like Clay was an anomaly, and her personal command of information on Shakespeare was most readily explained in computational terms. Between 1949 and 1991, Shakespeare had become an information domain where the boundary between human and machine was contested.[49]

The Turing example is no exception, but part of a pattern in explanations of information as a measure of disambiguation rather than a quantity of knowledge. G. H. Hardy's *A Mathematician's Apology* (1940), while predating information theory as such by a few years, nonetheless sets the tone by using Shakespeare's texts to explain the difference between pure and applied mathematics. Hardy argues that it would be fallacious to suppose that one's understanding of a theorem should be affected by the physical character of the means one uses to represent it, like imperfectly drawn shapes on a lecture-hall blackboard: "It would be like supposing that a play of Shakespeare is changed when a reader spills his tea over a page. The play is independent of the pages on which it is printed, and 'pure geometries' are independent of lecture rooms, or of any other detail of the physical world."[50] Here Hardy applies a version of the conduit metaphor to information, to which Worthen and others have objected (as discussed above).

Similar idealism appears in a 1956 book by one of the founders of information theory, the physicist Léon Brillouin, who mentions

---

[48] "Machines Who Think: Contest and Competitions," *Scientific American Frontiers*, season 2, episode 5; broadcast 23 October 1991, www.pbs.org/saf. See also Shieber, "Lessons," p. 72.

[49] On science's recruitment of Shakespeare in more general terms, see Garber's chapter "Who Owns 'Human Nature'?," in her *Quotation Marks*, pp. 243–67.

[50] Hardy, *Mathematician's Apology*, p. 126.

Shakespeare when he explains (following Shannon) that information theory does not deal with "the human value of information," or what one would call meaning, but only with the quantifiable behaviour of information in a communications system.[51] Brillouin states that one can quantify the amount of information in any arbitrary string of 100 letters, regardless of whether they are (in his words) "a set of 100 letters selected at random ... a sentence of 100 letters from a newspaper, a piece of Shakespeare or a theorem of Einstein."[52] Information is to be distinguished from knowledge, with knowledge represented by Einstein, Shakespeare, and a newspaper.[53] Compare this comment from the unpublished 1959 notebook of French biologist Jacques Monod: "From the point of view of the theory of information, the works of Shakespeare, with the same number of letters and signs aligned at random by a monkey, would have the same value ... What could be considered as 'objective' in the Shakespearean information that would distinguish it from the monkey's information? Essentially the transmissibility."[54] Monod alludes to the commonplace idea of infinite monkeys at typewriters reproducing the works of Shakespeare by accident, although in popular culture Shakespeare's texts have somehow substituted themselves for the books in the British Museum, which was the original example popularized by British physicist Arthur Eddington.[55]

These are just a few examples among many.[56] The pattern that emerges reveals certain assumptions: that Shakespeare is ideal text, not material text or performance; that the plays are the products of a single authorial source (Cynthia Clay was unwilling to discuss *The Two Noble Kinsmen* as a coauthored play and correctly guessed that human judges would not recognize the possibly collaborative play *Pericles*);

[51] Brillouin, *Science and Information Theory*, p. 9.   [52] *Ibid.*
[53] Cf. Alexander Graham Bell's juxtaposition of Shakespeare with newspaper stories in his demonstrations of the telephone, as discussed in Chapter 5 (see pp. 173–86).
[54] Quoted in Kay, *Book of Life*, p. 220.
[55] Butler, "Monkeying Around with Text," pp. 113–33.
[56] For similar examples, see Singh, *Great Ideas*, p. 209; Winograd and Flores, *Understanding Computers and Cognition*, p. 122; Layzer, *Cosmogenesis*, p. 31; Dembski, *Design Inference*, p. 216; MacKay, *Information Theory*, p. 490; Yockey, *Information Theory*, p. 5; Floridi, *Short Introduction*, pp. 105 and 108; and Gleick, *The Information*, pp. 328, 331, and 360. A more detailed engagement with the plots of *Macbeth*, *Hamlet*, *Romeo and Juliet* and other works appears in an article on the modelling of analogy for artificial intelligence; see Patrick H. Winston, "Learning and Reasoning."

that Shakespeare's texts possess no more internal complexity of transmission than any other book on the shelf; and that despite whatever cultural power one may locate in Shakespeare – what Brillouin calls "the human value" – information theory holds a greater power to make information strategically mobile by asserting a fundamental equivalency among all texts.

Information theory's claims for Shakespeare's *un*exceptionality might seem as provocative as Benjamin Jowett's controversial claim a century earlier that the Bible could be interpreted "like any other book."[57] This approach also resonates with the contemporary thinking about literary texts that was coming from the New Bibliographers. For example, F. P. Wilson's 1945 work *Shakespeare and the New Bibliography* exemplifies this sympathy in a claim similar in spirit to the Weaver epigraph to the preceding section: "To a formal bibliographer a book is not the life-blood of a master spirit but a collection of pieces of paper with printing on them."[58] Wilson hearkens back to W. W. Greg's stronger formulation of this dictum: "What the bibliographer is concerned with is pieces of paper or parchment covered with certain written or printed signs. With these signs he is concerned merely as arbitrary marks; their meaning is no business of his."[59] Such bracketing of meaning for the purpose of determining a mechanical process mirrors Shannon's similar gesture in most respects, including its contentiousness in the eyes of critics. D. F. McKenzie's answer to Greg's statement about "arbitrary marks" applies equally well to Shannon's theory: "the moment we are required to explain signs in a book, as distinct from describing or copying them, they assume a symbolic status. If a medium in any sense effects a message, then bibliography cannot exclude from its own proper concerns the relation between form, function, and symbolic meaning."[60]

The indivisibility of encoding from meaning is no surprise to Shakespeare editors, as distinct from pure bibliographers, considering that editors have long wrestled with received text that sometimes wavers on the border between sense and nonsense. A major blind spot in Shannon and Weaver's communications model – at least as it applies to

---

[57] Benjamin Jowett, "Interpretation of Scripture," p. 504, emphasis removed.
[58] F. P. Wilson, *Shakespeare and the New Bibliography*, p. 42.
[59] Greg, "Bibliography – An Apologia," in *Sir Walter Wilson Greg*, p. 141.
[60] McKenzie, *Bibliography*, p. 10; see Greg, "Bibliography – An Apologia," in *Sir Walter Wilson Greg*, p. 141, quoted above.

literature, as it supposedly does to all human communication – is its mistaking of where complexity lies, not just in signal and noise but especially in encoding and decoding.[61] This mistake accounts for a problematic tendency in the digital humanities: the assumption that the encoding of humanities material into machine-readable form should be straightforward, subject to a global set of rules underpinned by rationality and consistency.[62] However, once information theory extends itself into cultural matters, it cannot separate the solving of problems from the bestowing of value. Day argues that one sees such power at work "in the privilege that a certain 'factual' and 'clear' information is given in communication (in writing in general, in the media, in organizations, in education, and in politics), in the demand that the arts represent reality rather than 'distort' it (realism), and even in the claim that history is the transmission of the past to receivers in subsequent generations (cultural heritage)."[63] Whatever virtues computing humanists might make of encoding as a field for inquiry and illuminating problems, day-to-day practice feels the pressure of information theory's legacy: the technical assumption, even cultural conviction, that a text can be transmitted, encoded, and received with little difficulty so long as noise, ambiguity, and error are minimized to acceptable levels. As we shall see, what counts as noise depends upon human choices, especially ideological ones.

Warlike noise: code, machines, and the weaponizing of literature

> Professors back from secret missions
> Resume their proper eruditions,
> Though some regret it
> W. H. Auden, "Under Which Lyre" (1946)[64]

---

[61] See Hayles, *How We Became Posthuman*, p. 54.
[62] This notion informed a great deal of the early work on the Text Encoding Initiative (TEI) Guidelines, though the TEI community has become much more open to the materiality of texts in recent years. For example, the online teaching resource *TEIbyExample.org* contains a rich set of examples that challenge normative models of textuality.
[63] Day, "Conduit Metaphor," p. 810.
[64] Auden, "Under Which Lyre: A Reactionary Tract for the Times," in *Collected Poems*, pp. 333–4.

Mid-century bibliography and information theory were caught up in the same emergent tendency to regard texts as virtual.[65] Their concern with the Shakespeare text as an information pattern latent in physical documents manifested itself in the profiling of hypothetical manuscript copy behind real printed books, as well as the profiling of the work habits of the compositors who read and set from that copy. Matthew Kirschenbaum points out that "for both textual scholars and information theorists the immediate post-war years were a period dedicated to codifying their respective disciplinary methodologies," and he suggests that Greg's treatment of accidentals and substantives in his theory of copy-text editing resembles the kind of thinking occurring at the same time in information theory.[66] While Kirschenbaum reports finding no direct historical links, I suggest there does not necessarily need to be evidence of direct communication for there to be epistemological links of consequence to textual studies and digital humanities in the present. Although the New Bibliographers were not necessarily doing information theory, they were involved in analogous textual sciences.

The pattern of analogy also extends to their failures, especially their failure to account for the complex connections between what texts mean and how acts of communication – whether editing, performance, digitization, or rare book exhibitions – generate new meanings in their reception. Shakespeare's texts, as a cultural symbol like the Bible, carry a surplus of meaning in the form of the transmission narratives that accompany them. The transmission narrative most relevant to Shakespeare's emergence as information holds his texts to be conduits of meaning in the face of catastrophic conflict. This section will explore the wartime epistemology that serves to triangulate information theory and bibliography, and which also produced the idea of Shakespeare as machine-readable code.

Throughout the Second World War, military communication and intelligence practices invested in a conduit metaphor for information in ways that suited strategic planning and tactical responsiveness. Shannon's communications model rendered information mobile in

---

[65] On prewar tendencies toward information theory in bibliography, see Kirschenbaum, "Editing the Interface," and Maguire, *Shakespearean Suspect Texts*, pp. 21–71. Recent examples of literary scholars using information theory include McLeod, "Information on Information"; Robinson, "Is There a Text"; and Davis, "Monsters."

[66] Kirschenbaum, "Editing the Interface," pp. 19–20, n. 12.

ways that suited strategic thinking. Managing information was a tactical challenge, and one that had proven decisive in modern warfare. Information pioneers like Norbert Wiener and Vannevar Bush played major roles in the mobilization of science during the war, and the interdisciplinary field of cybernetics developed directly out of research on the interface between humans and machines in anti-aircraft targeting systems.[67] To the extent that information theory and its descendants conceive of physical documents, that conception has its prototype in the strategic mobility of microfilm. Microfilm had a vital application in military logistics as the technology of mobile libraries that could stand in for the masses of paper documents required in wartime correspondence. Vernon D. Tate's description of this technology's military value, in a 1942 article in the *Journal of Documentary Reproduction*, equates it with a weapon because it could free up space on a cargo plane for troops and supplies, as well as provide an encyclopedic reference for technical maintenance in the field: "In modern warfare the library accompanies even the most advanced fighting forces in the field."[68] Bush's own wartime vision for a device called the Memex, a proto-hypertext browser dependent upon microfilm, should be remembered as part of a wider project to use microfilm and microphotography to standardize and regulate flows of information that would otherwise necessitate the physical management of material documents.[69] The military and strategic legacy attached to the concept of information in this period created a barely submerged identity for cybernetics, which Mark Poster pointedly characterizes as "a theory for an armed camp preparing for a final struggle."[70]

---

[67] See Mahoney, "Cybernetics and Information Technology," and Galison, "Ontology of the Enemy."

[68] Tate, "Microphotography in Wartime," p. 133. On the wartime microfilm infrastructure that eventually made its way into the digital *Early English Books Online* (EEBO) project, see Mak, "Archaeology of a Digitization."

[69] Bush's article about the Memex, titled "As We May Think," was published in *Atlantic Monthly* (July 1945) and *Life* (November 1945). On the historical context for the two versions of the essay, including the atomic bombings of Hiroshima and Nagasaki, which took place in the interval between their publication, see Harpold, *Ex-foliations*, pp. 71–2. Bush's essay has since been republished in Nyce and Kahn (eds.), *Memex to Hypertext*. On the Memex's largely uncredited antecedents in the history of microfilm, see Buckland, "Emmanuel Goldberg"; on the Memex's relation to reading machines more broadly, see Harpold, *Ex-foliations*, pp. 20–43.

[70] Poster, *Mode of Information*, p. 29.

Within this wartime epistemology, which viewed documents as containers for meaning, Shakespeare's texts were subject to various kinds of encoding and decoding. Anti-Stratfordian hobbyists had searched for ciphers within Shakespeare's texts since the nineteenth century, and cryptography was a long-established profession, but the Second World War's impact on cryptanalysis was to raise the stakes of analyzing documents such that human lives depended on the flow and interception of coded information. During the war, Shakespeare's texts became code-bearing patterns of information in contexts far more consequential than the imaginations of Baconians and Oxfordians. According to Alice Brittan, "The most famous works of Shakespeare, Keats, Tennyson, Molière, Racine, and Rabelais became favorites among the Allied spies; they were easy for agents to remember, even under duress, because they were taught and studied in schools as exemplars of English or French literature."[71] Milton's image of Shakespeare's "easie numbers," like Twain's example of Captain Ealer's recitations on the Mississippi, takes on new meaning in light of these uses of Shakespeare's texts, which nonetheless depend upon the "deepe Impression" of the texts in the national consciousness, as Brittan suggests,

A British agent who as a student was asked to memorize Shakespeare's sonnet 55, or to write an essay in defense of its claim to immortality, could use the poem's opening lines – "Not marble, nor the gilded monuments / Of princes shall outlive this powerful rhyme" – to send information in defense of the country that claimed Shakespeare as its national bard. Code makers believed that the agent would recall this sonnet even in panic, because to forget was virtually an act of treason.[72]

In this one can see a type of Shakespearean code existing independently of the authorship debates in a bibliographic strain distinguishable from, though obviously related to, the better-known wartime recruitment of plays like *Henry V* to bolster English patriotism.[73]

Just as Shakespeare's texts became a sort of informatic weapon to help the Allies, so did wartime information techniques come to the rescue of Shakespeare. Former US Army cryptanalysis experts William

---

[71] Brittan, "War and the Book," p. 203. See also Marks, *Silk and Cyanide*, pp. 11–12.
[72] Brittan, "War and the Book," pp. 203–4.
[73] See Hoenselaars, "Shooting the Hero."

and Mary Friedman became two of the most respected debunkers of anti-Stratfordian cipher theories in their 1958 book *The Shakespearean Ciphers Examined.*[74] Cambridge University Press's dust-jacket description takes pains to establish the Friedmans not only as neutral arbiters of the authorship debate because of their dissociation from the academy, but also as expert witnesses on the subjects of cryptography in the light of their wartime achievements. Supposedly, the minds that helped break Japan's Purple Code had found a suitable postwar challenge in theories about Shakespeare's texts. Their book represents a form of textual and informatic rationalism confronting the irrationalism of anti-Stratfordian cipher hunting. Cryptographic historian David Kahn uses especially vivid terms to describe the Friedmans' encounter with the anti-Stratfordian cryptographic imagination in search of provable ciphers:

They find no such proof. But they have a fascinating trip. They pass through a surrealist landscape where logic and the events of history both resemble and do not resemble the real things, like the oozing watch of Salvador Dali, where supermen of literature outperform the most harried hacks in volume and the most thoughtful of philosophers in profundity – and then sit up nights enciphering secret messages to tell about it.[75]

Given the symbolic stakes of the Friedmans' work, outlined here in no uncertain terms by Kahn, it is perhaps not surprising that one of the Friedmans' biggest accolades came from the chief Shakespearean archive in the form of the 1955 Folger Shakespeare Library Prize.[76] Kahn's description is also illuminating because it holds a mirror up to the rational side of Shakespearean code. If the world of Baconian ciphers looks like a Dali landscape, the world of authentically Shakespearean code must be defined by right angles, with messages squared away and objects in their proper spatial relations.

Shakespearean archive fever makes for strange bedfellows, and the so-called Folio method discussed in Chapter 3 – which infuses every typographic detail of the Folio (presumably regardless of press variants)

---

[74] Friedman and Friedman, *Shakespearean Ciphers Examined.* William H. Sherman is currently working on a project dealing with the Friedmans and cryptography, and I am grateful to him for discussing his unpublished work with me; see his article "How to Make Anything Signify Anything."
[75] Kahn, *The Codebreakers*, p. 879.
[76] Rosenheim, *Cryptographic Imagination*, p. 151.

with Shakespearean authority – finds a counterpart among the many cryptanalytical conspiracy theories that the Friedmans confronted in their work. In order to demonstrate the presence of ciphered information in early printed books, Shakespeare's or Bacon's, many anti-Stratfordian theories mirror the Folio method in presuming an unrealistic level of accuracy and standardization among early print. For example, in the course of disproving Elizabeth Wells Gallup's bilateral cipher hypothesis in Shakespeare's works, the Friedmans make a key point about early printing: in order for certain kinds of cipher to be encoded in print, "careful setting by a compositor who knew what he was doing, followed by a careful proof-reading and correction before printing, were essential if the message were not to be garbled by errors."[77] (This particular refutation of the cipher theory was not new; Shakespeare Variorum editor Horace Howard Furness mentions it in a letter of 1885.[78]) The form of the Friedmans' refutations deserves attention since it depends on discoveries about the Folio made mid-century by the bibliographer Charlton Hinman. His landmark collation of Folio copies was far enough along in 1954 for the Friedmans to solicit personal correspondence from him to support their point about the impossibility (or high improbability) of ciphers in a medium where error is so much a part of the substance of information. The Friedmans also cite Hinman's 1953 *Shakespeare Quarterly* article on "Variant Readings in the First Folio of Shakespeare" at great length, in which Hinman argues that "It is perhaps not yet fully appreciated that 'the First Folio text' is, strictly speaking, only an abstraction, since individual copies of the First Folio in fact present us with a great variety of different texts."[79] Making the now-familiar argument about stop-press correction and the practice of binding corrected and uncorrected sheets together, Hinman arrives at two clear conclusions: "(1) that no two copies of the First Folio selected at random should ever be supposed

---

[77] Friedman and Friedman, *Shakespearean Ciphers Examined*, p. 227. William Friedman and Elizabeth Wells Gallup shared an interesting history that included Friedman helping her with her early researches into the Folio. See Rosenheim's account of the life of Friedman in his chapter "Deciphering the Cold War: Toward a Literary History of Espionage," *Cryptographic Imagination*, pp. 143–4 and 151.

[78] Horace Howard Furness, *Letters*, vol. I, p. 229.

[79] Hinman, "Variant Readings," pp. 281; quoted in Friedman and Friedman, *Shakespearean Ciphers Examined*, p. 228.

textually identical throughout; and (2) that no single copy is likely to preserve anything that can properly be considered '*the* First Folio text.'"[80]

For the Folio or any other early modern book to serve as a substrate for weapons-grade encryption, or even for encryption for civilian use, it would need to live up to the bibliographically impossible ideal summed up by Bruno Latour's term for inscriptions: "immutable moblies."[81] Such things are a fantasy of print culture, as the Friedmans demonstrate in concert with Hinman, and with more recent textual scholars such as Adrian Johns and David McKitterick.[82] Combined with previous insights of analytical bibliography that the Folio texts derive from different types of copy, Hinman's point that "*the* First Folio text" is only an abstraction – and only ever was – marks a significant step away from the early modern archive as a determinant of Shakespeare's reception. It would also lead to Hinman's 1968 Norton facsimile's assemblage of page images into a composite that represents the Folio as it might have been, and perhaps should have been, but not as it was in any single surviving copy. The Friedmans observe that Gallup "did not even bother to work from a true copy of the First Folio, but from a facsimile – made at a time when facsimiles were not good." In some sense the Folio is already an abstraction, an imaginary archive, in the minds of those with a radical investment in a transcendental Shakespeare text and its legitimate descent into material books.

The rational world represented by the Friedmans was also the one occupied by Bowers and Hinman during their years as cryptanalysts for the US Navy from 1942 to 1945. The connections between their wartime cryptanalytical expertise and their postwar advances in compositor analysis are noted by G. Thomas Tanselle in his retrospective of Bowers's career. Tanselle observes that even prior to the United States' entry into the war, Bowers had received "secret instruction as a

---

[80] Hinman, "Variant Readings," p. 283, emphasis in original; quoted in Friedman and Friedman, *Shakespearean Ciphers Examined*, p. 228. I have removed emphasis added by the Friedmans when they quoted Hinman, but retained Hinman's emphasis in "*the* First Folio text."

[81] Latour, "Visualization and Cognition."

[82] Adrian Johns critiques Latour and Elizabeth Eisenstein in *Nature of the Book*, pp. 11–14, and McKitterick offers a critique of the over-emphasis of the fixity of print in *Print, Manuscript, and the Search for Order*, pp. 99–100, 136, 224–5, and *passim*.

cryptanalyst in a naval communications intelligence group" at the University of Virginia. During the war, he supervised a naval communications group working on Japanese ciphers.[83] Whatever the reason, Bowers's group was heavy with Shakespeareans, with Hinman a member, along with two other experts from the Folger Library staff, Giles Dawson and Ray O. Hummel. The congruence between Shakespearean bibliography and military cryptanalysis was only natural, according to Tanselle:

It seems appropriate that several of the scholars interested in analytical bibliography after the war, including the two leaders of the field (Bowers and Hinman), spent their wartime years performing cryptanalytic work together, for the goal of both activities is to find meaningful patterns in what at first seem to be chaotic data, and the bent of mind required for both is obviously similar.[84]

Noting the war's disruption of scholarly work, Jeffrey Masten takes these links further by arguing that "compositor analysis wasn't so much suspended as *produced* by the war," as part of a paranoid culture of error-detection that also encompassed the detection of supposed communists and homosexuals hiding within the ranks of US government service.[85]

Masten's reading of this episode in bibliography's history also raises questions that join the cultural construction of information with the basic principles of information theory. Responding to Tanselle's comment about finding "meaningful patterns in ... chaotic data," Masten asserts, "Surely there are other questions to ask: what are the differences between intentionally produced codes disclosing the locations of Japanese warships, and the codes, or inscriptions, of seventeenth-century spellings? What if chaotic data ... is instead data that lies outside our standards for the behaviour of the chaotic and ordered?"[86] As a universal theory of human communication, the model proposed by Shannon and Weaver should encompass encoded reports of troop movements and imprinted words in early modern spelling with equal ease, supposedly proving that what matters most is the underlying sameness, not particularity, of different forms of information. This

---

[83] Tanselle, "Fredson Bowers," pp. 32–3.
[84] Tanselle, "Fredson Bowers," p. 34.
[85] Masten, "Pressing Subjects," p. 88, emphasis in original.
[86] Masten, "Pressing Subjects," p. 88.

perception of information's role in the standardization of communication – now a core concept in standards-based digital humanities projects – is fundamentally mechanistic and has as much to do with the machines of Shakespeare's time as with those of today.

Cybernetics emerged as a science at the same time as Shakespearean bibliographers made a concerted turn toward compositor analysis, the study of human–machine interface in the printing house, in order to understand the manuscripts behind Shakespeare's Folio and quartos. For cyberneticists like Wiener, the human–machine interface between a gunner and his anti-aircraft system is measurable and predictable in the same ways that the interface between an early modern compositor and the apparatuses of the press are for Hinman. There is a good fit between these domains of knowledge not only in terms of "bent of mind," as Tanselle says, but also between their technological applications. Hinman's optical collating device, an indispensable tool in his subsequent research on the First Folio, had its genesis in the intelligence group's technique for comparing photographs of enemy fortifications to detect changes. F. P. Wilson connects just such technologies to the overall shape of the New Bibliography in this period:

If [the study of dramatic manuscripts] has been peculiarly the work of the twentieth century, one reason has been that the inventions of science have only in recent years placed within the reach of the scholar photostats, photographs, and collotype facsimiles of manuscripts as of printed books which for many purposes are as good as the originals; while scientific instruments have enabled the scholar who has access to the originals to decipher documents hitherto indecipherable.[87]

Whether in the form of reliable reconnaissance or accurate facsimiles, reproducible information played an essential role in a New Bibliographic network of tools and methods for deciphering the indecipherable. Documents were encoded messages to be cracked with the help of machines to supplement the human cognitive system.

Analytical bibliography, like cybernetics, could be regarded as the study of the threshold spaces where the human meets the mechanical, and where the two function together in a complex, variable, and yet to a degree also predictable system of information transmission. For another representative example of the mathematical predictability of

---

[87] F. P. Wilson, *Shakespeare and the New Bibliography*, p. 50.

human–machine interfaces, one can turn to the New Bibliography's chronicler, F. P. Wilson, writing in 1945:

> it is often imperative to resort to hypothesis and conjecture, but often, as we have seen, the bibliographer reaches conclusions that are demonstrable and irreversible. The reason is that he is dealing with an Abel Jeffes or a James Roberts not in his relations with other human beings, whether of the government, or the Stationers' Company, or the playhouse, but in *his relations with a mechanical process*. Strange accidents can indeed happen to type, and human error plays its part in causing them, but the accidents are often analysable and explicable with a completeness that approaches mathematical proof.[88]

It would have been difficult to conceive of a human relationship with a mechanical process in this way prior to cybernetics – except in analytical bibliography, which may explain why the two fields seem so congruent after the late 1940s.[89] McKenzie exemplifies the metaphorical traffic between bibliography and information theory when he states that the "full primary evidence" of analytical bibliography, when available, "has revealed a geometry of such complexity that even an expert in cybernetics, primed with all the facts, would have little chance of discerning it."[90]

There is a good fit between these domains of knowledge not only in terms of "bent of mind," as Tanselle claims, but also between their technological applications. A bit of disciplinary history well known to Shakespearean bibliographers is that Hinman's photographic collating device, an indispensable tool in his subsequent research on the First Folio, had its genesis partly in his wartime intelligence experience. As Steven Escar Smith relates, Hinman's work with the cryptanalysis group probably exposed him to stories about experiments in optical comparison of aerial surveillance photographs of enemy emplacements. From these stories and earlier bibliographic experiments in mechanical collation, Hinman drew the underlying principles that linked photography, mechanical collation, and human cognition.[91] To look through the eyepiece of a Hinman Collator – one of which still resides at the Folger

---

[88] F. P. Wilson, *Shakespeare and the New Bibliography*, p. 34, emphasis added.

[89] See Henry S. Turner's similar claim with regard to Shakespearean performance and *A Midsummer Night's Dream*: "If Bottom and his company tell us anything, they tell us that Shakespeare's theatre was the first modern cybernetic system, a machine in which the poet grafted the living body of the actor to the props and prosthetics that fabricated personhood"; *Shakespeare's Double Helix*, p. 85.

[90] McKenzie, "Printers of the Mind," p. 63.

[91] Steven Escar Smith, "Eternal Verities."

Shakespeare Library – and see a press variant blinking on and off, as though the Folio page before you was itself digital, is to become part of one human–machine interface built to decode patterns of impression left by another, the printing house of William and Isaac Jaggard.

The point, however, is not simply to compare a Renaissance printing press to a computer or information system; the question is how the governing conceptual model shapes the possible relationships between humans and machines. Bibliographers study humans not merely as extensions of machines, or media as "extensions of man" (in Marshall McLuhan's phrase), but rather the two together in a complex system.[92] In the case of the Folger's Hinman Collator, that system would also have an institutional dimension in the form of the Folger Library itself, in that the machine's nature and purpose is defined in large part by its collocation with the world's largest collection of Shakespeare folios: systemically speaking, the library and the machine are different interfaces to parts of the same archive. Similarly, in the New Bibliography's epistemology, it is an abstract model of communications, not any particular machine, that affords the forensic and predictive power that matters for bibliographic work. The New Bibliography's investment in the virtuality of early modern texts was more than a cultural perception that the information patterns were simply there for the detecting. Analytical bibliography sought to backtrack the signal through the communications channel right to the source, and in so doing helped to produce that source as an indivisible unity.

Bibliography and the archives of Babel

Only a practising textual critic and bibliographer knows the remorseless corrupting influence that eats away at a text during the course of its transmission. The most important concern of the textual bibliographer is to guard the purity of the important basic documents of our literature and culture. This is a matter of principle on which there can be no compromise. One can no more permit "just a little corruption" to pass unheeded in the transmission of our literary heritage than "just a little sin" was possible in Eden.

Fredson Bowers, *Textual and Literary Criticism* (1959)[93]

---

[92] The phrase embodies the central thesis of McLuhan's *Understanding Media*, and furnishes its secondary title.

[93] Bowers, *Textual and Literary Criticism*, p. 8.

With the foregoing history in mind, one can appreciate with new eyes the ideological weight behind statements such as Bowers's call for bibliographers to dedicate themselves to purity. In one sense, Bowers's vivid, anthropomorphic description of textual noise evokes many of the depictions of knowledge's corruption in Renaissance texts. His career represents a bibliographic quest against the "remorseless corrupting influence" of what Edmund Spenser called "cursed Eld the Cankerworme of writs."[94] However, information theory and the New Bibliography alike combatted that influence by means of models and methods to detect corrupting noise, trace it to its source, and eradicate it. Bowers here moralizes textual work, just as Spenser did; there is a metaphysical surplus in the language of both. I would draw attention to two specific implications: first, that the "purity" of encoded inscriptions is not just attainable, but also imperative; and second, that the original context for these statements in Bowers's *Textual and Literary Criticism* is the textual transmission of Shakespeare, and of *Hamlet* specifically – Bowers generalizes from *Hamlet* to the condition of all texts that constitute cultural heritage threatened in transmission.

But what exactly was the threat? Spenser imagined Error personified as a heresy-spreading monster whose "vomit full of bookes and papers was," requiring heroic effort to slay.[95] Warren Weaver identified the threat in 1949 not as Germans or Russians but as Babel itself: the tendency toward communicative idiosyncrasy, producing otherness, dissensus, and ultimately conflict. Weaver expounded this view of communication in a memorandum about the possibility of machine translation from 1949, the lynchpin year whose effects have been the subject of this chapter. In a remarkable metaphor, Weaver likens humanity to

individuals living in a series of tall closed towers, all erected over a common foundation. When they try to communicate with one another, they shout back and forth, each from his own closed tower, . . . and communication proceeds very poorly indeed. But, when an individual goes down his tower, he finds himself in a great open basement, common to all towers. Here he establishes easy and useful communication with the persons who have also descended from their towers.[96]

[94] Spenser, *The Faerie Queene*, 4.2.33.6.
[95] Spenser, *The Faerie Queene*, 1.1.20.6.
[96] Weaver, "Translation," p. 23. See also Weaver's foreword to the same volume, titled "The New Tower." For critiques of Weaver's statements on language, see Golumbia, *Cultural Logic of Computation*, pp. 85–93, and Hayles, *My Mother*, pp. 110–1.

Ironically, Weaver's analogy reverses the original symbolism of the Tower of Babel, which in the Biblical source represents an attempt at human overreaching enabled by the unity of Adamic language, the perfect correspondence of names to things. Linguistic diversity emerges amid the rubble of the Tower of Babel only after God casts it down. In these terms, the threat becomes literally nonsense, the postlapsarian alienation of writing and utterance from the origin of meaning.

Weaver's Babel metaphor calls to mind the symbolic role of inscription as idealized writing, but the context of his comments points to the reconceptualizing of Shakespeare as *code*, a term Hayles defines as the "system of correspondences that relate the elements of one symbol set to another symbol set, [as] for example, when Morse code associates dots and dashes with alphabetic letters."[97] In all of the preceding examples of Shakespeare's translation into machine-readable code – from the code-bearing sonnets of Allied spies; to the code-breaking mindsets of Hinman, Bowers, and the Friedmans; to the New Bibliographers' proto-cybernetic interest in the human–machine interface of the early modern printing press – a kind of informatic sublime takes shape in which the words and bibliographic features of Shakespeare's texts assume special status even as they affirm their transmissibility within universal systems. In this view, Shakespeare's texts hold a surplus of meaning that exceeds the capacities of any medium yet also underwrites the authenticity of the transmission. Combined with this Shakespearean transmissibility in the wake of information theory is the desire for regularity embodied by Shannon and Weaver's communications model, in which we can find analogues in Hinman's and Bowers's cryptanalytic missions to find meaningful patterns in chaotic data, and even in Greg's determination to see regularity and order in early modern documents like Henslowe's diary. (In his edition, Greg normalized all Sunday performances to fall on other days, on the assumption that theatre performances on Sundays were not permitted and therefore must not have happened.[98])

What makes Shakespeare such a vexing case for digitization is that minimizing static, so to speak, escalates from a technical possibility to a cultural imperative – even, in Bowers's case, to a defense of a culture that images itself under threat. To Shakespeareans, as students of an author frequently troped as divine, Bowers's anxieties are nothing new, especially

---

[97] Hayles, *My Mother*, p. 108.
[98] Maguire, *Shakespearean Suspect Texts*, pp. 53–5.

when one considers how Shakespeare editors have wrestled with received text that seems to hover on the border between sense and nonsense. Witness the desperate patterns of editorial emendation of dialogue spoken by psychologically distressed characters, such as Leontes with his enigmatic phrase "Affection? thy Intention stabs the Center" and its seemingly incoherent surrounding lines in *The Winter's Tale* (discussed in Chapter 3).[99] Or take the rationalizing of the seemingly nonsensical "Chough's language" in *All's Well That Ends Well* by editors and translators, who, as Randall McLeod illustrates in "Shakspear Babel," seem compelled to find (or quietly create) internal logic even in a language with no history or documents apart from its original printed appearance in the 1623 Folio.[100] In both examples, one sees editors driven by motives similar to Weaver's in the 1949 memorandum on translation when he tells the story of a Second World War cryptographer who succeeded in decrypting a message written in Turkish, despite not speaking Turkish or even knowing the encoded message was *in* Turkish. The desire to make sense of nonsense is a powerful one, and lends appeal to the idea that all language – and with it, culture – has what Weaver calls a "common foundation" and "great open basement" where difference resolves into an ordered sameness. As I have discussed in this book's exploration of various Shakespearean basements, real and imagined, Weaver's proposed route to perfect communication passes through the disordered space of the archive.

Strangely enough, one of the clearest statements in appreciation of an archival way of thinking about literature and textuality comes from the very centre of the New Bibliography, in a lecture given by Greg to the Bibliographical Society in 1932 and published as "Bibliography – An Apologia":

We have in fact to recognize that a text is not a fixed and formal thing, that needs only to be purged of the imperfections of transmission and restored once and for all to its pristine purity, but a living organism which in its descent through the ages, while it departs more and more from the form impressed upon it by its original author, exerts, through its imperfections as much as through its perfections, its own influence on its surroundings. At each stage of its descent a literary work is in some sense a new creation, something different

---

[99] See p. 113. The commentary notes for these nine lines span eight pages in the New Variorum Shakespeare edition.
[100] McLeod, "Shakspear Babel."

from what it was to an earlier generation, something still more different from what it was when it came from the author's hand.[101]

This chapter has measured some of the distance, historically and epistemologically, between Greg's 1932 statement in praise of noise and Bowers's 1959 declaration of war against error. Yet the distance between Greg and present thinking about texts and archives seems not so great in the passage above, which reminds us that the New Bibliographers were wrestling with many of the same problems we face today, and that our understanding of texts is no less bound by history and technology than theirs. Joseph Loewenstein turns this point into a challenge to present textual scholars when he calls the above passage "Greg's prolegomenon to the New Cultural History, to Gadamer, Jauss, and McGann," and goes on to argue, "When we casually attribute a monological, idealized, and stipulative attitude to textuality to pre-postmodern critics, we should not suppose ourselves to be referring to Greg."[102] What may be most remarkable about Greg's statement, however, is that it comes from the same article as his strongest expression of affinity with information theory. Within a few pages of this passage we find his declaration that the meaning of texts is no business of bibliographers (to which McKenzie objected, as discussed above), as well as his repeated assertion that bibliography is "the science of the transmission of literary documents."[103] For Greg there was no contradiction.

Milton's encomium to Shakespeare, quoted at the opening of this chapter, reminds us that technical challenges like digital preservation and interface design may be understood through the lenses offered by literature, in which the rational and the irrational can be in focus simultaneously, resulting in a useful blurring of distinctions between form and content, text and reader, interface and data – just as meanings of the word "numbers" overlap in a post-digital reading of Milton's own poem. The note of potential loss that Milton sounds resonates with one of the strongest themes shared by Shakespeareans and information

---

[101] Greg, "Bibliography – an Apologia," in *Sir Walter Wilson Greg*, pp. 150–1.
[102] Loewenstein, *Author's Due*, p. 259. See also the reassessment of Greg in the special issue of *Textual Cultures* (4.2 [2009]) devoted to a collection of articles marking the fiftieth anniversary of Greg's death.
[103] Greg, "Bibliography – An Apologia," in *Sir Walter Wilson Greg*, pp. 135, 137, 140, and 141.

theorists alike: anxiety about what is recoverable and what is irrevocably lost in the material transmission of texts. That anxiety must have struck Milton as he looked back to the First Folio, one of the first great experiments in interfaces for the Shakespeare texts, along with the Elizabethan public playhouse itself. Milton's epitaph validates a kind of readerly collaboration in the continuance of the Shakespeare text: the leaves of Shakespeare's "unvalued book" are a preservation format, but only when they provoke a further circulation of texts among communities of readers, building networks of "deepe Impression." As Milton's poem suggests, Shakespearean information persists only through transformission in numbers yet unknown.

7 | Data and the ghosts of materiality

Henry V begins with a media allegory about databases. The play's entire political plot, not to mention the consequences that reverberate through the *Henry VI/Richard III* tetralogy (written earlier but set after *Henry V*), depends upon a scene that stages acts of archival research, textual scholarship, and even a form of early modern response to information overload. Act 1, scene 2, begins with the Archbishop of Canterbury and the Bishop of Ely reporting to Henry and his court on the results of a research assignment on the legitimacy of Henry's claim to France – and, by extension, of the justness of the war that will be required to enforce it. Following Henry's injunction not to "fashion, wrest, or bow [their] reading," or to proceed upon "titles miscreate, whose right / Suits not in native colours with the truth" (1.2.14–17), the churchmen present a convoluted and not altogether honest rationale for invading France that closely follows Shakespeare's source in Raphael Holinshed's *Chronicles*. That rationale takes sixty-two uninterrupted lines for Canterbury to unfold, a mass of expository information that creates a potential dead zone for audience engagement. (It is often cut down in performance, or punctuated by stage business such as the pratfalls and document-juggling to which Laurence Olivier resorts in his 1944 film version.) From an archival perspective, however, the speech is fascinating: it represents a research process that would have required the textual disciplines of diplomatics and philology – note the lynchpin moment of textual criticism when Canterbury questions a gloss: "Salic land" does not mean France itself (1.2.40–1) – and renders an archival search among records into a narrative deployed with purpose.

Henry's response is thoroughly digital. After Canterbury's sixty-two-line disquisition on the intricacies of the Salic law and the succession to the French throne, Henry responds not with another speech but with a single question that demands a one-bit answer: "May I with right and conscience make this claim?" (1.2.96). Thinking like a programmer *avant la lettre*, Henry structures a query

236

to simplify the volume and complexity of information returned by his initial information request, thereby forcing an information system (embodied by Canterbury and Ely, as archival interfaces themselves) into a constrained set of responses that a programmer would call Boolean variables: true or false, expressible as the numbers 1 or 0 – a binary structure that reflects the present capacity of consumer-grade transistors to distinguish between two voltage states but no more. In a performance that plays Henry straight, as opposed to one in which Henry is complicit with the churchmen's scheming and only plays up his skepticism for appearances, this Boolean query may be interpreted as a strategy to force an ethical commitment from someone hiding behind masses of data. Yet Canterbury's response to Henry's query is thoroughly human: not an outright yes or no, but "The sin upon my head, dread sovereign" (1.2.97), followed by an exhortation to war that leaves the word *yes* tacit, forcing Henry, the court, and the audience and reader to become complicit by filling it in themselves. Such are the data that send nations to war, even today.

In politically orthodox readings of the play such as Olivier's 1944 film and Kenneth Branagh's 1989 update, the anxiety about right and con-science never fades from the play, and indeed Henry's binary question leads right back to textual questions about the transmission and editing of the play itself. The complexities of textual and possibly memorial transmission resulted in a 1600 quarto version of the play with numer-ous errors in the Salic law speech, and with the highly consequential omissions of the play's ironizing Chorus scenes as well as scene 1.1, in which Canterbury and Ely reveal to the audience their ulterior motives for pushing Henry into war with France despite questionable justifica-tion.[1] Textual labour is both the scene's subject and the precondition for its existence within modern editions based on the Folio text. Henry seeks to establish for the record, as his representative to the French court asserts later in the play, that his is

> no sinister nor no awkward claim,
> Picked from the worm-holes of long-vanished days,
> Nor from the dust of old oblivion raked.

> (2.4.85–7)

---

[1] On the 1600 quarto's differences from the First Folio text, see Gary Taylor's introduction and appendices to his single-volume Oxford edition, especially pp. 20–6.

Henry V's archival metaphor of an overwhelming and error-ridden mass of documents, brought into order by a single digitally minded authority, stages the tensions between data, interpretation, and historicity that this chapter will explore.

Shakespeare may well seem like ideal content for information networks, as transmissible cultural heritage, just as computers may seem ideal venues for Shakespearean study because they, like Shakespeare, are just as prone to essentialization. As we have seen, however, Shakespeare's texts both underpin and trouble the twentieth century's normative concepts of transmissibility. An example from the world of databases can be found in the old logo for the popular open-source XML database software *eXist*, which until recently used XML-tagged text of *Hamlet* by way of background texture, ghosted behind the word "eXist" in light grey.[2] The presence of Shakespeare text here, as well as among the sample XML files that were included with the *eXist* download package (*Hamlet*, *Macbeth*, and *Romeo and Juliet*), was likely the result of the *eXist* team's collaboration with the humanities computing community. However, the integration of one of Shakespeare's most problematic play-texts into this database's logo makes for an ironic echo of prior uses of *Hamlet* to signify transmissibility and technological stability (compare, for example, Alexander Graham Bell's use of *Hamlet* described in Chapter 5). In many ways the ghostly presence of Shakespeare's text in a database logo emblematizes the tensions I wish to explore in this chapter with regard to digital data. Understanding digital Shakespeare is not just a matter of using digital tools to read Shakespeare differently; it is equally a matter of using Shakespeare to read digital technologies differently.

These relationships would be simpler if the metonymy of texts, artifacts, and performances we call *Shakespeare* was limited to, say, performance as an unreachable quintessence, or the content of a file in an XML database. In practice, however, the Shakespeare metonym usually takes a messier hybrid form, entangling performances with documents, texts, technologies, information patterns, and the materials of that other capacious metonym, code.[3] I seek to understand that entanglement

---

[2] As of the time of writing, the original *eXist* logo remains visible at the University of Vermont's Center for Digital Initiatives mirror of the old download page: cdi.uvm.edu/exist/index.xml.

[3] In addition to the references on literature and code in the preceding chapter, see Aschoff, "Early History of the Binary Code," and Heath, "Origins of the Binary Code." I am grateful to Jonathan Hope for these references.

as a kind of cultural work, a collective preoccupation with the virtuality of the received texts that implicates all aspects of digital Shakespeare scholarship. Although that might seem to be a digital humanities question, it does not sit comfortably alongside the digital humanities' traditional definition itself as a field concerned with the application *of* digital tools *to* the study of humanities materials. By 2013, this unidirectional impact-model of technology had become so tacitly unquestioned that Andrew Prescott, a leading figure in the field, had to exhort digital humanists not to neglect the material bases of their data and knowledge. That Prescott needed to say this at all tells us something; that his saying it was received as controversial tells us even more.[4]

Applying digital tools to humanities materials can lead to a comfortable sense of mastery and instrumental power – not to mention usefulness in a climate of fiscal utilitarianism – thus many digital humanists find it threatening to reverse the terms of engagement, and to regard our materials as the active, disruptive element in digital scholarship. The older tool-building and data-analyzing branches of the digital humanities therefore have little intellectual affinity with newer approaches that focus on the nature of digital textuality itself, such as Matthew Kirschenbaum's influential book *Mechanisms* and other forms of digital textual scholarship that do not limit themselves to making digital editions. The paradox, which Prescott recognized, is that digital tools are rarely applied to humanities materials directly, but rather to digital surrogates. When a researcher uses digital text analysis to study linguistic patterns in Shakespeare's *Sonnets*, he is likely to be relying upon a digital edition or corpus that is just as much a material artifact as any copy of the 1609 quarto *Shake-speares Sonnets*. The same researcher may feel little need to inquire too deeply into how his digital corpus was made, especially when the culture of big data in the digital humanities places all its emphasis on the analytical power of tools. (Ironically, actual data scientists are often far more concerned with data quality than their humanist counterparts, and therefore readier to ask the kinds of questions that textual scholars would about the histories of their digital texts.) In this light, the kind of bibliographic scrutiny that Kirschenbaum and other textual scholars have been applying to born-digital texts also needs to be applied where it may be least welcome, in

---

[4] See Prescott, "Making the Digital Human," and the many comments to this blog post; he articulates similar ideas in "An Electric Current of the Imagination."

digital humanities projects too busy planning their own future con-
quests to question what they call their data.

Spectres at the banquet: material remainders in computational models and databases

The reciprocal approach to the critical reading of tools and materials
alike, which I advocate in this chapter, is closely related to the long-
running tendency, explored throughout this book, of taking
Shakespeare's texts as prototypical material for information-based
methods and theoretical frameworks. One of the most well-known
examples in the library and information science world is a conceptual
model called Functional Requirements for Bibliographical Records
(FRBR), which maps the entities and relationships that librarians nav-
igate in information environments.[5] In its way, FRBR is a theory of
textuality in that it distinguishes between works, expressions, manifestations, and items, similar to the taxonomies of textual scholars such as
G. Thomas Tanselle and Peter Shillingsburg.[6] The report that originally
introduced the FRBR model, completed in 1997 by a study group of the
International Federation of Library Associations and Institutions,
makes a passing reference to *Hamlet*'s quarto and Folio texts in explaining the term *expression*, and subsequent explanations of FRBR often
take *Hamlet* as a core example.[7] The play makes for a good test of any
ontology, given its textual complexity and rich performance traditions
in diverse media. Yet models such as FRBR always raise the vexing
questions of exhaustiveness and instrumentality: what does the model
leave out, especially in its blind spots? What is the model *for*, and how
does it discipline the hand that wields it as a tool?

The FRBR example and the questions it raises point to modelling as
one of the most interesting applications of computing, and one that
is distinct from more easily essentialized forms of computing such as

---

[5] See *Functional Requirements* (IFLA report). For an application of the FRBR model
that shows its limits in a humanities context, see McDonough, *et al.*, "Twisty Little
Passages."

[6] See Tanselle, *Rationale*, and Shillingsburg's chapter "Ontologies," in *Scholarly
Editing*, pp. 41–51.

[7] To let one example stand for many, see Weng and Mi, "Towards Accessibility,"
pp. 225–7.

data-analysis or multimedia content-delivery. Modelling is a form of conjectural world-building in order to answer prior questions but also to discover new ones; as Michael Mahoney argues, modelling means "designing an *operative representation* [of a portion of the world] that captures what we take to be its essential features."[8] In the context of Shakespeare, the unavailability of an essential or ideal text, combined with the persistent cultural desire to have one nonetheless, can make for revealing experiments in modelling. This productive difficulty is enriched – or worsened, depending upon one's investment in instrumentality – by the traditions of Shakespearean performance and scholarship that challenge the ontological primacy of print, and explore alternatives to regarding Shakespeare performances as straightforward derivations from print. That position is best represented in the work of W. B. Worthen, and his work in particular raises the disconcerting possibility that some forms of meaning cannot be modelled, archived, or reduced to entity-relationship maps.[9]

We can test the difference a performance-oriented perpective makes to modelling in relation to Franco Moretti's application of network theory to *Hamlet*. Moretti and his collaborators at Stanford's Literary Lab follow in the tradition outlined throughout this book of recruiting Shakespeare to demonstrate a new information-based method, theory, or tool, yet participate equally in the parallel tradition of being upstaged by the complexity and irreducibility of the materials they recruit. In Moretti's chapter "Network Theory, Plot Analysis" in his book *Distant Reading*, which previously appeared as a digital pamphlet self-published by his lab, Moretti describes the creation of a map of *Hamlet*'s networks of speech acts, in which characters who address each other on stage are connected by graphical lines, with Hamlet and Claudius (unsurprisingly) appearing as busy vertices at the centre, and the Ghost (unsurprisingly) hovering at the periphery of the network.[10]

---

[8] Mahoney, "Histories of Computing(s)," p. 129, emphasis added. See also McCarty, *Humanities Computing*, and Brian Cantwell Smith, "Limits of Correctness."

[9] See Worthen, "Performing Shakespeare," and his chapter on "Cyber-Shakespeare," in *Shakespeare and the Force of Modern Performance*, pp. 169–215, as well as the chapters in Holland (ed.), *Shakespeare, Memory and Performance*. For a discussion of performance and the archive beyond Shakespeare, see Diana Taylor, *The Archive and the Repertoire*.

[10] Moretti, *Distant Reading*, p. 213 and *passim*.

The interpretive insights that Moretti draws from these maps tell us little that is new about *Hamlet*, but the value of Moretti's experiment lies in the way it exemplifies modelling as an activity. This is especially apparent when he arbitrarily subtracts Hamlet, Claudius, and Horatio from the network to see how other relationships change; this kind of playful, experimental manipulation to see what happens exemplifies the "operative" part of Mahoney's "operative representation." Understandably, one of Moretti's *Hamlet* network maps serves as *Distant Reading*'s cover image, emblematizing his approach as a whole.

Modelling requires a certain arbitrariness in the selection of features to model, which in turn can illuminate ambiguities that the modelling process forces one to formalize. For example, Moretti's map shows only two lines of connection to the Ghost, from Hamlet and Horatio, indicating that "some words have passed between them," which Moretti acknowledges could be modelled differently: one might also add lines if characters have speaking parts while on stage together, or simply occupy the same stage space without speaking (given that performance is more than merely the exchange of spoken language); the lines might also have been weighted somehow to reflect the amount of words that pass between characters.[11] A model such as this provokes questions about its non-equivalence to the object it models; indeed, those questions are the point.

For example, the seemingly minor character of Marcellus, the watchman present just before and after Hamlet's first encounter with the Ghost, raises questions about the model given the absence of a speech line connecting him with the Ghost. What of the Ghost's disembodied injunction to all present to swear their loyalty to Hamlet (1.5.149–63), and their reciprocal acts of swearing by Hamlet, Horatio, and Marcellus that answer the Ghost? What does it mean to include Marcellus in this bit of stage business? Must the Ghost be visible as some kind of full-torso apparition to count as being on stage, or may characters exchange meaningful speech acts with non-localized phenomena (the Ghost speaks from somewhere *under the stage* as the Oxford's stage directions have it)? For that matter, what is the stage in question, and what differences would it make to the scene's possible meanings? Are we dealing with *Hamlet* as pure work (in the FRBR sense)? If we were to

[11] Moretti, *Distant Reading*, p. 214–15.

measure Moretti's map against the textual territory it describes, where would we have to look?

As these questions indicate, acts of modelling can reveal assumptions and blind spots in the modeller. Moretti is no exception, and indeed he willingly critiques his own model at the outset, as noted above. Yet there remains a blind spot in the form of his near-total silence on the question of his data's relationship to material texts. Neither version of his chapter makes any mention of the source of the text that furnishes *Hamlet* as an object for network analysis, and he drops only a passing hint that changes in the network would look different if applied to the Q1 text (1603).[12] Presumably Moretti is using a text based on the Folio (1623) or the Second Quarto (1604–5), or a modern edition that may conflate the two, perhaps along with stage directions from Q1 and emendations by the editor that affect who speaks to whom. In a similar hypothetical modelling experiment that, say, attempted to map sequences of action to character motivations, the differences between the F and Q2 texts of *Hamlet* would be consequential due to the different motivations that Laertes has in each text for avenging himself upon Hamlet, as Paul Werstine has shown.[13] It is worth remembering the lesson that the US Army codebreakers William and Elizabeth Friedman learned from the bibliographer Charlton Hinman (see pp. 225–6 in Chapter 6): if *the* First Folio text of Shakespeare can only ever be an abstraction, because of the multiplicity of variant copies of the same book, how can we speak of *the* text of a play like *Hamlet* except as a network of textual and performative relations? The *Mona Lisa* may be in the Louvre, but *Hamlet* is not containable within any single text, and calling it data does not make it so.

Let us consider one interpretive complication that emerges from Moretti's apparent lack of interest in textual history and thus, in this

---

[12] Moretti, *Distant Reading*, p. 220.

[13] Werstine, "Textual Mystery." Moretti shows some appreciation of the textual complexity of *Hamlet* in a footnote in his 1994 article "Modern European Literature" (reprinted as the first chapter in his *Distant Reading*) in which he mentions the differences between Q1, Q2, and F *Hamlet*, and acknowledges that "The *Hamlet* we read is based on Q2 and F; it's from them that it draws its 'strangeness,' its tragi-comic web, the enigmatic structure which has turned it into a key text of modernity" (p. 105, n. 39). Curiously, Moretti goes on to repeat the bibliographical chestnut that Q1 *Hamlet* originated from a stripped-down touring version for the provinces, which by 1994 had been contested by numerous textual scholars. What is less curious is that Moretti cites no scholarly sources for his account of *Hamlet*'s textual history.

case, data quality: what is the name of the character who killed his brother, the rightful King, married his brother's wife, and displaced Hamlet in right of succession to the throne? Readers of the play know this character as Claudius, as he is named on Moretti's map (where, curiously, Gertrude remains "Queen"), yet in Q1 *Hamlet* he has no personal name and is called only by his title, "King," in all of his speech prefixes. The result for Q1 *Hamlet* is that this character becomes depersonalized and thus indistinguishable from the position he occupies. This may be a subtle dramatic technique, or it may simply be an interesting accident, though one could find evidence for dramatic technique in *Cymbeline*, where the chief villain, a wicked stepmother, is known only as "The Queen." Similarly, in the Folio and Q2 texts of *Hamlet* at no point does any character ever call Hamlet's uncle by name, and the name "Claudius" appears only in stage directions and speech prefixes printed in the early texts, as well as the *dramatis personae* lists of modern editions, and for that matter the programs given out at performances – all artifacts of the material print culture through which *Hamlet* is transmitted to the present, and which Moretti tends to ignore. The consequence is that this character is Claudius when we read *Hamlet* in a modern edition that prints this information in the text – in the 1986 Oxford Shakespeare, for example, he is always "King Claudius" in speech prefixes – but in performance, on stage, on film, on audio recording, and in other media he lacks a name, just as it was in Q1. Consequently, this character's identity is primarily relational, as uncle to Hamlet, brother to King Hamlet, brother-in-law and then husband to Gertrude, and King to Denmark.[14]

Ironically, this interpretation of Claudius, which reflects some of network theory's interests, is unlikely to become available through Moretti's experiment because of his decision to detach *Hamlet* from the messiness of its texts and performances. Such bracketing of history and materiality is typical of computational approaches in the parts of the digital humanities associated with big data, yet, like Shakespeare's many ghosts, history and materiality return unbidden to the stage of computational modelling when least expected or wanted. Lene Petersen's recent work *Shakespeare's*

---

[14] Compare the different relational names used for Lady Capulet in the second quarto of *Romeo and Juliet* (1599), including abbreviations for *Mother*, *Lady*, *Old Lady*, *Wife*, and *Capulet's Wife* depending on her function in the scene; see George Walton Williams, *Shakespeare's Speech-Headings*, pp. xii–xiv.

Errant Texts, for example, makes an attempt to reconcile computational stylistics with textual scholarship in its case studies of multiple-text plays such as *Titus Andronicus, Hamlet*, and *Romeo and Juliet*, but does not go far enough in considering the implications of Petersen's own caveat that "It is very easy, and perhaps also convenient, to underestimate the extent to which the textual instability of some of the early modern dramatic canon might impact on the 'purity' of the sample texts used in attribution studies."[15] The mistake is to miscategorize these kinds of questions as methodological problems to be solved; rather, they are epistemological and ideological positions to be negotiated, not taken for granted. Openly declining to engage these questions would be one thing, but Moretti's silence is a different matter, and symptomatizes a prevalent tendency in the digital humanities to idealize forms of computing in service of an instrumentalist narrative of the impact of new technologies upon the humanities.

That narrative has been especially strong in relation to the idea of the database as both an instrument and a product of scholarly labour. Some of the most debated claims about databases have come from Lev Manovich, who asserts that the emergent structure of the database is antithetical to the traditional structure of the narrative – an antithesis with profound consequences for literary studies and for the conceptualization of knowledge in a digital world.[16] For example, to adopt Manovich's point of view for a moment, one might say that Henry's pointed response to Canterbury in the Salic law scene dramatizes the incompatibility of narratives and databases, in that Henry suspects that Canterbury's narrative about the Salic law cannot capture the multiplicity of readings that the database-like structure of the archive of legal records and commentaries might support. (However, such a reading might find itself on shaky ground by conflating databases with archives.) The idea of data is central to the traditional conception of computing that Manovich draws from computer science, in which "data structures and algorithms are two halves of the ontology of the world according to a computer"; as he explains, "Examples of data structures are arrays, linked lists, and graphs. Algorithms and data structures have a symbiotic relationship. The more complex the

---

[15] Petersen, *Shakespeare's Errant Texts*, p. 193.
[16] Manovich, *Language of New Media*, pp. 225–8.

data structure ... the simpler the algorithm needs to be, and vice versa."[17] Even a snippet of XML-tagged Shakespeare text, such as the one depicted in the old *eXist* logo, may be considered as a data structure in that it imposes an order that makes it tractable to querying and other algorithmic methods.

This is all conventional wisdom in programming and computer science, but Manovich's arguments become more controversial when he extends them into traditionally humanistic realms, as for example in his claim that "A library, a museum – in fact, any large collection of cultural data – is replaced by a computer database. At the same time, a computer database becomes a new metaphor that we use to conceptualize individual and collective cultural memory, a collection of documents or objects, and other phenomena and experiences."[18] Such a reckless claim is difficult to accept if one understands libraries and museums to be more than warehouses of data – a mistake that politicians and university administrators seem to make with disappointing regularity. Yet Manovich nonetheless makes a valuable point about the power that databases have come to wield in the cultural imagination, especially in the conceptualization of memory and preservation.

For these and other reasons, Manovich's characterization of databases became the subject of focused debate in a 2007 issue of *Publications of the Modern Language Association*, in an article cluster that featured Ed Folsom's application of Manovich's ideas to his *Walt Whitman Archive*, juxtaposed with responses from other scholars.[19] Two of the most pointed responses came from Jerome McGann and N. Katherine Hayles, with the former pointing out that no database exists without an interface, and the latter pointing out that it is essential to understand the differences between kinds of databases, and not to assume that relational databases are the only kind (others include object-oriented databases and XML databases like *eXist*, both of which support very different kinds of ontologies).[20] Both of these nuanced responses to Manovich highlight the importance of technically

---

[17] Manovich, *Language of New Media*, p. 223.

[18] Manovich, *Language of New Media*, p. 214.

[19] See the articles by Ed Folsom, Peter Stallybrass, Jerome McGann, Meredith L. McGill, Jonathan Freedman, and N. Katherine Hayles in *Publications of the Modern Language Association*, 122.5 (2007).

[20] McGann, "Database, Interface, and Archival Fever," p. 1588; Hayles, "Narrative and Database," p. 1603–4.

informed commentary – McGann in particular takes Manovich and Folsom to task for their looseness in depicting databases, libraries, and archives – but also point to the weakness in many of the claims made for databases: the fallacy of computing essentialism, or the notion that computers have a single, identifiable, and immutable form that enables some generalizations and forecloses others.

As with *Henry V*'s database allegory described at the outset, it may be more useful to think of computing as a practice that is not necessarily localizable within computers as devices.[21] For example, among the other respondents in the *PMLA* cluster, Peter Stallybrass argues that Shakespeare's compositional habits reveal that he may have understood more about database structures than we realize, which he demonstrates by breaking the opening lines of Hamlet's "To be, or not to be" soliloquy into a table of quotable phrases that Shakespeare may have assembled and adapted from multiple sources.[22] Stallybrass's purpose is not to pin down the sources for Shakespeare's most famous dramatic speech – in the manner, say, of Edmund Malone's epistemological fantasy as expressed in my first chapter's opening epigraph – but rather to demonstrate the kind of aggregative database thinking that Shakespeare and other early modern authors employed in their writing. To uncover historically proto-digital forms of thinking and textuality in this way, as Stallybrass does, is to complicate the easy narratives of technological succession that posit databases as the telos of a providential order of history.

Just as Stallybrass's table of Shakespeare's authorial creation-by-aggregation renders "To be, or not to be" newly strange to our eyes, so is it worthwhile to see computers with different eyes by looking at the construction of digital data in the cultural imagination. As Derrida famously argues in *Archive Fever*, "archivization produces as much as it records the event" – an observation closely connected to Derrida's speculations elsewhere in the book about what it means to use the "Save" command while writing on a word processor.[23] What has

---

[21] On avoiding device-history accounts of computing, see McCarty, *Humanities Computing*, pp. 14–15, and Mahoney, "Histories of Computing(s)," pp. 121–3.

[22] Stallybrass, "Against Thinking," pp. 1581–2.

[23] Derrida, *Archive Fever*, pp. 17 and 25–6. For a discussion of Derrida's comments on digital writing and inscription in relation to *Hamlet*, see Galey, "Tablets of the Law," pp. 85–6.

Derrida (or anyone else) saved in these ubiquitous moments of digital writing that are repeated countless times in a working day? Is there a fundamental ontological condition shared by all digital texts, including Shakespeare's? The word *data* tends to provide the easy answer, but the rest of this chapter will question the universal applicability of the term by reading examples of digital textuality through the lenses of Shakespearean textual studies, in which materiality always returns like an unquiet ghost to trouble succession narratives.

Shakespearean data

> So long as the magnetic flux on this disk has not been disturbed,
>> and so long as humans retain the appropriate size and speed disk drives
>> and so long as they have hardware controllers and software device drivers capable of reading the bits from this disk,
>> and so long as they have access to the software that encoded the file structure and character codes employed in the bit stream of this document,
>> and so long as they can still find or recreate the computing environment necessary to run that software,
>> *and* so long as they can still breathe or see,
> So long lives this, [and this gives life to thee.]
>> Jeff Rothenberg's adaptation of the final couplet of Shakespeare's Sonnet 18, "Ensuring the Longevity of Digital Information" (1999)

As we have seen throughout this book, there is a cultural predisposition to conceptualize Shakespeare in the terms of digital technology. Yet, as the preceding chapters have also shown in different ways, there is a less obvious but persistent tendency to conceive of information technologies in Shakespearean terms. An example from the world of modern computing is an article by Jeff Rothenberg, a computer scientist with the RAND Corporation, in a 1995 issue of *Scientific American*, which helped to bring popular and scholarly attention alike to bear upon the problem of digital preservation. Rothenberg's "Ensuring the Longevity of Digital Documents" did so in part by including a colour photographic facsimile of Shakespeare's Sonnet 18 as printed in the 1609

Sonnets.[24] In the caption, he points out that the sonnet "exemplifies the longevity of the printed page: the words are legible after almost four centuries ... but digital media can become unreadable within a decade."[25] Shakespeare functions in this example not only as a familiar reference point that thematizes preservation – especially in the final couplet, "So long as men can breath or eyes can see, / So long liues this, and this giues life to thee," – but also as an image of material textuality. The image from the 1609 quarto shows bibliographic phenomena such as running titles, page breaks (emphasized by Sonnets 17 and 19 appearing in the same image, though incompletely on the page), early modern orthography and typography, and a possible compositorial error (or instance of brilliant authorial rule-breaking) in the form of the comma that ends the sonnet instead of the usual period. In Rothenberg's expanded version of his article, Shakespeare's sonnet even becomes material for adaptation, providing a venue to recast digital preservation in poetic terms through the rewriting of Sonnet 18's final couplet. In Rothenberg's example, Shakespeare is not only an object of preservation but also a means for thinking through what it means to preserve digital data.

More recently debate has focused not only on what the humanities can bring to the understanding of data, but also on whether computing necessarily requires humanists to accept the idea of data as the fundamental condition of our materials, and quantification as the fundamental basis of knowledge. As a modern counterpart to the many nineteenth-century newspaper accounts of new media quoted in Chapters 3 and 4, consider this extract from a *New York Times* story of 16 November 2010, part of a series of articles by *Times* arts reporter Patricia Cohen on the digital humanities:

A history of the humanities in the 20th century could be chronicled in "isms" – formalism, Freudianism, structuralism, postcolonialism – grand intellectual cathedrals from which assorted interpretations of literature, politics and culture spread.

The next big idea in language, history and the arts? Data.

---

[24] See p. 7, n. 16. Rothenberg's article exists in two versions, the one published in *Scientific American* in 1995, and an expanded version from 1999 available on the Council of Library and Information Resources website under a slightly different title. The poem quoted in the epigraph appears in the 1999 version, p. 3.

[25] Rothenberg, "Ensuring the Longevity of Digital Documents," p. 45.

Members of a new generation of digitally savvy humanists argue it is time to stop looking for inspiration in the next political or philosophical "ism" and start exploring how technology is changing our understanding of the liberal arts. This latest frontier is about method, they say, using powerful technologies and vast stores of digitized materials that previous humanities scholars did not have.[26]

This is a flawed assessment on many levels, not least in its failure to name the particular "ism" that underwrites the position of the article itself: positivism. It makes sense, however, that Cohen and the digital humanists she interviewed would wish to leave the word unspoken. Being reminded of it undermines the liberatory narrative by relocating this particular vision of scholarship back within the history of "isms" – the "grand intellectual cathedrals" of the twentieth century – from which some digital humanists seek to escape through an appeal to technology. Positivism has a history that took shape in the nineteenth century and developed throughout the twentieth, as many scholars in science and technology studies have documented, and that history is thoroughly entwined with the "isms" that Cohen lists.[27] Indeed, following her approximate chronological order, we would need to locate positivism's heyday at the earliest point on the timeline, before formalism, not at the forward-pointing end where "the next big idea" would happen.

A related form of historical forgetting shows through in the assumption that the "isms" from which digital technology and methods provide liberation were not, themselves, thoroughly immersed in questions of method, technology, and the need to understand massive amounts of information. Whether we conceive of these and other theoretical traditions as grand cathedrals, dusty archives, or messy workshops, they serve to reminds us, as Rothenberg does, that the humanities have intersected with information technologies in many ways over their long history together, and that the one-way application *of* technology *to* humanities research is not the whole story. The preceding chapters have sought to highlight other facets of that relationship in ways that trouble the progressivist sense of digital humanities as a relentless

---

[26] Patricia Cohen, "Digital Keys for Unlocking the Humanities' Riches," *New York Times* (16 November 2010).

[27] On the complex history of positivism in a range of disciplines, see the essays collected in Steinmetz (ed.), *Politics of Method*.

forward march into the future that sheds its past like an advancing army's detritus. As Paul Duguid remarks of technological liberationism, "Dismissals of history always recall the history of dismissal."[28] What liberationist and revolutionary positions tend to overlook is the complicating factor that computing already has a history, and a long one at that; indeed, computing is just as historically imbricated as the traditional humanistic activities of reading, writing, and the making of books.

This returns us to what I called in Chapter 1 the forgotten basement of the word *computer*, in the form of its long history prior to becoming the name of an electronic device.[29] In an instance of uncanny reverse-anachronism, Shakespeare comes one letter short of using a word we consider proper to our time, not his. The word appears in act 4, scene 3, of *The Winter's Tale* as Autolycus prepares to gull the Clown, who is trying to reckon up the expenses for the coming sheep-shearing feast. Here is the 1623 First Folio text:

> *Clo.* I cannot do't without Compters. Let mee see,
> what am I to buy for our Sheepe-shearing-Feast? Three
> pound of Sugar, fiue pound of Currence, Rice ...[30]

The Folio almost reads *Computers* here; we are only one *u* short. It would not take much for a digital forger, in the spirit of John Payne Collier, to emend a digital image of the Folio text to confirm the perception of Shakespeare's transcendent proto-modernity. After all, Shakespeare apparently knew the noun *computation*, which appears in both *The Comedy of Errors* and *Richard III*.[31] The noun *computer* might have been available to him, too, having been printed just a few years after the probable composition of *The Winter's Tale* in a 1613 book called *The yong mans gleanings* (which also supplies the OED's earliest attestation of the word, and the earliest instance of it that I can discover in EEBO). The word appears in a section titled "Of the

---

[28] Duguid, "Material Matters," p. 69.   [29] See pp. 21–2.

[30] F1, sig. Bb1v, TLN 1705–7.

[31] *The Comedy of Errors*, F1 text: (Antipholus of Syracuse) "[T]he heedful slaue / Is wandred forth in care to seeke me out / By computation and mine hosts report" (sig. H2v, TLN 396–8). *Richard III*, F1 text: "My Princely Father, then had Warres in France, / And by true computation of the time, / Found, that the Issue was not his begot" (sig. f1v, TLN 2175–7).

Mortalitie of Man," appropriately enough in support of a quantitative reminder of the limits of the human:

What art thou (O Man) and from whence hadst thou thy beginning? What matter art thou made of, that thou promisest to thy selfe length of daies: or to thy posterity continuance. I haue read the truest computer of Times, and the best Arithmetician that euer breathed, and he reduceth thy dayes into a short number: The daies of Man are threescore and ten.[32]

It is at least possible that Shakespeare could have encountered this most proleptic of words in his lifetime, perhaps pausing to reflect upon this particular computer's cheerful message about his own mortality.

Here the word *computer*, like the machines it now denotes, holds out the promise of bridging the distance between Shakespeare's time and our own. Like the imaginary device conjured by the title of Neil Rhodes and Jonathan Sawday's collection *The Renaissance Computer*, the word seems unstuck in time, hovering just on the edge of anachronism. This passage also reminds us that the first computers were humans, though even in this example the significance of "computer," paired with the living, breathing "Arithmetician," metaphorically elides the human "computer of Times" with the book or almanac in which the author of *The yong mans gleanings* presumably looked up this piece of information. When that author "read" this "truest computer," he or she may have done so using bibliographic technologies such as indexes, page numbers, or commonplace marks, which, according to Stallybrass, work in concert with the codex form as manipulated by human digits to demonstrate the literal digitality of early modern books.[33] (Such features presumably aided the archival research expedition undertaken by Canterbury and Ely, or their assistants, whose results we considered above.) As Stallybrass convincingly demonstrates in his study of book-marking and discontinuous modes of reading, the connection between digits and digital reading cannot be dismissed as mere wordplay: books and other textual artifacts can be digital without being electronic – indeed they could not have been otherwise before the late twentieth century.[34]

---

[32] *The yong mans gleanings ... By R. B., Gent.* (London, 1613), sig. B1r.
[33] Stallybrass, "Books and Scrolls."
[34] On digits and the digital, see also Sherman's chapter "☞: Toward a History of the Manicule," in his *Used Books*, pp. 25–52, and Bialkowski, DeLuca, and Lafreniere, "Manicules."

One can put similar pressure on the word *data*, taking Shakespeare as a test-case for the *New York Times*'s assertion that humanists have only recently discovered data. The database *Eighteenth Century Collections Online* indicates that the first Shakespeare edition to use *data* in its modern sense is Edmund Malone's variorum of 1790 – no surprise, considering his zeal for separating the reliable from the spurious, and for establishing the data (in the sense of the historical givens) of subsequent Shakespeare scholarship. Malone's "Historical Account of the Rise and Progress of the English Stage," included among the ancillary materials in his 1790 edition, uses the term to conclude a discussion of the economics of the English stage: "On all these *data*, I think it may be safely concluded, that the performers of the first class did not derive from their profession more than ninety pounds a year at the utmost."[35] *Data* here is a threshold word, like *compters*: still Latin enough to warrant the plural and italic type, but English enough to be used in the vernacular and in the sense recognizable to modern eyes. Here, data is the category of evidence that settles a factual question once and for all, and does so quantitatively, by counting the countable – in this case, prices, shares, profits, and other amounts.

However, it is also necessary to reckon with the cultural formation of the idea of *data* that allows the word to function in the *New York Times* story as a monolithic one-word answer to the question of the humanities' future – a future which, as Jussi Parikka warns in his critique of the same article, is mistakenly regarded as "beyond theory in the sense of going directly to data."[36] Yet the *New York Times* article also asks a good question:

This alliance of geeks and poets [working together via the digital humanities] has generated exhilaration and also anxiety. The humanities, after all, deal with elusive questions of aesthetics, existence and meaning, the words that bring tears or the melody that raises goose bumps. Are these elements that can be measured?

Cohen's question happens to echo a legend attached to Saint Jerome, the basis of Vittore Carpaccio's painting *The Vision of Saint Augustine* (*c.* 1502). At the moment of Jerome's death, his spirit is said to have appeared to Saint Augustine, who was attempting to quantify the soul's

[35] Malone (ed.), *Plays and Poems*, vol. I, part II, p. 155.
[36] Parikka, "Archives in Media Theory," p. 85.

joy in the presence of God. As Jerome says in his gentle rebuke, "Augustine, Augustine, what are you seeking? Do you think that you can put the whole sea in a little vase? ... By what measure will you measure the immense?"[37] Jerome should know, being a textual scholar: that is, a species of humanist whose materials call for regular traversal of the boundary between hermeneutic and empirical scholarship. Jerome might also have pointed out that these questions are much older than they seem.

Humanists have recently called attention to the historicity of the idea of data, as well as the value systems that are operative within the term. Johanna Drucker, for one, has argued forcefully against uncritical takeup of the word *data* by humanists, pointing out that

The experimental approach to scientific investigation ... gives shape to the phenomena to be observed and then designs the apparatus suitable for their detection. In the sciences this distinction is reinforced by the difference between concepts of 'data' and 'capta.' Data are considered objective 'information' while capta is information that is captured because it conforms to the rules and hypothesis set for the experiment.[38]

Compare this definition of capta to the language of Mahoney's description of modelling, quoted above, as an activity that "*captures* what we *take* to be ... essential features."[39] Compare also Daniel Rosenberg's observation that one of *data*'s meanings in pre-modern mathematics was "quantities *given* in mathematical problems, as opposed to *quaestia* [a term from Euclid], or quantities *sought*."[40] Rosenberg's valuable historical inquiry into the changing meanings of *data* (and their relation to the meanings of words like *fact* and *evidence*) also emphasizes that the semantic status of *data* – about which Drucker is so wary – results from a change in meaning over the course of the eighteenth century:

At the beginning of the century, "data" was especially used to refer either to principles accepted as a basis of argument or to facts gleaned from scripture that were unavailable to questioning. By the end of the century, the term was most commonly used to refer to facts in evidence *determined* by the

---

[37] Roberts, "St. Augustine," p. 292; the quotation comes from Roberts's translation from *Hieronymus. Vita et transitus* (Venice, 1485). See also Galey, "Human Presence," pp. 97–8.

[38] Drucker, "Graphesis," p. 6.

[39] Mahoney, "Histories of Computing(s)," p. 129, emphasis added.

[40] Rosenberg, "Data Before the Fact," p. 19, emphasis in original.

experiment … It had become usual to think of data as the result of an investigation rather than its premise … Still today we think of data as a premise for argument; however, our principal notion of data as information in numerical form relies on the late eighteenth-century development.[41]

A crucial point shared by all these terminological observations is that the noun *data* always involves pronouns and verbs that imply configurations of subjects and actions – configurations that are always epistemological and historical in nature.

For Drucker, the answer to the question of what *data*, as a term, puts at stake is nothing less than the humanities' epistemological distinctiveness. In particular, she defends the humanistic embrace of constructivist conceptions of knowledge in contrast to realist approaches, which, as she puts it, "depend above all upon an idea that phenomena are *observer-independent* and can be characterized as *data*."[42] The recent rush within the digital humanities to conceive of materials as data, she argues, commits the error of treating observations as though they are identical to observed phenomena, thereby "undoing the basis of interpretation on which humanistic knowledge production is based."[43] For Drucker, the word *data* functions as a Trojan Horse, smuggling an invasive epistemology into the humanities that does its work before its presence is fully comprehended.

The blanket use of *data* to which Drucker objects is captured in Alan Liu's term *transcendental data*, which puts a name to the desire to conceive of content separable from material form, and of data separable from human subjectivity.[44] My own critique in this chapter is similar in spirit to Drucker's and Liu's, though in the context of Shakespearean textuality I am interested in a more mundane Trojan-Horse effect of the term *data*: the creeping tendency of the word to refer to any volume of digital materials, and of any kind. For example, if I copy some digital Shakespeare texts – say, XML-tagged transcriptions of playtexts from the First Folio – onto a USB drive and share it with a colleague, one might describe my action as the sharing of data. This workaday use of *data* has a less epistemologically interesting history than the meanings

---

[41] Rosenberg, "Data Before the Fact," p. 33, emphasis added.
[42] Drucker, "Humanities Approaches," ¶ 1, emphasis in original.
[43] Drucker, "Humanities Approaches," ¶ 1.
[44] See Liu's chapter "Transcendental Data: Towards a Cultural History and Aesthetics of the New Encoded Discourse," in his *Local Transcendence*, pp. 209–39; previously published in *Critical Inquiry*, 31.1 (2004), 49–84.

that Drucker and Rosenberg unpack, and probably derives from the tendency of programmers to describe as data any volume of information too large for a computer to store in active RAM (Random Access Memory, of which most personal computers have enough surplus to go unnoticed by users), requiring the creation of an external file to hold it all.[45] When I was a computer science student learning programming languages such as Pascal and C++ in the late 1980s and 90s, I and my classmates would label files of comma-separated values with the suffix ".dat" for "data file," blissfully ignorant of any ontological implications. For us, as for many, data was merely stuff that an algorithm would operate upon.

However, the easy semantic slide of terms like *text, transcription,* and *play* into the catchall word *data* elides the sometimes intractable aspects of texts, namely their historical and bibliographical specificity – in other words, the differences that enable literary and historical texts to arrest our attention, and to make meaning in ways modern readers might not expect. The popularization of *data* to mean not only quantitative measures, but also any mass of digital information that may be moved around and subjected to computational analysis has supported the misconception of digitized texts as buckets of words that may be poured from one container to another without change. As Willard McCarty describes this tendency as it has been encouraged by mass digitization, "the torrent rushing out of computers into the various disciplinary heartlands pull[s] attention away from the difference between cultural artifacts and the data derived from them – away from the analytic concerns of earlier work ... to a great stocking of the shelves."[46] (Note that Rothenberg's article, in contrast to this tendency, is explicitly concerned with the difference between artifacts and their representation as digital data.) The danger, McCarty warns, is the reduction of humanities computing projects to digitization factories; or, as he puts it in a complementary metaphor of consumption, the reduction of computers

---

[45] I am grateful to my colleague Periklis Andritsos for pointing out this origin of the more casual meaning of *data*, which vexes data scientists as well, especially those concerned with what they call data quality. On the RAM-vs-data distinction, compare Pierre Nora's point that modern archival memory may be regarded as a societal effort to "store the material vestiges of what we cannot possibly remember" as individuals; *Realms of Memory*, vol. I, p. 8. See Chapter 1, p. 3.

[46] McCarty, *Humanities Computing*, p. 5.

to "knowledge jukeboxes."[47] The project-factory model of digital humanities that has taken hold in recent years calls to mind Thomas Richards's characterization of knowledge in the Victorian imperial archive. This earlier "great stocking of the shelves," as McCarty calls it, privileged data in the form of the fact; as Richards describes,

> The fact was many things to many people, but generally it was thought of as raw knowledge, knowledge awaiting ordering. The various civil bureaucracies sharing the administration of Empire were desperate for these manageable pieces of knowledge. They were light and movable. They pared the Empire down to file-cabinet size. The British may not have created the longest-lived empire in history, but it was certainly one of the most data-intensive.[48]

As we have seen, however, and as Richards shows in the late Victorian context, the figure of the archive unsettles idealistic notions of data, given that archives – in practice and in theory – are spaces for materials that cannot easily be normalized and reduced to the condition of data.

Just as the word "computer" appears in a text printed in 1613, and as the form of a sonnet appears in a modern article on digital preservation, so do the past and present become entangled in digital artifacts. The rest of this chapter will turn to the ways that the digital contents of those figural knowledge jukeboxes may be understood as artifacts with histories, which bear the traces of their making.

The archaeology of digital Shakespeare texts

In a recent article on print-on-demand books made from out-of-copyright and supposedly plain texts taken from Project Gutenberg, Whitney Trettien asks how such hybrid artifacts are "redrawing the boundaries between books, facsimiles, electronic files and databases and, in the process, reconfiguring the relationships between readers, authors and editors, both living and dead."[49] Trettien's example is a reprint of Milton's *Areopagitica*, but, as she demonstrates, Shakespeare once again serves to validate new information networks in the form of one

---

[47] McCarty, *Humanities Computing*, p. 27.
[48] Richards, *Imperial Archive*, p. 4. On the history of the concepts of data versus facts, see Rosenberg, "Data Before the Fact."
[49] Trettien, "Deep History," ¶3. Trettien's article subtly enacts the textual conditions it describes, with what appear to be scripted deformations appearing in the text as one reads it on the *Digital Humanities Quarterly* website.

publisher's inclusion of two verses of Shakespeare's obscure poem "The Phoenix and the Turtle" (misattributed to Bacon) on its version of a copyright page.[50] As Trettien shows, these seemingly nameless texts come from somewhere, producing and reconfiguring historical connections rather than transcending them. How, then, do supposedly plain digital texts of Shakespeare function within the larger imagined totality of the Shakespearean archive, and how might that relationship trouble the idea of transcendental data?

Part of the answer may be found in an example from Marilyn Deegan and Kathryn Sutherland's *Transferred Illusions*, in which they take *King Lear* as a test case to explore a set of broad questions about digital textuality: "What do we gain in digitization, and what do we lose? What are the effects of decoupling a text from its physical carrier? What does it mean for a work, a text or a book to be digital, and how are users to make sense of the many different kinds of digital offerings available?"[51] Applying these questions to examples of full-text versions of *King Lear* found in Google Book Search, they find identifiable editions from 1770, 1811, and 1860, but have to undertake some bibliographical detective work to identify a version published by Plain Label Books, which gives no explanation of its text of *Lear*. Deegan and Sutherland discover that Plain Label Books appears to be one of the many supposed publishers that simply repackage digital texts from Project Gutenberg – texts that are themselves often selected with no reference to scholarly criteria for textual accuracy, and keyed in by volunteers concerned more with sharing out-of-copyright materials than with establishing their reliability. Although their detective work does not uncover the full history of this particular digital Shakespeare text, they use the example to frame important questions: "What text is this of *King Lear*, a highly contested play in its textual forms and status? Who is its implied user/reader? And how does a text move through four centuries of scholarship and become 'plain' [having no textual apparatus at all]?"[52]

The questions posed by Trettien, Deegan, and Sutherland embody the recent turn toward regarding digital code as human artifact, which in

---

[50] Trettien, "Deep History," ¶22.
[51] Deegan and Sutherland, *Transferred Illusions*, p. 145.
[52] Deegan and Sutherland, *Transferred Illusions*, p. 147. I explore similar questions with regard to *Hamlet*, including a digital version similar to the Plain Label Books example, in "The Tablets of the Law," pp. 91–3.

turn reflects the influence of textual studies, such as the unediting practiced by Randall McLeod and Leah Marcus, as well as the critical
analysis of born-digital electronic texts and databases practiced by
Liu and Kirschenbaum. Bonnie Mak's recent article "Archaeology of a
Digitization" is another provocative example of this turn, and its title,
like that of the field of media archaeology, signals its debt to Michel
Foucault's earlier inquiries into the grammars of power that underlie
discourses.[53] Mak and others exemplify what McKenzie called the bibliographer's imperative to "show the human presence in any recorded
text," and especially to reveal the decisions of human agents where their
presence is most effaced, such as the construction of digital data.[54] Mak's
test case for this approach is the digitization project *Early English Books
Online* (EEBO), whose imperfect remediation of decades-old microfilm
images we briefly considered in Chapter 4 (see p. 119), though the point
of her exercise in reading the layers of agency in a digitization echoes that
of Deegan and Sutherland: what matters is that these kinds of questions
are applicable to the full range of digitized texts.

EEBO's digitized books have come under sufficient critical scrutiny
that the project has become a recognized example of the gains and
losses of digitization. The photographic accidents in EEBO's microfilmed
images, such as the presence of fingers and other objects, even have their
own Twitter hashtag thanks to Trettien's blog *Facsimile Fail* (facsimilefail.
tumblr.com). What has received less critical attention, however, is the
tension between approaches to digital Shakespeare that value the materiality of texts – of which Trettien's blog is a prime example – versus those
that value the computational tractability of data for the purposes of
quantitative analysis. Throughout much of the history of humanities
computing, this latter perspective went by the innocuous name of text
analysis, though in recent years it has become associated through
literary history with concepts such as big data, macroanalysis, and
distant reading.[55] The larger the scale of the analysis, the more likely it is
that some version of Claude Shannon and Warren Weaver's model of
information will govern the project's thinking about the transmission
of texts, with author and reader equivalent to sender and receiver (see

---

[53] Mak, "Archaeology of a Digitization." For Foucault's clearest statement of his
archaeological approach, see *Archaeology of Knowledge*.
[54] McKenzie, *Bibliography*, p. 29.
[55] See Moretti, *Graphs, Maps, Trees*, and Jockers, *Macroanalysis*.

Chapter 6, pp. 206–8). Even text-analysis scholars with expert knowledge of philology and computation have advocated a separation of the concerns of computational tractability from the materiality of texts. For example, that separation of concerns lies behind what Martin Mueller and his team have called the Nameless Shakespeare, a digital corpus that makes no claims for textual authority beyond being simply good enough for linguistic, thematic, and stylistic analysis.[56] Like the supposedly plain text of *King Lear* from Plain Label Books or whatever text underlies Moretti's experiment, any Shakespeare text that aspires to transcendental namelessness invites a closer look.

The proto-digital word "Compters" in the Folio text of *The Winter's Tale* serves as a case in point for the contesting claims of data and materiality in the way digital Shakespeare texts are deployed in projects. Like many early modern words, including *travail* – which cannot be modernized to *travel* without losing its reference to labour, as in the French *travailler* – meanings are lost and gained in modernization. The *OED* lists *compter* as an archaic spelling for the noun *counter*, especially in the sense of objects used for reckoning quantities and performing other arithmetical operations (*counter*, n.[3]), often in the form of pieces of metal or ivory – these are likely the compters which Shakespeare's Clown seems unable to do without. (Curiously, in its archaic form *compter* could also mean a prison, where people are reckoned up, as in William Fennor's 1617 narrative *The Compters Common-wealth, or A Voiage Made to an Infernall Land* [London, 1617]). As Gary Taylor describes in his note explaining his emendation of "accompt" to "account" in *Henry V*'s opening chorus, *compter* also reaches back to the Latin *computāre*, the root of the modern word for the machines that have become ubiquitous in modern life.[57] As with "accompt" in *Henry V*, editors often emend (or modernize) "Compter" to "counter," as for example in Stephen Orgel's 1996 Oxford edition.[58] It is the kind of historically tangled word that materially oriented

---

[56] See Mueller, "Nameless Shakespeare."   [57] Taylor, (ed.), *Henry V*, p. 92.
[58] Orgel (ed.), *The Winter's Tale*, 4.3.35; neither his collation nor his commentary note indicate the original form of the word, unlike Taylor's emendation of "accompt." Curiously, the most recent New Variorum Shakespeare edition of *The Winter's Tale* (ed. Robert Kean Turner, Virginia Westling Haas, *et al.*, 2005) also omits emendations to "Compters" from its collation, though H. H. Furness's Variorum of 1898 indicates that "counters" was the preferred emendation after Capell.

Shakespeareans like Stallybrass and Marcus often use to support their points about modern interventions into the histories of early modern texts. *Compter/counter/computer* is not exactly a crux, but it is the kind of philological tangle that points beyond itself to questions about history, theories of textual transmission, and the limits of our knowledge. However, if one Googles the words "search shakespeare" and looks for "compters" at the top-ranked sites, whatever they may be, the results will probably indicate that Shakespeare's texts say nothing about "Compters."[59] There is a sad irony in the fact that the most ubiquitous digital version of Shakespeare's texts actually erases this link between his works and the history of computing.

We lose words like *compter*, or at least the record of their having existed at all in the text, thanks to the tendency to use texts innocently thought to be good enough for computational purposes, whether those purposes are intricate analyses or simply online publishing. The various nameless Shakespeare texts that circulate digitally tend to derive from a single source: the Moby Shakespeare, a plaintext digital transcription released into the public domain in 1992 by Grady Ward, and sometimes attributed to Ward's project Moby Lexical Tools.[60] The brief readme file distributed with the texts is an artifact of its time, archived together with the texts in the now-archaic .tar format (named for "tape archive"), and giving minimal information about the provenance and nature of the texts: "These unabridged, complete works of William Shakespeare are supplied on two 1.4MB MSDOS operating system disks." The file at least includes some key elements of metadata, including the creator's name (Ward), the date of creation (17 May 1993), and a public domain statement. The single text file containing the plays offers a curious digital echo of the 1623 First Folio in seeming to provide

[59] Relying arbitrarily on Google's rankings, the top three results for "search shakespeare" in my region (Toronto, Canada) in July 2014 were *RhymeZone Shakespeare Search* (www.rhymezone.com/shakespeare), *OpenSource Shakespeare* (www.opensourceshakespeare.org), and *Shakespeare Searched* (shakespeare.yippy.com). All read "counters" for "Compters" in their texts of *The Winter's Tale*, and only *OpenSource Shakespeare* provides anything resembling a rationale for its texts.

[60] The only official website for Moby Lexical Tools appears to be this site hosted by the University of Sheffield's Institute for Cognitive Informatics: icon.shef.ac.uk/Moby. The Moby page indicates that it was last modified on 24 October 2000. Quotations from the Moby Shakespeare files are taken from copies downloaded from this website in August 2013.

an exhaustive archive of Shakespeare's works, including claims to completeness ("The Complete Moby Shakespeare") and a prefatory list of Shakespeare's works divided generically, like the Folio's Catalogue page, into histories, comedies, and tragedies – in this case ordered by approximate sequence of composition within generic categories, unlike the Folio's approximate ordering by reign within the histories.[61]

However, despite the Moby Shakespeare's recruitment by projects that exploit the liberatory potential of post-print media – such as the *OpenSource Shakespeare*, whose title implicitly substitutes Shakespeare texts in place of the application code distributed by open-source programmers – the Moby Shakespeare itself is thoroughly an artifact of nineteenth-century print culture. Andrew Murphy and Michael Best, among others, have noted the Moby text's direct derivation from a print edition known as the Globe Shakespeare, an out-of-copyright text that apparently furnished the source for Ward's transcription.[62] The Globe text, edited by William George Clark and William Aldis Wright and published by Macmillan in 1864, was itself a derivative of Clark and Wright's multivolume Cambridge edition published between 1863 and 1866, the first Shakespeare text to be edited by professional university-based scholars. (Their Cambridge text was the one that Horace Howard Furness originally proposed to use as the basis of his New Variorum Shakespeare editions, at least until Wright publicly warned him off the idea; see Chapter 3, pp. 103–4.) The publisher Macmillan repackaged Clark and Wright's text, dispensing with their intricate textual collation notes, reducing the edition to a single volume, and repricing it for the mass market. In the history of Shakespeare editing, the significance of the Globe text is overshadowed by its siblings, the scholarly Cambridge volumes, and rendered obsolete by the reconceptualizing of Shakespeare editing brought about by the New Bibliographers in the decades following. But like many forms of scholarly infrastructure, it has importance that may otherwise go unnoticed: Fredson Bowers asserts that the Globe

---

[61] The Moby's equivalent to the Folio's Catalogue is slightly more complete in that it includes *Pericles* and the poems, though it strangely groups the poems among the histories. On the significance of the Folio's Catalogue and its omissions, see Chapter 3, pp. 89–91.

[62] Murphy, "Shakespeare Goes Digital," pp. 402–6; Best, "Electronic Text," pp. 149–50. On the editorial usefulness of Clark and Wright's text, see Werstine, "Modern Editors," and Bowers's response, "Historical Collation."

"may be properly called the first modern edition"; Murphy points out that it "served as the standard reference text for several decades, with many subsequent scholarly editions keying their own citation systems to its act, scene, and line numbers"; and de Grazia calls it "a typographic marvel that dominated the world market for the better part of a century."[63]

Notably, in the same sentence de Grazia also calls the Globe "the best example of an idealized [Shakespeare] text," and goes on to consider the 1864 Globe volume as a material object, noting its resemblance to contemporary King James Bibles in format and portability, and its iconographic assertions of universality and globalized Englishness in the logo on its title page.[64] As she points out, the title-page logo shows a blank globe marked with lines of longitude – implicitly with the Prime Meridian running through the Royal Observatory at Greenwich, England, at the centre (established there only a few years before in 1851) – all encircled by the universalizing Shakespearean motto "One touch of nature makes the whole world kin."[65] This logo, long detached from the digital Moby text, reminds the reader that the Globe Shakespeare is named not for its origins in Shakespeare's theatre, but for its intended destinations as a cultural instrument of empire. This was a book made to be carried, along with King James Bibles, by civil servants, soldiers, merchants, and colonists to places like India, Australia, South Africa, Jamaica, and other territories under the British Empire's never-setting sun. As de Grazia notes, the Globe Shakespeare helped fulfill this function by eschewing nearly all visible signs of scholarly labour:

All traces of the Cambridge's daunting scholarship were concealed ... so that the Globe edition gave the impression of being no edition at all. It seemed as if nothing intervened between the reader and Shakespeare – except sheer text. With the contingent and material subsumed, the edition appeared almost transparent, as if the reader could see through the text to the mind in which it originated. One Shakespeare for one world.[66]

---

[63] Bowers, "Historical Collation," p. 255; Murphy, "Shakespeare Goes Digital," p. 403; and de Grazia, "The Question of the One and the Many," p. 246.

[64] De Grazia, "The Question of the One and the Many," pp. 246–7.

[65] On the ironies of recontextualizing this famous line from *Troilus and Cressida*, and its use in an Edison phonograph advertisement, see Chapter 5, pp. 162–4.

[66] De Grazia, "The Question of the One and the Many," p. 247.

This "one Shakespeare" also took the form of one book, in contrast to the increasingly copious multivolume Shakespeare editions of the late eighteenth century and early nineteenth. In contrast to the multivolume format that allowed Edmund Malone to imagine an ever-increasing paratext of editorial notes, the Globe edition offered the illusion of the Shakespearean archive made graspable.[67] It seems entirely appropriate, then, that a Shakespeare text designed to assert its universality and make a quiet conquest of the globe has succeeded in its mission nearly a hundred and fifty years later.[68]

This brief and incomplete archaeology of the Moby Shakespeare does not answer all the pressing questions about the text as a digital object. (For example, a question answerable only through collation is how much the digital Moby text deviates from the printed Globe text.) It should at least be clear that the Moby Shakespeare does not provide a transparent window into the mind of Shakespeare, or the texts he presented to his playing companies, or a record of what was acted on his stages. Indeed, digital projects that take the Moby Shakespeare to be a reliable data set are just as likely to make generalizations based on a Victorian adaptation of Shakespeare's texts, made to serve distinctly Victorian agendas.

My main purpose, however, is not to discredit the Moby and projects based upon it, but to demonstrate the value of what Mak calls the archaeology of digitization in a Shakespearean context. As Kirschenbaum, Drucker, and many other digital textual scholars have been demonstrating, digital artifacts – texts and data sets alike – are material things even if their substrates are not immediately recognizable or intelligible. The Moby Shakespeare that resides on my laptop's hard drive is a copy of one that

---

[67] I am paraphrasing Tom Stoppard's quip about the British Library, quoted in Chapter 2, p. 64. On editorial encyclopedism, see pp. 106–15, and the discussion of Malone at the beginning of Chapter 1.

[68] One of the ironies of the history of the Globe, however, is that the first edition of 1864, which was designed to become ubiquitous, has since become a rare book. Its rarity, however, seems to have been produced by massive reprinting, which made the first edition redundant in the eyes of many libraries (and reasonably so). As far as I can determine, even the Folger Shakespeare Library does not hold a copy of the first edition of this historically significant Shakespeare text, and my attempts to call it up at the New York Public Library repeatedly resulted in the wrong Globe edition being sent up from the stacks. I was finally able to locate a first edition through a rare book dealer in Australia, which I purchased and donated to the Thomas Fisher Rare Book Library at the University of Toronto.

resides on a Sheffield University server, and before that (according to the readme file) on "two 1.4MB MSDOS operating system disks," and through a longer chain of transmission on a copy of the Globe Shakespeare that probably matched de Grazia's description. All of these versions are material, in that they are venues where physicality interacts with human agency to shape the meaning of the textual artifact.

The Nameless Shakespeare text thus has a very specific name and history. Rather than accepting the Moby Shakespeare's immensely successful instantiation of the Shakespearean archive on its own terms, then, one might ask to what extent the Globe edition, via the Moby text, gives a distinctly mid-Victorian shape to the default digital Shakespeare text of the early twenty-first century. The Moby text is a refurbished artifact in many important respects, as Murphy illustrates in an automotive metaphor that critiques digital projects based on the Globe: "while one could probably fit a Model-T Ford with power steering, antilock brakes, and airbags, it would still remain, in essence, a Model T."[69] Mueller, probably speaking for many text analysis scholars, attempts to neutralize such questions on the grounds that "if one stands a few feet away from the passionately contested minutiae of Shakespearean editing," the Globe and the major modern editions "do not differ a great deal in their treatment of cruxes or choice of variants."[70] However, phenomena such as variants, emendations, and modernizations are reminders that texts change in transmission, and that the agents responsible for those changes are part of a sociology of the text that extends beyond any particular localization, whether framed as data or edition. More is at stake, therefore, in objections to the Globe Shakespeare than the question of which text is the most authoritative, or how many corrections or emendations would be necessary to create a Shakespeare text good enough for quantitative analysis. Shakespeare is not a data set to be massaged into a tolerable margin of error, like the linguistic corpora for which text-analysis methods were developed. Shakespeare's texts are always human artifacts travelling through time, and they carry their histories with them.

---

[69] Murphy, "Shakespeare Goes Digital," pp. 404–5. Compare de Grazia's similar metaphor of Theseus's ship, which was rebuilt so many times during his voyages that it raised the question of whether it was the same ship in the end; "The Question of the One and the Many," p. 245.

[70] Mueller, "Nameless Shakespeare," p. 63.

Shakespeare after computing essentialism

In 1946, W. H. Auden used Shakespeare to think through the problem of the changing politics of knowledge. The title of his poem "Under Which Lyre: a Reactionary Tract for the Times," an occasional piece for the first commencement at Harvard since the end of the Second World War, refers to a line from *Henry IV, Part II* in which Pistol challenges Justice Swallow to declare "Under which king" he bears his authority, "Harry the Fourth, or Fifth?" (5.3.114–15).[71] It is a comic moment loaded with seriousness, as the violence surrounding the contestation of the English throne appears poised to end, though partly at the price of the new king's rejection of Falstaff in the next scene. Auden takes Henry the Fifth (he of the sober interrogation of archives prior to invasions, as discussed at the outset) and Falstaff as examples of the different conceptions of postwar education. In the poem they correspond to Apollo and Hermes, the former signifying centralized order and instrumental reason, the latter signifying undisciplined creativity and the trickster's disregard of authority, and yet both making music of their own kind. Auden knew which side he was on:

> thou shalt not sit
> With statisticians nor commit
> A social science

was his poem's pointed response to the humanities' postwar displacement by the sciences, part of a "Hermetic Decalogue" which includes another commandment regularly ignored by digital humanists today: "Thou shalt not worship projects."[72] Although Auden knew he was fighting a losing battle, and acknowledged that a world run by Hermes would be as unlivable as one run by Apollo, his 1946 depiction of the humanities' permanent crisis nonetheless puts names to ideological forces operating today. Yet, then as now, the real enemy was rarely scientists themselves, but rather the culture of bureaucratic managerialism that held its own narrow conception of science to be the one true form of research. Whenever digital humanists trace their field's lineage

---

[71] For a discussion of the circumstances of the poem's composition and delivery, see Kirsch, "A Poet's Warning," *Harvard Magazine* (Nov.–Dec. 2007), harvardmagazine.com/2007/11/a-poets-warning.html.
[72] Auden, *Collected Poems*, pp. 337–8.

back to Vannevar Bush – popularizer of the Memex proto-hypertext system, head of the wartime Office of Scientific Research and Development, architect of the Manhattan Project, and witness to the first atomic bomb test – they wittingly or not take Apollo's side in the same ongoing contest.[73]

Ronald Day describes some of what Auden was up against in his account of the constitution of information science and modern computing, whose formation was defined by the needs of postwar corporate and military power in America. The consequence, which endures today, was that many approaches to the study of information still suffer from what Day identifies as "willful ignorance of Marxist, nonquantitative, non-'practical,' and, largely, non-American analyses of information"; as he argues, "analyses of information and society and culture have almost totally been given over to so-called information specialists and public policy planners, mainly from computer science, business and business schools, the government, and the quantitative social sciences."[74] The optimism that usually attends new media can lead us to forget that our everyday acts of individual communication, supported by mobile devices and social networks, are governed by master narratives that should not go unquestioned. Digital encryption, for example, has become so ubiquitous as to seem mundane, but as Tarleton Gillespie describes, every encoded Tweet and Facebook update invokes a cultural history related to the militarization of information described in the preceding chapter: "The paradigmatic relationship between participants that encryption has required in its traditional application – secret military communication – is being forced upon public, commercial, and cultural exchanges that never before worked on such terms."[75] In this light, even the most mundane of digital interactions fulfills Auden's fears by deepening the militarization of all human communication.

Recruiting Shakespeare to any cause – political, religious, aesthetic, disciplinary – can have unforeseen consequences, as every modern performance has the potential to show us. By interrogating the idea of Shakespearean data in this chapter, my purpose has been to show that the message that computing necessarily means a turn toward quantitative methods – and, implicitly, away from other approaches favouring

---

[73] On Bush's Memex essay, "As We May Think," and its wartime contexts, see Harpold, *Ex-foliations*, pp. 20–43 and esp. 70–2.

[74] Day, *Invention of Information*, p. 5.   [75] Gillespie, *Wired Shut*, p. 247.

things like history, materiality, gender, ideology, and performance – is simply false. Its promulgation within sectors of the digital humanities is less about recognizing *the* computer's essential nature, and more about a disciplinary sleight-of-hand by which materialist and constructivist approaches are displaced by a positivism that is more amenable to the cyberinfrastructure model of big science and an administered world.

Yet computing is not an alien technology that impacts the humanities from some distant beyond, like a meteorite hitting the earth, but is more productively conceived as a set of practices that have long been adapted and reinvented by different communities for their own purposes.[76] One disciplinary and epistemological consequence of this argument is that digital Shakespeare researchers need not feel constrained by the idea that digital technologies are inherently scientific instruments, on loan to the humanities on the condition that they be used scientifically – or pseudo-scientifically, as is often the case in the most conservative sectors of the digital humanities.[77] In many ways it was unfortunate that the first widely publicized use of computing to solve an interpretive problem in Shakespeare studies was a question of authorship attribution, Don Foster's computer-assisted analysis of the contested authorship of the "Funeral Elegy" – unfortunate not because of any particular deficiency in Foster's methods (which I am not qualified to judge), but simply because it presented computers in their old postwar role as answer-machines. Stephen Booth likely spoke for many Shakespeareans in his response: "As to the [computer] tests themselves, I don't pretend to understand them."[78] Who can blame him? In retrospect, it is difficult to see the past decade's proliferation of social media and Web-based computing drawing much inspiration or energy from the "Funeral Elegy" episode. Even at the time, it seemed an old-fashioned use of computing (statistical analysis) applied to an old-fashioned critical

---

[76] See Mahoney, "Histories of Computing(s)," and Hobart and Schiffman, *Information Ages*.

[77] Textual scholarship has had its own fraught relationship with science, which Greetham summarizes in "What Is Textual Scholarship?", pp. 21–3.

[78] Booth, "A Long, Dull Poem," p. 237. The participants who did succeed in taking the debate somewhere interesting tended to be those who, like Booth, focused less on computational and statistical methods, and more on the critical assumptions about authorship and canon that the debate had exposed; examples may be found in other articles in the same issue of *Shakespeare Survey* in which Booth's appears.

question (authorship attribution in the service of regulating cultural heritage), fought out in divisive polemics that led nowhere.

As an alternative, it is worth remembering some of the developments that succeeded in animating mainstream Shakespeare studies during the rise of personal computing and, later, the World Wide Web: the versioning of *King Lear* and, subsequently, other plays; the reevaluation of the so-called bad quartos; performance as a generator of meaning, not just a conduit for it; early modern theatre as what Gary Taylor calls "the most socialized of all literary forms," involving collaboration and revision[79]; the importance of Shakespeare's neglected contemporaries, such as Middleton and Heywood; and the materiality of texts, especially as mediated (or elided) by the interventions of editors. Not surprisingly, all but the last two emphasize Shakespeare as playwright, company shareholder, and actor, rather than Shakespeare as individualized poet, dramatic or otherwise. Using the terms of information theory, we could say that all of these areas of activity focus on noise, not just message. Instead, they treat Shakespeare's texts not as signals from the past to be purged of interference, but as bearers of the imprints of non-authorial agents (collaborators, players, audiences, readers, editors) and their meaning-making processes as they intervened in "what Shakespeare actually wrote" (as the saying goes). Put another way, these approaches self-consciously deal with materials that resist straightforward digital representation and modelling. The resulting gap between representation and artifact is the kind of space where humanists work best. What would digital Shakespeare criticism look like if the digital tools supporting it could also account for the complexity of textual transformission? That is an exciting prospect to contemplate, but it requires that ambitions of disciplinary conquest be set aside.

Preservation and performance alike provoke new ways of thinking about the nature of cultural texts through modelling, each in their way being forms of world-building. To regard computing as a negotiation between preservation and loss, and between the sometimes intractable world and our models of it, is to recognize the role of the archive in the way we imagine digital technology. As Pierre Nora provocatively states, "Archive as much as you like: something will always be left out."[80] Yet

---

[79] Wells and Taylor, *Textual Companion*, p. 15.
[80] Nora, *Realms of Memory*, p. 9. See also Ricoeur, *Memory, History, Forgetting*, p. 169

as we have seen, something can often get in unbidden, as well, even with digital data. The digital EEBO images of the 1613 edition of *The yong mans gleanings* (discussed above) embody McKenzie's sociology of text graphically by inadvertently capturing the photographer's thumbs in the lower corners of the images, probably a result of the octavo's small size preventing it from lying flat without help. Although EEBO's texts, images, and metadata might all be swept up by the catchall term *data*, the page image showing the *OED*'s earliest reference to a computer as a human also shows human digits, required to hold open an artifact whose design presupposed manipulation by human hands. This hybrid image of the overlap of past and present, and of human and artifact, hints that the digital Shakespeare texts of the future will be as time-bound, as mutable, and as human as the computers who made them.

8 | *Conclusion: sites of Shakespearean memory*

This book has considered, directly and indirectly, what it means to be a digital Shakespearean caught between two kinds of history. Michel de Certeau describes these two ways of relating to history, which are also different ways of understanding archives: "one type . . . ponders what is comprehensible and what are the conditions of understanding; the other claims to reencounter lived experience, exhumed by virtue of a knowledge of the past."[1] This first kind, in Certeau's words, "examines history's capacity to render thinkable the documents which the historian inventories. It yields to the necessity of working out models which allow series of documents to be composed and understood: economic models, cultural models, and the like."[2] This first mode of historical thought always has a by-product in the form of the questioning of the methodological and epistemological conditions in which history is written. Shakespeare studies has been defined by that questioning since the historical turn of the 1980s.

The second kind of history moves in a different direction; as Certeau says, it "valorizes the relation the historian keeps with a lived experience, that is, with the possibility of resuscitating or 'reviving' a past. It would like to restore the forgotten and to meet again men of the past amid the traces they have left."[3] Think of one of humanism's primal scenes: Machiavelli alone in his study at the end of the workday, entering (via his books) "the courts of ancient men" and conversing with them as though they were present – Machiavelli's point being that they are present, in a way.[4] The by-product of this second kind of history tends to be narrative (like Machiavelli's) which uses literary genres to shape the received past.

---

[1] Certeau, *The Writing of History*, p. 35. [2] *Ibid.*
[3] Certeau, *The Writing of History*, p. 35–6.
[4] Machiavelli describes this in a 1513 letter to Francesco Vettori; see Allan Gilbert (ed.), *The Letters of Machiavelli*, p. 142.

This book's analysis of various Shakespearean sites of memory –
Pierre Nora's *lieux de mémoire* – has operated mainly within the first
of these two historical modes, attempting to "render thinkable" information experiments such as Teena Rochfort Smith's *Four-Text Hamlet*,
the Royal Ordnance Survey's facsimiles, Thomas Edison's kinetophone
performance of *Julius Caesar*, Cynthia Clay's Shakespearean Turing
Test at the Boston Science Museum, and digital projects based on the
multilayered textual artifact that has become the Moby Shakespeare. In
the spirit of Certeau's first kind of history, one of the most convincing
rationales offered for the supersession of print editions by digital ones is
that print was never Shakespeare's only medium, or even his primary
medium in the case of his plays. Lukas Erne has recently reopened the
question of Shakespeare's intentions with regard to print – did he
compose his plays with an eye to print publication? was he indifferent
to the post-performance appearance of his plays in print? – but regardless of one's position on these debates, digital editing nonetheless calls
into question Shakespeare's relationship to all media, not just digital
media.[5] Discussions of digital editing should therefore never simply
remain discussions of digital editing, hence my deliberate displacement
of digital editions from the centre of this account, despite this book's
origins with the Electronic New Variorum Shakespeare. Contrary to the
present tendency of the digital humanities, I believe there are better
ways of telling the story than through our own project-histories.[6]

As much as textual scholarship demands rigour and empirical objectivity – recall Greg's definition of bibliography as "the science of the
transmission of literary documents" – it also demands a subjectivity that
takes pleasure in the uncanny pastness of the present, and presentness of
the past (as the etymology of the field's older name, *philology*, implies).[7]
An example we have encountered already is the shared sense of wonder
evoked by the preservation of performances in the form of early
recorded speech acts, as we encountered in Chapter 5, and evidenced
by widespread media coverage. As the Smithsonian and its collaborators at the Lawrence Berkeley National Laboratory, Indiana University,
and the Library of Congress uncovered and released more of Alexander

[5] Erne, *Shakespeare as Literary Dramatist*.
[6] See, for example, Burdick *et al.*'s assertion of "the project as [the] basic unit" of
digital humanities research, which they at least distinguish from "Big Humanities
projects built along the lines of Big Science"; *Digital Humanities*, p. 124.
[7] See pp. Chapter 6, pp. 203 and 234.

Graham Bell's recordings, the public gained an opportunity to appreciate not only what digital forensics and computational analysis could achieve, but also the sense of wonder evoked by a meeting of old and new media. Hearing Bell's voice seemed to bridge historical distance while at the same time emphasizing the vastness of the gap (as bridges tend to do).

With the recovered inscriptions of the Bell recordings, the recent past has furnished few better examples of the bibliographer D. F. McKenzie's point about the value of finding the "human presence in any recorded text."[8] The changing substrates of those recorded texts and their reconfiguration of remembered human presence have been the preoccupation of this book, just as it has preoccupied Shakespearean textual scholars working in the digital humanities. I will conclude by considering two final *lieux de mémoire*, both of which dramatize and complicate this book's overall arguments about archives, substrates, and human presences in their own ways. Each also embodies Certeau's different ways of relating to history.

The first comes from the margins of Shakespeare editing, and confronts editors (print and digital alike) with inscriptions on one of humanity's oldest substrates. Our natural emphasis on Shakespearean media such as print, performance, and film can lead us to forget that Shakespeare evidently wrote for the medium of stone with at least two of his poetic works, one being his own epitaph:

GOOD FREND FOR IESVS SAKE FORBEARE,
TO DIGG THE DVST ENCLOASED HEARE.
BLESE BE Y^E MAN Y^T SPARES THES STONES,
AND CVRST BE HE Y^T MOVES MY BONES.[9]

With this inscription, Shakespeare's grave in Holy Trinity Church at Stratford-upon-Avon becomes the most literal convergence of document and monument. The irony, at least for those wishing to hear Shakespeare speak to the present in his own voice, is that these words are addressed not to Shakespeare's literary posterity but to generations

---

[8] McKenzie, *Bibliography*, p. 29.
[9] The other is "Verses Upon the Stanley Tomb at Tong." This and the inscription on Shakespeare's grave are two among a number of epitaphs attributed to Shakespeare, but these are the only two whose copy-text tends to be the stone monuments themselves, not manuscript sources; see Wells and Taylor, *Textual Companion*, pp. 457–60.

of church sextons, who would normally relocate old graves to create space for new ones: we only overhear this message.[10] Taken at face value, these four lines bear less resemblance to, say, John Donne's funeral sermon than to a modern author's instructions to future archivists on the handling of his or her unpublished literary remains – or, in this instance, mortal remains. Nonetheless, Shakespeare's epitaph is usually collected among his literary works, in which case the stone itself is the copy-text. The attribution is more a matter of tradition than evidence: Sam Schoenbaum cites affirmations of Shakespeare's authorship of his own epitaph from late seventeenth-century correspondence, as do the Oxford editors.[11] It seems ungenerous not to grant to Shakespeare this one last textual transmission into the future – a future that he evidently imagined as being crowded with the dead.

Rather than subjecting this four-line inscription to metrical tests, rare-word analysis, or any other statistical attribution methods (which at best can only indicate probability), one might instead note that, for many visitors to this site, authenticity works in other ways entirely. The codes that produce this text's authority are both material and imaginative: this is an inscription in stone that speaks in Shakespeare's voice, and it is the Shakespearean text most physically proximate to the author's bodily remains. However, this most literal of Shakespearean inscriptions becomes a picture of textual mediation even for those standing right in front of it. The positioning of the grave in Stratford's Holy Trinity Church forces viewers to read the gravestone's text upside down, and those unwilling to contort themselves may instead read the epitaph on a small plaque that sits upon the gravestone. The effect is not unlike encountering an archivist's transcription of a hard-to-read holograph letter in a record box. With the epitaph's transcription as a surrogate for the inscription itself, even Shakespeare's grave has been edited.

The example of Shakespeare's epitaph holds out the promise of Certeau's second kind of history, in which the present communes somehow with the past. However, the layered materiality of these inscriptions demands that we engage with Certeau's first kind of history, and examine "history's capacity to render thinkable the documents" that

---

[10] Schoenbaum, *Documentary Life*, pp. 250–1.
[11] Schoenbaum, *Documentary Life*, pp. 250–1; Wells and Taylor, *Textual Companion*, pp. 459–60.

make up the Shakespearean archive, including documents that are also monuments.[12] The textuality of this particular monument (to recall Andrew Prescott's term) makes itself clear in the circulation of the epitaph beyond its original material context, and especially its inclusion among the canon of Shakespeare's works.[13] For example, the *Norton Shakespeare*, whose archival orientation is signalled by its reproduction of several historical documents, places the epitaph not among the "Documents" section in the appendix, but among the "Works" (in the subsection "Various Poems").[14] Following the 1986 *Oxford Shakespeare* upon which it is based, the *Norton Shakespeare* completes the transformation of inscription into literary text by giving it a title ("Epitaph on Himself"), modernizing the spelling ("Blese" becomes "Blessed"), adding a diacritical pronunciation cue to "enclosèd," and dutifully giving the poem an entry in the "Textual Variants" section. The epitaph's control text is specified as "Shakespeare's grave at Stratford."[15] This epitaph, along with the one included as "Verses upon the Stanley Tomb at Tong," is unique among Shakespeare's works in being preserved not by the two dominant media of early modern literary transmission – print and manuscript – but by stone.

This example of Shakespeare's textualized tomb shows Heather MacNeil's concept of archivalterity at work in its encrustations of historical meanings upon an original act of inscription.[16] The construction of authenticity in these examples also illustrates a basic premise about the interpretation of cultural artifacts, one associated with D. F. McKenzie but best expressed by Walter Benjamin in "The Work of Art in the Age of Mechanical Reproduction": "The authenticity of a thing is the essence of all that is transmissible from its beginning, ranging from its substantive duration to its testimony to the history which it has experienced."[17] Yet the very idea of the transmissible is put at stake with changes in media and substrates. For example, the originating moment of the stone inscriptions' creation, when transmissible textual information was chiseled into a symbolically enduring substrate, becomes paradoxically overshadowed by the accumulations of

---

[12] Certeau, *Writing of History*, p. 35.
[13] Prescott, "Textuality of the Archive"; see Chapter 2, pp. 46–56.
[14] Greenblatt, *et al.* (eds.), *Norton Shakespeare*, p. 2007.
[15] Greenblatt, *et al.* (eds.), *Norton Shakespeare*, p. 2009.
[16] MacNeil, "Archivalterity"; see Chapter 2, p. 70.
[17] Benjamin, "Work of Art," p. 221.

their history: the gesture of fixing a text in stone simply generates more copies, variants, and paratexts, re-initiating rather than arresting the Shakespeare text's passage through time. Shakespearean archive fever, however, has only occasionally manifested itself in a desire to inscribe Shakespeare's texts once and for all, as in the First Folio's or Edmund Malone's claims to definitiveness through encyclopedic textual management. Rather, the attraction of the Shakespearean archive as an imagined totality has tended to lie in the accumulations themselves, or in what Derrida called consignation: the gathering-together of signs within a single coordinating episteme.[18]

The substrates change and multiply in my final Shakespearean *lieu de mémoire*: Jorge Luis Borges's short story "Shakespeare's Memory," which captures the wonder and uncanniness of the Shakespearean archive in the form of a cautionary tale. The story, set in the years following the First World War, concerns a Shakespearean textual scholar named Hermann Sörgel, author of "a scattering of critical and philological 'notes,'" a Shakespeare chronology, a drafted but unpublished article on George Chapman's language, and a "diatribe against an emendation inserted by Theobald into his critical edition of 1734."[19] While attending a Shakespeare conference, Sörgel receives the gift of Shakespeare's own memories from a mysterious stranger. Shakespeare's memory, which exists in the possessor's mind alongside his own, was given to this stranger by a dying man on an eastern battlefield, who presumably had received it in turn from someone else. The gift of Shakespeare's memory comes with certain conditions, as the giver describes: "The one who possesses it must offer it aloud, and the one who is to receive it must accept it the same way. The man who gives it loses it forever" (p. 125).

Sörgel accepts via this exchange of speech acts, and receives further instructions about how Shakespeare's memory operates: "The memory has entered your mind, but it must be 'discovered.' It will emerge in dreams, or when you are awake, when you turn the pages of a book, or turn a corner" (p. 125). Part of the advice even appears directed at Sörgel's scholarly instincts: "Don't be impatient; don't *invent*

---

[18] On the concepts of consignation and textual management, see pp. 62–3.
[19] Borges, "Shakespeare's Memory," p. 122; page numbers are cited parenthetically hereafter.

recollections. Chance in its mysterious workings may help it along, or it may hold it back" (p. 125–6; emphasis in original). Predictably enough, Sörgel then embarks upon an antiquarian's fantasy, experiencing memories that may or may not be authentically Shakespearean, but which hold the promise of unique insight into the mysteries of the Sonnets, Shakespeare's embarrassment at not keeping up with Ben Jonson's Greek and Latin hexameters, and even fragments such as odd melodies that Shakespeare might have whistled while out walking.

In this way Borges's character experiences the ultimate form of Certeau's version of history as the re-encounter with lived experience, even to the point of Shakespeare's quotidian life leaving its marks in Sörgel's own. The nearly empty archive of Shakespeare's private life here becomes an overflowing storehouse of memory. Eventually the gift of memory turns sour, as supernatural gifts often do in this kind of *Twilight Zone* narrative, and Sörgel finds himself staggering under the weight of two memories that have begun to mingle, his own and "the incommunicable other's" (p. 130). Overburdened by the weight of the Shakespearean archive as live memory, Sörgel, turns to information technology:

I have forgotten the date on which I decided to free myself. I hit upon the easiest way: I dialled telephone numbers at random. The voice of a child or woman would answer; I believed it was my duty to respect their vulnerable estates. At last a man's refined voice answered.

"Do you," I asked, "want Shakespeare's memory? Consider well: it is a solemn thing I offer, as I can attest." (p. 130)

Sörgel apparently makes the offer with the determination to maintain the patriarchal link of bequeathing Shakespeare's memory to an adult male heir, who inherits a crisis of knowledge. The man at the other end of the line accepts, and Borges's version of the Shakespearean archive slips through the telephone network to a new recipient, like a computer network virus in the era of dialup modems. Nowhere in Borges's story appears any single monument, gravestone, or book that localizes Shakespeare's memory: for Borges, the Shakespearean *lieux de mémoire* are networks themselves, both the furtive human network of Shakespearean memory-survivors and the technological network of phone lines. As we have already seen, those wires have been transmitting the memory of Shakespeare's texts, if not Shakespeare's actual memories, from the telephone's earliest moments.

Borges illustrates the dilemma of Certeau's two kinds of history in ways that expose the paradoxes of memory. In the course of the story, Sörgel reflects on the operations of memory, initially subscribing to the theory that "our brain is a palimpsest. Every new text covers the previous one, and is in turn covered by the text that follows – but all-powerful Memory is able to exhume any impression, no matter how momentary it might have been, if given sufficient stimulus" (p. 127). In this case the stimulus turns out to be more books, namely Shakespeare's sources in Chaucer, Gower, Spenser, and Marlowe. However, this dream of mastery soon gives way to a sense of fragmentation and disorientation: "The man who acquires an encyclopedia does not thereby acquire every line, every paragraph, every page, and every illustration; he acquires the *possibility* of becoming familiar with one and another of those things" (p. 128; emphasis in original). Like the palimpsest, the encyclopedia provides another archival metaphor that should by now be familiar, similar to Borges's metaphor of the archive as a chaotic basement: "A man's memory is not a summation; it is a chaos of vague possibilities. St. Augustine speaks, if I am not mistaken, of the palaces and the caverns of memory. The second metaphor is the more fitting one. It was into those caverns that I descended" (p. 128).[20] The actual experience of Shakespeare's lived experience cannot take the form of a narrative, at least for Sörgel, and the lived experience of memory becomes a burden.

A striking feature of this story is the almost offhand way that Sörgel solves his memory overload problem by turning to information technology. Similarly, Borges chooses to imagine the externalization of memory by metaphorical recourse to a machine, which recalls the discussion of Derrida, Freud, and the Mystic Writing-Pad from Chapter 2. Despite not knowing what Shakespeare's "magical memory" (p. 128) really is, or where it came from, Sörgel nevertheless transmits it electronically over the telephone, connecting randomly and anonymously in a manner we now associate with the Internet and before that with amateur radio. In an even stronger digital parallel, Sörgel, like his predecessors, in the end finds he can only erase Shakespeare's memory by overwriting it with something else, like a computer's magnetic disc.[21] In Borges's story, one

---

[20] Book ten of Augustine's *Confessions* deals substantially with memory.
[21] On overwriting as erasure in digital media, see Kirschenbaum's chapter "Extreme Inscription: a Grammatology of the Hard Drive," in *Mechanisms*, pp. 73–110.

cannot displace Shakespeare with alternate objects of study, such as William Blake, because Shakespeare's connectivity means that all network paths lead back to him – except one: the "strict, vast music" of Bach, in which Sörgel finds relief at the end (p. 131). Given the presence of these media allegories for memory, it is all the more striking that Borges does not fall back on the literary trope of the lost inscription: there is no relic or Stratford gravestone to fetishize in the story, and Shakespeare's memory is never materialized like a found manuscript in a Gothic romance. There are only the unknown and undistinguished hosts of Shakespeare's memory who have become media themselves.

This book has similarly concerned itself with many of those agents of transmission who have left few traces behind them, at least in the traditional histories of Shakespeare editing. Some of the names of the experimenters in new media and information technology that populate this book are well known in the history of Shakespeare textual scholarship, such as Jaggard, Collier, Furness, and Furnivall. Others names such as Rochfort Smith, Colonel James, Edison, Bell, Field, Turing, the Friedmans, Kolkowski, and Rothenberg do not form a canon, yet their engagements with Shakespeare, large and small, add up to an alternate history of experimentation and inquiry at the intersection of the human and the mechanical. My aim in bringing their stories together has been to persuade digital Shakespeareans, particularly the next generation of digital textual scholars, that the history of what they undertake is varied, complex, and not to be found in any one telling of the story.

That brings us to Certeau's most important point, which is that, despite appearances, the two forms of history he describes are not in opposition, though they are in tension. The result is a historiographical paradox that also frames all speculation about the future of information: "Thus founded on the rupture between a past that is its object, and a present that is the place of its practice, history endlessly finds the present in its object and the past in its practice."[22] It becomes difficult to sustain digital Shakespeare as a distinct category of inquiry when considered in these terms, in which proto-digital experiments can take place in the nineteenth century, and centuries-old editorial infrastructure manifests itself in supposedly plain digital texts. That difficulty is productive, and the reward for engaging with this tension is the uncanny feeling one gets upon realizing that the past does not always stay put;

---

[22] Certeau, *Writing of History*, p. 36.

sometimes it connects with the present in arresting ways, like the appearance of a ghost.

Shakespeare haunts our technological infrastructures like a ghost, much like the one he may have played, himself, in *Hamlet*. Textual scholars, as counterparts to Borges's Hermann Sörgel, desire to interrogate the ghostly presences hovering at the edges of rational systems. Digital tools, like the nineteenth-century positivism that many of them embody, often hold out the prospect of compelling stones to speak. Derrida identifies that desire in Freud, himself an amateur archaeologist: "It is the nearly ecstatic instant Freud dreams of, when the very success of the dig must sign the effacement of the archivist: the origin then speaks by itself ... [The archive] comes to efface itself, it becomes transparent or unessential so as to let the origin present itself in person. Live, without mediation and without delay."[23] Hamlet and Horatio could sympathize, as could Shakespeareans who have shared Greenblatt's conflicted desire to speak with the dead.[24] The stone inscriptions on Shakespeare's tomb might seem to hold out the same promise, like the Ark of the Covenant described in the Introduction's reading of *Raiders of the Lost Ark* – a radio for talking to God, as Indiana Jones's archaeological nemesis, Belloq, calls the chest that holds whatever remains of Moses's tablets. That wonderfully anachronistic metaphor, in its conflation of an ancient medium of inscription with a modern one of transmission, serves as a reminder that our theories about the transmission of Shakespeare's texts are indivisible from deeply felt investments of desire and faith. What matters is how we respond to the gap between material records and the substantiation of what we desire to know about Shakespeare's texts. The Shakespearean archive is the substance of things hoped for, the evidence of things not seen.

---

[23] Derrida, *Archive Fever*, pp. 92–3, emphasis removed.
[24] Greenblatt, *Shakespearean Negotiations*, p. 1.

Bibliography

Allen, Woody, "The Condemned," in *Side Effects*, New York: Ballantine, 1975, pp. 11–22

Armstrong, Carol, *Scenes in a Library: Reading the Photograph in the Book, 1843–1875*, Cambridge, MA: MIT Press, 1998

Armstrong, Nancy, *Fiction in the Age of Photography: The Legacy of British Realism*, Cambridge, MA: Harvard University Press, 1999

Aschoff, Volker, "The Early History of the Binary Code," *IEEE Communications Magazine*, 21.1 (1983), 4–10

Asheim, Lester, "New Problems in Plotting the Future of the Book," *Library Quarterly*, 25.4 (1955), 281–92

Assmann, Aleida, "Texts, Traces, Trash: The Changing Media of Cultural Memory," *Representations*, 56 (1996), 123–34

Auden, W. H., *Collected Poems*, ed. Edward Mendelson, London: Faber and Faber, 2007

Auslander, Philip, *Liveness: Performance in a Mediatized Culture*, 2nd edn., London: Routledge, 2008

Ayers, P. K., "Reading, Writing, and *Hamlet*," *Shakespeare Quarterly*, 44.4 (1993), 423–39

Bal, Mieke, *Travelling Concepts in the Humanities: A Rough Guide*, University of Toronto Press, 2002

Ball, Robert Hamilton, *Shakespeare on Silent Film: A Strange Eventful History*, London: George Allen and Unwin, 1968

Balsamo, Anne, *Technologies of the Gendered Body: Reading Cyborg Women*, Durham, NC: Duke University Press, 1996

Barthes, Roland, *Camera Lucida: Reflections on Photography*, trans. Richard Howard, New York: Hill and Wang, 1981

  "The Death of the Author," in *Image – Music – Text*, trans. Stephen Heath, New York: Hill and Wang, 1977, pp. 142–8

Bateson, F. W., "Modern Bibliography and the Literary Artifact," in G. A. Bonnard (ed.), *English Studies Today*, 2nd series, Bern: Francke Verlag, 1961, pp. 67–77

  "The New Bibliography and the 'New Criticism,'" in *Essays in Critical Dissent*, London: Longman, 1972

Bateson, Gregory, *Steps to an Ecology of Mind*, 1972; repr. University of Chicago Press, 2000

Beaumont, Francis, and John Fletcher, *Comedies and Tragedies*, London, 1647

Bell, Alexander Graham, "Researches in Telephony," *Proceedings of the American Academy of Arts and Sciences*, 12 (1876), 1–10

Bell, Alexander Melville, *English Line-Writing: A New, Simple, and Exact System of Phonetics*, New York: E. S. Werner [1886]

Bell Family Papers (see Abbreviations on p. xv, above)

Benjamin, Walter, "The Work of Art in the Age of Mechanical Reproduction," in Harry Zohn (trans.), *Illuminations*, New York: Schocken Books, 1968

Berger, Thomas L., "The New Historicism and the Editing of English Renaissance Texts," in W. Speed Hill (ed.), *New Ways of Looking at Old Texts: Papers of the Renaissance English Text Society, 1985–1991*, Binghamton, NY: Medieval and Renaissance Texts and Studies, 1993, pp. 195–7

Bergeron, David M. (ed.), *Reading and Writing in Shakespeare*, Newark, DE: University of Delaware Press, 1996

Best, Michael, "Shakespeare and the Electronic Text," in Andrew Murphy (ed.), *A Concise Companion to Shakespeare and the Text*, Oxford: Blackwell, 2007, pp. 144–61

Best, Michael, and Eric Rasmussen (eds.), *Monitoring Electronic Shakespeares*, special issue *of Early Modern Literary Studies*, 9.3 (2004)

Bialkowski, Voytek, Christine DeLuca, and Kalina Lafreniere, "Manicules," in Alan Galey, *et al.* (eds.), *Architectures of the Book*, University of Toronto, http://archbook.ischool.utoronto.ca/archbook/manicules.php.

Bjelland, Karen, "The Editor as Theologian, Historian, and Archaeologist: Shifting Paradigms Within Editorial Theory and their Sociocultural Ramifications," *Analytical and Enumerative Bibliography*, 11.1 (2000), 1–43

Black, Matthew W., and Matthias A. Shaaber, *Shakespeare's Seventeenth-Century Editors: 1632–1685*, New York: Modern Language Association; Oxford University Press, 1937

Blair, Ann M., *Too Much to Know: Managing Scholarly Information Before the Modern Age*, New Haven, CT: Yale University Press, 2010

Blake, Erin C., and Kathleen Lynch, "Looke on his Picture, in his Booke: The Droeshout Portrait on the Title Page," in Owen Williams with Caryn Lazzuri (eds.), *Foliomania!: Stories Behind Shakespeare's Most Important Book*, Washington DC: Folger Shakespeare Library, 2011, pp. 21–39

Blayney, Peter W. M., *The First Folio of Shakespeare* [exhibition catalogue], Washington DC: Folger Shakespeare Library, 1991

The First Folio of Shakespeare: The Norton Facsimile, 2nd edn., New York: W. W. Norton, 1996

"The Publication of Playbooks," in John D. Cox and David Scott Kastan (eds.), *A New History of Early English Drama*, New York: Columbia University Press, 1997, pp. 383–422

Blouin, Francis X., Jr., and William G. Rosenberg, *Processing the Past: Contesting Authority in History and Archives*, Oxford University Press, 2011

Bolter, Jay David, and Richard Grusin, *Remediation: Understanding New Media*, Cambridge, MA: MIT Press, 2000

Booth, Stephen, "A Long, Dull Poem by William Shakespeare," *Shakespeare Survey*, 25 (1997), 229–37

Borges, Jorge Luis, "The Aleph," in Andrew Hurley (trans.), *The Aleph*, New York: Penguin, 1998, pp. 118–33

"Shakespeare's Memory," in Andrew Hurley (trans.), *The Book of Sand and Shakespeare's Memory*, New York: Penguin, 1998

Borggreen, Gunhild, and Rune Gade (eds.), *Performing Archives/Archives of Performance*, Copenhagen: Museum Tusculanum Press, 2013

Bornstein, George, "How to Read a Page: Modernism and Material Textuality," *Studies in the Literary Imagination*, 32.1 (1999), 29–58

Bowers, Fredson, "The Historical Collation in an Old-Spelling Shakespeare Edition: Another View," *Studies in Bibliography*, 35 (1982), 235–58

Principles of Bibliographical Description, Princeton University Press, 1949

Textual and Literary Criticism, Cambridge University Press, 1959

Bowker, Geoffrey C., *Memory Practices in the Sciences*, Cambridge, MA: MIT Press, 2008

Bowker, Geoffrey C., and Susan Leigh Star, *Sorting Things Out: Classification and Its Consequences*, Cambridge, MA: MIT Press, 2000

Bradshaw, Graham, "Precious Nonsense and the Conduit Metaphor," *Shakespearean International Yearbook*, 4 (2005), 98–122

Braunmuller, A. R., "Shakespeares Various," in Ann Thompson and Gordon McMullan (eds.), *In Arden: Editing Shakespeare*, London: Arden Shakespeare–Thompson Learning, 2003, pp. 3–16

Brillouin, Léon, *Science and Information Theory*, 2nd edn., 1962; repr. New York: Dover Phoenix, 2004

Bringhurst, Robert, *The Elements of Typographic Style*, ver. 3.1, Point Roberts, BC: Hartley & Marks, 2005

Bristol, Michael D., *Shakespeare's America, America's Shakespeare*, London: Routledge, 1990

Brittan, Alice, "War and the Book: The Diarist, the Cryptographer, and *The English Patient*," *Publications of the Modern Language Association*, 121.1 (2006), 200–13

Brockbank, Philip J., "Shakespearean Scholarship: From Rowe to the Present," in John F. Andrews (ed.), *William Shakespeare: His World, His Work, His Influence*, vol. III, New York: Scribner, 1985, pp. 717–32

Brothman, Brien, "The Past that Archives Keep: Memory, History, and the Preservation of Archival Records," *Archivaria*, 51 (2001), 48–80

Brown, Richard Harvey, and Beth Davis-Brown, "The Making of Memory: The Politics of Archives, Libraries and Museums in the Construction of National Consciousness," *History of the Human Sciences*, 11.4 (1998), 17–32

Bruce, Robert V., *Bell: Alexander Graham Bell and the Conquest of Solitude*, London: Victor Gollancz, 1973

Buchanan, Judith, *Shakespeare on Silent Film: An Excellent Dumb Discourse*, Cambridge University Press, 2009

Buckland, Michael K., "Emmanuel Goldberg, Electronic Document Retrieval, and Vannevar Bush's Memex," *Journal of the American Society for Information Science*, 43.4 (1992), 284–94

Bunbury, Henry, *Correspondence of Sir Thomas Hanmer*, London, 1838

Burdick, Anne, Johanna Drucker, Pete Lunenfeld, Todd Presner, and Jeffrey Schnapp, *Digital_Humanities*, Cambridge, MA: MIT Press, 2012

Burnett, Chris, "A Scene in a Digital Library: Imaging Literature," in Timothy H. Engström and Evan Selinger (eds.), *Rethinking Theories and Practices of Imaging*, Basingstoke: Palgrave Macmillan, 2009, pp. 227–51

Burt, Richard, and Julian Yates, *What's the Worst Thing You Can Do to Shakespeare?*, Basingstoke: Palgrave Macmillan, 2013

Busa, Roberto, *Index Thomisticus: Sancti Thomae Aquinatis operum omnium indices et concordantiae in quibus verborum omnium et singulorum formae et lemmata cum suis frequentiis et contextibus variis modis referuntur*, Stuttgart-Bad Cannstatt: Frommann-Holzboog, 1974

Bush, Vannevar, "As We May Think," in James M. Nyce and Paul Kahn (eds.), *From Memex to Hypertext: Vannevar Bush and the Mind's Machine*, Boston: Academic Press, 1991, pp. 85–107

Butler, Terry, "Monkeying Around with Text," *TEXT Technology*, 15.1 (2007), 113–33

Capell, Edward (ed.), *Mr William Shakespeare his Comedies, Histories, and Tragedies*, 10 vols., London, 1768

Carlyle, Thomas, "On History Again," in G. B. Tennyson (ed.), *A Carlyle Reader*. Cambridge University Press, 1984, pp. 104–12

Carson, Christie, "The Evolution of Online Editing: Where Will It End?," *Shakespeare Survey*, 59 (2006), 168–81

Cary, Elizabeth, *The Tragedie of Mariam, the Faire Queene of Iewry*. London, 1613

Casanova, Eugenio, *Archivistica*, Siena: Lazzeri, 1928

Certeau, Michel de, *The Writing of History*, trans. Tom Conley, New York: Columbia University Press, 1988

Chartier, Roger, *Inscription and Erasure*, trans. Arthur Goldhammer, Philadelphia: University of Pennsylvania Press, 2007

Chartier, Roger, and Peter Stallybrass, "What Is a Book?," in Neil Fraistat and Julia Flanders (eds.), *The Cambridge Companion to Textual Studies*, Cambridge University Press, 2013

Chaudhuri, Sukanta, *The Metaphysics of Text*, Cambridge University Press, 2010

Clanchy, M. T., *From Memory to Written Record: England 1066–1307*, 2nd edn., Oxford: Blackwell, 1993

Clark, Hilary A., "Encyclopedic Discourse," *SubStance*, 67 (1992), 95–110

Clark, William George, and William Aldis Wright (eds.), *The Globe Edition [of] the Works of William Shakespeare*, Cambridge and London: Macmillan, 1864

   The Works of William Shakespeare, 9 vols., Cambridge and London: Macmillan, 1863–6

Cloonan, Michéle V., "Preserving Records of Enduring Value," in Eastwood and MacNeil (eds.), *Currents of Archival Thinking*, pp. 69–88

Cobley, Evelyn, "Hard Going After Theory," *English Studies in Canada*, 30.4 (2004), 188–204

Codebò, Marco, *Narrating from the Archive: Novels, Records, and Bureaucrats in the Modern Age*, Madison, WI: Fairleigh Dickinson University Press, 2010

Cohen, Adam Max, *Shakespeare and Technology: Dramatizing Early Modern Technological Revolutions*, Basingstoke: Palgrave Macmillan, 2006

Coldiron, Anne, *Printers Without Borders: "Englishing" Texts in the Renaissance*, Cambridge University Press, 2014

Comay, Rebecca (ed.), *Lost in the Archives*, Toronto: Alphabet City Media, 2002

Cook, Terry, "The Archive(s) is a Foreign Country: Historians, Archivists, and the Changing Archival Landscape," *Canadian Historical Review*, 90.3 (2009), 497–534

   "What Is Past Is Prologue: A History of Archival Ideas Since 1898, and the Future Paradigm Shift," *Archivaria*, 43 (1997), 17–63

Cook, Terry, and Joan M. Schwartz, "Archives, Records, and Power: From (Postmodern) Theory to (Archival) Performance," *Archival Science*, 2 (2002), 171–85

Crary, Jonathan, *Techniques of the Observer: On Vision and Modernity in the Nineteenth Century*, Cambridge, MA: MIT Press–October Books, 1992 d'Alembert, Jean Le Rond, *Preliminary Discourse to the Encyclopedia of Diderot*, trans. Richard N. Schwab, University of Chicago Press, 1995

Daniel, P. A. (ed.), *King Henry V: Parallel Texts of the First Quarto (1600) and First Folio (1623) Editions*, London: N. Trübner [for the New Shakespeare Society], 1877

   Romeo and Juliet: Parallel Texts of the First Two Quartos, London: N. Trübner [for the New Shakespeare Society], 1874

Daston, Lorraine, and Peter Galison, *Objectivity*, Brooklyn, NY: Zone Books, 2007

Davis, Tom, "The Monsters and the Textual Critics," in Laurie E. Maguire and Thomas L. Berger (eds.), *Textual Formations and Reformations*, Newark, DE: University of Delaware Press, 1998

Dawson, Anthony, "The Imaginary Text, or the Curse of the Folio," in Barbara Hodgdon and W. B. Worthen (eds.), *A Companion to Shakespeare and Performance*, Malden, MA: Wiley-Blackwell, 2005, pp. 141–61

Day, Ronald E., "The 'Conduit Metaphor' and the Nature and Politics of Information Studies," *Journal of the American Society for Information Science and Technology*, 51 (2000), 805–11

   The Modern Invention of Information: Discourse, History, Power, Carbondale, IL: Southern Illinois University Press, 2001

DeCook, Travis, and Alan Galey (eds.), *Shakespeare, the Bible, and the Form of the Book: Contested Scriptures*, New York: Routledge, 2011

Deegan, Marilyn, and Kathryn Sutherland, *Transferred Illusions: Digital Technology and the Forms of Print*, Farnham: Ashgate, 2009

Dembski, William A., *The Design Inference: Eliminating Chance Through Small Probabilities*, Cambridge University Press, 1998

Derrida, Jacques, *Archive Fever: A Freudian Impression*, trans. Eric Prenowitz, University of Chicago Press, 1996

   "Freud and the Scene of Writing," in Alan Bass (trans.), *Writing and Difference*, University of Chicago Press, 1978, pp. 196–231

   Paper Machine, trans. Rachel Bowlby, Stanford University Press, 2005

Dibdin, Thomas Frognall [as Mercurius Rusticus], *Bibliophobia: Remarks on the Present Languid and Depressed State of Literature and the Book Trade*, London: Henry Bohn, 1832

Domesday Book, or, the Great Survey of England of William the Conqueror, AD MLXXXVI, Fac-simile of the Part Relating to Somersetshire, Southampton: Ordnance Survey Office, 1862

Donaldson, Peter S., "Cinema and the Kingdom of Death: Loncraine's *Richard III*," *Shakespeare Quarterly*, 53.2 (2002), 241–59

   "Digital Archive as Expanded Text: Shakespeare and Electronic Textuality," in Kathryn Sutherland (ed.), *Electronic Text:*

Investigations in Method and Theory, Oxford: Clarendon Press, 1997, pp. 173–97

Donnellan, Declan, *The Actor and the Target* [New York]: Theatre Communications Group, 2002

Douglas, Jennifer, "*Archiving Authors: Rethinking the Analysis and Representation of Personal Archives*," PhD thesis, Faculty of Information, University of Toronto, 2013

Douglas, Jennifer, and Heather MacNeil, "Arranging the Self: Literary and Archival Perspectives on Writers' Archives," *Archivaria*, 67 (2009), 25–39

Drucker, Johanna, *A Century of Artists' Books*, 2nd edn., New York: Granary Books, 2004

   "Graphesis: Visual Knowledge Production and Representation," *Poetess Archive Journal*, 2.1 (2010), 1–50

   "Humanities Approaches to Graphical Display," *Digital Humanities Quarterly*, 5.1 (2011), www.digitalhumanities.org/dhq/vol/5/1/000091/000091.html

   SpecLab: Digital Aesthetics and Projects in Speculative Computing, University of Chicago Press, 2009

Duff, Wendy M., and Verne Harris, "Stories and Names: Archival Description as Narrating Records and Constructing Meanings," *Archival Science*, 2 (2002), 263–85

Duguid, Paul, "Material Matters: The Past and Futurology of the Book," in Geoffrey Nunberg (ed.), *The Future of the Book*, Berkeley, CA: University of California Press, 1996, pp. 63–101

Duranti, Luciana, "The Archival Bond," *Archives and Museum Informatics*, 11 (1997), 213–18

Eagleton, Terry, *After Theory*, New York: Basic Books, 2003

Earhart, Amy, *Traces of the Old, Uses of the New: the Emergence of Digital Literary Studies*, Ann Arbor, MI: University of Michigan Press, 2015

Eastwood, Terry, "A Constructed Realm: The Nature of Archives and the Orientation of Archival Science," in Eastwood and MacNeil (eds.), *Currents of Archival Thinking*, pp. 3–21

Eastwood, Terry, and Heather MacNeil (eds.), *Currents of Archival Thinking*, Santa Barbara, CA: Libraries Unlimited, 2010

Egan, Gabriel, *The Struggle for Shakespeare's Text: Twentieth-Century Editorial Theory and Practice*, Cambridge University Press, 2010

Eggert, Paul, "Brought to Book: Bibliography, Book History, and the Study of Literature," *The Library*, 13.1 (2012), 3–32

Elsaesser, Thomas, "Freud and the Technical Media: The Enduring Magic of the Wunderblock," in Erkki Huhtamo and Jussi Parikka (eds.), *Media Archaeology: Approaches, Applications, and Implications*, Berkeley, CA: University of California Press, 2011, pp. 95–115

Erne, Lukas, *Shakespeare as Literary Dramatist*, Cambridge University Press, 2003

Ernst, Wolfgang, "Archival Action: The Archive as ROM and Its Political Instrumentalization Under National Socialism," *History of the Human Sciences*, 12.2 (1999), 13–34

   Digital Memory and the Archive, Minneapolis: University of Minnesota Press, 2013

Esmail, Jennifer, *Reading Victorian Deafness: Signs and Sounds in Victorian Literature and Culture*, Columbus: Ohio University Press, 2013

Estill, Laura, "Commonplace Markers and Quotation Marks," in Jon Bath, Richard Cunningham, Alan Galey, and Paul Werstine (eds.), *Architectures of the Book*, www.archbook.ca

Evans, Frank B., Donald F. Harrison, Edwin A. Thompson, and William L. Roffes, *A Basic Glossary for Archivists, Manuscript Curators, and Records Managers*, reprinted in *American Archivist*, 37.3 (1974), 415–518

F1, F2 (see Abbreviations on p. xv, above)

Facsimiles of National Manuscripts, from William the Conqueror to Queen Anne, Selected under the direction of the Master of the Rolls and Photozincographed by Command of Her Majesty Queen Victoria by Colonel Sir Henry James R.E., Director of the Ordnance Survey, 4 vols., Southampton: Ordnance Survey Office, 1865–1868

Flanders, Julia, "The Body Encoded: Questions of Gender and the Electronic Text," in Kathryn Sutherland (ed.), *Electronic Text: Investigations in Method and Theory*, Oxford: Clarendon Press, 1997, pp. 127–43

   "Data and Wisdom: Electronic Editing and the Quantification of Knowledge," *Literary and Linguistic Computing*, 24.1 (2009), 53–62

Flint, Kate, *The Victorians and the Visual Imagination*, Cambridge University Press, 2000

Floridi, Luciano, *Information: A Very Short Introduction*, Oxford University Press, 2010

Foucault, Michel, *The Archaeology of Knowledge*, New York: Routledge, 2002

   Discipline and Punish: The Birth of the Prison, trans. Alan Sheridan, New York: Vintage, 1979

   "Of Other Spaces," trans. Jay Miskowiec, *Diacritics*, 16.1 (1986), 22–7

   "What Is an Author?," in Paul Rabinow (ed.), *The Foucault Reader*, New York: Pantheon, 1984, pp. 101–20

Freeman, Arthur, and Janet Ing Freeman, *John Payne Collier: Scholarship and Forgery in the Nineteenth Century*, 2 vols., New Haven: Yale University Press, 2004

Freeman, Neil (ed.), *The Taming of the Shrew*, New York: Applause, 1998

Freud, Sigmund, "A Note upon the 'Mystic Writing-Pad,'" in James Strachey (trans.), *The Standard Edition of the Complete Psychological Works of Sigmund Freud*, vol. XIX, London: Hogarth Press, 1955, pp. 226–32

Friedman, William F., and Elizabeth S. Friedman, *The Shakespearean Ciphers Examined: An Analysis of Cryptographic Systems Used as Evidence that Some Author Other than William Shakespeare Wrote the Plays Commonly Attributed to Him*, Cambridge University Press, 1958

Frye, Northrop, *The Educated Imagination*, Toronto: Anansi, 2002
  "Literary and Mechanical Models," in Ian Lancashire (ed.), *Research in Humanities Computing*, vol. I, Oxford: Clarendon Press, 1989, pp. 3–12

Functional Requirements for Bibliographic Records: Final Report, International Federation of Library Associations and Institutions, 1997, www.ifla.org/publications/functional-requirements-for-bibliographic-records

Furness Family Papers (see Abbreviations on p. xv, above)

Furness, Horace Howard, *The Letters of Horace Howard Furness*, ed. Horace Howard Furness Jayne, Boston: Houghton Mifflin, 1922

Furness, Horace Howard (ed.), *Othello*, 2nd edn., Philadelphia: J. B. Lippincott, 1886

Furness, Horace Howard, *et al.*, "How Did You Become a Shakespeare Student?," *Shakespeariana*, 5.58 (1888), 439–40

Furness, Walter Rogers, *Composite Photography Applied to the Portraits of Shakespeare*, Philadelphia: Robert M. Lindsay, 1885

[Furnivall, Frederick J.], *Teena Rochfort-Smith: A Memoir, with Three Woodbury-Types of Her, One Each of Robert Browning and F.J. Furnivall, and Memorial Lines by Mary Grace Walker*, Suffolk: Clay and Taylor, 1883

Gadd, Ian, "The Use and Misuse of *Early English Books Online*," *Literature Compass*, 6.3 (2009), 680–92

Galey, Alan, "Dizzying the Arithmetic of Memory: Shakespearean Documents as Text, Image, and Code," *Early Modern Literary Studies*, 9.3 (2004): http://purl.oclc.org/emls/09-3/galedizz.htm
  "Encoding as Editing as Reading," in Margaret Jane Kidnie and Sonia Massai (eds.), *Shakespeare and Textual Studies*, Cambridge University Press, [forthcoming]
  "The Human Presence in Digital Artifacts," in Willard McCarty (ed.), *Text and Genre in Reconstruction: Effects of Digitalization on Ideas, Behaviours, Products, and Institutions*, Cambridge: Open Book, 2010, pp. 93–117
  "The Tablets of the Law: Reading Hamlet with Scriptural Technologies," in DeCook and Galey (eds.), *Shakespeare, the Bible, and the Form of the Book*, pp. 77–95

Galey, Alan, Jon Bath, Rebecca Niles, and Richard Cunningham, "Imagining the Architectures of the Book: Textual Scholarship and the Digital Book Arts," *Textual Cultures*, 7.2 (2012), 20–42

Galey, Alan, and Ray Siemens (eds.), *Reinventing Digital Shakespeare,* special issue of *Shakespeare*, 4.3 (2008)

Galison, Peter, "The Ontology of the Enemy: Norbert Wiener and the Cybernetic Vision," *Critical Inquiry*, 21 (1994), 228–66

Galton, Francis. *Inquiries into Human Faculty and Its Development*, London: Macmillan, 1883

Garber, Marjorie, *Profiling Shakespeare*, New York: Routledge, 2008
  Quotation Marks, New York: Routledge, 2003

Gaskell, Philip, *A New Introduction to Bibliography*, New Castle, DE: Oak Knoll Press, 1972

Gernsheim, Helmut, with Alison Gernsheim, *The History of Photography: From the Camera Obscura to the Beginning of the Modern Era*, revised edn., London: Thames and Hudson, 1969

Gibson, James M., *The Philadelphia Shakespeare Story: Horace Howard Furness and the New Variorum Shakespeare*, New York: AMS Press, 1990

Gilbert, Allan (ed. and trans.), *The Letters of Machiavelli*, New York: Capricorn Books, 1961

Gillespie, Tarleton, *Wired Shut: Copyright and the Shape of Digital Culture*, Cambridge, MA: MIT Press, 2007

Gitelman, Lisa, *Always Already New: Media, History, and the Data of Culture*, Cambridge, MA: MIT Press, 2006
  Scripts, Grooves, and Writing Machines: Representing Technology in the Edison Era, Stanford University Press, 1999

Given, Lisa M., and Lianne McTavish, "What's Old Is New Again: The Reconvergence of Libraries, Archives, and Museums in the Digital Age," *Library Quarterly*, 80.1 (2010), 7–32

Gleick, James, *The Information*, New York: Pantheon, 2011

Goldberg, Jonathan, *Writing Matter: From the Hands of the English Renaissance*, Stanford University Press

Golumbia, David, *The Cultural Logic of Computation*, Cambridge, MA: Harvard University Press, 2009

Grady, Hugh, *The Modernist Shakespeare and After: Critical Texts in a Modern World*, Oxford: Clarendon Press, 1991

Grazia, Margreta, de, "The Question of the One and the Many: The Globe Shakespeare, The *Complete King Lear*, and The New Folger Library Shakespeare," *Shakespeare Quarterly*, 46.2 (1995), 245–51
  Shakespeare Verbatim: The Reproduction of Authenticity and the 1790 Apparatus, Oxford: Clarendon Press, 1991

Grazia, Margreta de, and Peter Stallybrass, "The Materiality of the Shakespearean Text," *Shakespeare Quarterly*, 44.3 (1993), 255–83

Greenblatt, Stephen, *Shakespearean Negotiations: The Circulation of Social Energy in Renaissance England*, Berkeley, CA: University of California Press, 1988

Greenblatt, Stephen, Walter Cohen, Jean E. Howard, and Katharine Eisaman Maus (eds.), *The Norton Shakespeare*, New York: W. W. Norton, 1997

Green-Lewis, Jennifer, *Framing the Victorians: Photography and the Culture of Realism*, Ithaca, NY: Cornell University Press, 1996

Greetham, David C., *The Pleasures of Contamination: Evidence, Text, and Voice in Textual Studies*, Bloomington: Indiana University Press, 2010

Textual Scholarship: An Introduction, New York: Garland, 1994

"What Is Textual Scholarship?," in Simon Eliot and Jonathan Rose (eds.), *A Companion to the History of the Book*, Malden, MA: Wiley–Blackwell, 2009), 21–32

Greg, W. W., *The Editorial Problem in Shakespeare: A Survey of the Foundations of the Text*, 3rd edn., Oxford: Clarendon Press, 1954

Sir Walter Wilson Greg: A Collection of His Writings, ed. Joseph Rosenblum, Lanham: Scarecrow Press, 1998

Greg, W. W. (ed.), *The Merry Wives of Windsor, 1602*, Oxford: Clarendon Press, 1910

Grigely, Joseph, *Textualterity: Art, Theory, and Textual Criticism*, Ann Arbor, MI: University of Michigan Press, 1995

Groden, Michael, *Ulysses in Focus: Genetic, Textual, and Personal Views*, Gainesville, FL: University Press of Florida, 2010

Groth, Helen, *Victorian Photography and Literary Nostalgia*, Oxford University Press, 2003

Gupta, Abhijit, "We Can List You: Bibliography and Postcolonialism," in David William Foster and James R. Kelly (eds.), *Bibliography in Literature, Folklore, Language and Linguistics*, Jefferson, NC: McFarland, 2003, pp. 70–88

Hamilton, Carolyn, Verne Harris, Jane Taylor, Michele Pickover, Graeme Reid, and Razia Saleh (eds.), *Refiguring the Archive*, Dordrecht, Netherlands: Kluwer, 2002

Harding, Robert Coupland, "Concerning Fashion and Taste," *Inland Printer*, 15 (1895), 486–8

"A Hundred Years Hence," *Typo*, 8 (27 January 1894), 1

Hardy, G. H., *A Mathematician's Apology*, 1940; repr. Cambridge University Press, 2001

Hardy, Thomas, *A Laodicean*, New York: Penguin, 1997

Harpold, Terry, *Ex-foliations: Reading Machines and the Upgrade Path*, Minneapolis: University of Minnesota Press, 2009

Harris, Verne, *Archives and Justice: A South African Perspective*, Chicago: Society of American Archivists, 2007

Hayles, N. Katharine, *As We Think: Digital Media and Contemporary Technogenesis*, University of Chicago Press, 2012

   How We Became Posthuman: Virtual Bodies in Cybernetics, Literature, and Informatics, University of Chicago Press, 1999

   My Mother Was a Computer: Digital Subjects and Literary Texts, University of Chicago Press, 2005

   "Narrative and Database: Natural Symbionts," *Publications of the Modern Language Association*, 122.5 (2007), 1603–8

   Writing Machines, Cambridge, MA: MIT Press, 2002

Heath, F. G., "Origins of the Binary Code," *Scientific American*, 227.2 (1972), 76–83

Hedstrom, Margaret, "Archives, Memory, and Interfaces with the Past," *Archival Science*, 2 (2002), 21–43

   "Understanding Electronic Incunabula: A Framework for Research on Electronic Records," *American Archivist*, 54.3 (1991), 334–54

Heims, Steve Joshua, *The Cybernetics Group*, Cambridge, MA: MIT Press, 1991

Hinman, Charlton, *The Printing and Proof-Reading of the First Folio of Shakespeare*, 2 vols., Oxford: Clarendon Press, 1963

Hinman, Charlton, "Variant Readings in the First Folio of Shakespeare," *Shakespeare Quarterly*, 4.3 (1953), 279–88

Hobart, Michael E., and Zachary S. Schiffman, *Information Ages: Literacy, Numeracy, and the Computer Revolution*, Baltimore: Johns Hopkins University Press, 1998

Hobbs, Catherine, "Reenvisioning the Personal: Reframing Traces of Individual Life," in Eastwood and MacNeil (eds.), *Currents of Archival Thinking*, pp. 213–41

Hoenselaars, Ton, "Shooting the Hero: The Cinematic Career of *Henry V* from Laurence Olivier to Philip Purser," in Sonia Massai (ed.), *World-Wide Shakespeares: Local Appropriations in Film and Performance*, London: Routledge, 2005, pp. 80–7

Holland, Anna, and Richard Scholar, introduction to *Prehistories and Afterlives: Studies in Critical Method*, London: Modern Humanities Research Association and Maney Publishing, 2009, pp. 1–13

Holland, Peter (ed.), *Shakespeare, Memory and Performance*, Cambridge University Press, 2006

Hope, Jonathan, and Michael Witmore, "The Hundredth Psalm to the Tune of 'Green Sleeves': Digital Approaches to Shakespeare's Language of Genre," *Shakespeare Quarterly*, 61.3 (2010), 357–90

Horkheimer, Max, and Theodor W. Adorno, *Dialectic of Enlightenment*, New York: Continuum, 1988

Horsman, Peter, "Taming the Elephant: an Orthodox Approach to the Principle of Provenance," in *The Principle of Provenance: Report from the First Stockholm Conference on the Archival Principle of Provenance, 2–3 September 1993*, Stockholm: Swedish National Archives, 1994

Horton, Bob, review of *Lost in the Archives* (ed. Comay), *American Archivist*, 67.2 (2004), 296–9

Huhtamo, Erkki, and Jussi Parikka (eds.), *Media Archaeology: Approaches, Applications, and Implications*, Berkeley, CA: University of California Press, 2011

Hunt, Maurice, "New Variorum Shakespeares in the Twenty-First Century," *Yearbook of English Studies*, 29 (1999), 57–68

Hunter, G.K., "The Marking of Sententiae in Elizabethan Printed Plays, Poems, and Romances," *The Library*, 6, 5th series (1951–2), 171–88

Israel, Paul, *Edison: A Life of Invention*, New York: Wiley, 1998

Jenkinson, Hilary, *A Manual of Archive Administration*, Oxford: Clarendon Press, 1922

Jennings, Edward M. (ed.), *Science and Literature: New Lenses for Criticism*, Garden City, NY: Doubleday–Anchor Books, 1970

Jockers, Matthew, *Macroanalysis: Digital Methods and Literary History*, Champaign, IL: University of Illinois Press, 2013

Johns, Adrian, *The Nature of the Book: Print and Knowledge in the Making*, University of Chicago Press, 1998

Jones, F.W., "A Review of Certain Claims to the Art of Telephony," *Electrical World*, 10 (3 December 1887), 296–7

Jowett, Benjamin, "On the Interpretation of Scripture," in Victor Shea and William Whitla (eds.), *Essays and Reviews: The 1860 Text and its Reading*, Charlottesville: University of Virginia Press, 2000

Jowett, John, *Shakespeare and Text*, Oxford University Press, 2007

Jowett, John, (ed.), *Sir Thomas More*, Arden Shakespeare, 3rd series, London: Methuen, 2011

Jowett, John, William Montgomery, Gary Taylor, and Stanley Wells (eds.), *The Oxford Shakespeare*, 2nd edn., Oxford University Press, 2005

Jussim, Estelle, *Visual Communication and the Graphic Arts: Photographic Technologies in the Nineteenth Century*, New York: Bowker, 1974

Joyce, James, *Ulysses: a Critical and Synoptic Edition*, Hans Walter Gabler with Wolfhard Steppe and Claus Melchior (eds.), 3 vols., New York: Garland, 1986

Joyce, Patrick, "The Politics of the Liberal Archive," *History of the Human Sciences*, 12.2 (1999), 35–49

Kahn, David, *The Codebreakers: The Comprehensive History of Secret Communication from Ancient Times to the Internet*, rev. edn., New York: Scribner, 1996

Kastan, David Scott, *Shakespeare and the Book*, Cambridge University Press, 2001

Kay, Lily E., *Who Wrote the Book of Life?: A History of the Genetic Code*, Stanford University Press, 2000

Kerby-Fulton, Kathryn, "The Women Readers in Langland's Earliest Audience: Some Codicological Evidence," in Sarah Rees Jones (ed.), *Learning and Literacy in Medieval England and Abroad*, Turnhout, Belgium: Brepols, 2003, pp. 121–34

Kermode, Frank, *Shakespeare's Language*, New York: Penguin, 2000

Ketelaar, Eric, "Archival Temples, Archival Prisons: Modes of Power and Protection," *Archival Science*, 2 (2002), 221–38

  "Writing on Archiving Machines," in Sonja Neef, José van Dijck, and Eric Ketelaar (eds.), *Sign Here! Handwriting in the Age of New Media*, Amsterdam University Press, 2006, pp. 183–95

Kichuk, Diana, "Metamorphosis: Remediation in *Early English Books Online (EEBO)*," *Literary and Linguistic Computing*, 22.3 (2007), 291–303

Kidnie, Margaret Jane, *Shakespeare and the Problem of Adaptation*, New York: Routledge, 2009

Kinney, Arthur F., *Shakespeare's Webs: Networks of Meaning in Renaissance Drama*, New York: Routledge, 2004

Kirschenbaum, Matthew G., "Editing the Interface: Textual Studies and First Generation Electronic Objects," *TEXT: an Interdisciplinary Annual of Textual Studies*, 14 (2002), 15–51

  Mechanisms: New Media and the Forensic Imagination, Cambridge, MA: MIT Press, 2008

Kirschenbaum, Matthew G. (ed.), *Image-Based Humanities Computing*, special issue of *Computers and the Humanities*, 36.1 (2002)

Kittler, Friedrich, *Discourse Networks, 1800/1900*, trans. Michael Metteer and Chris Cullens, Stanford University Press, 1990

  Gramophone, Film, Typewriter, trans. Geoffrey Winthrop-Young and Michael Wutz, Stanford University Press, 1999

Knights, L. C., "Shakespeare and Shakespeareans," in *Explorations: Essays in Criticism Mainly on the Literature of the Seventeenth Century*, London: Chatto and Windus, 1958, pp. 78–91

Knowles, Richard, "Variorum Commentary," *TEXT: an Interdisciplinary Annual of Textual Studies*, 6 (1994), 35–47

Lahusen, Thomas, "An Archival Journey into Stalin's Russia," in Comay (ed.), *Lost in the Archives*, pp. 612–19

Lanier, Douglas, "Encryptions: Reading Milton Reading Jonson Reading Shakespeare," in David M. Bergeron (ed.), *Reading and Writing in Shakespeare*, Newark, DE: University of Delaware Press, 1996, pp. 220–50

"Shakespeare on the Record," in Barbara Hodgdon and W. B. Worthen (eds.), *A Companion to Shakespeare and Performance*, Malden, MA: Blackwell, 2005, pp. 415–36

Lastra, James, *Sound Technology and the American Cinema: Perception, Representation, Modernity*, New York: Columbia University Press, 2000

Latour, Bruno, *Science in Action: How to Follow Scientists and Engineers Through Society*, Cambridge, MA: Harvard University Press, 1987

"Visualization and Cognition: Thinking with Eyes and Hands," *Knowledge and Society*, 6 (1986), pp. 1–40

Layzer, David, *Cosmogenesis: The Growth of Order in the Universe*, Oxford University Press, 1990

Lepore, Jill, *A Is for American: Letters and Other Characters in the Newly United States*, New York: Vintage, 2007

Lesser, Zachary, *Hamlet After Q1: An Uncanny History of the Shakespearean Text*, Philadelphia: University of Pennsylvania Press, 2015

Lesser, Zachary, and Peter Stallybrass, "The First Literary *Hamlet* and the Commonplacing of Professional Plays," *Shakespeare Quarterly*, 59.4 (2008), 371–420

Levy, David M., *Scrolling Forward: Making Sense of Documents in the Digital Age*, New York: Arcade Publishing, 2001

Liu, Alan, *The Laws of Cool: Knowledge Work and the Culture of Information*, University of Chicago Press, 2004

Local Transcendence: Essays on Postmodern Historicism and the Database, University of Chicago Press, 2008

Loewenstein, Joseph, *The Author's Due: Printing and the Prehistory of Copyright*, University of Chicago Press, 2002

Mabillon, Jean, *De re diplomatica*, Paris, 1681

MacKay, David J. C., *Information Theory, Inference, and Learning Algorithms*, Cambridge University Press, 2003

MacNeil, Heather, "Archivalterity: Rethinking Original Order," *Archivaria*, 66 (2008), 1–24

"Picking Our Text: Archival Description, Authenticity, and the Archivist as Editor," *American Archivist*, 68.2 (2005), 264–78

"Trusting Records in a Postmodern World," *Archivaria*, 51 (2001), 36–47

Maguire, Laurie E., *Shakespearean Suspect Texts: The "Bad" Quartos and their Contexts*, Cambridge University Press, 1996

Mahaffey, Vicki, "Intentional Error: The Paradox of Editing Joyce's *Ulysses*," in George Bornstein (ed.), *Representing Modernist Texts: Editing as Interpretation*, Ann Arbor: University of Michigan Press, 1991, pp. 171–91

Mahoney, Michael S., "Cybernetics and Information Technology," in R. C. Olby, G. N. Cantor, J. R. R. Christie, and M. J. S. Hodge (eds.), *Companion to the History of Modern Science*, London: Routledge, 1990, pp. 537–53

"The Histories of Computing(s)," *Interdisciplinary Science Reviews*, 30.2 (2005), pp. 119–35

Mak, Bonnie, "Archaeology of a Digitization," *Journal of the American Society for Information Systems and Technology*, 65.8 (2014), 1515–26

How the Page Matters, University of Toronto Press, 2011

"On the Uses of Authenticity," *Archivaria*, 73 (2012), 1–17

Malone, Edmund (ed.), *The Plays and Poems of William Shakespeare, in Ten Volumes*, London, 1790

Manoff, Marlene, "Theories of the Archive from Across the Disciplines," *Portal: Libraries and the Academy*, 4.1 (2004), 9–25

Manovich, Lev, *The Language of New Media*, Cambridge, MA: MIT Press, 2001

Marcus, Leah S., *Puzzling Shakespeare: Local Reading and Its Discontents*, Berkeley, CA: University of California Press, 1988

Unediting the Renaissance: Shakespeare, Marlowe, Milton, London: Routledge, 1996

Marks, Leo, *Between Silk and Cyanide: A Codemaker's War, 1941–45*, New York: Touchstone, 2000

Marvin, Carolyn, *When Old Technologies Were New: Thinking About Electric Communication in the Late Nineteenth Century*, Oxford University Press, 1988

Massai, Sonia, "Scholarly Editing and the Shift from Print to Electronic Cultures," in Lukas Erne and Margaret Jane Kidnie (eds.), *Textual Performances: The Modern Reproduction of Shakespeare's Drama*, Cambridge University Press, 2004

Shakespeare and the Rise of the Editor, Cambridge University Press, 2007

Masten, Jeffrey, "Pressing Subjects; or, the Secret Lives of Shakespeare's Compositors," in Masten, Peter Stallybrass, and Nancy J. Vickers (eds.), *Language Machines: Technologies of Literary and Cultural Production*, New York: Routledge, 1997, pp. 75–106

Textual Intercourse: Collaboration, Authorship, and Sexualities in Renaissance Drama, Cambridge University Press, 1997

McCarty, Willard, *Humanities Computing*, Basingstoke: Palgrave Macmillan, 2005

McDonough, Jerome, Matthew Kirschenbaum, Doug Reside, Neil Fraistat, and Dennis Jerz, "Twisty Little Passages Almost All Alike: Applying the FRBR Model to a Classic Computer Game," *Digital Humanities Quarterly*, 4.2 (2010), www.digitalhumanities.org/dhq/vol/4/2/000089/000089.html

McGann, Jerome J., *A Critique of Modern Textual Criticism*, Charlottesville: University Press of Virginia, 1992

"Database, Interface, and Archival Fever," *Publications of the Modern Language Association*, 122.5 (2007), 1588–92

"Information Technology and the Troubled Humanities," *TEXT Technology*, 14.2 (2005), 105–21

"A Note on the Current State of Humanities Scholarship," *Critical Inquiry*, 30.2 (2004), 409–13

Radiant Textuality: Literature After the World Wide Web, Basingstoke: Palgrave Macmillan, 2001

"Textonics: Literary and Cultural Studies in a Quantum World," in Andrew Nash (ed.), *The Culture of Collected Editions*, Basingstoke: Palgrave Macmillan, 2003, pp. 245–60

McLeod, Randall [as Random Clod], "Information upon Information," *TEXT: an Interdisciplinary Annual of Textual Studies*, 5 (1991), 241–81

[as Random Cloud] "Shakspear Babel," in Joanna Gondris (ed.), *Reading Readings: Essays on Shakespeare Editing in the Eighteenth Century*, Madison, WI: Fairleigh Dickinson University Press, 1998, pp. 1–70

McKenzie, D. F., *Bibliography and the Sociology of Texts*, Cambridge University Press, 1999

"Printers of the Mind: Some Notes on Bibliographical Theories and Printing-House Practices," in Peter D. McDonald and Michael F. Suarez (eds.), *Making Meaning: "Printers of the Mind" and Other Essays*, Amherst: University of Massachusetts Press, 2002, pp. 13–85

"'What's Past is Prologue': The Bibliographical Society and the History of the Book," in Peter D. McDonald and Michael F. Suarez (eds.), *Making Meaning: "Printers of the Mind" and Other Essays*, Amherst: University of Massachusetts Press, 2002, pp. 259–75

McKerrow, R. B., *An Introduction to Bibliography for Literary Students*, Oxford: Clarendon Press, 1927

McKitterick, David, *Old Books, New Technologies: The Representation, Conservation and Transformation of Books since 1700*, Cambridge University Press, 2013

"Old Faces and New Acquaintances: Typography and the Association of Ideas," *Papers of the Bibliographical Society of America*, 87.2 (1993), 163–86

Print, Manuscript and the Search for Order, 1450–1830, Cambridge University Press, 2003

McLuhan, Marshall, *Understanding Media: The Extensions of Man*, 2nd edn., New York: Signet, 1964

Millard, Bailey, "Pictures that Talk," *Technical World Magazine*, 19.1 (March 1913), 16–21

Menke, Richard, "The Medium Is the Media: Fictions of the Telephone in the 1890s," *Victorian Studies*, 55.2 (2013), 212–21

  Telegraphic Realism: Victorian Fiction and Other Information Systems, Stanford University Press, 2008

du Moncel, Count, *The Telephone, the Microphone and the Phonograph*, New York: Harper, 1879

Moretti, Franco, *Distant Reading*, London: Verso, 2013

  Maps, Graphs, Trees: Abstract Models for a Literary Theory, London: Verso, 2005

  "Modern European Literature: A Geographical Sketch," *New Left Review*, no. 206 (1994), 86–109

  "Network Theory, Plot Analysis," Stanford Literary Lab, Stanford University, http://litlab.stanford.edu/

Mowat, Barbara, "The Problem of Shakespeare's Text(s)," in Laurie E. Maguire and Thomas L. Berger (eds.), *Textual Formations and Reformations*, Newark, DE: University of Delaware Press, 1998, pp. 131–48

Mueller, Martin, "The Nameless Shakespeare," *TEXT Technology*, 1 (2005), 61–70

Muller, S., J. A. Feith, and R. Fruin, *Handleiding voor het Ordenen en Beschrijven van Archieven*, Groningen: Erven B. van der Kamp, 1898 [known informally as the Dutch Manual and translated by Arthur H. Leavitt as *Manual for the Arrangement and Description of Archives*, Chicago: Society of American Archivists, 2003]

Murphy, Andrew, "Electric Shakespeares [review of *The Arden Shakespeare CD-ROM*]," *Computers and the Humanities*, 32.5 (1998), 411–20

  "Shakespeare Goes Digital: Three Open Internet Editions," *Shakespeare Quarterly*, 61.3 (2010), 401–14

  Shakespeare in Print: A History and Chronology of Shakespeare Publishing, Cambridge University Press, 2003

Nesmith, Tom, "Still Fuzzy, But More Accurate: Some Thoughts on the 'Ghosts' of Archival Theory," *Archivaria*, 47 (1999), 136–50

Nolen, Stephanie (ed.), *Shakespeare's Face*, Toronto: Knopf, 2002

Nora, Pierre, *Realms of Memory: The Construction of the French Past*, vol. I, trans. Arthur Goldhammer, New York: Columbia University Press, 1996

Norton, David, *A Textual History of the King James Bible*, Cambridge University Press, 2005

[Norton, Thomas, and Thomas Sackville], *The Tragidie of Ferrex and Porrex*, London, 1570

Novak, Daniel A., *Realism, Photography, and Nineteenth-Century Fiction*, Cambridge University Press, 2008

Nunberg, Geoffrey, "Farewell to the Information Age," in *The Future of the Book*, Berkeley, CA: University of California Press, 1996, pp. 103–38

O'Driscoll, Michael J., "Derrida, Foucault, and the Archiviolithics of History," in Tilottama Rajan and Michael J. O'Driscoll (eds.), *After Poststructuralism: Writing the Intellectual History of Theory*, University of Toronto Press, 2002, pp. 284–309

O'Driscoll, Michael, and Edward Bishop, "Archiving 'Archiving,'" in *The Event of the Archive*, special issue of *English Studies in Canada*, 30.1 (2004), 1–16

Orgel, Stephen (ed.), *The Winter's Tale*, Oxford University Press, 1996

The Papers of Thomas A. Edison, Vol. I: The Making of an Inventor, February 1847–June 1873, ed. Reese V. Jenkins, Leonard S. Reich, Paul B. Israel, Toby Appel, Andrew J. Butrica, Robert A. Rosenberg, Keith A. Neir, Melodie Andrews, and Thomas E. Jeffrey, Baltimore: Johns Hopkins University Press, 1989

The Papers of Thomas A. Edison, Vol. IV: The Wizard of Menlo Park, ed. Paul B. Israel, Keith A. Neir, and Louis Carlat, Baltimore: Johns Hopkins University Press, 1998

Parikka, Jussi, "Archives in Media Theory: Material Media Archaeology and Digital Humanities," in David M. Berry (ed.), *Understanding Digital Humanities*, Basingstoke: Palgrave Macmillan, 2012, pp. 85–104

"Mapping Noise: Techniques and Tactics of Irregularities, Interception, and Disturbance," in Erkki Huhtamo and Jussi Parikka (eds.), *Media Archaeology: Approaches, Applications, and Implications*, Berkeley, CA: University of California Press, 2011, pp. 256–77

Parrott, T. M., "Errors and Omissions in the Griggs Facsimile of the Second Quarto of *Hamlet*," *Modern Language Notes*, 49.6 (1934), 376–9

Petersen, Lene B., *Shakespeare's Errant Texts: Textual Form and Linguistic Style in Shakespearean "Bad" Quartos and Co-Authored Plays*, Cambridge University Press, 2010

Phillips, Angus, "Does the Book Have a Future?," in Simon Eliot and Jonathan Rose (eds.), *A Companion to the History of the Book*, Malden, MA: Wiley-Blackwell, 2009

Picker, John M., *Victorian Soundscapes*, Oxford University Press, 2003

Pierce, John Robinson, *Symbols, Signals, and Noise*, New York: Harper, 1961

Poovey, Mary, *A History of the Modern Fact: Problems of Knowledge in the Sciences of Wealth and Society*, University of Chicago Press, 1998

Poster, Mark, *The Mode of Information: Poststructuralism and Social Context*, University of Chicago Press, 1990

Prescott, Andrew, "An Electric Current of the Imagination: What the Digital Humanities Are and What They Might Become," *Journal of Digital Humanities*, 1.2 (2012), http://journalofdigitalhumanities.org/1-2/an-electric-current-of-the-imagination-by-andrew-prescott

"Making the Digital Human: Anxieties, Possibilities, Challenges," lecture given at the Digital Humanities Summer School, Oxford University, 6 July 2012, http://digitalriffs.blogspot.com.au/2012/07/making-digital-human-anxieties.html

Representing Texts: Manuscripts and Archives in the Digital Age, Faculty of Humanities Philology Research Group, University of Calgary, 2000

"The Textuality of the Archive," in Louise Craven (ed.), *What Are Archives? Cultural and Theoretical Perspectives: A Reader*, Farnham: Ashgate, 2008

Rabinovitz, Lauren, and Abraham Geil (eds.), *Memory Bytes: History, Technology, and Digital Culture*, Durham, NC: Duke University Press, 2004

Ramsay, Stephen, *Reading Machines: Toward an Algorithmic Criticism*, Champaign: University of Illinois Press, 2011

Ranson, Nicholas, "Indian/Iudean Again," *Analytical and Enumerative Bibliography*, 10.1 (1999), 29–35

Raven, James (ed.), *Lost Libraries: the Destruction of Great Book Collections Since Antiquity*, Basingstoke: Palgrave Macmillan, 2004

Read, Oliver, and Walter L. Welch, *From Tin Foil to Stereo: Evolution of the Phonograph*, 2nd edn., Indianapolis: Howard W. Sams & Co., 1976

Rée, Jonathan, *I See a Voice: Deafness, Language and the Senses – a Philosophical History*, New York: Henry Holt–Metropolitan Books, 1999

Rhodes, Frederick Leland, *Beginnings of Telephony*, New York: Harper, 1929

Rhodes, Neil, and Jonathan Sawday (eds.), *The Renaissance Computer: Knowledge Technology in the First Age of Print*, London: Routledge, 2000

Richards, Thomas, *The Imperial Archive: Knowledge and the Fantasy of Empire*, London: Verso, 1993

Ricoeur, Paul, *Memory, History, Forgetting*, trans. Kathleen Blamey and David Pellauer, University of Chicago Press, 2004

Ridener, John, *From Polders to Postmodernism: A Concise History of Archival Theory*, Duluth, MN: Lutwin Books, 2008

Roberts, Helen I., "St. Augustine in 'St. Jerome's Study': Carpaccio's Painting and Its Legendary Source," *Art Bulletin*, 41 (1959), 283–97

Robinson, Peter, "Is There a Text in these Variants?", in Richard J. Finneran (ed.), *The Literary Text in the Digital Age*, Ann Arbor: University of Michigan Press, 1996, pp. 99–115

Rochfort Smith, Teena (ed.), *A Four-Text Edition of Shakespeare's Hamlet: In Parallel Columns*, London: N. Trübner & Co. [for The New Shakespeare Society], 1883

Ronell, Avital, *The Telephone Book: Technology – Schizophrenia – Electric Speech*, Lincoln, NB: University of Nebraska Press, 1989

Rosenberg, Daniel, "Data Before the Fact," in Lisa Gitelman (ed.), *"Raw Data" Is an Oxymoron*, Cambridge, MA: MIT Press, 2013, pp. 15–40

Rosenheim, Shawn James, *The Cryptographic Imagination: Secret Writing from Edgar Poe to the Internet*, Baltimore: Johns Hopkins University Press, 1997

Rothenberg, Jeff, "Ensuring the Longevity of Digital Documents," *Scientific American*, 272.1 (January, 1995), 42–7; posted in expanded form in 1999 as "Ensuring the Longevity of Digital Information," Council on Library and Information Resources, www.clir.org/pubs/archives/ensuring.pdf

Rothwell, Kenneth S., and Annabelle Henkin Melzer, *Shakespeare on Screen: an International Filmography and Videography*, New York: Neal-Schuman, 1990

Rouse, Richard H., and Mary A. Rouse, "Wax Tablets," *Language and Communication*, 9.2/3 (1989), 175–91

Rowe, Katherine, "Shakespeare and Media History," in Margreta de Grazia and Stanley Wells (eds.), *The New Cambridge Companion to Shakespeare*, Cambridge University Press, 2010, pp. 303–24

Sawday, Jonathan, *Engines of the Imagination: Renaissance Culture and the Rise of the Machine*, London: Routledge, 2007

Scharnhorst, Gary, *Kate Field: The Many Lives of a Nineteenth-Century American Journalist*, Syracuse University Press, 2008

Schellenberg, Theodore, *The Management of Archives*, New York: Columbia University Press, 1965

   Modern Archives: Principles and Techniques, University of Chicago Press, 1956

Schoenbaum, Sam, *William Shakespeare: A Documentary Life*, New York: Scolar Press; Oxford University Press, 1975

Schreibman, Susan, Ray Siemens, and John Unsworth (eds.), *A Companion to Digital Humanities*, Malden, MA: Blackwell, 2004

Schwartz, Joan M., and Terry Cook, "Archives, Records, and Power: the Making of Modern Memory," *Archival Science*, 2 (2002), 1–19

Schweppenhäuser, Gerhard, *Theodor W. Adorno: An Introduction*, trans. James Rolleston, Durham, NC: Duke University Press, 2009

Sconce, Jeffrey, *Haunted Media: Electronic Presence from Telegraphy to Television*, Durham, NC: Duke University Press, 2000

Scott, A. de C. *On Photo-zincography and other Photographic Processes Employed at the Ordnance Survey Office, Southampton*, 2nd edn., London: Longman, Green, Longman, Roberts & Green, 1863

Scott, Charlotte, *Shakespeare and the Idea of the Book*, Oxford University Press, 2007

Sekula, Allan, "The Body and the Archive," *October*, 39 (1986), 3–64

Shapin, Steven, and Simon Schaffer, *Leviathan and the Air-Pump: Hobbes, Boyle, and the Experimental Life*, new edn., Princeton University Press, 2011

Shannon, Claude E., and Warren Weaver, *The Mathematical Theory of Communication*, Urbana: University of Illinois Press, 1949

Sherman, William H., "How to Make Anything Signify Anything," *Cabinet Magazine*, 40 (Winter 2010/2011): www.cabinetmagazine.org/issues/40/sherman.php

  Used Books: Marking Readers in Renaissance England, Philadelphia: University of Pennsylvania Press, 2008

Shieber, Stuart M., "Lessons from a Restricted Turing Test," *Communications of the Association for Computing Machinery*, 37.6 (1994), 70–8

Shillingsburg, Peter L., *From Gutenberg to Google: Electronic Representations of Literary Texts*, Cambridge University Press, 2006

  Scholarly Editing in the Computer Age: Theory and Practice, 3rd edn., Ann Arbor, MI: University of Michigan Press, 1996

  "The Semiotics of Bibliography," *Textual Cultures*, 6.1 (2011), 11–25

Singh, Jagjit, *Great Ideas in Information Theory, Language, and Cybernetics*, New York: Dover, 1966

Sisk, John P., "The Cybernetics of Othello," *New Orleans Review*, 11 (1970), 74–7

Smith, Brian Cantwell, "Limits of Correctness in Computers," in Rob Kling (ed.), *Computerization and Controversy: Value Conflicts and Social Choices*, 2nd edn., San Diego, CA: Academic Press, 1996

Smith, Jonathan, *Charles Darwin and Victorian Visual Culture*, Cambridge University Press, 2006

Smith, Steven Escar, "'The eternal verities verified': Charlton Hinman and the Roots of Mechanical Collation," *Studies in Bibliography*, 53 (2000), 136–8

Snow, C. P., *The Two Cultures*, Cambridge University Press, 1998

Spenser, Edmund, *The Faerie Queene*, ed. Thomas P. Roche, Jr., London: Penguin, 1978

Spieker, Sven, *The Big Archive: Art from Bureaucracy*, Cambridge, MA: MIT Press, 2008

Stallybrass, Peter, "Against Thinking," *Publications of the Modern Language Association*, 122.5 (2007), 1580–7

"Books and Scrolls: Navigating the Bible," in Jennifer Andersen and Elizabeth Sauer (eds.), *Books and Readers in Early Modern England: Material Studies*, Philadelphia: Pennsylvania University Press, 2002, 42–79

Stallybrass, Peter, Roger Chartier, J. Franklin Mowrey, and Heather Wolfe, "Hamlet's Tables and the Technologies of Writing in Renaissance England," *Shakespeare Quarterly*, 55.4 (2004), 379–419

Steedman, Carolyn, *Dust: The Archive and Cultural History*, New Brunswick: Rutgers University Press, 2002

Steinmetz, George (ed.), *The Politics of Method in the Human Sciences: Positivism and Its Epistemological Others*, Durham, NC: Duke University Press, 2005

Sterne, Jonathan, *The Audible Past: The Cultural Origins of Sound Reproduction*, Durham, NC: Duke University Press, 2003

Stoppard, Tom, *The Invention of Love*, New York: Grove Press, 1997

Svensson, Patrick, "Envisioning the Digital Humanities," *Digital Humanities Quarterly*, 6.1 (2012), www.digitalhumanities.org/dhq/vol/6/1/000112/000112.html

"From Optical Fiber to Conceptual Cyberinfrastructure," *Digital Humanities Quarterly*, 5.1 (2011), www.digitalhumanities.org/dhq/vol/5/1/000090/000090.html

"The Landscape of Digital Humanities," *Digital Humanities Quarterly*, 4.1 (2010), www.digitalhumanities.org/dhq/vol/4/1/000080/000080.html

Talbot, William Henry Fox, *The Pencil of Nature*, New York: Da Capo Press, 1969

Tanselle, G. Thomas, "The Life and Work of Fredson Bowers," *Studies in Bibliography*, 6 (1993), 1–154

A Rationale of Textual Criticism, Philadelphia: University of Pennsylvania Press, 1989

"Reproductions and Scholarship," *Studies in Bibliography*, 42 (1989), 25–54

"The World as Archive," *Common Knowledge*, 8.2 (2002), 402–6

Tate, Vernon D., "Microphotography in Wartime," *Journal of Documentary Reproduction*, 5.3 (1942), 129–38

Taylor, Diana, *The Archive and the Repertoire: Performing Cultural Memory in the Americas*, Durham, NC: Duke University Press, 2003

Taylor, Gary, *Reinventing Shakespeare: A Cultural History from the Restoration to the Present*, London: Hogarth Press, 1989

Taylor, Gary (ed.), *Henry V*, Oxford University Press, 1982

Telephone Suits: Circuit Court of the United States, District of Massachusetts, In Equity: Bell Telephone Company et al. v. Peter A. Dowd, Boston: Alfred Mudge and Son, 1880

Terdiman, Richard, *Present Past: Modernity and the Memory Crisis*, Ithaca, NY: Cornell University Press, 1993

Terras, Melissa M., *Digital Images for the Information Professional*, Aldershot: Ashgate, 2008

Theimer, Kate, "Archives in Context and as Context," *Journal of Digital Humanities*, 1.2 (2012), n.p.

Thompson, Ann, "Teena Rochfort Smith, Frederick Furnivall, and the New Shakespeare Society's Four-Text Volume of *Hamlet*," *Shakespeare Quarterly*, 49 (1998), 125–39

Thompson, Ann, and Neil Taylor (eds.) *Hamlet* [based on the 1623 First Folio text], London: Thompson–Arden Shakespeare, 3rd series, 2006
   Hamlet: The Texts of 1603 and 1623, London: Thompson–Arden Shakespeare, 3rd series, 2006

Thompson, Emily, "Machines, Music, and the Quest for Fidelity: Marketing the Edison Phonograph in America, 1877–1925," *Musical Quarterly*, 79.1 (1995), 131–71

Thompson, Silvanus P., *The Life of William Thompson, Baron Kelvin of Largs*, 2 vols., London: Macmillan, 1910

Thompson, Sir William, address to the British Association, Glasgow, *Nature* (14 September 1876), 426–31

Traister, Daniel, "The Furness Memorial Library," in *The Penn Library Collections at 250: From Franklin to the Web*, Philadelphia: University of Pennsylvania Library, 2000, pp. 62–79

Trettien, Whitney, "A Deep History of Electronic Textuality: The Case of *English Reprints Jhon Milton Areopagitica*," *Digital Humanities Quarterly*, 7.1 (2013), http://www.digitalhumanities.org/dhq/vol/7/1/000150/000150.html

Tschichold, Jan, *The Form of the Book: Essays on the Morality of Good Design*, ed. Robert Bringhurst, trans. Hajo Hadeler, Vancouver: Hartley and Marks, 1991
   The New Typography, trans. Ruari McLean, Berkeley, CA: University of California Press, 2006

Tucker, Jennifer, *Nature Exposed: Photography as Eyewitness in Victorian Science*, Baltimore: Johns Hopkins University Press, 2005

Turing, A. M., "Computing Machinery and Intelligence," *Mind*, 59, new series (1950), pp. 433–60

Pure Mathematics: Collected Works of A. M. Turing, ed. J. L. Britton, Amsterdam: North-Holland, 1992

Turner, Henry S., "Life Science: Rude Mechanicals, Human Mortals, Posthuman Shakespeare," *South Central Review*, 26 (2009), 197–217

Shakespeare's Double Helix, London: Continuum, 2007

Turner, Robert Kean, Virginia Westling Haas, *et al.* (eds.), *The Winter's Tale*, New York: Modern Language Association, 2005

Twain, Mark, *1601, and Is Shakespeare Dead?*, ed. Shelly Fishkin Fisher, Oxford University Press, 1996

Twyman, Michael, *Early Lithographed Books: A Study of the Design and Production of Improper Books in the Age of the Hand Press, with a Catalogue*, London: Farrand Press; Private Libraries Association, 1990

Urkowitz, Steven, "'Well-sayd olde Mole': Burying Three Hamlets in Modern Editions," in Georgianna Ziegler (ed.), *Shakespeare Study Today: The Horace Howard Furness Memorial Lectures*, New York: AMS Press, 1986), pp. 37–70

Urrichio, William, and Roberta E. Pearson, *Reframing Culture: The Case of the Vitagraph Films*, Princeton University Press, 1993

Velz, John W., "*Judean* and *Indian* Yet Once Again," *Analytical and Enumerative Bibliography*, 10.1 (1999), 21–9

Voss, Paul J., and Marta L. Werner (eds.), "Toward a Poetics of the Archive," *Studies in the Literary Imagination*, 32.1 (1999), i–viii

Wade, Nicholas, "Droeshout's First Folio Shakespeare," *Word and Image*, 1 (1985), 259

Waibel, Günter, and Ricky Erway, "Think Globally, Act Locally: Library, Archive, and Museum Collaboration," *Museum Management and Curatorship*, 24.4 (2009), 323–35

Wakeman, Geoffrey, *Aspects of Victorian Lithography: Anastatic Printing and Photozincography*, Wymondham, UK: Brewhouse, 1970

Warren, Michael (ed.), *The Complete King Lear 1608–1623*, Berkeley, CA: University of California Press, 1989

Weaver, Warren, "The Mathematics of Communication," *Scientific American*, 181.1 (1949), 11–15

"Translation," in William Locke and A. Donald Booth (eds.), *Machine Translation of Languages*, New York: Wiley, 1957, pp. 15–23

Weingust, Don, *Acting from Shakespeare's First Folio: Theory, Text, and Performance*, New York: Routledge, 2006

Wells, Stanley, and Gary Taylor, with John Jowett and William Montgomery, *William Shakespeare: A Textual Companion*, New York: W. W. Norton, 1997

Weng, Cathy, and Jia Mi, "Towards Accessibility to Digital Cultural Materials: A FRBRized Approach," *International Digital Library Perspectives*, 22.3 (2006), 217–32

Werner, Sarah, "Where Material Book Culture Meets Digital Humanities," *Journal of Digital Humanities*, 1.3 (2012), 2–9

Werstine, Paul, *Early Modern Playhouse Manuscripts and the Editing of Shakespeare*, Cambridge University Press, 2013

    "Modern Editors and Historical Collation in Old-Spelling Editions of Shakespeare," *Analytical and Enumerative Bibliography*, 4 (1980), 95–106

    "Narratives About Printed Shakespeare Texts: 'Foul Papers' and 'Bad Quartos,'" *Shakespeare Quarterly*, 41 (1990), 65–86

    "Post-Theory Problems in Shakespeare Editing," *Yearbook of English Studies*, 29 (1999), 103–17

    "The Textual Mystery of *Hamlet*," *Shakespeare Quarterly*, 39.1 (1988), 1–26

West, Anthony James, *The Shakespeare First Folio: The History of the Book. Vol. I: An Account of the First Folio Based on its Sales and Prices, 1623–2000*, Oxford University Press, 2001

    The Shakespeare First Folio: The History of the Book. Vol. II: A New Worldwide Census of First Folios, Oxford University Press, 2003

West, Anthony James, and Eric Rasmussen (eds.), *The Shakespeare First Folios: A Descriptive Catalogue*, Basingstoke: Palgrave Macmillan, 2012

Whitehead, Anne, *Memory*, New York: Routledge, 2009

Williams, Franklin B., "Photo-Facsimiles of *STC* Books: A Cautionary Check-List," *Studies in Bibliography*, 21 (1968), 109–30

Williams, George Walton (ed.), *Shakespeare's Speech-Headings*, Newark, DE: University of Delaware Press, 1997

Williams, Grant, and Christopher Ivic, "Sites of Forgetting in Early Modern English Literature and Culture," in Ivic and Williams (eds.), *Forgetting in Early Modern English Literature and Culture: Lethe's Legacies*, London: Routledge, 2004, pp. 1–17

Williams, Owen, and Caryn Lazzuri (eds.), *Foliomania!: Stories Behind Shakespeare's Most Important Book*, Washington DC: Folger Shakespeare Library, 2011

Wilson, F. P., *Shakespeare and the New Bibliography*, rev. and ed. Helen Gardner, Oxford: Clarendon Press, 1970

Wilson, John Dover, "The Task of Heminge and Condell," in *Studies in the First Folio: Written for the Shakespeare Association in Celebration of the First Folio Tercentenary*, London: Humphrey Milford; Oxford University Press, 1924, pp. 53–77

Winograd, Terry, and Fernando Flores, *Understanding Computers and Cognition: A New Foundation for Design*, Norwood, NJ: Ablex, 1986

Winston, Brian, *Media, Technology and Society: A History from the Telegraph to the Internet*, New York: Routledge, 1998

Winston, Patrick H., "Learning by Reasoning and Analogy," *Communications of the Association for Computing Machinery*, 23.12 (1980), 689–703

Worthen, W. B., "Performing Shakespeare in Digital Culture," in Robert Shaughnessy (ed.), *The Cambridge Companion to Shakespeare and Popular Culture*, Cambridge University Press, 2007, pp. 227–47

Shakespeare and the Authority of Performance, Cambridge University Press, 1997

Shakespeare and the Force of Modern Performance, Cambridge University Press, 2003

Wurman, Richard Saul, "Introduction," in Richard Saul Wurman and Peter Bradford (eds.), *Information Architects*, New York: Graphis, 1997, pp. 15–37

Wurman, Richard Saul, and Joel Katz, "Beyond Graphics: The Architecture of Information," *American Institute of Architects Journal*, 64 (1975), 40 and 56

Yeo, Geoffrey, "The Conceptual Fonds and the Physical Collection," *Archivaria*, 72 (2012), 43–80

"Debates About Description," in Eastwood and MacNeil (eds.) *Currents of Archival Thinking*, pp. 89–114

Yockey, Hubert P., *Information Theory, Evolution, and the Origin of Life*, Cambridge University Press, 2005

Young, Alan, "*Hamlet* and Nineteenth-Century Photography," in Holger Klein and James L. Harner (eds.), *Shakespeare and the Visual Arts*, Lewiston, NY: Edwin Mellon, 2000, pp. 260–307

Index